D0015615

THE ICE MAIDEN

It was a pleasure sailing with you on the NG Endeavour.

Johan Reinhard

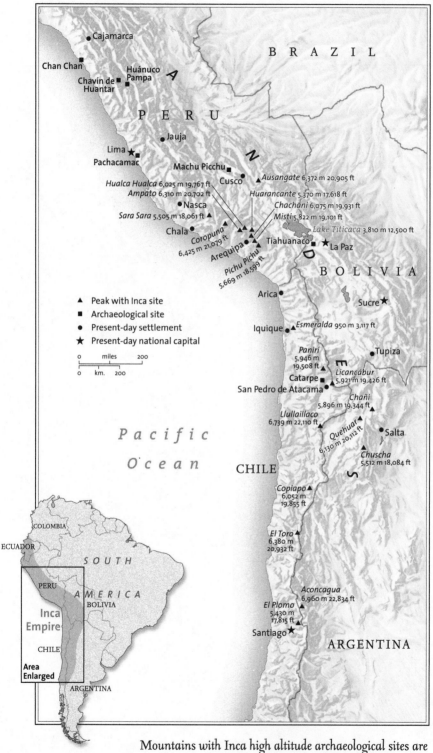

Mountains with Inca high altitude archaeological sites are
marked on this map of the Central Andes.

THE ICE MAIDEN

Inca Mummies, Mountain Gods,
and Sacred Sites in the Andes

JOHAN REINHARD

 NATIONAL GEOGRAPHIC

WASHINGTON, D.C.

Published by the National Geographic Society

All rights reserved. Without limiting the rights under copyright reserved above, no part of this publication may be reproduced, stored in or introduced into a retrieval system, or transmitted in any form, or by any means (electronic, mechanical, photocopying, recording, or otherwise), without the written permission of both the copyright owner and the above publisher of this book.

Copyright © 2005 Johan Reinhard

Printed in the U.S.A.

Library of Congress Cataloging-in-Publication Data Available Upon Request
ISBN: 0-7922-6838-5

All photographs by Johan Reinhard except as noted: Pg. xiv Illustration by Ronsaville Harlin Inc.; Pg. 142 Graphic courtesy the Carrier Corporation; Pg. 165 CT scan courtesy Johns Hopkins Hospital; Pg. 278 Photograph by Gordon Wiltsie; Pg. 307 Artwork by Bob Pratt © Johan Reinhard; Pg. 310 CT scan courtesy Tomografia Computada Sociedad del Estado (Salta); Color Insert Illustrations #5 and #9 by Christopher A. Klein

One of the world's largest nonprofit scientific and educational organizations, the National Geographic Society was founded in 1888 "for the increase and diffusion of geographic knowledge." Fulfilling this mission, the Society educates and inspires millions every day through its magazines, books, television programs, videos, maps and atlases, research grants, the National Geographic Bee, teacher workshops, and innovative classroom materials. The Society is supported through membership dues, charitable gifts, and income from the sale of its educational products. This support is vital to National Geographic's mission to increase global understanding and promote conservation of our planet through exploration, research, and education.

For more information, please call 1-800-NGS LINE (647-5463) or write to the following address:
National Geographic Society
1145 17th Street N.W.
Washington, D.C. 20036-4688 U.S.A.

Visit the Society's Web site at www.nationalgeographic.com.

CONTENTS

A man descends a glacier after making offerings to the mountain gods during the festival of Qoyllur Riti.

Dedicated to my companions during climbs in the Andes and to all those whose support helped make this research possible.

Quechua villagers reenact an Inca ceremony involving the simulated sacrifice of a girl.

PROLOGUE

Individual dramas are reflections of the universal ones.
—ANAÏS NIN

Finish with me now because the celebrations
they held for me in Cuzco were enough.
—WORDS SPOKEN BY A GIRL ABOUT TO BE SACRIFICED,
AS TOLD TO RODRIGO HERNÁNDEZ DE PRÍNCIPE, 1621

THE PRIEST RAISED THE WOODEN CUP TOWARD THE SUN AND asked for its blessing. The assembled group lowered their heads and placed their hands to their lips, making kissing sounds as they opened them and stretched their arms out to the sun. Gesturing toward the snow-capped peaks surrounding him, the priest invoked them to accept the offerings that lay nearby. Then, while others sang solemn songs and played flutes and drums, he tilted the cup so that the liquid in it poured slowly onto the ground. Turning to the young girl by his side, he told her it was time for her to drink from an identical cup. She lifted it to her lips in hands that had begun to freeze in the cold wind. Exhausted and unaccustomed to the bittersweet taste of maize beer, she had difficulty swallowing it.

The girl wore a finely woven dress of alpaca wool. It was held by an elaborately woven belt around her waist and two silver pins at her shoulders. A shawl with bright red and white stripes was draped around her shoulders and held in place by another pin. She wore a light and dark brown colored head cloth over her black hair.

She felt overwhelmed as her eyes took in the panorama before her. She stood on the summit of Ampato, one of the highest peaks in Peru, looking down on a vast field of ice and beyond it to a sea of mountains that gradually disappeared in the distance. Yet until yesterday she had never touched snow.

Her journey had begun months ago when she was sent to Cuzco, capital of the Inca Empire. She was a virgin without blemish and had been especially selected by the Incas to participate in one of their most important ceremonies. She had been feted during days of rituals that included dancing and drinking, and then set off on her pilgrimage to the sacred mountain. Priests and their assistants led the way with llamas carrying supplies of food and ritual offerings. As the ritual procession passed through the villages along the way, people averted their eyes and prostrated themselves on the ground.

After days of travel, the procession reached Kallimarca, the last Inca settlement on their way to Ampato. Built on a ridge above the Colca Canyon, Kallimarca had a small plaza with a ceremonial platform built adjacent to it. The girl was led three times around the platform; then she climbed up its stairs to the top. There the priests first made offerings to the Inca deities, especially Inti, the sun. Then they invoked Ampato and the volcano Hualca Hualca, visible in the distance, along with other sacred peaks in the region.

Once the offerings at Kallimarca had been completed, the procession continued up a river valley. Gradually the pilgrims ascended to a pass where they were met with their first view of Ampato in all its grandeur. They wound their way to the *tambo*, a group of buildings the Incas had built as a way station at the foot of Ampato at 16,000 feet.

From here, only the priests and their assistants continued on with the girl as they climbed up to a small plateau at 19,200 feet, where they spent the night in tents. The next day the little band followed a trail that zigzagged up a steep slope, bordered by a massive wall of ice.

The group was relieved to reach their goal for the day, a hillock on the crater's rim that was covered with grass matting. As soon as she set foot on it, the maiden saw the highest point of the summit. The group spent another night in tents, insulated from the ice by the matting. The next morning the girl ate a simple meal of vegetables.

During her ascent up the 20,700-foot mountain, the maiden had been disoriented by the inhospitable and unfamiliar terrain. The altitude not only exhausted her, it also nauseated her and gave her a headache. She needed to be helped on the last steep section leading to the summit. Finally she walked along with the priests to the end of the summit ridge. There she saw the low walls of a small stone structure.

When they reached it, the priests pulled out the offerings they had brought, many of them all the way from Cuzco. They included bags of coca leaves, wooden drinking vessels, maize, beans, peanuts, jerky, jars with maize beer, weaving implements, and beautifully clothed female figurines made of gold, silver, and spondylus shell. An assemblage of specially made pottery, consisting of storage jars, pots, bowls, and shallow plates, was carefully set to the side.

The group chewed coca leaves in honor of the gods. Smoke rising from the burning incense alerted the people waiting at the tambo below, who began dancing and singing as they realized the ritual was reaching its climax.

The priests then helped lower the girl into the structure. She had earlier felt honored by being selected to enter the realm of the gods, but now she was frightened at what she knew would happen next. Suddenly her vision turned black as a priest placed a cloth over her head. His face was the last thing she would ever see.[1]

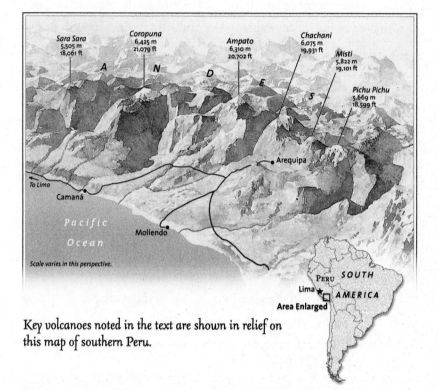

Key volcanoes noted in the text are shown in relief on
this map of southern Peru.

CHAPTER ONE

DISCOVERY on AMPATO

Every beginning ends something.
—PAUL VALÉRY

*There is a snow mountain called Ampato . . . which has its own order of
people dedicated to its service.*
—CRISTÓBAL DE ALBORNOZ, 1583

THE ERUPTING VOLCANO OF SABANCAYA SPEWED OUT CLOUDS OF ash
more than a mile into the sky, blanketing even its higher neighbor,
Ampato. Eventually the weight of melting snow caused a section of
Ampato's steep summit ridge to collapse. As it swept down the slope,
the mix of ice and rock carried with it an ancient cloth-wrapped bundle. Smashing against an icy outcrop 50 yards below, an outer cloth
was torn open and 500-year-old Inca artifacts were strewn over the
rugged landscape. But the most important part of the bundle
remained intact as it came to rest on top of the ice—the frozen body
of an Inca child. With its exposure, a race against time began.

I knew nothing of this, but by chance I was to become involved
in the rescue of the mummy that came to be called the Ice Maiden.
Her discovery made headlines in the world press that eventually
reached almost a billion people. Few finds have cut across so many
cultural and age boundaries, fascinating young and old alike in
countries across the globe. The small frozen mummy of an Inca
girl captured the interest of men and women from all walks of life,
ranging from taxi drivers to world leaders.

I had spent the previous 15 years as an archaeologist in the Andes, climbing more than a hundred mountains. A new field had developed called "high-altitude archaeology," and its focus was naturally on the Inca culture of 500 years ago—it was the only society known to make offerings on the summits of peaks more than 20,000 feet high.[1] In 1995 much work still remained to be done before we would know the location of all the sites they had built, let alone understand why they made these sacrifices on top of some of the world's highest mountains.

Ironically, when I landed in the Peruvian city of Arequipa late in August of that year, I thought my research had ended for the summer. I would soon head back to the United States after completing a series of expeditions. Discoveries of Inca ruins in eastern Peru had been followed by more in Bolivia—it had been one of my best field seasons ever. I expected that my stay in Arequipa would be an anticlimax.

I called ahead to arrange to meet with an old friend of mine in Arequipa, the archaeologist José Antonio Chávez. He was as keen as I was on planning excavations of high-altitude sites in 1996. José and I had co-directed two expeditions to excavate ruins on Pichu Pichu, one of the region's highest volcanoes, in 1989 and 1991.[2] We found skeletal remains from a human sacrifice outside an Inca structure at 18,600 feet, but frozen soil had stymied our attempts to excavate the summit platform. It was time to return to this and other mountain sites in the region.

Many of Arequipa's most impressive buildings were constructed with a light-colored volcanic stone—the remains of ancient eruptions—hence it is often referred to as the *ciudad blanca*, or "the white city." Arequipa retains much of its original colonial charm, even though it has nearly a million inhabitants and has sprawled out into the desert for miles in all directions. From a distance it looks as if buildings, like desert plants after a rain, have sprouted in the barren terrain of the moon.

Arequipa is a city with a reputation for being independent. The locals joke that they have their own passport for the "Republic of

Arequipa," and indeed imitation passports can be bought in stores. Some Peruvians outside of Arequipa think the city's inhabitants are arrogant, and rivalries between Arequipa and other cities can become intense. José once told me about a time he gave a lecture in northern Peru: "I was showing slides of the active volcano Misti and described how an eruption could easily bury the city. At this, the audience erupted in applause!"

I met with José and his then wife Ruth (Charo) Salas on a pleasant side street close to Arequipa's renowned plaza. José was director of Catholic University's archaeology department and had been conducting excavations in the region for more than 30 years. Ruth was also a trained archaeologist, but now was running a store that focused on the beautifully worked gemstones obtained from a family mine. Lean and hardened from years of fieldwork, José had not lost a bit of his fascination with archaeological exploration. We sat down and began considering mountaintop sites that we might investigate in 1996.

We knew from the early Spanish writings (known as the chronicles) that when the Incas entered this region in the late 1400s, mountains were the principal deities of the peoples they conquered.[3] The Incas believed that statues of precious metals and, especially, human sacrifices were the most important offerings they could make to the gods. The chroniclers were told that there were several reasons why the sacrifices had been conducted. Some of them were undertaken at times of key events in the life of the Inca emperor, such as illness, death, birth of a son, preparation for war, and his succession to the throne. They were also made to prevent natural calamities, such as bad weather, epidemics, earthquakes, and volcanic eruptions, and were performed annually during major festivals at several important ceremonial sites throughout the empire.[4]

The Incas made annual offerings to major mountain deities at special times in the year. If the peaks were too difficult to ascend, the offerings would be made from a place within view of them. Otherwise, the Incas climbed to their summits, carrying the sacrificial offerings with them. Clearly, weather affected such sites differently, depending upon their locations. To avoid storms and deep snow, ceremonies on the high summits would have taken place during the dry summer months (the Northern Hemisphere winter) in the southern part of the Inca Empire (central Chile and Argentina) and the dry winter months in Peru.

Two volcanoes, Chachani and Misti, dominate Arequipa's skyline. We knew that the Incas had made offerings on both their summits. However, I had been to them years before and seen the results of the looting carried out by treasure hunters at these sites. Thus, I was surprised when José said, "Human bones strewn about the summit have recently been seen by climbers. Looters used dynamite to break up the frozen ground and uncovered an intact burial."[5] Since the peak is regularly climbed and no one had reported this before, it could only have happened within the past few weeks.

"If looters dynamited the site on Chachani, they may have done this on Pichu Pichu, as well," I said in frustration. We had not been to the peak since 1991 and had no idea as to the condition of the ruins. "Pichu Pichu will have to be on our list," I said, "but we need carry out excavations on other mountains before their sites are looted." One of the mountains that most interested us was Sara Sara, because I had found ruins on its summit in 1983 that looked virtually untouched. Its main drawback was its location in an isolated area a full day's drive to the north of Arequipa.

That obstacle was overcome after a friend of ours, Dante Lucioni, said he could join us. His four-wheel-drive vehicle would bring us closer to the mountain, and that meant we would have to make only a short trek with heavy packs. At the last minute, though, he had to cancel and, worse, José couldn't go because of work that had come up. Plans would have to be changed.

In the meantime I had run into Miguel (Miki) Zárate, who had worked as an assistant on some of my expeditions near Arequipa in the past, including those on Pichu Pichu. He said he was free to join me. I was relieved, as none of the other climbers I had worked with before was available, and I had no desire to climb Sara Sara alone.

Miki's father was a renowned local climber, and three of his sons had been literally following in his footsteps, becoming accomplished climbers themselves. Miki's small size and genial nature belied a tough interior formed during years in the mountains. Even in the city he walked slightly bent over as if he had a pack on his back. Although he had no formal training, he was keenly interested in my high-altitude archaeological research. This made for a rare combination.

Since I was using my personal funds and little remained after two months of work in the Andes, I could offer to pay Miki a salary for only five days, plus expenses. I assumed that no ascent of a mountain would take longer than that. Realizing how rough the sharp volcanic rock was on footwear, he said, "OK, but I'd rather you paid the money in advance so that I can get a new pair of boots." With that, he left to start buying supplies we needed for the trip.

Several mountains close to Arequipa had possible Inca sites on them, but those bordering the Colca Canyon, twice as deep as the Grand Canyon, especially attracted my interest. The inhabitants of the Colca Canyon had worshipped mountains long before the arrival of the Incas. The Spaniard Juan de Ulloa Mogollón reported in 1586 that the Cavana and Collagua peoples who lived in the Colca bound the heads of their children in order for them to take on the shapes of the mountains from which they believed they were descended.[6] One of the volcanoes was the flat-topped mountain massif of Hualca Hualca. It was the legendary ancestor of many of the people living nearby.

Miki and I had climbed its easternmost summit in 1982, but Hualca Hualca's westernmost peak had most caught my attention. It stood out by itself from the rest of the flat-topped massif with vertical walls surrounding it. Although the Spaniards had banned head deformation, I had been told in the early 1980s that to this day the women in the Colca Canyon wore hats with shapes similar to the mountains. It was no surprise that Cabanaconde, the center for

Hualca Hualca's worship during the Inca period, was located in an area known for its flat-topped hats.

Something else drew me to the region of Hualca Hualca. At the time the volcano Sabancaya was erupting daily. Next to it was Ampato, the highest volcano in the area of the Colca Canyon. Miki had tried to interest me in climbing Ampato in 1991. While guiding clients during an ascent of the mountain, he had seen at 19,000 feet two circles of stones about a yard in diameter, along with some pieces of wood and a few shards. The site lay on the volcano's western flank, far below the summit, and he thought the Incas must have ascended it using this side. He had tried to interest others in investigating the peak, but something had always intervened to prevent it.

Miki also told me that his brother Carlos, a well-known local guide, had seen woven grass in the ice field below the summit. Miki believed it might be the outer wrapping of a mummy bundle. We went to talk with Carlos, but he thought differently. "The grass was a good distance from the summit near a lower section of the crater rim. It did not appear associated with anything indicating a mummy," he said. Whatever it had been used for, it would be a miracle to locate it amid the ever-changing ice field.

Miki still wanted to climb Ampato. "Why take the time and effort to climb a peak that is permanently snow covered?" I asked him. "I've climbed several such peaks, and I've never seen anything to indicate the Incas had reached their summits, let alone built anything in the snow." Even if the summit had been free of snow during the time of the Incas, we wouldn't be able to see anything if the mountain was blanketed with it now. Of all the mountains in the region, I thought that Ampato was the one with the greatest certainty of not finding anything on its summit. That was the reason I didn't include it among the peaks I'd climbed during the 1980s.

However, I had a desire to see an active volcano up close, and Ampato was perfectly positioned for this. Sabancaya had begun erupting in 1990, and in 1991 I had often observed its atom bomb–like mushrooming clouds erupting while directing an archaeological excavation on the summit of Huarancante, 20 miles to the east.[7] An ascent of Ampato meant I would be able to look down on an eruption.

Miki and I met at a French coffeehouse, and he mentioned a final tidbit that clinched my decision. In the early 1980s I had had to take a 4 a.m. bus for an all-day ride to reach the inner part of the Colca Canyon. Since then, both the road and the bus service had been dramatically improved. "Now comfortable buses go directly to Cabanaconde in only six hours and they even leave at midday," he said. My mind was made up. Hualca Hualca and Ampato it would be. By such simple inducements are decisions made that can change the course of people's lives.

ON SEPTEMBER 2 WE WERE READY TO GO. THE BUS WAS BETTER than expected, even showing a movie in English. Unfortunately, it was Toxic Avenger, a low-budget American film full of the predictable blood, gore, and half-naked women. Worse, it was being shown on a bus full of village women and children. The lone gringo sank low in his seat.

We arrived that evening in Cabanaconde and went to the town's best "hotel." It consisted of a few rooms fronting a central courtyard whose distinguishing characteristic was a toilet bowl set in the middle. The disarray of other junk and weeds somehow made the toilet seem less out of place, almost a work of avant-garde art. Our room had moldy spring beds and a light bulb—it was the best one to be had.

The unfamiliar sound of burros braying kept me awake on and off during the night. In the morning Miki went to search for some-one with a burro to carry supplies to the place we would set up base camp. He returned with Henri Wamani, who had the reticent air of a man accustomed to hard times.

That afternoon we watched as villagers plowed and strewed

seeds as part of a sowing festival. The villagers were led by musicians and dancers, including one dressed as a clown. Off to the side, each family assembled at their respective fields to pour libations on the ground while facing toward Hualca Hualca. When I asked some villagers what this was for, they said, "We make offerings to Pachamama [Mother Earth] and the mountain gods for water and good crops." We, too, made our offerings, except ours were for a successful climb.

By six o'clock the next morning Henri still hadn't appeared, and Miki went to search for him. They returned leading two burros. Henri said we needed them both, not because we had so much equipment, but because, he explained, "One burro won't go alone so far from the area he knows." As we loaded them with meager supplies of camping gear and food, I grumbled to myself about such an unnecessary expense. It turned out to be one of the best bargains I ever made. I couldn't know then the value of the load that extra burro was going to bring back down.

Because Cabanaconde lies at 10,800 feet, we were able to acclimatize ourselves to the mountains for two nights. Although some Western scientists define "high" as any level above 10,000 feet, people in the Andes routinely live well above this altitude (even cities such as La Paz and Cuzco are about 11,000 feet). Scientists have a rule of thumb that working capacity decreases about 3 percent per 1,000-foot gain in altitude about 5,000 feet.[8] Even staying months at higher elevations only slightly improves this percentage. So when climbers work at 20,000 feet, they usually are functioning at just half their normal working capacity. Such extremes mean that acclimatizing yourself at each new height is crucial.

I awoke at 3 a.m. and lay awake until the sun came up. Even after so many expeditions, I still couldn't sleep well the night before leaving on one. This is not unusual. In a study of skydivers, interviews revealed that their highest levels of anxiety were not when they jumped from the plane, but when they made the decision to leave for the airport. Despite the casual way that both Miki and I approached the trip, at a subconscious level I knew anything could happen. We planned to climb new routes on two 20,000-foot peaks only a few days apart.

We left before eight and were soon trekking high above Cabanaconde on a hill slope to the south. Although Cabanaconde is located on a rim above the Colca River, the gorge drops off so steeply that there is no indication it is flowing below. The view over the town loses nothing for this, however. Snow-capped peaks and sheer cliffs dominate the northern horizon and tower over villages thousands of feet below.

By midday Miki and I reached a pass at 14,500 feet and waited for the burros. When Henri caught up with us, he said, "This is a dangerous place. People believe that at night a ferocious bull comes out of that hill," he nodded to the south, "to harm anyone nearby." I noticed a large mound of casually stacked stones nearby. Called *apachetas*, these are often found at high points, and many were begun long before the Spanish conquest. I say "begun" because they continue to grow. Travelers place stones on them as a way of showing respect to the local gods—and to ask for success in their journeys.[9] Following Henri's lead, we did the same.

Soon, as we passed amid volcanic boulders, we came upon a small depression filled with sand, looking like a dried-up lake bed. Clearly, water would accumulate here in the rainy season, and rough stone walls along the sides indicated that that this had been used for centuries, if not since Inca times. "Maybe this is the route the Incas used to reach the mountain," I said to Miki. We continued on until Mukurka Lake appeared in the distance. A legend is associated with it. Originally it was a mountain that turned into a lake after being beaten in a battle with Hualca Hualca. Still considered sacred, the lake gleamed while Ampato rose through the haze beyond.

We walked across a plain with a steady wind blowing dust into our faces. All along the Peruvian coast, the cold Humboldt Current causes the moisture-laden winds to rise and not form clouds until they hit the Andes. The result is that this region is one of the most barren on earth, with less rainfall in the Atacama Desert of northern Chile than in the Sahara.[10] Burros raced across the barren landscape. "They escaped and have turned wild," explained Henri. They reminded me of the wild asses of Tibet, fleeing at the slightest movement.

In 1990 Paul Gelles had written of a large canal, called Huataq, that the Incas had reportedly built and that was still being used until recent times. Indeed, control of the canal had been a bitter source of contention between the communities of Cabanaconde and Lluta during the first half of the 20th century.[11] Walking across the plain, I could see the remains of it traversing the side of a hill to the south. I was beginning to think we might actually be following in the footsteps of the Incas.

We set up our tents in an empty corral near a trickle of water that miraculously ran through the desert rock and sand. It felt good to crawl back into my old tent. I had left it behind in Arequipa when I'd gone to the U.S. three years before. It is hard to describe the feeling that comes with being in a tent that you have lived in over the course of years. Everyplace you visit, no matter how remote, seems like home once you close the tent flap. I settled down to read the novel *River God*, and let my mind escape to the world of Egypt. After the sun went down and darkness enveloped the camp, the moon came out and the wind died down. I was glad to be back in the mountains.

It dawned clear, and at 6:00 I called out to Miki and Henri to wake up. The sun lit our tents at 6:30, and soon we had a simple breakfast of bread and cheese with tea. I pulled out the yellow plastic sheet I had brought to protect the tent floor and cut it so that it fit the tent's shape. I put the leftover scraps in my pack thinking that they might be used to mark our ascent up the mountain, a minor precaution that would prove critical later.

By the time we loaded the burros, it was almost nine o'clock. Henri and Miki thought that a lower approach to the mountain would be easier on the burros. This route had been used since ancient times to carry salt between villages in the region. I went ahead and waited, but they disappeared behind some hills and did not reappear. After waiting for a while, I went in search for them, wondering if one of the burros had had an accident. I discovered that they had abandoned the trail and cut cross-country without informing me. When I caught up with them, I asked what had happened.

"We shouted to you and thought you'd heard. The wind must have drowned out our calls," explained Miki. That answer hardly satisfied me. He knew better than to make a last-second change of plans without making sure I knew what was happening. I was in a foul mood as we continued onward.

After lunch, we spent hours crossing ridges that led down from Hualca Hualca before finally reaching a stream. As I continued on ahead, I saw that it was turning muddy. We knew we would not have any water where we were planning to set up our base camp, so I backtracked to tell Miki and Henri to fill our five-gallon container with water from a side stream. I found out too late that they had only half filled it, despite our estimating we needed two days' worth. I was beginning to regret my decision to go to Ampato.

As we came over a ridge and once more could see the volcanoes, Sabancaya let loose with a gigantic eruption, blocking the sun and rekindling my desire to see it up close. The route Miki had climbed before on Ampato looked steep at the top, where it met a wall of ice cascading off the summit ice field. Miki felt we would find small, eroded sections that would serve us as "steps," but I thought this unlikely. Based on past experience, I knew it could just as easily prove to be the opposite, and the eroded ice could be terribly difficult to cross.

The melting of ice had turned Ampato's large crater area into a seemingly impenetrable field of ice pinnacles. Now that I had come this close, I remembered why Ampato had never been a popular peak for climbers. Mountains closer to Arequipa, such as Misti (19,416 feet) and Chachani (19,960 feet), were much more accessible. If Ampato did contain ruins, they likely remained undiscovered.

A cloud of volcanic ash is carried by the wind over the summit of Ampato (on the right) from the erupting Sabancaya.

Ampato was one of the most important deities of the region during Inca times. It was one of the mountains described in an account written by the Spanish priest Cristóbal de Albornoz around 1583.[12] In 1967 the Andean scholar Pierre Duviols published this document, but it passed largely unnoticed. When I first came across the document in 1980, I thought it was one of the little-known gems of Andean history.

Albornoz had listed the most important deities worshipped by the peoples conquered by the Incas, and I was initially stunned to read that the majority were mountains (or stones in mountains—usually representing them). This supported the information I was collecting at the time about current-day beliefs. Mountain gods were consistently more important than the primary deities named in the usual accounts of Inca religion, such as Inti (the sun) and Illapa (weather). These latter deities were ones that could "exist" everywhere, because they were so generalized—no small advantage to a state wanting to dominate a variety of ethnic groups, who worshipped their localized gods.

The name Ampato is probably derived from the native word *hampattu*, which means "frog." Although it seems an odd name for such a massive volcano, some indigenous people thought it was derived from the shape the mountain has when viewed from an Inca road that ran by it to the east. I thought it was not merely a coincidence that, throughout the Andes, frogs were considered ritually important for attracting water—an attribute they shared with mountains.[13]

We set up our tents at more than 16,000 feet in a sunken, dried-out streambed where we were protected from the wind. We finished setting up camp in the dark, using our headlamps. Although there was little water for the burros down below, Henri said he could wait with them here for another day. Miki and I settled down for the night. From this camp we felt we would be able to climb the remaining 4,000 feet to the summit the next day and return by nightfall.

The light had still not hit our tents when we started dressing for the climb in the morning. Until now we had been wearing relatively light clothing and did not need any special gear. But today we would be climbing over unfamiliar terrain covered in ice and subjected to high winds. Cold weather parkas, wind pants, gaiters, gloves, and balaclavas were de rigueur. For the first time we pulled on our heavier mountaineering boots. Miki had his new leather pair and I my double plastic boots. They had proven ideal for withstanding the abuse of climbing over sharp volcanic rocks. Ice axes, crampons (pointed metal spikes worn on boots for climbing steep ice), headlamps, and spare clothing were added to our packs, along with some food and water bottles. Miki took the rope, while I carried a medical kit, binoculars, camera, emergency blanket, and other miscellany, which included what I called "the gang of four" (to help me remember): an altimeter, a tape measure, a map, and a compass.

"I don't believe it," I groaned. "I forgot the compass." My embarrassment was compounded by having told Miki before we left Arequipa that I would bring two along. Neither of us expected to need one to keep from getting lost, but how could we now make accurate plans of any sites we might come across if we didn't know their orientations?

After plastering on sunscreen, we set off just after first light. Soon we got into a spirited discussion. Miki thought we should go directly up the route he had used before. I noted that we had already agreed on trying the north ridge. I was annoyed that he had brought this up just as we were about to start up the mountain. I had wanted to ascend the northern slope, because that way I could always keep Sabancaya in view. I couldn't know ahead of time where the best photos could be taken of the eruption, and even a view from the summit might not provide the best angle. If we went up Miki's western route, Sabancaya would be blocked from sight for much of the time by the intervening bulge of the slope. I could end up not getting any good photos, and that was the reason I had decided to climb Ampato in the first place.

Much to his disgust, we continued toward the northern ridge, then veered off and started climbing up a steep slope. In order to ease the way for him, I went ahead, making footsteps in the loose scree. Similar to breaking trail in snow, this meant a considerable savings in energy for the person climbing behind. The air was still, and in the silence all we could hear was the "crunch, crunch" of our boots as we kicked them into the slope. As if to demonstrate his independence, Miki made some of his own steps off to the side.

The northern slope did prove to be easy going, but when we reached its high point at more than 20,000 feet at 11:30, we were confronted with an ice field. Ice pinnacles or penitentes (aptly named for "penitence") two to three feet high extended in an upward jumble for nearly a mile to the summit. Miki, unhappy at seeing this field of ice spread out before us, suggested that we go back down. "You've taken your photos of Sabancaya," he said, "and you obviously won't get better ones crossing through ice in the opposite direction." He was right, but we still had plenty of time to get back. I thought we might as well give the penitentes a try, even if we failed to reach the summit itself.

So I forged ahead, knowing he would be too proud to give up if I kept going. I stepped carefully between the pointed edges of the pinnacles wherever possible and kicked the tops off them for footholds when not. At 20,000 feet this process was physically draining, worse than postholing in deep snow.

Miki had an even harder time, since he was shorter and couldn't step over some of the same pinnacles I could, even if he had been able to follow me directly. Formed at odd angles and widths, the treacherous field was impossible to pass through in a straight line.

I soon lost sight of Miki and two hours later had made my way out of the penitentes. I waited, but after nearly a half hour had passed, I began to worry that he might have given up or, worse, been injured. I started to go search for him when he appeared from behind a large outcrop of ice. After resting a moment, he said, "You disappeared and then reappeared on a hillock in the middle of the penitentes. I couldn't figure out how you'd gotten there." He'd resigned himself to breaking his own way through the ice pinnacles to reach me, but by then I'd disappeared again. I didn't tell him that I'd done this deliberately to pressure him into following me.

To my surprise he barely complained about the crossing. Perhaps he was as relieved as I that the way was open to the summit and we were over the worst of the climb. But he did realize that one problem still remained. How were we going to descend the mountain without having to go back through the penitentes?

While I had been waiting for him, I had scouted the area in vain for a way off the rim of the ice field. Now we walked along it farther, only to find sheer drops below. We had a rope, but some time passed before we found ground close enough below for the rope to reach it, if we needed to rappel off.

With an escape route established, we continued on toward the summit, which to our amazement appeared to be free of snow. Nearby, the west ridge reached the crater rim, and we had a clear view over the small plateau where Miki had seen the two circles. It was nearly a thousand vertical feet below us, but even from this distance, I could make out a large, rectangular structure more than 30 feet long. When I looked at it through my binoculars, I had little doubt that it was Inca.

"How did you miss seeing it?" I asked. "That area must have been covered in snow," he replied.

We soon came upon another surprise. Just before reaching one of the lower summits on the crater rim at 20,300 feet, we saw a layer of dead grass running through the ice. How had so much of this wild-growing grass (called *ichu* [*Stipa ichu*]) made it to more than 20,000 feet? Batches of grass extended upward, and I started to follow them. This explained what Carlos had described to us in Arequipa. He said he'd seen a bundle of ichu grass on this part of the mountain, and the melting of the past two years had exposed much more of it.

"It is getting late, and we should start back down. Otherwise, we will get caught out in the dark," said Miki. This made sense, but I hated to leave without seeing what became of the grass. We had reached the top of the slope that led down to the plateau, and climbing down did not look difficult. Reaching camp in the dark did not bother me either, since the moon would be full, providing enough light. "You go ahead. I'll start down as soon as I check out this last hilltop," I said, pointing up.

I started zigzagging up the scree slope, and after a few minutes Miki caught up. I was not surprised. We might not always agree, but he was a determined climber and would not quit while I continued on. We kept together for another ten minutes until we reached the top of the hill, where we found hundreds of square yards of thick grass. Scattered on top of it were pieces of Inca pottery and clothing, sections of ropes, chunks of wood, and even leather and wool sandals. "Do you believe this?" I exclaimed in wonder.

I took a photo as Miki held up one of a number of flat slabs of rock that the Incas had carried up from more than a thousand feet below—the rope they used still ran around it. The slabs must have been used to make floors and the thick layers of grass as insulation from the cold ground. Remains of wood posts suggested that tent structures had been built. The Incas probably employed llamas to help carry all this material, which would have weighed over a ton. They must have used this rounded, lower summit as a resting place before attempting the steep, final section to the highest point of the volcano, half a mile distant. The ichu grass was so plentiful, we would ever after refer to the place as Punta Ichu.

We could not reach the summit before dark, so I went over alternatives in my mind. We could climb to the top if we returned the next day, especially since this time we would take the more direct western route. It still looked steep, but the Incas must have managed it in order to reach this spot. We could also explore the ruins on the plateau during tomorrow's ascent.

Then another idea struck me—if we carried a tent up and camped on the plateau, we would have time the following day not only to climb to the summit, but to make a reasonably thorough search of the area. We could still return to base camp in time to meet Henri with the burros on September 9. To my relief, Miki agreed to this plan without the slightest hesitation.

Our problem now was getting down. Although a better alternative than the escape route we'd looked at earlier, the slope below us turned out to be not only steep but also covered with scree that only barely covered the ice beneath. We wondered how the Incas managed to get up, let alone down, it. But climb it they did, for, as we descended, we found wood scattered along the route, indicating they had once made a trail in the center of the slope. It had long since been swept away by avalanches. While we watched, rocks careened down the slope, and we continued with feelings of unease. When we eventually had to cross this section, we worked our way across it as fast as possible. We bypassed the little plateau and continued in the fading light straight down the face to the foot of the mountain. It was well past nightfall when we finally reached the gentle terrain leading to base camp. By then the moon had appeared from behind the ridge and its light was so bright, we had no further need for our headlamps. We reached our tent grateful to eat for the first time since morning. After our exertions, we easily fell asleep.

When I awoke the next morning, I couldn't open my eyes. They felt like they had been glued shut. After a moment I realized that the "sleep" in my eyes had solidified during the night. Doctors refer to this as "lachrymal goo," in a mix of slang and medical terminology. Wiping my eyes cleared up the problem, but left them burning. It was the beginning of one of those days.

"I have to take the burros down to a side valley where there is water and grazing," said Henri.

"Fine," I replied, "and if we aren't in base camp when you return September 9, you can continue on home. Assuming we haven't had an accident, it will mean that we decided to stay longer on Ampato. We will simply make our way back to Cabanaconde on our own."

Leaving Henri loading the burros, Miki and I slowly climbed up to the ruins on the small plateau located at more than 19,000 feet. There we found not only the two circles, but the remains of a few other Inca structures. We were surprised to see the desiccated body of a small animal, likely a coati, on the surface of one of the circles. It may have followed the Incas and died trying to dig for food offerings they had buried or it may have been an offering itself. Although it was a strange thing to find, it was the elevated stone-walled platform that most attracted our attention. With a tape we measured it at 3x15 yards. Clearly this was the rectangular structure we had seen from above yesterday.

The Incas traditionally buried most of their most important offerings. However, at times they encountered the problem of digging in rocky and frozen terrain. They solved this by building stone walls up from the ground. They would place the offerings in the space formed by the walls and then fill the structure with stones and sand until it became even at the top. Only a few of these artificial platforms had been excavated by archaeologists.[14] I wondered if we would ever learn what lay inside it.

Not far beyond the platform we found wood poles that were the remains of what could only have been tent structures. I knew the chroniclers referred to the Incas using tents, but I was not aware of any remains of them having survived. This discovery alone made our climb worthwhile. That is one of the joys of archaeology—finding physical evidence confirming what was written in ancient accounts.

After exploring the site, we set up camp. Water was not a major problem, as we could obtain it from the melting snows of the nearby ice field. Before long, though, we realized that this wasn't an ideal solution, since it was filled with dirt. I had brought a filter, but it was soon clogged, and I didn't have a brush to clean it. I'm not sure it would have helped in any case. Once I melted chunks of ice in a pot, the water still had the taste of sulfur, which no filter could have removed.

Even so, we had to drink it. Dehydration is one of the worst afflictions you can suffer when climbing high mountains. Beyond the obvious reason that your body needs water, drinking fluids is the key to avoiding cerebral edema. High-altitude cerebral edema (HACE) often proves deadly. It occurs when fluid leaks from blood vessels in the brain and causes it to swell. Mental acuity and motor skills quickly deteriorate—often in only a matter of hours and sometimes faster. Symptoms can include loss of balance and a strong desire to do nothing. People affected by HACE rarely realize it, and, if they don't descend within hours, they will die.[5] I had known climbers who died of it in the Himalayas, and one partner of mine barely escaped with his life during an expedition with me in Chile.

Unfortunately, in our present case drinking the water caused the onset of diarrhea. Until we could find an area of ice not so badly mixed with minerals, a vicious cycle would take place. The more water we drank, the longer we would have diarrhea and the more water we would need to replace the liquids lost.

I didn't sleep well, not surprising in view of the altitude. Worse, Miki did not sleep at all because of the fumes from the nearby sulfur source. They not only stank, they actually ate up oxygen. "I felt like I was suffocating," he told me, dead tired. "I sat up for hours in order to breathe better."

I heated the butane can between my legs and finally got the stove going and melted the ice for some tea. For our meal we ate some of the local cereal (germen de trigo) and a piece of bread. We left the tent before seven o'clock and soon started up a gradual slope leading toward the summit. Along the way we found grass and pieces of wood that had been placed on the steeper sections to reinforce a trail, presumably to make it easier for llamas to ascend the steep slope. In the dozens of other high-altitude sites I'd studied, I had never seen climbing aids like this.

"They wouldn't have gone to so much trouble to make this trail and the ichu site, just to make a few simple offerings," I said to Miki. "They must have made a human sacrifice somewhere near the summit."

Human sacrifice seems horrific to people today, but it was even practiced in ancient times in the West, albeit infrequently. It played an important role in the Old Testament, however symbolically it might be interpreted. In one of the most famous of the biblical stories, Abraham is willing to sacrifice his son, Isaac, at God's request. The earliest historical sources describe human sacrifice among the Celts, and the Romans issued laws banning it—hardly necessary unless it was practiced.[16]

We may never know how widespread human sacrifice was during the early rise of European civilization, but human sacrifice figured prominently in ancient mythologies, including those of the Greeks.[17] Nor were Europeans surprised to find sacrifices among cultures of the Americas. What did surprise them was its extent, especially among the Aztecs of Mexico, where Spaniards observed sacrifices firsthand. This was not the case with the Incas, due to the relative rarity of human sacrifices and the locations where at least some of them took place. Although the Incas told early Spanish writers about human sacrifices and Spaniards found physical evidence of them, no Spaniard ever witnessed one while it was being performed.[18]

The higher we climbed, the more arduous the route became. We first tried reaching the summit by climbing through a rock buttress. This way we could avoid crossing a steep section of the slope, down which an occasional stone bounced. We had left the rope and crampons at base camp, because we thought we wouldn't need them for the summit. After nearly an hour, we realized that we would spend too much time finding a safe way through the boulders of the buttress. So we crossed an exposed section of the slope, while rocks sailed by, released by the warmth of the sun. We were relieved when we reached the grassy knoll of Punta Ichu.

We tried to climb directly up the last hundred yards to the summit via the steep north ridge, but without a rope and crampons, we gave up when the route proved too risky. So we skirted along a scree slope below a series of gullies that dropped off the summit's northeastern face. We were only a few yards above the bottom of the ice-filled crater when we heard the sound of running water below us. Amazingly, we were more than 20,000 feet high, yet the ice was melting and a stream was flowing beneath it. As we made our way behind the summit ridge, we encountered a section of ice looming above us. It abutted the rocky part of the cliff and blocked our way. We came to a halt, frustrated. We were so close to the summit.

While Miki tried to find a way through the ice, I attempted one of the rock gullies a hundred feet to the right. I tried straddling the gully's walls, but couldn't get a grip without crampons. I repeatedly swung my ice ax into the ice-covered rock, only to have its point bounce out. Once a slab of ice broke off and crashed down the cliffside, bringing back the memory of a fall I had once taken—a memory I would have preferred to forget.

That fall had occurred when I was 20 years old and climbing alone on the Jungfrau, a mountain in Switzerland. Unexpectedly, I started plummeting down a snow-covered slope, and I frantically used my ice ax to slow myself down. Putting my weight on its point and holding the head of the ax against my chest, I could hardly believe my luck when I gradually stopped. But to my horror, I soon felt myself falling again. Only then did I realize that I was lying on top of a slab of falling ice!

It was carrying me toward a vertical drop of 2,000 feet and certain death. There was nothing I could do. After what seemed like agonizing minutes—but actually must have been only seconds—the snow once again came to a stop. This time I knew I could not move, or it might start sliding down the mountain again. I waited awhile and then slowly—very slowly—made my way sideways until I reached a stable area of the slope. I was so shaken that I continued down using both my hands and feet, even though it was an easy descent the rest of the way.

I kept calling over to Miki, "How does it look?" and the answer kept coming back, "It's impossible this way." Finally he said, "We should head back and return later with a team and more equipment."

"We are so close to the summit, I'll give it one last try," I said.

When I joined Miki, I couldn't understand why he hadn't called me over earlier. Only one short section had stymied him. With my longer reach, I managed to sink in the point of my ice ax and pull myself up onto a shelf.

I helped Miki up, then I left for the summit while he caught his breath. After another short section that I angled up, I found myself standing on the volcano's highest point. To my surprise the 30-foot-wide ridge that Miki and Carlos had described no longer existed. The ridge was now barely a yard wide. It consisted of a thin layer of volcanic ash covering frozen ground that dropped off steeply on both sides. I took photos of Miki as he scrambled up and, partners again, we shook hands at having finally reached the top.

I began writing down notes about the time, altitude, and summit conditions. In the meantime, Miki continued along the ridgeline. Soon I heard a whistle and saw him raise his ice ax. Without a word he pointed down. Even from a distance of 50 feet, I spotted the reddish feathers sticking out of a steep slope about six feet below him. My heart started pounding as I realized that they could only be from a feathered headdress.

First we examined the ridge above the feathers. We saw remains of a stone wall and a wood stump that had formed part of a ceremonial platform. The thin ash layer must have absorbed too much heat and caused much of the frozen ridge to collapse. Along with it had fallen the rest of the Inca structure.

We had no rope, so we tied together two slings. I held Miki and took photographs as he stretched out from the steep incline. He extracted first one, then two more statues with headdresses. Classical Inca female figurines made of gold, silver, and the rare spondylus shell, they were all facing toward the highest point of the summit. Their miniature textile wrappings were so well preserved, they looked new.

"There are only about a dozen clothed statues this well preserved in the whole world," I said, filled with wonder. The feathers that had been exposed were still in excellent condition. This meant that the gravel surrounding the statues must have fallen away only days before. Otherwise, the sun would have caused the feathers to dry and shrivel. Indeed, the statues themselves were on the verge of plunging down the slope at any moment. We carefully wrapped them in plastic and my spare clothing and placed them in the top of my pack.

Originally the structure had been the kind of artificial platform I had seen on so many summits before. Looking down, I saw that it could have fallen down either (or both) of two naturally formed gullies. They narrowed down to sheer drops to the crater floor. Unable to see where these led, I said to Miki, "How will we know which gullies we will be looking up at once we are inside the crater? There are several of them and they all look alike from below."

Then I remembered the yellow scraps of plastic. They would be perfect for spotting where the structure had fallen. I felt like a genius, despite its being a simple enough idea. I wrapped two stones in the plastic, tied the bundles with adhesive bandage and threw them down the gullies. I knew that even if they did not get stuck on the way down, they would be falling into a maze of ice pinnacles inside the crater. "It'll be a miracle if we ever see them again," I said, while quietly feeling confident we would find something. We retraced our route to the summit, eventually making our way horizontally above the crater bottom's ice field.

Miguel Zárate points to the feathers of a statue protruding from just below the summit.

We soon spotted one of the stones where the rocky slope met the ice field. I stopped to take pictures of the gullies above, because I knew that the ice in the crater could shift by the time we could mount a follow-up expedition to the volcano, and we had to have some points of reference.

Miki continued looking for the other rock. He soon called out, "I see something inside the crater! It looks like a bundle."

When I joined him, I looked down where he was pointing. A mummy bundle was simply lying on top of the ice. This seemed so unlikely that we couldn't believe our eyes. For 15 years I had visited dozens of sites on peaks in the Andes, and had never even *seen* a mummy bundle on a mountain, let alone one lying out in the open. Only a couple of intact mummy bundles had ever been recovered from high mountains, and only one by an archaeologist.

"Maybe it's a climber's backpack," said Miki.

"Maybe it's a climber," I replied, only half joking.

I took more photos while Miki made his way down to the bundle. I watched as he approached pieces of wood strewn above it.

As he stopped to examine the items near the wood, I dropped down to join him. We found fragments of a torn cloth, a spondylus shell, two cloth bags containing food offerings (maize kernels and a maize cob), llama bones, and pieces of Inca pottery scattered about the slope. Clearly these remains had been buried in the platform that had fallen.

As we drew closer to the bundle, my pulse quickened. The outer cloth wrapping had stripes typical of Inca textiles. Given the other items we had already found, it seemed certain it would contain a mummy. This could mean only one thing: The Incas had performed a human sacrifice, and the bundle containing the victim had fallen when the platform collapsed. Perched on top of a pedestal of ice, it looked as if the mummy were on display. I took photos as Miki used his ice ax to cut the ice beneath the bundle to free it. He turned it on its side for a better grip, and as he did so the bundle revolved in his hands. Suddenly, we froze and time seemed to stop. We were looking straight into the face of an Inca.

Wrapped in insulated pads to protect her from the sun, the Ice Maiden is led away on a burro's back. Thus began the race to reach Arequipa before the ice melted.

CHAPTER TWO

RETURN of the MAIDEN

The past is never dead. It's not even past.
—William Faulkner

*Some of the huacas [sacred places] are hills and
high places which time cannot consume.*
—Joseph de Arriaga, 1621

I first saw the face of a frozen mummy when I was in Chile in 1980. It had been brought down by treasure hunters in the mid-1950s from El Plomo, the mountain overlooking Chile's capital, Santiago, and was on display in the city's National Museum of Natural History.[ ] Now, on Ampato, I couldn't take my eyes off the face of a mummy that seemed to be staring directly at me.

"It looks like it has dried out," I said, my awe quickly turning to disappointment. It was obvious that the mummy's face had been exposed when the cloth covering it had been ripped open. That must have happened as the bundle tumbled down the gully. Based on what I could see of the mummy's face and clothing, I said to Miki, "It looks like a female." Unfortunately, it also looked like we had arrived too late. At the very least, her face had been exposed to the sun for so long that it had become desiccated. If this were the case with the rest of the mummy, then we wouldn't have the frozen body we had imagined only moments before.

"See, my intuition was right that there could be something on this mountain," said Miki proudly.

"Yes, but if you had gone when you wanted to before, you never would have found anything because of the snow," I pointed out. An incredible set of circumstances had come together to make the discovery possible, and intuition was the least of them.

I asked Miki to move the bundle off the pedestal, while I continued taking photos from different angles. "Hey, I can barely lift this thing," he groaned. I thought maybe he had become weakened from the combination of the days of climbing, the altitude, the lack of sleep, the lack of food—quite a list under any circumstances. I went over and gave it a try myself. He had not complained for nothing. The bundle had to be full of ice to weigh so much. (Later in Arequipa it weighed 97 pounds, even with some of the ice removed.) I set it down and examined the cloth wrapping the mummy. Then another thought struck me—there wasn't enough ice to make it so heavy. I felt a surge of adrenaline as I realized what this meant.

Even a partially frozen body would be invaluable for science. Few frozen mummies had been found on mountains anywhere in the Andes and none in Peru, close to the heart of the Inca Empire, and those had been largely desiccated through a freeze-drying process. Here we had made a unique find. The mummy's intact body tissues and organs would allow complex DNA and pathological studies that had never been conducted on an Inca mummy before.

"If the mummy is a female, we have found the first frozen female in the Andes," I said to Miki. Inca female clothing had never been found in such good condition while still being worn. For the first time we could see exactly how a noblewoman dressed. Even if she had been a commoner originally, I knew she would be dressed in the finest garments, given the importance of the other offerings we had found. Our accidental discovery could provide information unique in our knowledge of the Incas.

ACCORDING TO THE CHRONICLERS, CHILDREN WERE SELECTED BECAUSE their purity made them more acceptable to live with the gods. After being sacrificed, these children became messengers or representatives of the people to the gods and could intervene on their behalf. The children became, in effect, deified and worshipped together with the gods with whom they were believed to reside. They would be honored for all time, unlike the majority of common people, who only received offerings for a few generations.[2]

It was considered an honor for the parents of the children selected, and some were known to have offered their children willingly. The parents were not supposed to show sadness, and it was even said to have been a major offense if they did. Not all parents felt the honor worth the price, however. Thus they were not opposed to their daughters losing their virginity, since in this way they avoided being taken away.[3]

As for the victims themselves, some may have gone to their deaths satisfied that they were to join the gods. In an account that had especially moved me, I read about a young girl, Tanta Carhua, who was sacrificed on a mountain north of Lima. In the early 1600s Hernández de Príncipe had been told that Tanta Carhua said, "*Acaben ya conmigo que para fiestas bastan las que en el Cuzco me hicieron* (Finish with me now because the celebrations they held for me in Cuzco were enough)."[4] However, many children would surely have been frightened, as indicated by their being given *chicha* (maize beer) to drink in order to "dull their senses," as one chronicler wrote.[5]

The Incas used the word *capacocha* when referring to this kind of ritual human sacrifice. Boys and young girls destined to be sacrificed were reportedly provided as tribute to the state by local communities on a yearly basis. If true, this would likely have been more the case for capacocha ceremonies undertaken at Cuzco, where the Inca emperor resided. We knew that annual ceremonial offerings were probably made at the places where capacocha ceremonies had been carried out, but we knew of only one case of a mountaintop site at which more than one child had been sacrificed.[6] Also, some of the children sent to Cuzco were not sacrificed there, but instead continued on to other religious sites—

or returned to the region where they originated. I wondered if this girl was an outsider or had been raised within view of Ampato.

The Inca Empire became famous for establishing a system for selecting virgins and making sure they remained so. These were called acllas ("chosen women") and were taken from their homes at a young age. They were kept in special buildings (acllahuasis), out of contact with the rest of the population. The girls were taught to weave fine garments and prepare maize beer for religious and political purposes. After the age of puberty, some of the young women were removed from the acllahuasis and were given as secondary wives to nobles—or sent to be sacrificed.[7]

I estimated that the girl we found was about 14 to 15 years old. Some chroniclers had noted this as the age of the acllas chosen for sacrifice. That meant that the bundle contained one of the purest of maidens.

BY NOW, THE SUN HAD LONG SINCE DISAPPEARED OVER THE NORTHERN summit and it would soon be dark. My mind raced with all the implications of the discovery. What was the next best step? If we left the mummy behind, the sun and volcanic ash would further damage it. Also, at this time of year a heavy snowfall could cover the summit any day and make recovery impossible, perhaps forever. I knew that obtaining an archaeological permit could take weeks, if not months, as could obtaining the funding to organize a scientific expedition. Nor could we save time by flying in with a helicopter. Most helicopters could not land safely even at the altitude of our base camp.

It would have been impossible for us to lug the mummy on our backs to Cabanaconde in a single day, but we could cover the distance if a burro carried it. The spare burro that I had grumbled about bringing had now turned into a godsend. We could pack the mummy in ice, wrap it in the insulated pads we used to sleep on, and return to Cabanaconde the way we had come. The pads would protect the mummy from the sun, and most of the trip across the plateau would take place in the chilly temperatures at 14,000 feet. By the time we descended to the village at 10,800 feet, it would be dark and cooler.

I voiced these calculations to Miki, as I plotted the trip out further. There was no telephone in Cabanaconde and only a few hours of generator-powered electricity. Thus no freezer would be available to store the mummy. "There is a bus leaving at 11:00 p.m. to Arequipa on September 10," I said to Miki, who realized immediately what I was thinking. "It would arrive in Arequipa at six the next morning." He agreed that we could probably make it to Cabanaconde in time to reach the bus. "Even if not," I added, "we could probably find a vehicle to take us to Arequipa." Since the bus would be traveling at night and cover most of the journey at altitudes of more than 12,000 feet, we would have enough time to transfer the mummy to a freezer before it began to thaw out.

One major problem remained, though. If I returned from the mountain with a mummy, the archaeological authorities would think I had carried out an excavation without a permit. I had been registered as a professional archaeologist with the government for years and had directed several expeditions to Peruvian mountains in the past. A find like this would create a sensation. The news would travel around the world. That meant the government would be scrutinizing every detail. As a climber and a Peruvian, Miki wouldn't get into trouble. However, I was a professional archaeologist and had organized the expedition. I might never work in Peru again—and a ban would harm my standing in other Andean countries as well.

Yet what was the alternative? To leave the mummy meant putting at risk one of the most important finds ever made in Peru.

It was impossible to bury the mummy in the rocky, frozen ground. Covering it with ice could only be a temporary solution. The running water only a short distance away and the warmer weather of the coming months meant that the mummy would suffer more from exposure. It is difficult for non-mountaineers to imagine how hot it can become at even 20,000 feet when the sun is out and reflecting off the ice. One of the hottest places I have ever been was at more than

19,000 feet amid seracs in the Khumbu Icefall on Mount Everest. The only reason we wore thin parka shells over our sweating bodies was to prevent sunburn.

Worse, the mummy was on the eastern, sun-facing side of the summit ridge, exposed to the full brunt of the sun's rays. Even under the best conditions it would deteriorate. If my obligation as an archaeologist was to help preserve the cultural patrimony of Peru, leaving the mummy behind was an unacceptable alternative.

"Under the circumstances, it seems to me the best course of action is to carry the mummy down the mountain," I told Miki. "Besides, we already have Inca statues, and I'm not about to leave them behind. So, I may be criticized for excavating without a permit in any event."

"I'm not feeling strong enough to carry it," Miki replied, and I couldn't fault him. I wasn't sure I could do it myself, and I had the advantage of being acclimatized from recent climbs in Bolivia.

I gave the extra items I'd been carrying to Miki. Since the statues were especially delicate and his small backpack lacked compartments, I kept them in the top pocket of mine. Then I turned my attention to the mummy. She was wrapped in such a small bundle, I thought she had to have been buried, like most Incas, sitting in a "seat-flexed" position. Her knees would have been drawn up close to her chest and her arms and legs crossed. This was just as well, since a stretched-out mummy would have been impossible to carry on my back.

Besides ice that had formed inside the folds of the outer cloth, there were two large chunks attached on the outside that we couldn't remove without risking damage to the cloth. We covered the bundle in plastic and struggled to fit it inside my Lowe Expedition pack, one of the largest made. Although this proved impossible, the bottom of the bundle fit snugly into a large lower section of the pack that could be unzipped. With the weight thus supported, we strapped it to the frame.

I couldn't hoist the pack directly off the ground, so I sat down, put the straps around my shoulders, and Miki pulled me to my feet. I could barely stand up, let alone navigate an ice-covered slope. "I'll be lucky to make it to the crater rim," I told Miki as I staggered to keep my balance.

In the fading light the volcano's cloud of ash seemed to take on a sinister aspect. Having a dead body on my back added to the surreal scene. Images of Incas struggling through the same terrain ran through my mind. For a moment I was transported back in time, and I had the eerie feeling that I was rescuing someone who was alive.

I remembered that during the dry season Andean peoples believe the mountain gods provide "gifts" to those who they feel merit them. We were in the height of the dry season, and some villagers would be searching the mountain slopes in search of stones that have the shape of animals, such as llamas and alpacas, which are thought to increase the fertility of herds.[8] But the gifts can take other forms— including a mummy. In other words, some villagers would believe that we had not "found" the mummy, but that the mountain god had given it to us. In truth, the circumstances were so unusual, I began to feel this way myself.

I do not believe in mountain gods, but I can easily understand why Andean people do. You can't spend years in the mountains without gaining respect for them, and often they seem to take on personalities of their own. I realized that with the discovery of the mummy, Ampato would soon become one of the most famous mountains in the Andes.

First, though, I had to get down it. I started by putting one foot carefully in front of the other. We had not gone more than a hundred feet when I fell. The weight on my back was so pressing that I hit the ground faster than I could extend my arms to break the fall. I had the wind totally knocked out of me, and I lay gasping for air. Miki waited patiently, but there was nothing more he could do.

The distance from where we found the mummy to the edge of the crater rim where we would begin to descend was only half a mile away. Without a load, that distance would have not presented a problem. But to reach it, I would have to climb around strips of ice that zigzagged vertically up and down along the bottom of the slope. Yet an ascent of only 50 feet required an effort that left me exhausted.

The lack of food didn't help. We hadn't eaten the entire day and barely had eaten anything the day before. Combined with the effects of diarrhea, the altitude of 20,500 feet, and the treacherous footing, the journey down became a nightmare. The weight on my back made my legs feel like they were ready to collapse. Every movement upward caused my calves and thighs to strain unbearably.

Worst were the falls. Each one left me bruised and panting. I cursed myself repeatedly for not having brought crampons. I almost gave up after each fall, and indeed Miki repeatedly said I should. He was patient throughout the ordeal, cutting steps with his ice ax. But as it grew ever darker, I thought I wouldn't be able to continue.

Luckily, as we neared the grassy knoll on the crater's rim, I began to feel a surge of strength. I would need it. Once started downward, instead of getting easier, the way became worse and at times dangerous. Part of the slope inclined at a steep 50°, which would seem nearly vertical to an inexperienced climber. Cutting footholds in the fading light of headlamps immediately below me, Miki kept pleading with me to leave the mummy behind and to return for it the next day. (I thought he was worried about my physical condition, but later he told me, "I thought you would fall on me with that heavy pack, and we would both be swept down the mountain.") But by that time I had passed through the I-will-never-make-it stage to one of barely controlled fury—that peculiarly satisfying mental state of burning clarity experienced by fanatics.

As time went on, though, even I began to realize that I couldn't continue in these conditions. The moon had not risen high enough from behind the ridge, and we had used up too much of our batteries. Soon our headlamps barely illuminated the steep mixed-ice and scree slope. We could hear, but not see, stones hurtling down nearby. Crossing the slope would require time and thus almost certainly mean getting hit by falling rocks. I gradually accepted that it was foolish to continue with the mummy. I left it firmly lodged among penitentes at 20,000 feet. Without the weight, we quickly crossed the slope and descended to our tent in the dark. We collapsed inside, too exhausted to eat.

The next morning dawned clear and sunny. I returned alone to carry the mummy down to the high camp. While I started up, Miki set off down a scree slope that proved to be much easier to scramble down than we could have hoped. He reached the foot of the mountain in only half an hour and arrived in base camp in time to catch Henri before he gave up on us and returned to Cabanaconde. Miki also directed him to bring a burro to the foot of the slope to cut down the length of my portage.

An hour and a half after starting the ascent, I reached the mummy. Once again I fit the bundle in my pack, dreading what was to come. As soon as I had it tied firmly, I pushed the load up the side of a serac. I had to reposition it a few times before I was able to slide my arms under the shoulder straps. I gritted my teeth as I slowly rose up and away from the ice. The pack was as onerous and bulky as before. I wobbled a bit, but with a wonderful sense of relief, I realized that I wouldn't fall. The memory of last night's ordeal had been so strong that this was the first time I felt certain I would be able to carry it the rest of the way down. I started the descent, slowly working my way over, around, and through the edge of the ice that protruded into the scree-covered slope. Difficult, at times exhausting, the trip nonetheless seemed like a cakewalk in the daylight and after a night's rest.

Suddenly I sensed someone coming along beside me. Who could it be? The hood of my parka blocked my peripheral view, but I could swear I caught a glimpse of movement. Had Miki climbed up for some reason? Or had a climber descended from the summit? I quickly turned, but no one was there. The second time I turned, I knew what was happening. I was experiencing an illusion that other climbers have described, when they were convinced of the presence of someone beside them. One climber pulled out food to offer his newfound companion. Even the knowledge that it was an illusion did not stop me from a subconscious conviction that I had a companion by my side. In a way, it was oddly reassuring—I felt I was not alone.

I decided to cross the exposed slope higher up than we had last night. I soon found that descending at night had had its advantage. The number of rocks falling had been less frequent, because more of the rocks were frozen due to the night cold. Now rocks were regularly bouncing down by me on all sides. I looked up trying to estimate their paths, but a bad bounce could send a stone in any direction, including mine. I felt like a moving bowling pin avoiding a series of balls. I soon stopped looking up and worked my way down and across the slope as fast I could. Just before the ordeal ended, Sabancaya erupted. The wind carried the ash overhead, and soon I felt it striking my face in hundreds of tiny needles. Once I was across, I caught my breath as I rested amid some boulders. What remained was an easy (downhill stroll), and a half hour later I was back at our tent. "I did it," I exclaimed, even though I knew it was still a long way to Cabanaconde.

While waiting for Miki to return, I took down the tent and searched the plateau for more ruins. An hour later, Miki appeared with Henri, whom he'd somehow convinced to climb up to the plateau with him. Yesterday, Miki had occasionally teased me about carrying the mummy, even saying, "What's the big deal? It's only a few kilograms." So I thought he should experience what it was like, however briefly. Besides, my knees had taken a beating and the downhill scree run would only make them worse. Henri agreed to trade off with Miki carrying the load. But he grew more and more somber as he realized the nondescript load contained a dead body.

We started the descent, and I went ahead. Soon Henri passed by some distance away without a word and without stopping. A light snow started to fall. I was in a quandary. If I stayed to help Miki with the mummy, Henri might leave with the burros, abandoning us. At the very least, I worried he would not bring one of the burros from the camp to the foot of the final slope. The descent was a short one, probably less than an hour even with the mummy. I signaled back to Miki that I was going ahead. He gave no sign to indicate he needed help, and I started half-running down the scree.

I caught up to Henri at the campsite, preparing loads for the burros. He denied he was planning to leave us. Maybe so, but I had to argue with him to persuade him to return with one of the burros to meet Miki, thus saving us from having to carry the mummy the extra distance to the camp. Henri was tense and kept averting his eyes. This guy is spooked, I thought. He begrudgingly left with a burro and met Miki just as he reached the bottom of the slope. Before long, we were making up the loads. Now all any of us wanted was to descend to civilization, the faster the better.

As I put my pack on, I noticed something distinctly odd: "Why are you putting a blindfold over the burro's eyes?" I asked Henri.

"Because he will bolt if he senses that he is carrying a dead body," he explained.

That sounded reasonable enough, and the possibility kept us alert for the next hour. In that time we made our way down to the stream at the foot of the mountain at 15,300 feet. We arrived just as it began to get dark. We fetched water from a nearby spring and felt revived after some hot tea and soup. We climbed into our sleeping bags, having placed the mummy near the side of the tent with some ice. Even though it was cold during the night, we were taking no chances.

We were nearly out of food, and we ate only a few bits of hard bread with some jam for breakfast the next morning. But if the day went as planned, we would return to Cabanaconde and by evening have a real meal. We packed the mummy in our insulated pads and tied the bundle together with our climbing rope.

It proved impossible to keep the mummy bundle balanced directly on top of the burro's back as it traversed such rugged terrain, and eventually we had to counterbalance it by adding a rock to make a load on the opposite side.

As we walked along, Miki told me that he had had a dream the night before we found the mummy. "A female mummy had asked to be saved.

Last night she came and thanked us for doing this," he said. This was the first I had heard of Miki's having a dream about a mummy on the summit, and I gave it no further thought at the time.

We descended into a small valley where, to our surprise, we passed a corral that was still being used. A woman appeared who looked even more surprised than we were. She was watching a herd of llamas that surrounded us with some curiosity. It turned out that one had given birth only hours before. A good sign, we thought.

As we continued on, Miki began to talk of what he would do once the discovery became known. "You don't know how to use the press," he noted correctly.

I didn't like the idea of press being considered at this stage at all, and I asked, "What do you mean? I thought that last night we had agreed nothing would be let out to the press until we had a chance to return to the mountain. It will be hard enough for this to be kept quiet locally, since Henri is bound to say something. We might well return to find the sites looted by villagers, even if no word gets into the press."

"No, I wasn't thinking of that. But when the discovery does become known, I know how to make it reach a much wider public. You only think about the science, but people want more a sense of the esoteric," he replied. From our previous discussions, I knew he meant tapping into the New Age market, and I was not pleased at the idea.

"Whatever happens, there can't be any distorting of the facts," I said. He agreed, but in an offhand way that left me wondering.

We reached the place we had camped the first night during our ascent. There we made the first and only stop of the day. The three of us took a ten-minute break and shared the contents of a can of sardines and a small piece of cheese, the last of our food. We then began the dreaded walk across the flat plain. Although the going was easy, the sheer tedium made it an ordeal. The afternoon wind accomplished its usual job of making us eat dust—literally.

By the time we reached the outskirts of Cabanaconde, we had been walking for nearly three hours in the cool of the night. There was no moon, and our headlamp batteries had by then weakened to the point that we could only switch them on briefly when urgently needed. It was so dark that we couldn't see our feet, but the burros smelled home and took off on the familiar path at a pace we could barely match.

We finally passed by a few buildings and entered town, having trekked for more than 13 hours. I paid Henri and he left, clearly relieved that the job was over. Our dreams of having a hot meal in a restaurant were quashed, however, for they had all closed. We did find a stand selling chicken and spaghetti, a favorite dish in the Colca Valley, and a gourmet meal for famished climbers.

As for the bus, we were relieved to find that it was leaving on time and there was plenty of room. Even better, it had an undercarriage where the mummy would remain cool. We placed the nondescript-looking bundle into the coolest part we could find.

While arranging our transportation on the bus, I had been thinking about how to store our valuables during the ride. We knew we were too exhausted to stay awake during the all-night bus ride. Night buses were notorious for the thefts that took place while passengers slept, and a gringo would be a prime target. The mummy would be locked in the storage compartment, not to mention being too bulky and heavy to be easily moved by a thief, but what about the statues? They were too fragile and valuable to put into storage, and my camera gear was valuable as well. The film rolls were irreplaceable.

I explained this to Miki and said, "I can't see how we can both go with the mummy."

"You can go alone with it," he replied.

"But that would mean the statues and camera gear would have to remain with you," I said. "If the police made a search of the bus, you would have a harder time of explaining their being in your possession than I would." I didn't say it, but I knew that if they were confiscated, it could prove a nightmare getting anything back, let alone the statues.

I weighed the options. The night bus was due to arrive in Arequipa around 6:00 a.m. Since it would be a Monday and thus a workday, I knew that José would leave home to go to the university at about 7:00. Once in the bus terminal, Miki could call him, and José could quickly take a taxi and move the mummy to a freezer. Even if José didn't personally have a freezer large enough to hold the mummy, he could call our friend Dante Lucioni, who by fortunate coincidence actually sold freezers—and big ones, at that. In the worst-case scenario, Miki could take the mummy to his house and then locate José. I didn't have a place to stay, let alone to leave a mummy.

In the end, we decided it made the most sense for him to go ahead with the mummy. Thus having settled—hopefully—the main contingencies, I arranged to take the first bus in the morning. Miki left at 11:35. No one else on the bus knew they had a mummy traveling with them through the night.

Despite being dead tired, I had an anxious night and woke a number of times to distant barking. Yet that wasn't the reason I had trouble sleeping. I kept thinking of Murphy's Law: if anything could go wrong, it would go wrong. I imagined the bus breaking down, a highway robbery, the police confiscating everything, an uprising of the passengers upon discovering a mummy was traveling with them, a workers' strike (not uncommon in Peru then) causing the road to be blockaded—the list went on and on.

My worries continued during the long bus ride the next day. Once I arrived in Arequipa, I immediately went to José's. He set my mind at ease. "Don't worry, the mummy is fine. The bundle even has ice still attached to it," he said.

It turned out that Miki's bus had not arrived until 6:45 in the morning, and he found that all the telephones at the bus station were occupied. So he had taken the mummy directly to his parents' house and then gone in search of José at the university. José contacted Dante, who immediately had a freezer delivered to Miki's home. "The mummy was safely stored in the freezer by nine o'clock," said José.

A wave of relief swept through me—we had done it. We had managed to get all the items safely to Arequipa in the same condition as we had found them. I've rarely enjoyed a supper more than the one I had that evening.

THE FROZEN INCA MUMMY WAS AN EXCEPTIONAL ARCHAEOLOGICAL discovery, but her death occurred within a historical context where such sacrifices were seen as vital. In order to understand how this girl would have been regarded at the time, it is necessary to briefly review who the Incas were and what they achieved. Even to this day discoveries are still being made about this culture that dominated South America when the Spaniards arrived in A.D. 1532—indeed, the Inca Empire was the largest to ever exist in the Americas. The Incas had conquered the entire central Andes, a region extending from northern Ecuador to central Chile, more than 2,500 miles in length.[9] To provide a sense of scale, if it were laid across a map of the United States, it would cover an area that extends from Los Angeles nearly to New York.

Archaeologists divide the history of the central Andes into time periods called "horizons" (when a particular art style was found extending over a broad area) and "intermediate periods" (when widespread art styles were absent). The Preceramic period (ca. 3000–2000 B.C.) was marked by the introduction of cotton on the Peruvian coast. During the Initial period (ca. 2000–1200 B.C.) people settled, and agriculture, pottery making, and textile manufacturing became common. The Early Horizon (ca. 1200–200 B.C.) was associated with the Chavin art style, which spread over a large area of central coastal Peru and the highlands. Regional art styles characterized the Early Intermediate period (ca. 200 B.C.– A.D. 600), with the Nazca and Moche being the best known. The Middle Horizon (ca. A.D. 600–1000) was established based on the Tiahuanaco-Huari art style that extended from the southern highlands to the north coast of Peru. During the Late Intermediate period (ca. A.D. 1000–1475) regional art styles again arose over limited areas, with the Chimu culture holding sway in the north coast of Peru. The Incas dominated the Late Horizon (ca. A.D. 1475–1535) before falling to the Spaniards.[10]

Thus, the Inca culture was only the last in a long line of civilizations that arose in the Andean region over three millennia. Many aspects of the Inca Empire had their origins in institutions and technologies that long preceded it. However, the Incas accomplished astounding feats of their own, all in less than a century before the arrival of the Spaniards.[11] One of the best-known examples is the Inca road system, which was one of the most extensive ever built in the ancient world, rivaling that of the Roman Empire. It has been estimated that the Incas built 20,000 miles of roads. Inca stonemasons became famous for fitting together multi-ton stones without mortar—and so well that a knife blade could not be slid between them. This caused wonder among the Spaniards, despite the great fortresses and churches they knew from Europe. Scientists are still trying to figure out how they achieved such precision.

The administration of such an extensive multiethnic state was itself a major feat, made possible by initiatives that incorporated conquered groups into a highly integrated economic, political, and religious system. Deities were believed to control the success of crops and herds, of wars, of illnesses, of business transactions, and so on—everything was intertwined. The Incas helped ensure their control of the state through several means, including the establishment of a single language, Quechua, as a principal means of communication. They established a system of posts or way stations (tambos) for travelers to stay and also to hold supplies. Runners (chasquis) were used for the rapid transmission of messages.

In broad terms there are two types of agriculture in the Andes. One is based on highland staple root crops, principally the potato, which can be grown up to 16,400 feet in some parts of the Andes. More than 200 varieties are known. Potatoes can be stored for long periods after having gone through a process of freezing and drying, and they do not require irrigation or the use of fertilizers. Tuber agriculture and herding were (and are) usually combined. Other highland crops include grain foods, such as quinoa, the world's most nutritious cereal.

The second type of agriculture takes place in the lower elevations and has evolved around maize. Although irrigation and fertilizers are usually necessary for a successful crop, there is no need to leave land fallow, as is necessary with potatoes, and the grain can be stored for long periods. The Incas are particularly associated with the spread of maize agriculture in their empire and into valleys in the highlands. It had a high status and played an important role in ceremonial contexts.

Although terracing was practiced long before the Incas, they became especially associated with its expansion and with developing it to a high standard. Terraces help to prevent erosion and to extend the amount of land available for cultivation. Irrigation has played a significant role in agriculture since at least the Early Horizon, and irrigation systems not only became important for obtaining successful harvests but also became the focus of much ritual attention, especially at the time that canals were cleaned. And that brings us back to the mountains, the origin of down-flowing water and the deities most widely venerated whenever water is involved.

In order to better control and develop the regions they conquered, the Incas moved entire communities to colonize them, thereby insuring local support groups and promoting integration. They educated local leaders and their children in Inca ways, often by having them spend time in Cuzco, capital of the Inca Empire. They supported local shrines, while keeping some of the main idols of the conquered peoples as virtual hostages in Cuzco. They undertook major public works in conquered regions, such as terracing, irrigation, and storehouses, in order to offset any food shortages. The Incas also promoted the expansion of herding into new areas and set up systems for the redistribution of products and services. They used a hierarchical system based on a decimal system for the division of labor, including military units.

No documents predate the arrival of the Spaniards, because the Andean peoples lacked writing. However, they developed an elaborate system of record keeping by using variations of knots and colors on cords, called quipus. Although the Incas did not have the wheel, thanks to their road system and llama caravans, products were transported throughout the empire. All this took place in one of the most rugged terrains on earth.

The Incas' organizational and logistical ability set their empire apart from any that had come before. This ability also enabled them to undertake a systematic campaign to climb to the summits of the highest peaks in the Americas.

The Incas had a precise knowledge of topography and were able to make models of the areas they conquered even at the extremes of their empire. One such model of the larger Cuzco region was so well done that the chronicler Garcilaso de la Vega wrote, "the best cosmographer in the world could not have done it better."[12]

The Inca emperor was regarded as the son of the sun deity, Inti. He was not only a secular ruler but also head of the Inca state religion, which was imposed throughout the lands they conquered. The Incas began to expand out of the Cuzco region sometime around A.D. 1438. The emperor Pachacuti (ca. A.D. 1438–63) undertook campaigns that soon brought a vast area of the central Andes under Inca control. The period of his reign is the first for which we have unambiguous historical and archaeological evidence. It marked the beginning of major building initiatives, including such well-known sites as Machu Picchu. The empire was divided into four (tawantin) quarters (suyus), hence its name Tawantinsuyu. The name Andes is thought to derive from the name of one of these quarters, Antisuyu.

Pachacuti's son Tupac Yupanqui (Topa Inca, ca. A.D. 1463–93) conquered more lands, until the borders stretched from modern-day Ecuador to central Chile. The limits of the empire were reached with Topa Inca's son Huayna Capac (ca. A.D. 1493–1525). His death was followed by a conflict between his sons over succession. The struggle resulted in a weakened empire at the time the Spaniards arrived in Peru. Taking advantage of this division (along with their superior armor, the dissatisfaction of some tribes against Inca rule, and the aftereffects of an earlier epidemic), the Spaniards were able to take over a state that rivaled any in Europe in size and riches.

ON THE MORNING OF SEPTEMBER 12, JOSÉ AND I WENT OVER TO MIKI'S parents' house to check on the mummy, and then we sat down to plan our next steps. The first priority had to be the mummy, and the sooner specialists were called in the better. Although simply ensuring that the mummy was kept below freezing was fine in the short term, for long-term conservation we needed to establish what the right temperature and relative humidity would be. I had been living in Chile in the early 1980s when specialists examined the frozen Inca mummy found by treasure hunters on the volcano El Plomo. The Canadian expert Dr. Patrick Horne had stressed to me then the importance of controlling humidity and maintaining a steady temperature.

We also had to consider the case of the Iceman. In 1991 two hikers had discovered the frozen body of a Neolithic man in the Alps. A large multinational team had convened to decide how to best preserve his body. We needed a team of our own.

I had met Dr. Sonia Guillen while in a village near Cuzco some years before, and I knew she was one of the few trained mummy specialists in Peru. When I learned that she had her own mummy research facility at Ilo, a few hours' drive from Arequipa, José and I decided to call her. Luckily, we were able to reach her that evening, and she agreed to come immediately to Arequipa.

José had called the rector and obtained his approval to store the mummy at Catholic University. But we still had to notify the authorities, and this caused us some concern. When I first arrived in Arequipa, I had intended to talk with one of the archaeologists I knew at Arequipa's branch of the National Institute of Culture (INC).

Before I did, though, I learned that a number of mummies and artifacts under the protection of the INC had been destroyed or stolen—and these included items I'd left with the institution years before. Directors of the local INC were political appointees, and while all had good intentions, they were rarely archaeologists. One new Arequipa INC director, pressed for space, had transferred mummies and artifacts to a military base for temporary storage. There they were left unattended for nearly a year. As a result, more than 50 mummies and hundreds of artifacts had been ransacked, and in some cases stolen or burned. José had been particularly affected, since he had carefully excavated dozens of mummy bundles that now no longer existed.

All archaeological finds ultimately belong to the government of Peru, but custody of the finds often lies with the institution that is willing to take responsibility for them. There was no doubt in either of our minds that Catholic University was the best place in Arequipa to have the mummy kept and conserved. It was independent, which meant that it was not nearly as susceptible to political pressures, such as the strikes that often crippled Peru's state-run national universities. It also was not as seriously affected by economic problems. In addition to having the only archaeology department in southern Peru, it had departments of other disciplines, such as medicine, which could be drawn upon for the kinds of specialized work that inevitably converged in studies of frozen mummies.

Another factor had to be considered as well. We wanted to keep the discovery out of the press at least until we organized an expedition and returned to the mountain. Otherwise the news could spur treasure hunters to loot the site. We needed to conduct a careful archaeological search of the summit site and the slope down which the mummy fell. Also, José was convinced that the site on the plateau would harbor at least one more burial.

Given past experience, I had no faith that INC personnel would keep quiet about our find. In the course of an excavation I directed in 1991 on Huarancante, a volcano near Arequipa, we had found a gold

Inca statue.[13] After depositing it with the INC, I asked its chief archaeologist, Pablo de la Vera Cruz, not to give any information out to the
press. Personnel at local INCs were always tempted to leak news of
a discovery because it reflected well on them. I made the request
because I did not want headlines in the papers about "gold" being
found, since this might spark the interest of looters. They might destroy
not only the site on Huarancante, which we had only partially excavated, but those on other mountains, including Sara Sara, which
was where we were headed next. Pablo reassured me, "Of course I
understand. And in any case, your permit guarantees that you have
first rights to publish on your finds."

We left the next morning for Sara Sara, and when we returned a
week later, we discovered to our dismay that the very day we had left,
the statue appeared on national television! When I questioned Pablo
about how this could have happened, he explained that he had been
hounded by the "press," and didn't want them to think the INC was
trying to keep something secret. Since he was still the chief archaeologist at the INC in Arequipa, I had no faith that he would keep quiet
about the discovery of the Ampato mummy.

Yet clearly we had to inform the INC at the national level as soon
as possible. Less than 24 hours after my return, José and I called Dr.
Roger Ravines, the national director of the archaeology section of the
INC. He immediately asked me the question I had been expecting
(and dreading) since first finding the mummy: "What were you doing
in the field without a permit?" After I explained the circumstances,
he claimed that he understood. He also said he realized the need to
issue a permit to return to the mountain as soon as possible. He
requested that we send him a report within a day or two. We assumed
that he would relay the information immediately to the INC in
Arequipa, and every morning I was afraid to open a newspaper lest
I see news of the mummy.

To help underscore the importance of the finds for the university,
we showed the statues to the vice rector that evening. José had thought

of temporarily keeping the freezer containing the mummy in one of his department's offices, but we needed a place to set up a laboratory and storage facilities. This couldn't be arranged as quickly as we would have liked, and so the mummy stayed at Miki's house for another day.

I debated whom to contact for help to fund both the conservation and an expedition to return to Ampato. There was little hope of obtaining support soon from the financially strapped Peruvian government or, for that matter, any other Peruvian institution. Several organizations in the U.S. provide support for archaeological research, but almost all require a lengthy process of submitting proposals and having them reviewed by specialists.

There was one obvious choice. In 1983 I had received a grant from the National Geographic Society to conduct research that year on high-altitude archaeology in the Andes, and I had published an article for its magazine about the topic in 1992. Best of all, the director of its Committee of Research and Exploration, Dr. George Stuart, was a friend of mine, and I knew the committee had the flexibility to make available a few thousand dollars immediately. Dr. Stuart was also a prominent archaeologist, and he would understand the importance of the mummy. Indeed, I had barely started to explain the discovery over the phone when he asked, "How much do you need?" Within minutes he promised to wire $7,500. Four thousand would cover urgent conservation concerns, and the remaining $3,500 would help pay the expenses of our return to the mountain.

We still had to obtain the permit, however. The climbing season ends by late September in most of Peru. The North American summer coincides with the winter months in South America, but as luck would have it, the South American winter is the period of the most stable weather in the central Andes. With spring come more rains at lower elevations and snow in the mountains. A heavy snowstorm could hit and the snows cover the site, not to melt off again for months—if ever. In short, the later we started, the more chance that snow on Ampato would impede our excavation.

Many archaeologists have to conform to the prevailing weather patterns in their work, but few have as short a window of opportunity as that in high-altitude archaeology. The problem was complicated further by the nature of our work. Finding people who had a combination of climbing ability and interest in archaeological research was difficult enough. Fewer still were able to get free for the lengthy periods away from home that were necessary. I had been frustrated before, watching an entire season slip away due to bureaucratic delays in obtaining permits. The central authorities never seemed to understand that high-altitude archaeology was different from most other archaeological work.

José lost the letter I had prepared to send Dr. Ravines on Wednesday, so I rewrote it, and we finished a proposal for obtaining a permit, sending them off together on Friday. We left messages for Dr. Ravines to contact us if he wanted additional information, but as time went on, we did not hear a word. I kept anxiously calling a friend in Lima who was in regular contact with him and was told, "Everything is fine. He is just busy." However, the days dragged on and still we heard no word about the permit.

We had transferred the mummy in its freezer to Catholic University that first Wednesday. It was placed with the artifacts in a locked room directly in view of a guardhouse that a watchman occupied 24 hours a day. A room had been cleared and turned into a temporary lab and storage facility. Now we could undertake preliminary research and documentation of the finds in a secure, private environment.

Dr. Sonia Guillen arrived and offered to bring her team later when the unwrapping of the mummy began. We were pleasantly surprised when she said, "I know members of the team that worked on the Iceman, and I feel certain they will be interested in helping." Soon I was on the phone with Dr. Konrad Spindler, an archaeologist who had written a detailed book on the Iceman.[14] He reassured me that the mummy would remain stable as long as it was kept in the freezer.

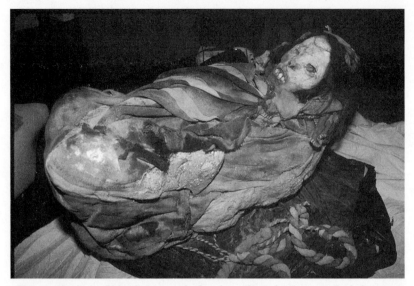

The Ice Maiden still had ice attached to her when she first reached the city of Arequipa.

Sonia arranged for material to cushion the mummy whenever it was moved from the freezer to a table in order to be examined. Based on our knowledge of what had been done in the past with frozen mummies and on discussions with the Iceman team members, we knew that sealing the mummy in a vapor barrier of plastic would help it stabilize at its own degree of relative humidity.

With the frozen girl in our care, the team made a seemingly innocuous decision. They thought that referring to her as la doncella ("the maiden") sounded too impersonal. They wanted to use an informal name until a permanent name could be chosen. José told me they had selected the name Juanita, because it was a familiar one among villagers and easy to remember. The name had even been used for Inca noblewomen shortly after the Spanish conquest and applied to a summit of one of the most sacred mountains of the Incas—Ausangate.[15] Also, we did not know where the girl had originally come from, and thus any name ran the risk of being from a language that she had never spoken. Much to our surprise, the name was later picked up by the press and stuck.

After more than a week had passed, we began to wonder why we still had not heard from the local INC. By now surely Dr. Ravines had called the local director, Franz Grupp, or Pablo de la Vera Cruz. On September 21 I decided to visit the INC to see why no one had contacted us. The office had closed by the time I stopped by at three o'clock, so I left my card for Pablo with my telephone number.

The next morning, José, Miki, and I met with the faculty heads and other authorities of Catholic University. I explained the importance of the finds, but also emphasized the problems that were sure to arise if the university decided to retain custody of the mummy. These ranged from the financial responsibility the university would have to assume to the pressure from people in positions of power who would want control. Since a frozen mummy was so rare, no uniformity of opinion would exist even among specialists as to how to conserve Juanita. That meant the university was bound to encounter some criticism. Much to their credit, later that day they decided to accept full responsibility. Also, at José's instigation, during the meeting the university formally offered Miki a full scholarship.

Miki and I left at ten to talk with the officials at the INC. Pablo still had not called, but I thought it best to meet before more time had passed. When we arrived, we were told that Pablo and Franz Grupp had heard about the mummy and left for Catholic University shortly before we arrived.

Back at the hostel, an official of the university called to say that Pablo and Grupp were angry they had not been informed earlier about the mummy. Miki and I went once more to the INC only to find that the director had just left. But Pablo was there and we were soon involved in a heated exchange.

"You deliberately withheld information from us, and you know that all archaeological artifacts are by law the property of the government," he said.

"I do know that. And that is why I immediately informed the national authorities. You should be asking them why they didn't notify you earlier," I shot back. "There is no law stating that the local

INC has to be informed first, nor is there a time limit on this. And how could I trust that you wouldn't let out the news immediately, when the last time I was here you had the Huarancante statue on national television within 24 hours?" (I refrained from mentioning the destruction of mummies in the INC's custody only a few years before, since Pablo had not been present then.)

We eventually calmed down, though not before Pablo informed me of his low opinion of Catholic University's archaeology department. I had long been aware of this, since a rivalry had existed between INC and Catholic University archaeologists for years. It did not help that Pablo and José had disliked each other since they were both students and that Pablo taught at National University, the main rival of Catholic University.

More days passed, and still we heard no word about the permit. Concerned, I finally asked a previous American ambassador to Peru, my friend Alec Watson, if he could contact the Peruvian ambassador in Washington. Peru had suffered severely from the bad press generated when the Shining Path guerillas were active, and now they risked losing the publicity and prestige that a National Geographic expedition would surely bring. Luckily, the Peruvian ambassador, Ricardo Luna, was not only a close friend of Alec's but also instantly grasped what was at stake. He contacted the INC, and on September 29 a colleague called to say that we had the permit. At last, we could finalize the timing of the expedition, the members of the team, and the supplies and equipment.

Finding an experienced crew with high-altitude filming experience was not easy, especially on such short notice. National Geographic Television had contacted David Breashears, who had just returned from one of his several ascents of Mount Everest, and he had soon mounted his own team. We agreed that the expedition would leave Arequipa on October 6. The pieces of the puzzle were coming together.

Our optimism was tempered on October 3 when I received a call informing me that the producer being sent by National Geographic TV was a woman without climbing experience, and she was planning to ascend the mountain with us. This added one more concern to an ever-growing list for this complex expedition.

That call was followed by one from *Der Spiegel* wanting a story. The best-known and most respected of the German weekly magazines, it was also an arm of a conglomerate that had its own TV company. They had made a film about the Iceman, and the Ice Maiden seemed like a natural for them. I soon heard that at least one of the Iceman team members had told *Der Spiegel* about our discovery in order to have his trip to Peru paid.

I was introduced that afternoon to Arcadio Mamani and Juan, Miki's brother. Arcadio was a local guide and had occasionally worked with Miki's older brother Carlos, who was overseeing buying supplies and plotting the logistics for the ever-rising number of team members. Juan was a genial young man, but he lacked the experience I had expected, given his family background. Arcadio looked every bit like the hardened mountaineer he was, but had the humility and calmness of a Buddhist monk. "He's the kind of man who made it possible for the Incas to build sites on mountaintops," I thought, little knowing the important role he would later have in studying them.

I still had not received any money from National Geographic, so I went with Miki to the bank the next morning to cash some travelers checks. "I've decided not to accept Catholic University's offer of a scholarship," he said as we walked along. "I don't want to take the entrance exam and do the work a degree would require." He also complained about feeling marginalized by José and Ruth Salas. She was an archaeologist in her own right, and I knew they both felt that Miki was too inexperienced to be involved in laboratory work.

"I'm not feeling well, and I will only go on the expedition if you insist on it," he said to my surprise. "I also don't think that the archaeology students will be strong at altitude, and I will end up having to do a lot of the work."

"I think it is important for you to be on the expedition, as long as you feel well enough to go," I replied. "I'll make sure you aren't left doing most of the work."

Yet this wasn't his main concern that morning. "My father wants to be on the expedition, and if he isn't, he will follow us and publish about it on his own."

"But three of his sons are already on the team, and he is too old to work on the summit," I said, annoyed at this demand. Nonetheless I agreed, understanding that his father, an important figure in the local climbing scene, would want to join one of the biggest expeditions ever to take place here.

That afternoon the film crew arrived, and I was reassured to discover all of them had participated in mountaineering expeditions before. Accompanying David Breashears, one of the world's top mountaineering cinematographers, were the soundman, James Brundage, the assistant cameraman, Joe Montgomery, and a climbing partner of David's, Mike Weiss. Stephen Alvarez, the photographer, had no high-altitude experience, but he was an accomplished caver and outdoorsman. The producer, Amy Wray, was the only one who lacked climbing experience, but she did not anticipate venturing much beyond base camp. David had especially insisted that National Geographic hire Mike for the trip, since he was not only a very strong climber but also had considerable experience handling logistics.

That would be needed, for the film crew had come with literally a ton of equipment. They wanted 20 burros to carry 100 pounds apiece. Added to this were another 10 burros for our own supplies and gear. "How will we get all this stuff to base camp, let alone up the mountain?" I wondered aloud to José. That night I sent Arcadio on a bus to Cabanaconde to see what could be arranged.

Sonia arrived that evening from Lima with money sent to her account by National Geographic. She also brought the permit. To my dismay, I discovered it was written in a way that I would never have accepted under normal circumstances. It noted concerns about other archaeological work carried out in the past under the auspices of Catholic University, and by placing my name in the same context, the permit made it sound as if I had undertaken unauthorized excavations and made "fraudulent use of documents." Nonetheless, it authorized the return expedition under the supervision of the INC in Arequipa.

"What are they referring to?" I asked José, who was as perplexed as I was about the accusations. "If they had concerns, why didn't they just talk to us?"

I decided to ask them the next morning, while the team organized gear and collected supplies. I walked over to the INC. We first went over details of the expedition, and Pablo said he would be joining us once we had established camp and begun the excavation. I agreed to send a guide and have horses meet him when he arrived in Cabanaconde.

I finally brought up the wording of the permit, which we knew had to have been based on what he had written to the INC in Lima. "I have never used a false document in my life," I said.

"That actually refers to another foreign archaeologist who had worked with Catholic University while using an expired permit," he replied. "The 'unauthorized excavations' refers to that person."

"In that case, what are these accusations doing in a permit issued in my name?" I asked.

"That was a mistake made by the INC in Lima. They combined two separate issues into one, since they both have to do with Catholic University," he replied. "They used the opportunity of your permit to make known their displeasure."

Your displeasure, I thought. After all, the national INC knew only what he had told them. But I did not have time to have the permit reworded before we left for Ampato—it would just have to wait.

Unfortunately, the intrigues and infighting over the Ice Maiden had only just begun. As soon as people heard about the rising star of Peru's patrimony, they wanted to be linked to her. Once the news became fully known, our mummy would become an international cause célèbre.

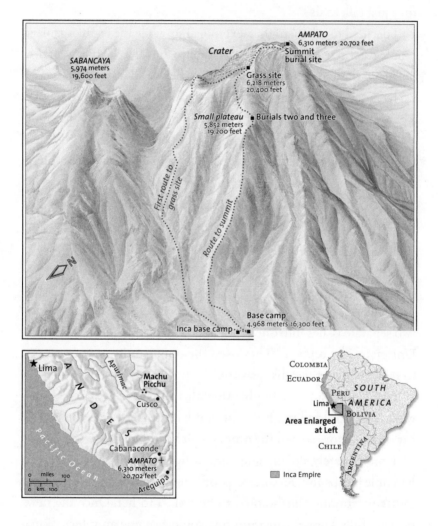

A relief plan of Ampato shows the two routes taken to its summit in 1995. The route
on the left kept to the northern slope in order to observe Sabancaya's eruptions

CHAPTER THREE

EXTREME ARCHAEOLOGY

Only the paradox comes anywhere near to comprehending the fullness of life.
—CARL JUNG

Human nature would not allow them to kill their own children . . .
if they did not expect some reward for what they were doing or if
they did not believe that they were sending their children to a better place.
—BERNABÉ COBO, 1653

THE NEXT DAY WE BOARDED A PRIVATE BUS RENTED BY THE FILM CREW, and that night piles of equipment filled the rooms of the little hotel in Cabanaconde. As we were leaving Arequipa, Sonia, swamped by the myriad problems presented by the frozen mummy, jokingly said, "Please don't bring back any more." The possibility seemed so remote that we all laughed.

We woke up early the following morning and spent a few hours arranging payments with a number of villagers, since no single person owned the caravan of burros and horses we needed. While the animals were being loaded, the whole village turned out to observe what seemed like a circus that had come to town. Despite the chaos, the burro drivers left in time for us to reach our previous campsite at 14,000 feet.

It felt good to be heading back into the mountains. Like many climbers who spend long periods in mountains, I do not feel at ease until I am amid them. I estimate that over one 17-year period, I did not spend more than three months without being on an expedition.

I have spent more than four years in tents in the mountains, and although I am now over 60, cities still seem foreign and temporary to me. Whenever I sling on a pack and start up a mountain, I feel a surge of satisfaction—I am going home.

The trudge across the desolate plateau seemed shorter than before. Some people grew fatigued, however, due to a lack of acclimatization, and reached camp only after dark. A few ended up riding the last couple of miles on horseback.

The morning sun rose in a cloudless sky, but most of us did not stir until its rays had warmed the insides of our tents. By the time we set out, the sun was high in the sky, and we felt the heat, thankfully lessened by a cool breeze. To our surprise, the weather was proving to be even better than it had been in September.

However, as the afternoon wore on, the breeze we had welcomed earlier turned into a strong wind. It swept up dust and fine volcanic ash that filled our mouths. Although a couple of the burros fell while crossing a stream, we made good time. Then, just as we neared the last slope to ascend to the site of our base camp, the burro drivers halted, insisting on staying the night there.

I learned to my consternation that Henri had told them it would take another three hours to reach the campsite. This meant they would not reach it before dark, let alone return back here, the last place with water. I knew that camping here would mean the loss of a full day. That was not merely an extra expense, but, more important, one less day of supplies for us to use higher on the mountain.

"I promise it will not take longer than half of Henri's estimate," I told the men. After much arguing back and forth, one of them finally said, "We will continue on one condition. If we don't reach the campsite in one and a half hours, we will drop the loads and turn back."

Our prospects did not bode well when one of the burros slipped on the way up and fell nearly a hundred feet. Fortunately, the animal was unharmed, and after a few minutes its load was readjusted and it continued on. I went ahead and waited anxiously out of the wind in a gully near the campsite. The minutes ticked by until I finally caught sight of movement over the rise in the distance. Wavering like a mirage, the shape slowly took form, and I breathed a sigh of relief when it turned out to be a burro. Eventually all the burros reached our campsite just under the deadline. We quickly unloaded the tents and began setting them up.

During the day's climb we had seen three condors circling above us. "That's good luck," noted Arcadio approvingly. Throughout the Andes traditional people believe that condors either represent the mountain gods or are the forms they take to oversee their terrain. We had come well prepared to make an offering to them. While in Arequipa I had asked Arcadio to buy a *pago* ("payment"). This bundle of ritual offerings usually includes coca leaves and seeds, small pieces of gold and silver foil (representing the minerals), pieces of starfish, incense, maize kernels, llama fat, and other foods deemed appropriate for the gods. The fetus of certain animals, such as llamas, vicuñas, and pigs, would also be added for important rituals, and Arcadio obtained one of these as well.[1] Traditional deities associated with the mountains and Pachamama, Mother Earth, would be pleased, he assured us.

One night Arcadio made the offerings to the gods, asking them to help us have a successful expedition. As a firm believer in their power and the only man from the Colca Valley planning to go with us to the summit, he felt a special responsibility. "Nothing should be taken from the mountain without something being given in return," he said.

The Incas had built their own base camp (tambo) a few hundred yards away from ours. This consisted of several roughly built circular and rectangular stone structures for sleeping, along with a corral for llamas.[2] Although our camp was well situated, water had to be carried up from a spring an hour's walk below. This would be the cause of a constant water shortage, as burro drivers repeatedly arrived too late with water for the morning meal. Climbers then had to carry supplies up the mountain with little or no water to drink— not the best way to adapt to high altitude.

We planned to encamp 18 people on the plateau at 19,200 feet for nearly a week, so we began ferrying loads up the 3,000-foot ridge. Although the climb amounted to basically a high-altitude hike, there was one spot with a ten-foot drop. Climbing alone with a top-heavy pack, I was thrown off balance and ignominiously landed with a thud, causing gashes in my leg and hand. Memories of carrying the mummy vividly came back to me. Too embarrassed to mention the fall to the others, I limped the rest of the way to Camp 1.

We were lucky to find a depression just below the plateau where we could set up all our tents in a protected area. The winds would still gust, but at least they lost some of their power whipping by overhead. We set up the cheap mess tent we had bought in Arequipa and kept our fingers crossed that it would survive until the end of the expedition.

To my mind lightning was of far more concern. The plateau was wide open and thus exposed to strikes, despite being situated well below the summit. I have dreaded lightning for years, ever since I was struck at age 17. While working on a railroad line gang in Iowa, I had fitted wires on the cross arms of telegraph poles. One day I was strapped on top of a 35-foot pole, putting in a "four-way." I was attached to the pole by a leather strap affixed to my harness. My boots had sharp metal shanks with spikes that I plunged into the wood for balance.

If telegraph wires are kept in parallel lines, they pick up interference from each other. A way to avoid this is to periodically have them cross through a series of insulators, hence the need for a four-way. Just as I was crossing one of the wires, lightning hit the lines some distance away. Swoosh—up shot a flame between my hands, exactly where I was twisting the wire. The next thing I knew I was hanging from my harness: I'd been knocked out cold.

During my ensuing years in the mountains, my hair had become electrified on several occasions and I had nearly been hit a half dozen times. Once, my climbing partner Luis Glauser and I had summited a Bolivian mountain and stood in the clouds with little sound, except for a sigh of wind. I heard a light "bzzz" and thought I had inadvertently set off the self-timer on the camera dangling from my neck. The second time I heard the sound I could see that the timer wasn't moving, and I realized with a start that the metal of the camera was reacting with the electrified air.

"Down!" I shouted, and started running. Luis didn't know what had happened until I passed and sharply cried out, "Lightning!" We had sprinted maybe 200 feet from the summit when it hit. The boom was tremendous, and I was thrown to the ground before I realized how I had gotten there—indeed, I must have been momentarily knocked unconscious again. To my consternation I later read that, under the right atmospheric conditions, lightning can travel horizontally— indeed it has done so more than ten miles.

As part of my further research, I learned that a lightning bolt could carry up to 30 million volts and reach a peak temperature of 55,000°F.[3] Compare that to the shock 120 volts can cause in your home, and you get the idea. So how do people survive a lightning strike? Despite its power, the strike is so brief—its peak temperature lasting only a few millionths of a second—that it might do no more than singe a person's clothing. Then again, more people are killed by lightning each year in the U.S. than by hurricanes or tornadoes.

That was why I always took precautions when placing a camp. Some of my companions thought I was being overly cautious. "It only takes one strike to kill you," I told them.

The day after we had set up Camp 1, Mike, one of the strongest men on the mountain, ironically became the first to have an accident. While he was climbing up the ridge over unstable rocks, a rock slab fell on his leg. David helped him as he hobbled back down in considerable pain, using two sticks to support him. His leg soon became badly swollen, and I cut ice to keep the swelling down. Fortunately, Mike was able to limp back to base camp under his own power. By coincidence, he arrived in time to meet Pablo, who had appeared on horseback from Cabanaconde the same evening.

As we expected, several members had difficulty adapting to the altitude. About a quarter of those who go quickly above 10,000 feet suffer acute mountain sickness (AMS). Its symptoms can include headaches, fatigue, disturbed sleep, nausea, vomiting, and shortness of breath. But it is not fatal and can dissipate as the body adapts. That is not the case with more serious kinds of altitude illness, such as cerebral and pulmonary edema.[4]

We tended to avoid the worst of the illnesses by following the adage "climb high, sleep low." Given the amount of archaeological work we would be conducting at a mountaintop site, we could not carry everything we needed to the summit in one trip. Thus, in the process of ferrying loads up the mountain, we became both better acclimatized and in better shape.

I have often been asked if we use oxygen, but this isn't feasible. We would have to carry an enormous quantity of bottles to use for the relatively long periods we work. The multiple carries needed would not be offset enough by the benefits. The better course was to simply acclimatize. After all, that's what the Incas did.

Also linked to acclimatization and high-altitude illness is dehydration. Humidity decreases the higher you climb, because the reduction in temperature and atmospheric pressure means a reduction in the water content of the air. Your body tissue's water balance is also thrown off due to a drop in the potassium levels in the cells as you ascend a mountain. For these reasons drinking an adequate amount of fluids becomes essential.

Add to this the cold: the temperature falls by roughly 3°F for every 1,000 feet you ascend. When you reside on a mountain, you are also more exposed to the winds. To give an example of what the windchill factor can mean: Imagine you are standing in the open and the temperature is at freezing (32°F). Then a wind of 40 mph comes up. Now the equivalent temperature is roughly −24°F—a drop of 56°. Any exposed flesh will soon freeze, even though the temperature still reads 32°F.[5]

During the first few days at 19,000 feet, Hector vomited several times, Mario had diarrhea, and José and Walter suffered from both nausea and headaches. Joe was constipated and, after taking a laxative, discovered that he had worms. The possibility loomed that the team might become too small to do any serious work before the supplies ran out.

Nonetheless, the first day we began surveying the structures on the plateau. This did not take long, and we next concentrated on excavating one of the stone circles. I was taking notes when I heard someone shout, "Feathers! My God, we've found a headdress of feathers!"

I walked over and stooped down beside José, who was bent over a row of reddish-looking feathers. "This must be on top of a mummy," he said with tenseness in his voice. By now the whole team had assembled, and all eyes anxiously watched as he cleared more soil from around the feathers. "Cloth!" he exclaimed. We instantly felt certain that it covered the head of a mummy.

It was if a primal source of energy had been released. Despite the extremes at 19,200 feet, we barely were able to contain our excitement as we took turns carefully excavating deeper around the body. The end of a shawl pin soon protruded from the opening, proving we had found the body of a female. "She is so small, she must be young, maybe no more than eight years old," said José. The textiles were in excellent condition. "We've done it. She must be perfectly preserved," I said optimistically as we all shook hands celebrating the find.

The largest feathers of the headdress appeared to have been flattened in order for the mummy to fit into the tomb. We later found that the mummy had been placed on top of a flat stone by the Incas. They had dug down as far as they could into the frozen ground.

A separate, much finer layer of feathers was so closely molded to the mummy's facial contours that at first we thought part of the headdress had served as a mask. Headdresses have been found on female Inca statues, but I knew of only two recovered from tombs of Inca women, and neither was well preserved.[6] This one would rank as Peru's finest.

The first few inches of the burial consisted mainly of a gray volcanic ash. Then we uncovered red earth that continued to the bottom of the burial three feet down. "The closest source for this dirt is hundreds of yards below," said José, who had immediately gone in search of it. I knew that red coloring had a ritual significance for the Incas. They had painted their faces red in certain religious ceremonies, and the coloring had also been found on Inca human sacrifices on mountains in Chile and Argentina.[7] But this was the first time we had seen red soil used in a burial.

The team soon began uncovering pottery as well. Some of the pots appeared to have been deliberately broken; pieces were found widely separated from one another. José pointed out that it could have been ritual breakage, although it didn't explain why so many other pots had remained intact. We knew that pottery intentionally broken in this way had been found at other sites in the Andes, including among cultures predating the Incas. But the reason for the breakage remains unclear.[8] We eventually uncovered nearly 40 pots of purely Inca origin. They appeared to have been deliberately chosen to represent most of the different types of pottery used by the Incas.

Pottery was another kind of offering the Incas made together with human sacrifices. Inca pottery is highly standardized in its forms of decoration and easy for us to recognize. We eventually freed *aribalos*, short-necked bottles, pots, shallow plates, and bowls. We knew that the aribalos and jars were used for the transportation, storage, and distribution of *chicha* (maize beer). The pots were devoted to cooking and the plates and bowls to the consumption of food.

However, the high quality, lack of use, and fine decorations of most of the pottery indicated its important symbolic role.[9] At the bottom of the burial, three aribalos had been placed with their openings facing in three cardinal directions, which Inca scholars have noted as being significant in Inca religion. Some of the pottery pieces were miniatures, and their use was clearly more symbolic than utilitarian. "Have you seen any collection this good found in a burial context?"

José asked me. He was referring to the fact that most Inca pottery on display in museums lacks information as to how it had originally been placed. "Seen? I haven't even heard of one," I replied, smiling.

We encountered a serious problem when we hit 500-year-old, rock-hard ice a third of the way down. How could we continue excavating without damaging artifacts or being forced to leave behind the mummified body and remaining objects to possible treasure hunters? We did not have time to wait for the sun to slowly melt the frozen earth as we picked away at it. In a way the ice was worse than concrete, since concrete cracks, while a strong blow with an ice pick left only a small dent in this mix of ice and gravel. We even briefly experimented with a blowtorch to melt ice along the side of the burial, but it had little effect. Even if it had, the lack of oxygen at this altitude meant that the blowtorch was difficult to keep lit.

"Let's try using water heated in the tea kettles," I finally suggested. "By pouring it around the artifacts we can gradually isolate them and free them up. In effect we will be doing what the sun would have done naturally."

Using this method, we also slowly melted a channel around the mummy. That way we could free it without directly soaking its priceless clothing. Foam packing materials were used as sponges to absorb the water. By wringing them out into a bucket and then reheating the water, we found we had a self-perpetuating system. This was no small accomplishment, as we would otherwise have had to constantly melt ice for the water—a time-consuming business that kept one man occupied just making our drinking water.

Not wanting to disturb the small stone-walled circle marking the upper boundary of the tomb, we eventually worked down to a depth where we had to stretch to reach bottom. Shorter team members had to be held by their ankles. We chose to work without gloves so that our fingers were more sensitive to any piece of cloth that might be mixed in with the water-soaked soil. We wanted to avoid as much as possible any potential damage to the fabrics.

As a result, though, our fingertips became cracked and sore for what turned out to be weeks afterward. The simplest task, such as buttoning a shirt or tying a bootlace, caused a grimace of pain. Fortunately, the excitement of slowly uncovering rare artifacts more than made up for the discomfort. Weaving tools, two wooden spoons, a small open wooden box (to hold medicine or hallucinogenic powder?), small wooden ceremonial drinking vessels, two offering bundles, and other items emerged, adding to our growing knowledge of the burial. But it was a pair of tiny sandals that gave us sad pause to reflect on the fate of this child.

Mike's leg improved enough for him to return on the 12th. That night in the mess tent he informed us that the archaeology group would have to help carry the film crew's equipment down the mountain once the expedition was over. Besides the problem that out of the six of us only three, Miki, Orlando, and I, felt strong enough to climb back up to make the carries, I was concerned about fairness. The archaeology team members were being paid less than the climbers working with the film crew, and I knew they did not like the perception that they could be used as "porters." Even the men hired to help the film team did not like being perceived this way, and it had been a sensitive issue when loads started to be ferried up the mountain.

Yet Mike had a point—we couldn't simply abandon the expensive gear. Thus we agreed to the time-honored tactic of postponing any decision and instead waiting to see how the course of events evolved.

Friday the 13th lived up to its reputation. The burro drivers went on strike for more pay. They were supposed to go back to Cabanaconde and return to meet us on the 17th. Now they refused unless we raised the pay for both them and the burros. The strike was made worse by the fact that, being at the high camp, we had to negotiate their demands through walkie-talkies. We felt betrayed, since this went against the agreement they all had signed. Of course, they knew they had us over a barrel.

Pablo had climbed up on the 12th to see how the work was progressing and to acclimatize, and he returned to stay on the 13th. The effort he made was impressive, and I sympathized with his complaints that the INC didn't appreciate how hard the climbing was, not even supplying him with the necessary equipment.

Pablo also told us that the discovery of the Ice Maiden had made the front page of El Correo, a local newspaper, soon after we had left Arequipa. "According to the story, Miki and you brought down a 'princess' and valuable statues."

The news didn't surprise me, but I wasn't happy to hear it. I knew the discovery was bound to get out sooner or later. Indeed, I'd been surprised that the arrival of the film crew hadn't alerted the media to something's being afoot. A ton of film gear didn't arrive at Arequipa airport every day. After the El Correo story appeared, the INC and Catholic University were deluged with calls, Pablo said. The rector had to reveal that they did have custody of the finds and that a return expedition was currently under way. We began to worry that newspapermen without climbing experience might try seeking us out while we were still on the mountain.

We suspected Pablo still harbored ill feelings about belatedly learning about the Ice Maiden, so we were not surprised when he immediately began criticizing our work. Perhaps he was spurred to action when he realized that his longtime rival José was in charge of the excavations. "The plans aren't being drawn well enough, and some parts of the wall have collapsed," he said as he pointed to the platform.

"The platform's wall was that way when we arrived," I replied. "You are right that better drawings could be made, but we have backed them up with photographs and video footage."

Pablo inspected the site some more, then said in a superior tone, "Archaeologists don't use picks and shovels. You should only be using trowels."

That was when we knew he was going out of his way to find fault. While trowels certainly play an important role in excavations, the use of picks and shovels to remove topsoil and gravel fill is a common archaeological practice throughout the world even at sea level, not to mention when attacking frozen ground at 19,000 feet. "Fine, you go ahead and work only using a trowel," I countered. After several fruitless attempts to scrape away frozen soil, he eventually gave up. He didn't broach the subject again.

However, he did insist that we not remove a section of the wall in order to remove the female mummy. Although we agreed that it wasn't ideal, we saw no alternative. The mummy was pressed up against the wall and without removing some of the stones, we would be forced to leave the mummy behind. This would likely mean its removal, destruction, or both by treasure hunters, who were sure to search the site once we had left. We went ahead excavating behind it, and eventually even Pablo agreed to the partial dismantling.

The time allotted for removing the mummy was running out, and everyone, including Pablo and the film crew, began helping with the excavation. After three days we were finally able to free the bundle. Miki and I climbed into the excavation pit and, with cameras clicking and the film crew bustling about for different camera angles, we began to lift the 500-year-old mummy out of its frozen tomb.

Even though we had been gazing down at the mummy bundle for days now, exclamations of "incredible" and "beautiful" filled the air. It seemed incongruous and yet somehow right when the entire team broke into applause. We felt we had saved a priceless gift for all Peruvians.

Unlike Juanita, this mummy had never been exposed. The clothes were exceptionally well preserved, and the mummy was so heavy that we were confident it contained a frozen body. Those of us who had climbed together over the years, and suffered numerous hardships, felt a special satisfaction. For one of the few times in history we had established the complete context of an Inca human sacrificial burial, and recovered what we thought would be one of the best preserved mummies in the world.[10]

Previously, Arcadio and I had carved out a hole in the ice to store the mummy bundle. After we deposited it inside, we packed ice around the outside. That would keep it frozen until we left the mountain. The sun was setting as we finished, and we returned to our tents feeling elated. Whatever happened now, the expedition was a tremendous success.

Since only a few men could work at any given time in the small, enclosed burial space, we had simultaneously been conducting another excavation. Orlando, Ruddy, and Walter had been working in a burial where skeletal remains were partly carbonized. Other aspects of its preservation were compromised as well. The only remains of textiles we found were under the bones and badly burnt. Like the first mummy, the body of this one belonged to a youth placed facing south, a direction some Andean scholars believe the Incas associated with death. Here, though, it also faced the direction of Ampato's summit.

Walter said to me, "Obviously the body has been in some way consumed by fire, but look at the plant fibers near its red-colored skull. Why did they remain virtually unscathed?" One possibility was that the Incas had deliberately burned the body, and the fibers were placed next to it when it was buried. But that didn't seem right. I had never heard of the Incas burning a human sacrifice.

Before long we found the clue that solved the mystery. A gold-alloyed statue was recovered from under the pelvic region of the skeleton. We knew immediately that it was of a male, since it had the classic elongated, pierced ear lobes. These were only permitted to men of Inca nobility and this practice was the reason the Spaniards called the Incas orejones ("long ears"). What we hadn't expected was to see a hole burned directly through it.

After drawing my attention to the hole, José pointed to a jar and said, "Now you can see what caused the body to be carbonized." At first I didn't understand what he meant, but then I looked more closely. Pumice had melted onto it. Lightning must have struck the mummy after it was buried at this high point on the plateau. That explained the small lumps of melted sand, called fulgurites, which we began to uncover. When lightning penetrates into sandy soil, the heat can fuse it into the shape of the path taken by the electricity. Fulgurites, which often look like corroded hollow tubes, have been found more than 60 feet down in sandy areas.[11]

Lightning clearly also caused the hole burned through a piece of gold lamina found in the lap of the other mummy. Despite the great heat generated by lightning, the holes left by strikes are usually quite small, only an eighth-inch in diameter.

Interestingly, throughout the Andes, lightning represents the power of the mountain gods, who use it to kill those who offend them or to strike down their livestock. A villager told me the mountain deities are also widely believed to use lightning to strike people selected to become priests devoted to their worship. The more strikes a person survived, the more power he possessed.[12] "If that is true," I quipped to José later, "I am obviously the exception to the rule."

Thus began a discussion that continues to the present day. Could the Incas have deliberately placed the human sacrifices so that they were likely to be struck by lightning? I didn't think so, because some had not been buried in the most exposed areas of a mountain and the items with them did not appear to have been buried with the intention of their being destroyed—rather the contrary. But some scholars continue to believe this theory, and we may never be able to prove it one way or the other.

The male statue and the lack of shawl pins both suggested to me that the skeleton was that of a male child, although its sex still remained to be determined. Its fewer offerings led us to think that it might have been viewed as an accompanying sacrifice to the female one nearby, perhaps as a pair. In 1551 the Spaniard Juan de Betanzos, who had married an Inca princess, wrote what he had been told about human sacrifices at a major ceremony in Cuzco: "Many boys and girls were sacrificed in pairs, being buried alive and well dressed and adorned. With each pair they buried . . . items that a married Indian would possess."[13]

Only a few yards away from the first mummy a piece of wood marked the location of a male gold statue. This meant that two of the first three stone circles had yielded sacrificial burials. Three other circles awaited us, and we hadn't even gone to the summit yet. "We might end up with a half dozen mummies to take back to Arequipa," José said, only half-joking. For transport reasons, if nothing else, we were relieved when the other circles proved not to contain bodies.

Not far from the other circles was another, where we excavated llama figurines made of both silver and spondylus, buried right above an intact spondylus shell. One of the film crew asked, "Why did the Incas use seashells to make statues?"

"Because the shells were linked with the ocean—Mamacocha, the mother of all water," I explained. "Spondylus shells and figurines were often used in rituals for rain in Inca times and have even been found in ritual deposits dating back 2,500 years ago." The Incas were said to have valued the shell more than gold. Because it could only be found in waters outside the cool Humboldt Current, it had to be obtained in trade from as far away as Ecuador.[14]

Other excavations in the same area yielded statues of a silver man and gold llama, while potsherds and textile and rope fragments were collected on the surface. Find after find was cataloged. We had recovered the richest collection of artifacts ever found at a high-altitude site.

We made test excavations at the two structures formed by wood poles, and the remains of fires and traces of common clothes and artifacts were uncovered. This supported our original hypothesis that the poles had been used as supports for tents. Although not as dramatic as the mummy burials, these were unique finds in their own right. In 1553 Cieza de León wrote an account of the hardships the troops of the Inca emperor Huayna Capac suffered when they traveled through the mountains, "Great snows fell upon them; they carried tents under which to protect themselves."[15] It was fascinating to view poles actually used by the Incas still in their original locations. To my knowledge, these were the first tent remains thus far discovered.

Ironically, one of the places where we had most expected to find offerings, the raised artificial platform, yielded the fewest results. Admittedly, we had only excavated in three test areas, leaving several square yards untouched. Still, nothing more than a small amount of carbon was uncovered. I took a compass bearing and found that the platform's orientation was toward the June solstice sunrise. Both of the solstices were important religious events for the Incas—not surprising, since they believed themselves to be the children of Inti, the sun. Perhaps the surface of the platform had been used as a place for offerings of foods and liquids. If so, these would have left little, if any, trace.

The platform did, however, provide us with one important piece of information. José discovered a layer of volcanic ash under it. Since Misti's eruption in the mid-1400s didn't reach this far and Ampato hadn't erupted during the past millennium, that left Sabancaya as the likely source.[16]

Nice coincidence, I thought. The main reason for the sacrifices was probably to placate the volcano itself. It looked like it was thanks to Sabancaya that a site was built originally and thanks to Sabancaya that the site was revealed.

One of the most difficult questions to answer has always been, why had the Incas made human sacrifices on the summits of high mountains? For the first time we had found three human sacrifices on a single mountain. Some historical accounts stress that human sacrifices took place mainly at major state events, such as the death or coronation of an emperor. Now we had hard evidence that the sacrifices were made either during a lengthy period of extreme drought, during (or just after) volcanic eruptions, or both. Only in such periods could the ground have been unfrozen enough to allow the Incas to build the sites and bury the offerings as they did. And this factor could explain their importance. Droughts and volcanic ash would kill off pasturage and pollute and deplete the water sources so critical to the villagers below. Irrigation canals extending several miles had been built in pre-Hispanic times to capture water from the slopes of Hualca

Hualca and Ampato and bring it to irrigate fields in the Colca Valley.

Indeed, Juan de Ulloa Mogollón noted in 1586 that human sacrifices were made to the mountains because they supplied water to the settlements below.[7] Of course, other Inca state deities, such as the sun, would likely have been invoked in the rituals, but the reason they took place at such heights probably had to do with the role of the mountains themselves in controlling weather and water—and thus the fertility of crops and herds alike.

Our work on the plateau left little time for research at the higher sites. While Pablo returned to base camp, ten of us climbed to the summit the morning of the 15th. The TV team was filming as we went, and by coincidence, David had us stop close to where I had left the mummy that first night. He chose the spot to film me climbing up, talking to the camera as I approached. A problem arose when it turned out that I was too well acclimatized—I wasn't breathing hard. He explained, "The average viewer won't believe that it's hard going at 20,000 feet, if you aren't breathing hard." He solved this easily enough. "Just go down a ways and run up," he said. Feeling like an actor in my own real-life drama, I complied with his request.

At Punta Ichu (the grass summit) we recovered a few objects from the surface, including woolen sandals and the frozen body of a mouse. I suspect that this was a hungry rodent that scampered up behind the Incas all the way to 20,300 feet. We had been plagued with live ones at altitudes not much lower.

We continued on to the place where we located the first mummy. After a brief search of the scree slope, Mike came back with a wooden box. David found a spondylus female statue with its miniature clothing dirty from the fall, but still intact. "Someday I would like to return without a camera. This is one of the most interesting times I've ever had in the mountains," said the man who had been on a half dozen expeditions to Mount Everest. When we later stood on the summit, David was awed by what the Incas had accomplished: "To have built all these sites, carried all that material, and climbed up such steep terrain is amazing."

Since our ascent that day had been basically a reconnaissance and film shoot, most of the archaeology team had stayed behind to finish the excavations below. While we were gone, they found llama statues of gold and spondylus shell. By this time all of the most obvious targets had been excavated and supplies were running out. I had thought of staying longer with a few men and then making our own way back to Cabanaconde, but that idea evaporated in the face of the quantity and importance of the finds we had made. We all needed to return with them. "It looks like it's time to end the expedition," I said to José, with some regret.[18]

The next day, José and Orlando had the well-earned opportunity to go to the summit. David kindly offered to climb with Amy as well. Originally, she intended only to venture as high as the grass site, but she did so well that they continued on and she made the summit. This was a considerable achievement for someone who had never climbed a mountain before, let alone one over 20,000 feet. One team member said to her later, with a touch of the macabre, "Congratulations, Amy, you are the first woman to have reached the top *and* made it back down alive."

Most of the team descended with loads that day, and the group that had gone to the summit arrived back in time to make the one-hour descent to base camp. Only David and I remained camped at 19,200 feet that night. As we sat in his tent waiting for water to boil, he pointed out to me, "The Peruvian archaeology students don't have enough mountaineering experience. They act too cocky. This isn't ordinary archaeology, it's *extreme* archaeology, and they should get more training before a serious accident happens."

I knew he was right, but there hadn't been time to train them. Then again, their very cockiness meant they were among the few men willing to participate in such difficult conditions in the first place. Still, if we were to continue with expeditions like this one, I agreed the men needed to be both better trained and better equipped. Above 18,000 feet we were indeed working in what some scientists call the "death zone." Our bodies can adapt for relatively brief periods above 18,000 feet, but not permanently. They slowly, inexorably deteriorate and eventually will die.[19]

The next morning we carried down what remained of the most important loads. We left behind inessential items, including food, picks, and shovels, hiding them so that looters wouldn't be able to use them. I stayed on to ensure that no trash was left lying about, so I was the last one to leave camp at four o'clock that afternoon. I walked alone among the ruins wondering what still lay to be discovered and what the site would look like when archaeologists were next able to return here. I had visions of the holes and scattered remains of looted sites I'd seen elsewhere, and I could only hope a better fate was in store for this one.

That evening at base camp we sat around a fire made of chunks of llareta (Azorella glabra), a resinous moss renowned for its high heat output. We discussed our concerns about the number of burros and horses that would come back for us, since a two-day festival was to begin tomorrow in Cabanaconde. What would we do if only a few showed up? Meanwhile, Amy and Mike tried to persuade Pablo to sign the agreement giving first rights of popular publication to the National Geographic Society. This was a standard form that was provided to all expeditions supported by the Society, and we had all signed it. "It's in English and I need more time to review it. I'll do this after we have returned to Arequipa," Pablo argued, reasonably enough. "Besides, as an employee of the government, I am bound by the terms of the excavation permit not to publish anything on your work anyway," he added. At the time I thought this sounded fine, but he never did sign the agreement—and only much later did we discover the reason why.

In a pleasant surprise, the burro drivers arrived on time the next morning with enough animals to carry all the loads and even a few extra horses to ride as well. José, Edwin, Miki, and Pablo trotted ahead on horseback with the mummy wrapped in insulation. Meanwhile the rest of us trudged over a pass into a strong wind filled

Team members cross the western slope of Ampato at 20,000 feet, with Coropuna visible in the background.

with the all-too-familiar mix of dust and ash. Dropping down beneath the massive hulk of Hualca Hualca, we stopped by a stream to have a lunch break and wash off the dirt. We continued on to make our last night's camp amid the brush. Not far below us were the Inca ruins of Kallimarca, which had been a focus of Pablo's research some years before.[20] That was likely the last permanent settlement the Ice Maiden had stayed at before she left for Ampato.

On the following day we made our way down to a side road where, to our relief, a pickup was waiting for us. As planned, José and Pablo had left the night before on a bus with the mummy. Our own rented bus eventually arrived in the afternoon and brought news that they had reached Arequipa that morning. The frozen mummy was now safely stored in a freezer. Soon we too were rumbling down the road to Arequipa. It seemed only appropriate that by the time we were driving past Ampato, the sun had sunk behind it: The volcano stood silhouetted on the horizon, surrounded by a golden hue.

CHAPTER FOUR

MUMMIES *and* MEDIA

I have yet to see any problem, however complicated, which, when you looked at it the right way, did not become still more complicated.
—POUL ANDERSON

These children [to be sacrificed] would be collected from all over the land and would be carried in litters together and by pairs to be buried. They should be very well dressed, paired up female and male.
—JUAN DE BETANZOS, 1551

I AWOKE IN THE EARLY LIGHT OF DAWN OCTOBER 20 TRYING TO FIGURE out where I was. First I was disoriented by the lack of tent walls. Gradually my eyes adjusted, and I realized that, wherever I was, it had four walls and a bathroom—the ultimate luxury. "Ah, yes, the Colonial Inn," I finally recalled. My next thought was of eggs and pancakes. The owners of the inn, Maria and Reynaldo Casos, provided their guests with one of the best breakfasts in Arequipa.

I finally struggled out of bed at 6:30 and started shaving. Just then the phone rang. It was to be the first in a series of calls from the press, the National Geographic, colleagues, and local authorities that continued nonstop for the next five hours. The first few times I hung up the phone, it rang so quickly that I thought it was malfunctioning. I finally finished shaving in time for lunch.

Pablo was one of the callers. While we had been working away in blissful ignorance on the volcano, a number of stories had appeared in the media. Some were less than accurate, and a few were downright sensational. The INC had been deluged with calls from reporters, and its national director, Pedro Gjurinovich, was arriving in Arequipa today. INC and university officials had explained to the press that they could not provide details about the expedition. By law, they noted, the director of the expedition had the right to be the first to publish the material he had found, and I had signed a contract with the National Geographic Society giving it exclusivity.

This provoked exclamations of disbelief that a foreigner, not to mention a foreign institution, had control over information that the newsmen viewed as belonging to the nation as a whole. For some, the arrangement brought back memories of colonialism and thus struck an underlying chord of anti-gringo sentiment that had a long history in Peru. One of Peru's best-known talk show hosts and documentary filmmakers, Alejandro Guerrero, complained that morning on his popular TV program *Buenos Días, Peru,* that Catholic University had sold out Peru's "cultural patrimony." Once I had eaten, I called the National Geographic Society to tell them about the strong feelings that had surfaced and to stress that basic information had to be given out about the expedition. This was the only way I could see to counter the wild rumors that were already circulating.

Even before we left for Ampato in early October, we had decided to hold a press conference on Tuesday, October 24. At the university I met with the rector Dr. Luis Carpio, José, Sonia, and other university authorities. We agreed that the press conference should be as complete as possible under the circumstances, including an exhibition of some of the key artifacts and the presentation of slides and a video. Although we decided not to risk putting one of the frozen mummies on display, we thought the skeletal remains of the male could be shown, since the bones did not need to be kept permanently frozen. We hoped the display would be enough to satisfy the media, but we doubted it.

At a late lunch with Pedro Gjurinovich and Frans Grupp, we reviewed the circumstances of the original discovery and discussed our finds of the second expedition. Before long one of the rumors was brought up. "I heard that National Geographic paid $20,000 for exclusivity about the expedition," said Mr. Gjurinovich.

"We have only received $7,500, and more than half of that was used for conservation," I replied. "The rest did not even cover the archaeology team's expenses on Ampato. In any event, the exclusivity solely relates to a popular magazine article, and even then basic information about our finds can be presented at the press conference." Then with some trepidation I asked him, "Do you have any other questions or concerns?"

"No, I'm satisfied, for now," he said. It was the "for now" that troubled me.

Later in the afternoon I met with a team of Austrian and German mummy specialists. They had come to Arequipa with a German Der Spiegel TV crew and been waiting for our return from Ampato. The scientists had worked on the famous 5,000-year-old Tyrolean Iceman, which was at the time being kept in a laboratory in Innsbruck. They had already published an impressive series of books and articles about the Iceman, having brought together an international team from a variety of scientific fields. They invited me to supper at La Posada, one of Arequipa's finest restaurants. It is situated on top of a cliff overlooking the Chili River, with city lights blinking in the distance. Piano music playing in the background added to an atmosphere in such contrast to the dinners I'd been having the past few weeks that I felt disoriented.

The dinner conversation began congenially enough. The German archaeologist Dr. Konrad Spindler of the University of Innsbruck's Institute for Prehistory and Early History had published a best-selling book about the Iceman. Dr. Kurt Irgolic had conducted studies of the Iceman's hair. Tillman Scholl was a personable cinematographer who had already made a well-received film about the Iceman. A freelance journalist working on the story for Der Spiegel magazine had traveled widely throughout Peru. Sonia, who had spent some time in Austria and knew the Iceman team, was present as well. It seemed an excellent opportunity to discuss conservation of the mummy and a possible collaboration with them on a number of research projects.

However, before long the discussion turned to restrictions placed on their filming and photography because of my agreement with the National Geographic Society. Spindler told about once having angered a writer contracted by the National Geographic to do a story on the Iceman. When the writer arrived in Innsbruck, he discovered not only that Spindler had changed his mind about working with the Society but also that he would not be allowed access to the Iceman, contrary to their agreement. Spindler had decided that the National Geographic's contract was too restrictive.

He asked how much the Society had offered to pay me to write the story. When I told him, he scoffed at the amount. "They offered me ten times that much and I wasn't even the one who found the Iceman," he said. Both he and the journalist proceeded to list the numerous ways they thought the National Geographic exploited scientists. After all their bad-mouthing, I began to feel sympathy for the writer sent by the Society.

The journalist then broached a subject that took me by surprise. "You could get a lot more money if you broke your contract with National Geographic and went with Der Spiegel instead."

I thought it insulting to even bring up the topic, and I looked hard at him and said, "I don't break contracts."

"Lawyers can break anything," he replied without missing a beat.

I repeated what I'd said, my annoyance growing. Although I had not spoken the language in years, I easily understood Spindler when he said to the journalist in German, "Let it go. He won't change his mind."

Spindler added that he had worked out an arrangement in Europe whereby he received six-figure sums in stages for his book, being published in different languages. In fairness, he couched this subject in terms of the need to obtain the funding to support the large expenses incurred in conserving the Iceman. But by then it was obvious what the real reason was for inviting me to supper. It was the kind of behind-the-scenes dealing I suppose I should have expected.

To my relief the conversation turned from money and National Geographic bashing to a discussion of conservation issues. The scientists said that research on the body tissues could be done for free, using expensive equipment available in Austria. They promised to try to raise funding for some of the research. Sonia said, "We might be able to complete the unwrapping while the film crew is here, but most of the work can only be done when a permanent laboratory has been built and specialists have become involved."

I agreed warily. We both knew, though, that there would be pressures to begin with at least some of the work as soon as possible. Given how slowly bureaucracies moved, it could be a long time, indeed, before we had a well-equipped lab at our disposal. We still were not even sure where the mummies would finally be stored. Rumors were swirling that the INC in Arequipa wanted to take control and ship the mummies to the national museum in Lima.

As preparations for the press conference continued, I was told that Miki still felt that he was being marginalized. We had tried to find ways for him to stay more involved, but he had no experience in lab work, and this was the work that remained when the expeditions were over. Unfortunately, he had openly criticized Catholic University, stating that it had done nothing to help him. Perhaps he did this as a way of pressuring the university, but it ignored their offer of a scholarship, and it naturally soured him in the eyes of university officials. A rift opened that was to widen in the days to come. Even so, I thought he should have a place of honor at the press conference.

When I arrived, I was led to a row of chairs arranged to face the audience, where José and key Catholic University officials were already waiting. The INC representatives were seated in the front row, looking decidedly glum. I was told that their chairs had not been ready, and they felt the university had slighted them. The room was full, not only with newspapermen and radio and TV crews but also with local authorities and even men wearing impressive military uniforms.

"Well, here we go," I mumbled to José.

After the introductions, José thanked the people and institutions that had helped us and proceeded to show slides and a video clip of the expedition. For the first time most of the audience saw the conditions in which we had worked, and this clearly made an impact. Then it was my turn.

I described the discovery and explained my decision to carry the mummy down. "It was my responsibility as an archaeologist to try and save Peru's cultural patrimony, not to leave it where it would be destroyed," I said. I was relieved to see a few people nod in agreement, including a military officer sitting in the front row. A glance in the direction of the INC representatives was less comforting. They continued to frown, and I sensed that I was a long way from convincing them.

I next presented the chronology of our informing the authorities and arranging for specialists. Then I dealt with the sensitive issue of why we had kept the news quiet until we could return to the mountain and the reason I had contacted the National Geographic Society.

"Aside from providing immediate financial support, the Society's involvement means greater scientific credibility for our work and an ability to reach a public of some 200 million people through the magazine and television programs. This will benefit not only the mummies but also Peru," I said. "The 'exclusivity' relates solely to the popular article." I thought the press conference was going well. They had now heard basic information about the work, seen photos and a video, and were about to view and photograph a collection of the key artifacts. "We welcome the financial support of other media institutions for future expeditions," I added. The silence that greeted this invitation spoke for itself.

After I had finished, I motioned to Miki, who had been standing by a wall to the side, to join us. The university had decided to have only "professionals" speak, but I explained that I would have had a hard time carrying down the mummy without his help. No matter what he might have done in the meantime, I felt he deserved to be with us. As he made his way to the podium, I told the audience of his role in the discovery. However, before he had a chance to take the microphone, a university official gave the sign for a curtain to be pulled aside. The artifacts and bones had been kept hidden behind it in order to provide a visually interesting way to wrap up the press conference. Once revealed, the media stampeded forward to see them, and the conference was over.

But not the interviews, which began with multiple microphones stuck in front of our faces. "When will we be able to see the other mummies? Will you be returning again to Ampato? Do you think there are other mummies on mountain summits near Arequipa?" were among the barrage of questions I was asked. These were relatively easy to answer, but then came a double zinger: "Is it true that you did not have a permit when you first went to Ampato, and how much did National Geographic pay you for exclusivity?" asked a journalist who worked for Panamericana, the same media company as Alejandro Guerrero, the talk show host.

"I didn't go to Ampato to excavate a site, and no one needs a permit to climb Ampato or any other mountain. Since when do archaeologists have fewer rights than everyone else?" I asked, rather testily to be sure. I explained about the $7,500 and the standard agreement I had signed, which was the same for anyone who received funding from National Geographic's Research Committee.

I was eventually led away to a small ceremony during which I was officially declared an honorary professor of Catholic University. Even the INC representatives shook my hand.

That this was nothing more than a courtesy was made abundantly clear when an article attacking me appeared the next day. It included a verbatim transcription of the INC permit, and noted the "call to attention" and the supposed use of a false document—without, of course, any explanation that it had nothing to do with me. Since it was an internal document of the INC, it obviously had been leaked by one of its officials.

When I learned from the reporters that Pablo was the source, I called him. "What you did was a serious violation of ethics, especially since you knew full well that the 'false document' charge had nothing to do with me." Then, for one of the few times in my life, I slammed down the phone on someone. Clearly, the accumulated pressures were getting to me. I was relieved that we would finally start to scientifically examine the source of all the controversy—the Ice Maiden herself.

"THE ICE MAIDEN IS NOT REALLY A MUMMY," ONE REPORTER SAID to me. "She wasn't artificially mummified the way the Egyptians treated their dead." He was right about that, but wrong about how the word "mummy" is generally defined. The term is also used in cases where the skin of a corpse has been preserved over a skeleton, whether through natural or artificial processes.[1]

I've sometimes been asked a question that follows on the tail of this explanation: "What prevents a body from becoming naturally mummified?" Two of the main causes of body decomposition are putrefaction and autolysis.[2] Putrefaction is what occurs when bacteria cause decay by acting on organic matter. The bacteria in our stomachs spread throughout our bodies, feeding on tissues. Not surprisingly, the intestines are the first parts of the body to putrefy and for this reason the Egyptians removed the internal organs before they embalmed their mummies.

Autolysis involves the decomposition of the internal body tissues caused by enzymes (and other chemicals) that are spread following death. The pancreas is particularly quick to decompose since it contains digestive enzymes. Thus, the presence of a pancreas in a frozen mummy is like a canary in a coal mine. In this case it indicates that the person froze soon after death and that other organs and their cells should be in an excellent state of preservation.

What makes frozen Andean mummies unique is their natural preservation. Some of the Egyptian mummies date back more than three millennia before the Incas, but these are usually desiccated bodies that have had their intestinal organs removed (even the brain) and embalming elements applied to the skin to help the mummification process. Though this is not generally known, artificially mummified bodies much older than those in Egypt have been recovered. The Chinchorro mummies found in northern coastal Chile date back some 6,500 years, and thus are the world's oldest known artificially mummified bodies.[3]

Naturally frozen mummies are far fewer. Thanks to their better-preserved body tissues and organs, they provide a wealth of human biological information and enable scientists to undertake more comprehensive studies. Especially well known is the frozen body of the Iceman found in the Alps, but others have been found as far apart as the 2,400-year-old Pazyryk woman from Siberia and the 500-year-old Utqiagvik Eskimo woman recovered in Greenland.[4]

One of the unusual aspects of Inca human sacrifices on mountaintops is that very little time elapsed between the time the victims died and their burial. Indeed, the chroniclers described most of them as being buried while they were still alive. On snow-laden mountains this allowed for an unprecedented scientific treasure—a body could be frozen with little decomposition having occurred.

"Yes, but what actually happens to the body when it freezes? Don't the cells break down?" I asked one specialist. He gave a long explanation, but here is the gist of it.[5] Ice crystals form in tissues as they cool to freezing and below. This withdrawal of water has a dehydrating effect, especially as temperatures reach 14–23° F. Although more than 90 percent of the body's water may turn into ice, chemical bonding with cellular compounds can prevent the remainder from doing so. Without fluidity, chemical reactions in general are slowed down.

The rate of cooling is important, but however fast it occurs there will be some dehydration and the potential for the cells to be damaged. Cells that were alive when they were frozen can survive this process much better than dead cells, which have already undergone changes. In short, the faster tissues are frozen, the less damage. The body cells and their DNA could be in such excellent condition that you would have what might be called a "perfect" mummy.

The Ampato Ice Maiden was not the only Inca human sacrifice to have been found frozen on a mountaintop.[6] The mummies recovered from the mountains El Plomo, Aconcagua, and El Toro were especially well preserved, being essentially freeze-dried. Less intact Inca human sacrifices had also been found on the mountains Chuscha and Esmeralda, while partial remains of Inca human sacrificial victims had been recovered from the summits of Chañi and Chachani. I had also participated in excavations of Inca human sacrificial remains on the summits of Pichu Pichu and Quehuar (where we later found a frozen mummy). What made the Ice Maiden mummy unique was its being a female and one of the best preserved of any yet found.

I should add that not everyone is convinced that the Incas performed human sacrifices. One of the most famous of the chroniclers, Garcilaso de la Vega, denied that it had ever occurred.[7] His account was widely read by Spaniards in the 1600s, and still is today. It has especially played a role in history courses taught in Peruvian schools. The result is that some people refuse to accept that the mummies we found had been killed as part of a ritual. In this version, they were children who died natural deaths and were carried up to the summits for burial.

On the other hand, dozens of chroniclers have described exactly what we are finding archaeologically.[8] This ranges from the children themselves to the kinds of artifacts, including rare statues, special pottery, and fine clothing, to the contexts and the types of sites they occur in. The physical evidence, such as frostbite and unhealed fractures, demonstrate that the children must have died when on or near the summits—hardly normal places for young girls and boys to be visiting by chance. Even if no one had ever described human sacrifice among the Incas, the archaeological and forensic evidence would prove that it took place. But, of course, the Incas provided numerous chroniclers with details about the practice, and we have found striking confirmation of what they described. Indeed, human sacrifices continued less frequently and in secret after the Spanish conquest, and they have even been reported in exceptional cases up to recent times.[9]

WHEN DR. SPINDLER EXAMINED THE ICE MAIDEN, HE SAID, "YOUR mummy is better preserved than the Iceman, and this makes it a discovery of worldwide importance." He was being modest in this evaluation, since the Iceman was 4,800 years older than "our" mummy and unique in itself. But his comments served to reinforce to everyone the Ice Maiden's importance.

Despite the considerable pressure to put her mummy on display, we continued to insist that Juanita could not be shown to the public until we had a suitable conservation unit. We needed one that would maintain a low temperature and a high relative humidity, while also allowing the mummy to be viewed. According to the Iceman team and others we contacted, however, such a unit had never been successfully built. The humidity always caused the glass to fog up. Nor did the government or the university have the financial resources to pay for the construction of custom-made freezer units.

The Iceman scientists thought that 22°F (–6°C) would be best for preserving the Ice Maiden. According to one study, this was the temperature of the glacier where the Iceman had been found and thus was the one chosen for his conservation. "Frozen is frozen," said Dr. Spindler.

But others said this temperature could only be an estimate, since the exact circumstances of the Iceman's preservation in the glacier were unknown. Several scientists thought that even if true, 22°F was too warm for the Iceman, since chemical processes aiding decomposition would not be slowed down sufficiently at this temperature. We had already thought of preserving the Ice Maiden at a lower temperature, given the conditions where she had been found. After all, we ourselves had been sleeping in temperatures far colder while camped even lower on the mountain. Thus we initially settled on 10°F

(–12°C). Although some members of the Iceman team thought this was unnecessarily cold, they did not think it would harm the mummy.

The more difficult problem was determining what percentage of relative humidity should be used. Relative humidity is the ratio of water vapor present in the air to the greatest amount possible at the same temperature, and it is difficult to maintain constant the colder it is. To complicate matters, the mummy's head was desiccated and for that reason would be better preserved at a relatively low humidity. We saw no way to maintain a different relative humidity for both parts of the body, that is, a relatively dry one for the head and high one for the rest of the body. Since the body was in greatest need of humidity to conserve its state, we initially decided that the mummy would need to be kept at 75 percent relative humidity. Later this would be raised to more than 90 percent—and in the process technology was pushed to a new limit.

PABLO, AS THE INC REPRESENTATIVE, LOOKED ON AS A VERY CAUTIOUS group of scientists began their examination of the Ice Maiden. Sonia Guillen brought her team from her mummy center, Centro Mallqui—archaeologist Nilda Juárez de Vargas, chemist Nelly Vásquez, and weaving specialist Rosa Choque. All had experience working with pre-Hispanic textiles. The physical anthropologist Silvia Quevedo had arrived from the Natural History Museum in Santiago, Chile. Together with José, Ruth, and myself, we began heating cloth pads with a hair dryer and applying them to the ice. The pads absorbed the water as it melted—a technique successfully employed on both the El Plomo and Aconcagua mummies. Scheduled for evenings to avoid the heat of the day, the sessions were limited to a half hour at a time.

We were thankful when Bill Conklin, an American specialist in pre-Hispanic Andean textiles, joined us on October 25. Assisted by Ruth and an archaeology student, he began the unromantic but necessary task of "stabilizing" the artifacts, especially the statues. Each of these was placed in its own foam-core box, where it would be better aerated and protected at the same time.

Bill also oversaw the preservation of the wooden objects. "Q-tips should be dipped in isopropyl alcohol," he explained to me, "but these then need to be shaken so that no free liquid remains on them. It is the odor of the alcohol, not the liquid that is necessary to stop the growth of mold." Having a person of Bill's experience on hand from the beginning was a great plus for ensuring the conservation both of the artifacts and the textiles.

As for the latter, he initially examined those from the first expedition. We had found scattered above the bundle fragments of what proved to be the outer wrapping of the mummy. The head cloth had also been damaged in the fall, but was nonetheless fairly complete. To our surprise, we could see where tears had been repaired, presumably before the sacrifice. Bill suspected that the cloth might have been made locally. It might even have belonged to the girl.

Chroniclers had noted that the standard female clothing consisted of a dress (aksu) wrapped around the body and fastened with a belt (chumpi) around the waist and two metal pins (tupus) at the shoulders. A shawl (lliclla) was worn on the shoulders and held in place by a metal pin, while sandals (ushutas) or moccasins were their footwear. A head cloth (ñañaca) was also worn, but apparently only by women of high status.[10]

Although the outer cloth of the mummy bundle had little ice adhering directly to it, the process of freeing it was still time consuming. This only worsened with the ice we found in the cloth folds. It was extremely hard "old" ice, the kind climbers find on exposed faces in the mountains—it is like rock and even the sharp pick of an ice ax can barely penetrate it. The ice slowed down the removal of the outer textiles, but at least we extended the time the mummy could be kept out by placing packs of ice over those parts of the mummy bundle not being examined.

The tension in the laboratory was high, since everyone knew that a mistake could be permanent and cause an avalanche of criticism from colleagues. At times the lab team was in high spirits and joking, but there were also periods when we were working so intently that it would have been possible to hear a pin drop.

We began to realize that the chunks of ice on the bundle must have turned into water and frozen again at least once, and perhaps multiple times, while the mummy lay exposed on the mountain. "When do you think she fell?" Bill asked me.

"Whatever occurred, the ridge must have collapsed after 1991, since it was still seen intact then," I said. "My guess is that it fell either in the South American spring of 1994 or in the winter of 1995. Plenty of ash from Sabancaya would have accumulated by then to help cause erosion, and the well-preserved feathers of the statues could not have been exposed for long or they would have dried out. Whenever she had been exposed, her surrounding clothing obviously had to have warmed enough for water to form and later freeze inside the folds." I began to wonder if her body would be as well preserved as I had hoped.

The snail-like pace was especially frustrating for the National Geographic film crew and photographer. Visually there was little to document. "It's difficult for us to get as excited as you scientists when another tiny piece of cloth is unfolded," said David with a wry smile.

Finally, we decided that we needed to wait until we had cooler temperatures and preferably a cold room to work in. Sonia had her own responsibilities to attend to, as did we all, and we didn't yet have the funds to cover the project's research needs. We wanted to contact more specialists, and we felt a break would be good for us all—including the Ice Maiden. Taking the advice of the specialists, we wrapped her in an acid-free cloth inside a vapor barrier of plastic, while keeping her stored in a freezer. The vapor barrier meant that she should reach a degree of stabilization that was appropriate for her own body.

Although the late-night work sessions were largely uneventful, reporters outside the laboratory became increasingly fractious. Some were annoyed that they could not observe the sessions, and they watched in exasperation as the National Geographic team entered unhindered. They could, however, interview the scientific team as it went in and out of the lab in a congested hallway. This opportunity led to arguments over positions outside the door. In the jostling two reporters nearly came to blows. While I sympathized with the reporters, there wasn't enough room to accommodate everyone in the lab, even assuming all other factors were equal—and they were not. The room was relatively small, and allowing several reporters in during sessions would have made it harder for the scientists to work. One film crew was plenty, and in any event the only way the National Geographic Society could finance the work was if it had a few new pieces of information and footage that had not already been made public. However, as the days passed and rumors ran wild about what we were supposedly uncovering, some newsmen lost an objective view of this arrangement.

Fortunately, I was able to take a break from the pressures of the lab when the Peruvian Air Force kindly offered to take some of us in a helicopter to Ampato. "We can't reach high enough to fly directly over it, but we can circle around the upper part of the mountain," the pilot told us as we piled in. "We could land at your base camp, but we couldn't be sure of being able to lift off."

We were happy to have the opportunity to examine the mountain's slopes and the terrain surrounding it. I still was curious about whether the Incas had ascended the summit from the pass on its north side. We couldn't help but wonder if we would discover another route used by the Incas. And then there was a more discomfiting thought: would we see looters scrambling amid the ruins?

Soon we were looking down onto the plateau where we had found the two burials. But it was difficult to make out structures, and if we hadn't known where to look, even the platform would have been hard to spot. We saw no other ruins, but we did get views of all sides of Ampato—and the menacing cliffs surrounding it. "That mountain does not look friendly," someone said above the roar of the helicopter blades. We returned impressed with the sense of power that the volcano gave off when seen whole.

"Why don't you just fly over peaks looking for ruins and save yourself a lot of time and trouble?" I have often been asked. But, as this flight showed, it isn't easy to distinguish ruins, especially relatively small ones built with stones from the same terrain. This holds equally for using aerial or satellite photographs. Like it or not, the only way to confirm the presence of ruins on a mountain is to make a physical search of it—virtually yard by yard.

The National Geographic team left October 31. It was hard to believe that only 11 days had passed since we returned from the mountain. The next day I joined the Colonial Inn's staff to watch Miki while he was interviewed on Alejandro Guerrero's *Buenos Días, Peru*, the most watched of Peru's morning television programs. Ever since being denied permission to film the mummies, Guerrero had been making biting attacks against Catholic University. Officials were understandably sensitive about more ammunition being handed to him and could only watch with frustration as Miki, among other things, once again denied being offered any help from the university. "It has not given me anything," he said. Unfortunately, by alienating the university, he had guaranteed that I would never be able to persuade them to include him in future work—or, for that matter, even to have his name appear in their museum materials about the discovery. It was a sad ending to his participation.

I had booked a flight from Arequipa to Lima the evening of November 1, and from there I would fly to the U.S. on November 3. I had already delayed more than a month beyond the departure date I had set when I first arrived in Arequipa. Besides personal matters, I needed to organize further research and the conservation of the mummies.

While walking along a street in Miraflores, a suburb of Lima, I saw a Lima tabloid with headlines about the "curse" of Juanita. Since it quoted Miki, I wondered if this was the beginning of his use of "esoteric" issues to reach a wider public that he'd mentioned while we had been walking back to Cabanaconde. Fortunately, the news in more respectable media sources was fairly accurate and uniformly more favorable. Less than an hour later, I saw the Latin American issue of Newsweek magazine. It had a factual account of the discovery as its cover story. The Peruvian ambassador to the U.S., Ricardo Luna, later told me, "The four-page story was the longest to ever appear about Peru in the magazine." Such is the power of a frozen mummy.

After returning to the U.S., I also received the copy of an article that had appeared November 5 in La República Domingo, the Sunday edition of Peru's most widely read newspaper. The article went into considerable detail about our discovery and included pictures showing finds made while we were still on the mountain. Pablo's photos had made it into print within 48 hours of my departure.

WHEN I RETURNED TO AREQUIPA ON DECEMBER 11, I FELT AS IF I had never left. Steve Alvarez had been contracted again by the National Geographic to do the photography. Ann Williams, then a researcher with the Society, came to document the work. Chris Klein, an artist, was getting the kind of background he would use to excellent effect in his paintings showing reconstructions of the sacrifice of the Ice Maiden and the burial of the second female. Bill Conklin soon arrived to continue his work on the textiles, and Sonia Guillen was on hand with her two assistants.

Part of the Iceman team was also present, and this time it included Dr. Horst Seidler, a specialist in bioanthropology at the University of Vienna, Austria. By coincidence, this was my alma mater, and we had even attended the university at the same time.

I met the Iceman team after they had been introduced at a press conference announcing an agreement to collaborate with Catholic University. We were all anxious to work with the mummies again. We gathered for a meeting in the university's staff cafeteria. The Iceman team stressed the urgency of removing the textiles from the bodies so that both could receive the independent treatment they required. Dr. Seidler pointed out the effects of the higher relative humidity on the dry face of Juanita. "That is why you need to unwrap the mummy as quickly as possible," he said. He emphasized this by hitting the table with his fist. "First, second, and third: You must remove the textiles."

Most specialists would agree with this under normal conditions. Textile needs a relative humidity of its own (usually above 40 percent). A mummy would normally need a different relative humidity—lower if a fully desiccated body and higher if a frozen one. We didn't realize until a few months later that when a mummy is kept well below freezing, this is not the problem it appears to be. However, at the time, Dr. Seidler's concern meant we focused on removing the outer textiles.

The team was no longer in harmony, however. The relationship between José and Ruth on the one hand and Sonia on the other had been growing steadily worse. During the month I was at home, I had found myself engaged in lengthy telephone conversations with one of them and then having to call the other to negotiate. They were within a couple of hours' drive of each other and I was on another continent, yet they were disinclined to talk to each other. Both found faults in the professionalism of the other, but to me it appeared to be more of a personality clash. Sonia had a Ph.D., experience working with mummies, and contacts in the international community. Since she spoke fluent English, scientists who did not speak Spanish naturally gravitated to her. Unfortunately, at times she could also be brusque and somewhat condescending toward others.

José, a reserved and proud man, tolerated no disrespect. Ruth shared these characteristics, which in her case occasionally was combined with a fiery Latin temper. Not only was José the chairman of the Archaeology Department of Catholic University and co-director of the project, he had overseen the establishment of the laboratory. He and Ruth (now chief of laboratory) had to take day-to-day care of all the materials. Thus, most of the responsibility fell on their shoulders, both for the lab work and for handling the interest generated among the public, politicians, and scientists. Given the intense pressure they were under, José and Ruth did not take kindly to someone they felt was undermining them.

Sonia eventually requested that Catholic University give authority over the mummy research to the Centro Mallqui, which she directed. Catholic University officials regarded this as an ultimatum and reacted accordingly. The mummies, they announced, would stay under the control of their university—and that meant José. Soon afterward Sonia decided to leave the project.

Drs. Spindler and Seidler, who continued to work closely with Sonia and her mummy center, were disappointed when she was no longer involved with Juanita. They were well aware of the professional and interpersonal difficulties that could arise in mummy research, having experienced their fair share with the Iceman. Thus they recommended that we draw up a contract for researchers to sign so that work would be better coordinated and everyone would be kept to the same set of rules. "We had problems with scientists who had worked with the Iceman and then published the material as they liked. They were supposed to hold the results for the volumes that we were to edit," said Dr. Spindler. Some of them reportedly even made money by selling publications about their research, without any of the profit going back to the project—which had significant expenses to cover.

Dr. Spindler and Dr. Seidler thought that scientists should not publish—or even comment publicly on—the research until they had received the agreement of the directors. They said they had had some unfortunate experiences with people criticizing the Iceman team's directors without notifying them first and giving them an opportunity to explain.

Based on their suggestions, we drew up a contract binding all researchers for a period of five years, the period a project director in Peru had intellectual property rights over the material recovered during his excavations. Once we had an agreement drawn up along the lines they suggested, we thought we had brought a degree of control to the research. Little did we imagine that the first ones to break the agreement would be those who had helped formulate it.

We finally began work again on December 13, which also happened to be my birthday. One of the first issues to resolve concerned the textiles. They had been kept frozen, but once taken out for scientific work, they would eventually unfreeze. The problem concerned refreezing them after each session. Could this potentially damage the fibers?

Ruth was especially concerned about this, but Bill thought it was a relatively minor issue. While in the U.S., he had tested a number of procedures, including having wet and dry cotton and alpaca textiles frozen and thawed repeatedly to see if there were any adverse effects. There were none. "After all," he pointed out, "this fiber is from alpacas and they live in those kinds of conditions."

Nevertheless, Ruth looked particularly tense as a well-preserved cloth bundle was being opened. It had been found inside the outer textile and lying along the Ice Maiden's side. I asked her if anything was wrong, and she said, "I haven't slept all night worrying about that bundle." It didn't help that some days work sessions lasted past midnight, once until 5:00 a.m.

Renate, a Polish volunteer, drew details of the bundle as it was slowly, painstakingly, opened. We would stop by her table to watch as the edges of the cloth were peeled back, reminding me of the blossoming of a flower. Items began to appear—fine clumps of hair, along with a carved piece of spondylus shell on a cord, a belt, and a small cloth bag.

These were likely personal items belonging to Juanita. Hair is often well preserved because it is made of keratin, which is the dry material that is left behind by dead cells. In Inca times it was a common practice for a person's own hair and nails to be buried with his body at death, since they were regarded as important for accompanying the soul in the afterlife. The outer layer of your skin and your nails are also made of keratin, and being lifeless, they are difficult for the enzymes of bacteria to destroy. These items survive together with bones long after the rest of the dead person's body has disappeared. We suspected that the hair we found might be from the Ice Maiden's first haircut.[11]

Another feather-covered bag found with Juanita contained coca leaves. The coca leaf was a common offering in Inca times, and still is in many areas of the Andes today. Thanks to plant DNA, scientists will one day be able to pinpoint the valley where the leaves were grown.

All the while José placed blankets of ice around the portions of the bundle that were not being examined. A constant monitoring of the body and textile temperatures was maintained. As soon as the body came to within a few degrees of unfreezing, work would be stopped for the day.

In addition to the hair dryer used to heat pads to apply to the ice, a few times we even tried a soldering iron on the hardest blocks. However, in the end neither of these tools was utilized during most of the work. The work was slow and frustrating. Steve said, "Echave [the photo editor] is going to love this. Rolls and rolls of film showing nothing but people bending over what looks like a sack of potatoes!"

As long as the ice blankets were applied elsewhere on the bundle, the ambient air temperature (usually about 70° F) was sufficient to thaw some of the outer textiles. Sometimes we pressed bags of hot water against the more frozen textiles to help the process along. This had the advantage of being easily monitored, but the process was so slow. That meant the mummy was out of the freezer for longer, which we wanted to keep to a minimum. Clearly a new method had to be found.

I was eyeing a syringe someone had brought, lying to the side, when a light went off in my head. It could be used to squirt tiny amounts of distilled hot water on difficult-to-reach ice that formed in folds. The moisture would then be quickly absorbed with a cloth pad. For some specialized tasks this new "technique" did prove useful. Still other techniques had to be invented as new problems arose during the days to come.

Despite the agonizing slowness, we were learning more about the personal items of the girl—her story was coming alive. The first cloth to be removed was the outer textile or mantle, which was woven of alpaca wool and was gray with white stripes. Damaged during the mummy's fall, it did not seem to have been especially made for ceremonial use. Wrapped up with it were a folded woolen belt, a cloth bag containing personal items, a bag of coca leaves, balls made from cords of human hair, some string, and a piece of spondylus shell.

The cloth used to cover her face had been badly torn in the fall. It had been well made, with a plain dark brown center flanked by a lighter, brownish gold color on each side. This kind of head cloth (ñañaca) seems to have been worn only by women of high status. "It's the first example found in context," said Bill approvingly. Such head cloths had been described at the time of the Spanish conquest and depicted in drawings of 1613, but the cloths displayed in museums had mostly been recovered by collectors and looters, who left no descriptions of how they had been worn.

What arrested our attention was how the ñañaca had been pulled down over her face and held in place by a tupu (metal pin). We soon realized that this was one of the three tupus that a woman traditionally used—one to hold together two ends of her shawl and two to hold the upper folds of her dress. The priests must have taken out the shawl's tupu and used it to pin down the head cloth. This meant she was probably already dead before she was buried. Many months would pass before CT scans made this a near certainty.

The next piece of clothing caused even more of a sensation. Once the head cloth had been removed, we could see the shawl (lliclla, pronounced "yikya") that the Ice Maiden had worn over her shoulders. Without hesitation Bill said, "This is one of the finest Inca woman's textiles in the world."

Its colors were a vivid red and white and, like the other clothing, it had been made of fine alpaca wool. This fit well with what Pedro de Cieza de León wrote in 1553 about Inca women's clothing in Cuzco: "In short, the dress of the ladies of Cuzco is the most graceful and rich that has been seen up to this time in all the Indies."[12]

As work proceeded, the girl's pigtail appeared, and to our surprise it was tied by a thread to her waistband. "Obviously she had

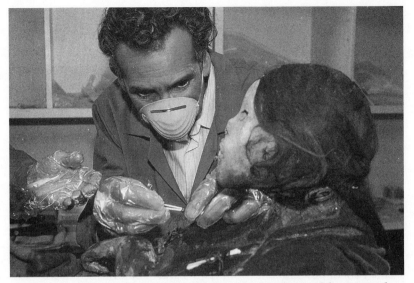

José Antonio Chávez removes ornaments from the shawl pins of the Ice Maiden in a laboratory at Catholic University in Arequipa.

been clothed, at least in part, by others just before—or very soon after—she died," said Bill. Shawl pins (apparently made of an alloy of gold and silver) were connected together by a plaited cord with diamond patterning. Each pin had woven cords attached to it along its shaft, which were held in place by half-hitch knots. The cords in turn had miniature wood carvings attached to them, and one was tied to a large needle made of the spine of a cactus. These carvings appeared to represent a box (with some substance in it, perhaps llama fat, a common offering), two drinking vessels, and what may have been a dog or fox. Although historical documents had noted "ornaments" being attached to the shawl pins, these were the first ones found still in place.

The last piece of the Ice Maiden's clothing to be examined was a dress (aksu), which was wrapped around her body and fastened with a thickly woven belt (chumpi) around the waist and by two tupus at her shoulders. (Women wore no undergarments.) "The tupus give the same flexibility as a man's suspenders. You can adjust them up or down with the ends of the dress for a better fit," said Bill, admiring them.

He estimated that the dress would have been about eight feet long when unfolded. We knew that Inca women had typically worn clothing in this style, but for the first time we could see it vividly in its original context. As more of the dress was unfolded, bands of bluish red (or plum) were revealed. Bill announced that they were "unprecedented for Inca textiles." Other bands of yellow, red, and orange further set these off. Bill later wrote, "The rainbow of colors which characterize the *aksu* were a shock to those who have previously only seen the Inca world only through the colonial black and white ink line drawings."

Once the clothing was lifted off the girl's shoulders and from above her folded arms, she became much more distinctly human to us all. She no longer was a mummy wrapped in a bundle. Whereas she had once seemed out of place amid the tools, lights, and people dressed in lab coats, she now "owned" the room. Our eyes were inexorably drawn to her.

What struck us most of all was her regal countenance. She appeared to have been gazing out serenely at the moment of her death—as if she accepted it, believing she would become one with the gods. I knew, however, that this was a subjective projection on my part. The look on the face of a mummy usually has little relation with how the person died. Normally the facial expressions of mummies are the result of muscle tissue relaxing after death, and the effects of decay can also cause the changes. (The gaping mouth displayed by some mummies is due mainly to the decay of the chewing muscles resulting in a sagging mandible—not because the person was horrified at the time of death.) But it was difficult to think in such a rational way when staring directly into the face of the Ice Maiden. "She looks so strong, it's as if she were saying, 'Wow, I'm on my way to heaven.' If we were part of the Inca culture, this would be like finding the tomb of the Virgin Mary," Bill said with awe.

For some team members Juanita was even assuming her own identity. A process of transference was starting to take hold. I had heard of this happening with other mummies. The scientists who spent time with them would sometimes become sentimentally attached, viewing the mummies almost as if they were still alive. Ruth in particular began to feel as if the Ice Maiden were a child who needed her care. "She has come to me in my dreams and given me advice on what to do."

Although the artifacts did not have the same psychological effect on us as the mummy, we were impressed with the great care the Incas had taken with them. The clothing of four of the female statues was intact and meticulously woven. After Bill finished looking them over, he said with a grin, "The figurines were completely color coordinated—really dressed for the ball."

One miniature textile was made of wool from a vicuña (a wild camelid that has the world's finest wool). I had read that the weave count of textiles made from this wool is as high as the finest machine-made clothing. Although many Inca statues have been found, at the time only a couple of dozen in the world had clothing that was so well preserved. The ones we recovered thus added to the importance of the Ampato finds. Thanks to Juanita, our knowledge of Inca burial customs had taken a major step forward.

WE HAD HIGH HOPES THAT THE SECOND MUMMY WOULD BE BETTER preserved than Juanita, perhaps even being completely frozen. Although the upper part of her body had been found in dry soil, her headdress could have provided insulation and x-rays seemed to confirm this. Before we could uncover the head, we had to remove an offering bundle from beneath the mummy. Its outer cloth had been badly damaged, but it contained a netted bag in which we saw a comb. Due to its fragile state, the bag was placed in a freezer and still has not been completely examined. We believe it contains the girl's personal effects.

One cloth had been frozen separately to the mummy's side and required the application of bags of warm water to slowly thaw and detach it from the mummy's clothing. Once it was freed, Bill told us with considerable surprise, "This is definitely an adult male's tunic. The quality of the textile is fabulous, and I don't recall ever seeing such a red-fringed tunic before." He examined it some more. "Inca tunics are not square, yet this one is perfectly so. And what is it doing together with a female sacrifice?"

It is one of the many questions that remain unanswered. We do have some sound hypotheses, however. One explanation is that the tunic was a symbolic offering from the child's father, for we know from historical documents that parents sometimes offered their own children to please the gods. Juan de Ulloa Mogollón described in 1586 that "beautiful daughters" of the Colca Valley headmen were given to the Inca emperor. In central Peru this included a girl who had been sent by her father to Cuzco and then returned by the Inca emperor to be sacrificed on a mountain near her village.[13]

As for the red-fringed tunic, I came across a line in a document of 1551 that described precisely such an item. Juan de Betanzos noted that the Inca emperor had ordered red-fringed tunics to be worn by the leaders of the people he had conquered in a region that included Arequipa.[14] That suggested that the girl was the daughter of one of these men.

The Incas also told Juan de Betanzos that boys and girls could be symbolically married and sacrificed. "These children were well dressed and looked like men and women."[15] If this had been the case with the boy and girl buried near each other at 19,000 feet, it would explain the adult-size clothing, which we also found on Juanita.

Bill offered another hypothesis, "Maybe it symbolized the marriage of the girl to someone in the next world."

"That could be a mountain god," I added. "I've been told that this belief is still held in some parts of the Andes."

However interesting such speculations are, though, at the time our attention was focused on more practical concerns, such as the removal of the girl's headdress. How could we do this if the feathers were frozen onto the child's face?

Fortunately, as the work continued, it became clear that the feathers were sewn onto a cloth cap placed on the child's head. Although a delicate operation, separating them was far easier than we had thought. Exposure to the ambient air temperature also helped. The headdress loosened without our having to unfreeze the outer part of the textile-wrapped mummy. These headdresses resemble the miniature ones worn by most of the female statues offered by the Incas. Feather headdresses had a ritual importance that probably was related to the status of the acllas.

Bill decided to give numbers to feathers that appeared insecurely attached, in case they fell off. Hector pinned on the tiny numbered flags with the delicacy of a surgeon, which in fact he was. Those of us in the room broke into spontaneous applause as the headdress was carefully lifted from the head cloth and placed over the black model of a head that Bill had prepared.

An ornithologist at the Smithsonian Institution would later state the headdress was made of macaw feathers, somewhat discolored by the red earth they had been buried in. They must originally have come from a tropical forest region, probably obtained as part of a long-distance trading pattern established centuries before the Incas came to power. An archaeology student, Fernando Velasquez, was put to work laboriously examining and, if necessary, treating and cleaning each of the feathers.

Given the lavish amount of fine Inca pottery found with this mummy, we were surprised that the girl's clothes were so common, not nearly as fine as those worn by Juanita. But that disappointment was nothing compared to what was to come.

While loosening the head cloth, I gently pulled it aside and shone my flashlight between one of the folds. I was startled to be looking directly into the mummy's open mouth. Only a few teeth were in place, and I spied little but bones and the telltale marks of carbonization. I sadly realized that the mummy had been struck by lightning, as the hole through the gold lamina in her lap suggested. I passed on the bad news. "It looks like nothing remains of any soft tissue—she was fried in her own body fat."

The gold lamina was probably a diadem or plume, since it resembled those depicted on the foreheads of Incas in Guaman Poma's drawings and was similar to the miniature versions of them we had found on male statues. "It may have, perhaps intentionally, functioned as a lightning rod," wrote Bill later.[16] However, being placed so low in the burial, I doubted that the plume had been used to deliberately attract lightning. The two mummies that had been hit were close together on a high section of the plateau, where lightning would be expected to strike.

We couldn't be certain where lightning had first entered the girl's body. It is easy to mistake burn marks for entry and exit points. Specialists have found that electricity often enters the body in a uniform way, with a strike flowing partly through the body and partly over its surface.[17] The amount of electricity that penetrates inside it determines how much damage occurs, and this in turn depends on the wetness of the body. In the case of the female it was extensive.

When we examined the x-ray, we did not observe any sign of a fracture in the girl's cranium, nor was any seen in the skull of the boy. Perhaps they had been strangled, or buried alive, or maybe one or both of them had been knocked unconscious, without leaving any signs, and then buried. Indeed, a person can die from such a blow. Called *commotio cerebri*, it acts like an electric short circuit in the brain.[18] A person gets hit on the head, dies instantly, and even a skilled medical examiner might not observe the injury.

We soon abandoned work on the clothes, since we could not continue unwrapping them without risking the bones' collapsing. We had misinterpreted the x-rays because of the multiple layers of textiles. Further work would now have to await the help of physical anthropologists.

Though we were disappointed, at least we still had two distinct sets of Inca female clothing. As Bill said, "This material will define Inca women's textiles." Later I talked with Dr. Ann Rowe of the Textile Museum in Washington, D.C., a world authority on Inca textiles. She concurred with Bill on how unusual the find was. "Although Inca male textiles are relatively common and examples of Inca female clothing also exist, our knowledge of how Inca women actually wore the clothing rests largely on what we have seen in the drawings of Guaman Poma in 1613, of miniature clothing from Inca statues, and our readings of the historical documents, most of which were written years after the Spanish conquest. Now you have found clothing actually being worn by women."

José had been documenting everything with a Hi-8 camcorder, but this would not provide the quality necessary for a television program. Since we were now beginning to make interesting discoveries regularly, National Geographic hired an old friend of mine, Peruvian cinematographer Jorge Vignati, to film the work, and he arrived the afternoon of December 20.

José and Ruth had rough copies of the Ice Maiden's clothes made, and José used himself as a model to determine how best to proceed whenever the decision was made to remove some items from her. The small ornaments, attached by knotted cords to the shawl pins, posed the biggest problem, because they prevented the pins from being removed. We did not want to undo the knots, but without the pins being removed, we wouldn't be able to work on the upper part of the Ice Maiden's aksu (dress). At first we could not see any way out of this quandary, then José came up with a clever solution. He used a Q-tip to replace the pin at the same time the cords were slid off it.

The Ice Maiden's humanity really hit home on December 21. We uncovered her right hand and found it holding the cloth in what looked like a death grip. Called a "cadaveric spasm," this is distinct from rigor mortis, which disappears after two days.[19] By grasping the textile so tightly, the Ice Maiden made it a seemingly impossible task to remove it without damaging her skin. This meant the temporary termination of our work. However, thanks to Bill, we had accomplished one of our principal goals. By making calculations and laboriously piecing together the data, he was able to reconstruct exactly how the girl had been clothed. In the process he also discovered that she had been dressed in the same sequence as that of the female statues.

By coincidence, the day we stopped work on the Ice Maiden, we received the news that Time had selected her as one of the world's ten most important scientific discoveries for 1995. We were pleased that this recognition had been given to a mummy that had become the center of our lives.

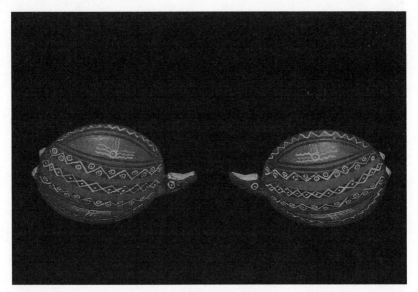

A pair of Inca plates was found in the boy's burial at 19,200 feet on Ampato. The pairing of some items was common in Inca culture and meant to indicate reciprocity in relationships between humans and between people and gods.

The next day I left for the U.S. and was met by my companion, Jackie. She had been patient and helping behind the scenes ever since the discovery of the Ice Maiden. Spending the holidays with her and her family at their home on the Chesapeake Bay was a badly needed change of pace. On Christmas Day their television happened to be on, and we were taken by surprise when we overheard someone mention an Inca mummy on one of the morning shows. The editor of *Discover Magazine* was being interviewed and he cited the Ice Maiden as one of the most important scientific discoveries made during the past year. After all our struggles to preserve her, it was hard to imagine a better present.

CHAPTER FIVE

The MOUNTAINS of POWER

Destiny is not a matter of chance, it is a matter of choice; it is
not a thing to be waited for, it is a thing to be achieved.
—WILLIAM JENNINGS BRYAN

Padre, don't you get tired of seizing idols? Well then,
take this mountain, if you can, for it is the god that I worship.
—COMMENT OF A VILLAGE LEADER, QUOTED BY PADRE FRANCISCO PATIÑO IN 1648

MORE THAN ONCE I HAVE THOUGHT BACK OVER THE EVENTS
that led to my becoming an anthropologist and ultimately to my
research in the Andes. When we reflect on how our lives have
evolved, it is usually difficult to pick a single turning point, and mine
is no different. Little in my childhood suggested that I would end
up living most of my life outside the United States, much less that
I would one day be carrying an Inca mummy down a mountain.

My name has thrown off people, who often assume I am foreign
born. My last name is of German origin, but my father's side also
includes Scotch and Irish, and no one in our family spoke German.
Despite having been born in Wisconsin, my mother's native tongue
was Norwegian, and it was she who named me Johan, the Norwegian
name for John. This has created no end of confusion throughout my
life. Once my name was mistaken for Joann and even appeared on
the list of girls to vote for as high school queen. (I got three votes.)
Johnny Cash's song "A Boy Named Sue" has always had a special
resonance for me.

Far from being a foreigner, I was born and lived the first 18 years of my life in New Lenox, a village smack in the middle of Illinois farm country. I never left the U.S. until I was 18—and did not climb a mountain until I was 20. This provincialism was somewhat offset by my parents' approach toward life. My mother's Norwegian background helped me gain a broader outlook on the world, although her attempts to teach me the language bore no fruit. More important were her wide-ranging interests and open-mindedness to other ways of thinking. For only one example, she collected the works of Freud when they were still considered scandalous reading for a woman.

My father was a detective for the postal service, responsible for mail robberies on trains and planes throughout the Midwest. This proved to have a major influence on how I viewed the world. In my mind his job combined scientific investigation with the excitement of a dangerous profession. Some of my earliest memories are of fingerprinting and playing with powders that showed up under ultraviolet light—my father used them to mark bills sent through the mail. He always carried a .38-caliber revolver, and he kept a variety of guns in our house, ranging from a German sniper's rifle to a semiautomatic that a robber attempted to turn into a full automatic by shaving down its firing pin. I owned my own gun by age 12, and all through my childhood imagined myself as a detective solving mysteries. Subtract the gun and, in a way, I've never changed.

By the time I started high school, I was reading about explorers and exotic places. My mother's fascination with the Norwegian explorer Thor Heyerdahl was contagious. Richard Halliburton's Book of Marvels in particular led me to focus on exploring foreign lands.[1] I dreamed of daring the feats that the author accomplished while he was still a boy. Swimming the Bosporus! Reaching the summit of the Matterhorn at age 14! I was soon determined to become an explorer. But how, without money and experience?

I had to start somewhere, so I leaped at the chance when a friend of the family said he could get me a job working on the Rock Island

Railroad traveling throughout the Midwest. During the summers of 1960, 1961, and 1963 I worked with Southerners on a railroad line gang. Our main job was to dig holes by hand, put up telegraph poles, and then climb up them to add cross arms. The men were all at least four years older than I and came from much different backgrounds—to put it mildly. To me they were like people from another world, and in a way they were. As a Northerner I had to act and talk like they did in order to become accepted. Without knowing it, I had begun to behave like an ethnographer (called in anthropological jargon "participant observation"), constantly learning more about how these strange men thought.

I had my share of "learning experiences" during those summers, but one would dramatically affect me for the rest of my life. One day in 1961 I climbed up a 35-foot pole that had been badly eaten by termites. My job was to untie the lines from their insulators so that the pole could be cut down and a new one put in its place. I strapped myself in and leaned out to undo the last wire on a cross arm, watching as it dropped below. The next thing I knew I was falling straight back—the termite-eaten pole had snapped off and was falling down with me dangling under it. Ironically, the belt that had kept me from falling, also kept me from throwing myself off the pole. I knew I was dead.

The fall must have taken two seconds, but I wasn't counting. Scenes went slowly through my mind taking me back to early childhood. My life passed before my eyes.

I survived. Although the wires had dropped down, they were still hanging above the ground. They were attached to the telegraph poles on both sides of me. The cross arms on my pole caught in the wires, and there was a "bwang" as the pole bounced up. It quickly fell back down, and I found myself dangling only a few feet above the ground.

Once my mind had cleared enough for me to realize what had happened, I slowly undid the belt. With a quick push, I threw myself off to the side, hoping the pole wouldn't somehow spring out and follow on top of me. I lay there shaking for several minutes, until I finally got enough strength to stand up. I walked slowly over to the pole and shoved it free of the wires. It landed with a loud thud, bounced a few inches, then lay still.

As paradoxical as it may seem, the experience underscored to me the importance of living life the way I wanted to. It crystallized in my mind, like nothing else could at that age, the reality that one day I would be dead, and I should not let my life be wasted on doing things I did not find interesting. In the years to come whenever I was in a difficult situation and asked myself the question, "Why am I doing this?" that scene on the telegraph pole would replay itself in my mind's eye. And I would know.

While in high school I read The Rivers Ran East and my attention was drawn to the Amazon.[2] This curiosity solidified when Steve Meyer, a high school friend, moved to Brazil. He would occasionally return to New Lenox with tales of a country that seemed full of possibilities for exploration. When I graduated from high school, I traveled alone to Brazil with money I had saved from working two summers on the railroad line gang.

My father could not understand why I would waste perfectly good money to visit a foreign country, and he refused to talk to me for weeks beforehand or even shake my hand when I left. But during that trip I realized that I was indeed interested in living in other cultures—I had not just been fantasizing while reading about them. I wanted to learn more about both ancient civilizations and the living cultures of people in other parts of the world. I couldn't believe my luck when I found out that there was an actual profession devoted to this—anthropology.

I began majoring in archaeology at the University of Arizona, but soon focused more on cultural anthropology, which seemed to better fit my interests. A documentary film, The Sky Above, the Mud Below, had a profound effect on me.[3] This movie depicted a team making the first crossing of New Guinea in order to search for tribes that previously had never seen Westerners. The more I read about cultural anthropology, the more I thought it provided wonderful opportunities to explore the world. It also seemed to provide the best way for me to make contributions to other disciplines, especially philosophy and psychology, which had begun to interest me in my late teens.

I decided to gain skills or "tools" that would be of help in a variety of situations. Thus, as soon as I entered the University of Arizona, I took up scuba diving, skydiving, mountain climbing, cave exploring, and karate. Some of the tools were academic ones, like linguistics (to learn unwritten languages), or were ones that helped in documenting tribal customs, such as cinematography. I could employ them anywhere in the world and they would enable me to undertake expeditions that led to new discoveries.

After two years at the University of Arizona, I thought it was time to gain anthropological field experience that would lay the foundation for research in New Guinea. A friend of mine, Bill Holz, and I planned an expedition in 1964 to skydive onto Mount Roraima, an uplifted plateau on the border of Brazil and Venezuela. It had become famous as the reputed model for Arthur Conan Doyle's book The Lost World.[4] At the time it was still relatively difficult to reach. We planned to gather information on the tribes we encountered as we made our way out through Brazil. As luck would have it, Bill's car was broken into and we were left without money to carry out our plan. In retrospect, that may have been just as well, but at the time the desire to do something original was a powerful driving force.

My next decision was more practical. I decided that if I was going to live in other cultures and speak other languages, I would learn more if I studied anthropology in a foreign country. In a sense I would be doing anthropology while learning it. I decided to learn German, since it would help me understand philosophy and psychology, while meeting my language requirement for graduate school. After taking intensive language training, I enrolled in anthropology at the University of Vienna. Vienna's location allowed me to easily escape to ski and mountain climb. I had no money, but I could hitchhike to some of the Alps' most famous mountains in a day. Vienna seemed the ideal choice for a total learning experience.

Before my first semester at Vienna in 1965, I left for Greece, where I contacted Peter Throckmorton. Together with George Bass, he had founded the field of underwater archaeology only a few years before and had set up his base for research in Piraeus. We surveyed shipwrecks and recovered Roman artifacts in the Mediterranean Sea off the coast of southern Italy. Later we surveyed a village site of the 3,000-year-old Villanovan culture. It was located in 16 feet of water in Lake Bolsena in northern Italy, and we uncovered artifacts that had never been seen before. By sheer luck, I participated in some of the most exciting archaeological research being undertaken at the time.

As interesting as these experiences were, I wanted to study a culture as different from my own as possible, and nomadic hunter-gatherers seemed ideal for that. Only a few such societies still existed in the world, yet 99 percent of man's time on earth was spent as a hunter-gatherer. Many of the basic building blocks of society were established during the change from this way of life to a settled agricultural one. I realized that within my lifetime the last of these societies would likely cease to exist, and the opportunity to study this kind of cultural change would be gone forever.

I wanted to conduct this research in New Guinea, but it was too far away and too expensive to reach. By chance, I read an article about the Kusunda, a hunter-gatherer tribe reported to roam throughout the foothills of Nepal. The Kusunda had been briefly noted in a text dating from the mid-1800s and were believed to have a language unrelated to any other. The tribe had disappeared from view until a Tibetan scholar reported in the mid-1950s the rumor that they were still wandering the hills of Nepal. If I could find the tribe, I could study how its members had managed to maintain their way of life and what happened if some groups of the tribe had already settled.

When my plane landed in Nepal in early 1968, I didn't have enough money to fly back. Although I did eventually locate the last few survivors of the Kusunda, there were not enough of them to do a truly ethnographic study. Fortunately, after months of searching, I was able to find different groups of the Raji who had been hunter-gatherers until recent times (and one, the Raute, that still was) and study their transition to settled life. I also investigated abandoned hunter-gatherer camps, searching for clues about their current-day customs and comparing them to what I knew of prehistoric hunter-gatherers. This type of study, called ethnoarchaeology, would play a key role in my later research in the Andes.[5]

I became especially interested in shamanism and how the tribe's belief system related to the natural world—the forests, rivers, and mountains. This focus on indigenous religious specialists would also influence my research in the Andes. Ironically, I was to find out more about a culture interacting with the environment (and associated religious beliefs) when I studied the Incas, a highly complex civilization, than I ever did with hunter-gatherers.

I lived in the Himalayas for more than eight years during the 1960s and 1970s, but in all that time I never focused on mountain worship. Like most climbers, I regarded mountains as physical challenges to be overcome. I began to gather information about current-day beliefs about mountains only after I participated in an American expedition to Mount Everest in 1976.[6] The Sherpas burned juniper boughs the entire time we were on the mountain in order to please the goddess believed to reside in it.

The next year I embarked on an expedition to an isolated area of eastern Nepal, where the legendary land of Khembalung was thought to be located. Tibetan Buddhists believe that mountain gods protect these "hidden lands" (beyul) and "hidden treasures" (ter) of sacred texts and objects meant to be revealed only at special times of need. I eventually visited six of these hidden lands myself. I worked with a Tibetan translating some of the ancient "guidebooks" (lamyig) to them. These provided directions for believers along with a mixture of omens, rituals, and mythical and actual places. Said to have been first passed on by the great Padmasambhava more than a millennium ago, the guidebooks described the mountains as being protector gods of the hidden lands.[7]

I was fascinated, and my interest in the importance of sacred mountains began to grow. But by 1980 it still had not become a focus of my research there, and it played no role whatsoever in my decision to go to the Andes. Indeed, I had not even thought of the Andes until late 1979. I was asked to join two different expeditions to the Andes. There my interests in mountains, religion, archaeology, and cultural anthropology would combine in a way that would change my life forever.

My journey to South America in January 1980 was a respite after five years of living in Nepal. The stage had been set by a climb I had made the previous summer. I had started thinking of becoming a more serious Himalayan climber, undertaking rapid ascents with small teams. When Dick Isherwood, an especially strong English alpinist, asked me to join him on an expedition to Pakistan, I seized the opportunity.

We made the first ascent of the western face on Buni Zom, the highest peak in the Hindu Raj range.[8] While we were on the summit a storm struck, and our metal climbing gear was buzzing with electricity as we made a long traverse to escape the exposed ridge. Then we rappelled down through spindrift avalanches, reaching the foot of the face at night in a blizzard. Dick fell in a crevasse, but he was able to get out unharmed. We literally stumbled over our tent after hours of searching in the dark. We were lucky to escape alive, and I began to reconsider my goals. Surviving a life-and-death struggle certainly helps you get your priorities straight. I had too many other goals I wanted to reach to subject myself to the risks involved in Himalayan climbing.

No sooner had I returned to Kathmandu than Jack Miller, a climbing friend, said, "I've heard that a group of boat nomads still exists in Tierra del Fuego. I'm leading an expedition there this February and you're welcome to join us." If the story were true, the group would be among the last nomadic hunter-gatherers in the Western Hemisphere. I hadn't abandoned my hope of investigating such people—it had, after all, been the reason I journeyed to the Himalayas in the first place.

Then, out of the blue, came an offer to join a British expedition in the mountains and jungle of a little-known region of eastern Ecuador.[9] With luck, we might come across a previously unknown tribe. I would have been hesitant to go to South America for only one expedition—but two! The extreme contrasts of jungle, mountains, and Fuegian islands, together with the possibility of new anthropological discoveries, were too tempting.

On the first expedition we trekked into the Llanganatis, a wild, jungle-draped mountain range in Ecuador. We ended up having to cut our way for weeks from it to the Amazon amid a constant downpour—and without seeing a single Indian on the way. The experience brought back unpleasant memories of living in the jungle during the monsoon in Nepal and reinforced my decision to do anthropology only in the mountains.

As luck would have it, I missed the second expedition by a day. I went to Tierra del Fuego anyway. Eventually I met another explorer and the two of us trekked through virgin forest while making our way to the Beagle Channel. It proved worse than the Amazonian jungle, blindly hacking and pushing our way through dense trees and vegetation. "This is what I swore I would never put myself through again," I complained to my companion. I now understood what Charles Darwin meant when he described how sailors would yell out soundings as they traveled through similar terrain.[10] You were sometimes walking on dead vegetation a dozen feet off the ground.

On my way back to the U.S. an odd item caught my eye while I was visiting an office in Santiago. As I studied the Chilean Andean Federation's glassed-in display of publications and climbing gear, I noticed a booklet with a map on its cover. I asked for the case to be opened, and soon I was reading about an expedition to an Inca site on the summit of Licancabur, a volcano in northern Chile." Within minutes, I was hooked.

The Andes is the world's youngest and longest mountain range—and one of the most rugged. The central Andes remind me of the Himalayas. When the South American continent "drifted" west, it forced a dense oceanic plate beneath it. This caused the uplift of rocks along the continent's western edge, forming mountains. It also pro-duced molten magma in the earth's mantle, and numerous volcanoes where it burst through. This process continues to this day—the Andes are still growing in altitude, albeit at a rate too slow for us to perceive without the help of sophisticated instruments."

The average tourist sees the Andean range for the first time through the window of a jet plane—and rarely forgets it. On a clear day, snow-capped peaks dominate the landscape for as far as the eye can see. This should be no surprise, as the Andes mountain chain extends for more than 4,500 miles. Furthermore, there are no higher mountains outside Asia. More than 60 peaks are over 20,000 feet, and Aconcagua (22,834 feet) is the highest mountain in the Western Hemisphere.

The region bordering the Andes is a study in contrasts. To the west of the Andes is found the world's driest desert, itself bordered by the Pacific Ocean. To the east lies the Amazon jungle, one of the largest on earth. It is possible to travel from the coast to the tropical forest in 124 miles (less than the distance from New York City to Philadelphia) and cross 20 of the world's 34 life zones. The Andes mountains are sandwiched between the most extreme climatical and ecological conditions on earth. Nonetheless, the highlands of the Andes form the most densely inhabited high-altitude region in the world.

The indigenous peoples who inhabit the Andes have fascinated anthropologists for more than a century. Most of the ethnic groups belong either to the Quechua or Aymara language families, but many possess their own, quite distinctive languages. And despite the con-siderable intermarriage with people of Spanish descent, indigenous groups make up large percentages of the populations of some Andean countries (e.g., 45 percent in Peru, 50 percent in Bolivia, and 25 percent in Ecuador).[13] Although most are Christians, traditional religious customs and beliefs that predate the Spanish conquest still hold sway. As one chronicler, Joseph de Arriaga, noted in 1621, they "carry water on both shoulders" because they had "recourse to both religions at once."[14]

I gathered more information about the ruins on mountain summits that predated the Spanish conquest of A.D. 1532, including well-built stone structures up to 22,000 feet. By 1980 climbers had reported more than 40 sites above 17,000 feet. This subject struck a special chord in me. Here was a way to combine my interests in climbing and anthropology. The result was that my stay in South America extended beyond those first few months to more than ten years—and now spans a quarter of a century.

Despite their uniqueness, the high-altitude sites were not even mentioned in North American archaeological textbooks. Indeed, little had been written about them in English at all. However, in South America a handful of Chilean and Argentine climbers had been investigating and writing about them for several years. These men were mostly untrained in archaeology, and only a few, especially the pioneer in the field, the Argentine Antonio Beorchia, had undertaken serious studies.[15] He helped transform high-altitude archaeology from an occasional topic of interest to professionals to a subfield of Andean archaeology. Among professional archaeologists, only the Argentine Juan Schobinger had conducted detailed research on more than a single high-altitude site, although a few others made valuable contributions to the analysis of materials that climbers had brought back down.[16]

Nonetheless, even the most basic questions remained unanswered. Who made the sites and how far through the Andes were they distributed? One question in particular kept repeating itself over and over in my mind: why? Why had men 500 years ago built a road and way stations through the world's driest desert, the Atacama, and then constructed buildings at altitudes that would not even be reached by others until nearly 400 years later? The only way to solve these puzzles was to combine an investigation of the high-mountain sites with historical research about Inca religion. Before long, I came to realize that ethnography needed to be added as well.[17]

The search for answers led to an odyssey that, after more than 200 ascents above 17,000 feet in five Andean countries and the discovery of more than 50 archaeological sites, still has not ended for me. In addition to trying to solve the mystery of why the sites had been made, I knew that some of the best-preserved artifacts, textiles, and even frozen Inca mummies had been found at these ruins. Because they were among the few intact Inca ceremonial sites to exist at any altitude, they promised to provide insights on Inca religious practices that could not be obtained in any other way.

THE FIRST MOUNTAIN I CLIMBED WAS LICANCABUR, THE ONE THAT had piqued my interest in Santiago. Inca ruins and artifacts had been found many years before on the crater's rim. This peak on the border of Bolivia and Chile is a striking cone-shaped volcano that dominates a vast region bordering the Atacama Desert. I knew a lake, the world's highest, was located within its crater, but was unprepared for the spectacular contrast of sparkling blue water surrounded by snow at 19,200 feet, with a backdrop of sheer cliffs and barren desert.

On the same trip I investigated structures that climbers had reported seeing on the summit of Paniri, a 19,508-foot volcano north of Licancabur. Sure enough, I found well-preserved Inca ruins on the summit. This marked my first "discovery" of a site, but I was no closer to answering the persistent question: why did the Incas climb to such heights? Could the sites have been signal stations as some people believed? Or, as most archaeologists thought at the time, were the sites dedicated to worship of the sun, a major deity of the Incas?

In one of those twists of fate that changes lives, the bag containing my camera gear (and worse, all my notes and slides) was stolen when I entered Peru. I could not redo the expeditions in Ecuador and Tierra del Fuego, but the volcanoes were close enough to reclimb. Equipped only with a pocket camera I bought in northern Chile, I returned to climb the peaks again. In the process, I began to find answers to my questions.

I was trekking back to the village of Socaire in Chile after having climbed three volcanoes when I passed a man leading his donkeys to a nearby lake. This humble villager provided the first clue that eventually led me to unraveling the mystery of high mountain sites. When I explained I had scaled some of the mountains in the area, he looked at me strangely and said, "In a few days we will be worshipping them. You see, we have to clean the irrigation canals, and before beginning the work we make offerings to the mountains asking them to send water for our crops and livestock."

When I asked which peaks were the most important, he named them in a hierarchy that paralleled exactly the significance—as based on the complexity of the structures—of the sites I had found. Yet no villager knew these sites existed. I was suddenly struck by the realization that a link existed between beliefs of today and those at the time of the Incas. A mass of disparate details commingled in my mind and for the first time made perfect sense—the deities residing in the mountains were their weather and fertility gods. Although the Incas worshipped the sun, the sites must have been built where they were on specific mountain summits because of the importance of the peaks themselves. This reasoning was based on ecological facts: the mountains do (at least to a degree) "control" weather and provide down-flowing water. Thus they directly affect the fertility of the crops and herds necessary for people to survive.

Still, the question remained: would this theory also help explain ritual sites on mountains in other areas of the Andes? Several of the early Spanish writers referred to sacred peaks as "mountains of power," but gave few details about the reasons why they were worshipped. Especially important for me was a little-known document written by the priest

Cristóbal de Albornoz in 1583. He listed major deities and sacred places throughout the Inca Empire. According to him, mountains were consistently the most important. In the early 1600s Guaman Poma made drawings of some of the sacred mountains that the Inca emperor personally supported. A book of the early 1600s—the only one written on traditional religion in the native Quechua language—described the gods of Huarochiri near Lima, and it provided further clues. In it are descriptions of rituals for worshipping the great mountain deity Pariacaca that were performed for water and fertility.

As I gathered more information from historical and ethnographic sources, this basic theme was consistently repeated. I began to understand why the anthropologist Joseph Bastien had called mountain worship the "keystone of Andean culture."[18] In my mind it was also the key to understanding the mystery of Inca high-altitude sanctuaries.

IN 1981 I RETURNED TO LICANCABUR WITH THE ARCHAEOLOGISTS Ana María Barón and George Serracino. We camped four days on its summit while surveying ruins, the first time an archaeological expedition had stayed more than a day at such a high site. We undertook a few exploratory excavations, but they were limited to one-meter squares less than three feet deep. We had not brought the tools for anything more ambitious.

I had heard the legend of a golden statue lying at the bottom of the lake. I doubted it was true, but the Incas might well have thrown offerings into the lake. To check out this possibility, I had carried up skin-diving gear. I was startled to find myself diving in and out of clouds of zooplankton colored brown, yellow, and—to my amazement—red.

A year later I was once again camped on the summit, this time as part of a much better equipped expedition. Five of us dove with scuba gear several thousand feet higher than had ever been done before, exploring the lake and collecting plankton, including a new species. We wore dry suits and our scuba equipment was specially adapted for use with pure oxygen. The idea was that oxygen would help our breathing and prevent us from blacking out when we surfaced. This had been a problem with divers at 15,000 feet, so how much more so for nearly a mile higher?[19]

We did not find Inca offerings in Licancabur's crater lake, but this work (and the scuba tanks a friend and I salvaged from those abandoned on Licancabur's summit) laid the basis for later underwater archaeological expeditions I led in Lake Titicaca, Bolivia. There was no doubt that the Incas had made offerings into that lake. We recovered not only Inca ritual artifacts, but pre-Inca ones as well.[20]

I continued climbing other mountains, soloing on more than 40 of them. This was not my preference—it was just that finding climbing partners was always a problem, one made worse because I rarely could pay more than expenses. But the solo ascents had their rewards for someone who loves mountains. Nothing makes me feel more attuned to my environment than being completely alone, with no possibility of rescue if an accident occurs. Climbing entails a unique combination of spectacular scenery, physical and mental challenges, and living on the edge. There is a tremendous satisfaction in having a sense of mastery of your mind and body in extreme conditions. My senses come alive, sensitive to the wind, the sounds, the slightest variations in terrain. If the weather changes, I might have to make my way back down with limited visibility, so I memorize as many of the mountain's myriad features as I can. Each mountain seems to have its own personality—peaceful, capricious, mean, generous, and stern were some of the adjectives I would attribute to them.

During the ascents of peaks in Chile, Argentina, Bolivia, and Peru, my teammates and I discovered dozens of high-altitude sites. Since I knew the Incas had reached more than 22,000 feet on Llullaillaco, the possibility existed that they might have made the summits of even higher peaks, including Aconcagua, the highest mountain outside Asia.

I made a solo ascent of the peak in 1981, but my search on the summit was cut short by an approaching storm. Four years later climbers found the frozen body of a child at 17,220 feet. The Incas had buried the body at the foot of a steep cliff, which they could not ascend. In a rare absence of greed, the climbers left the site intact and informed the archaeologist Juan Schobinger. "We recovered the body along with statues made of silver, spondylus shell, and gold," he told me later that year.

For only the second time a frozen body had been recovered by a professionally trained person on a mountain summit. The previous time occurred 21 years earlier by, appropriately enough, Dr. Schobinger, who had been called in after the initial discovery. Thanks in large part to his work, we have a much fuller picture of Inca human sacrifices.[21]

The naturally frozen bodies have provided bonanzas for scientists, who have conducted studies on everything from diseases to what food the children ate before they died. "I'd never seen anything so exciting," the Canadian paleopathologist Patrick Horne told me after examining a mummy found by treasure hunters on El Plomo in 1954. The mummy? Gold? No, he was referring to his discovery of a virus, which he said proved for the first time that one could be preserved in human tissue for more than 500 years.

Initially I focused more on finding and comparing sites than in excavating them. Years passed before I could obtain the funding that enabled me to organize expeditions able to remain for the lengthy periods necessary to scientifically excavate ruins at high altitudes. This was in large part due to the policies of the scientific institutions that supported archaeological research. In the early 1980s (and to a large extent, still today) it was very difficult to obtain funding for a project that was risky, not just physically but also in terms of the potential for obtaining new information. "I can't be certain we will even reach the summit, let alone find something when we excavate a site," I had to admit to skeptical proposal reviewers.

Thanks to my receiving the Rolex Award in 1987, I finally had enough money to undertake serious excavations. It could hardly have come at a better time, as I had only a little over a thousand dollars in the bank, no health insurance, no home, and no job on the horizon.

The first site I chose was one at 19,855 feet on the summit of Mount
Copiapo in central Chile. I had made a quick ascent of the mountain
in the mid-1980s and discovered it was one of the few peaks containing
a relatively untouched Inca platform. Among the team members on
our 1988 expedition were two friends from previous climbs, Louis
Glauser and Martin Erb; two Swiss alpinists, Thomas Schutz and
Harry Spiess; the Chilean climber Guillermo Gonzalez; and the
Chilean archaeologist Miguel Cervellino.[22]

Although the expedition took place during the South American
summer, the ground was frozen so hard that we broke an iron wedge
while trying to move a rock. For five days we barely loosened the soil.
Morale began to run low, as well as supplies. Then I heard cheers followed by, "Oh no, it's plastic!" One of the team had uncovered what
looked like a plastic figurine. Our hearts sank as we thought looters
had been there before us. In fact, the figurine proved to be that of a
llama carved from the spiny oyster (spondylus) shell. Soon we uncovered another shell figurine, this time of a human male with his
miniature clothing perfectly intact.

The next find caused the biggest sensation. We uncovered the top
of a feathered silver statue located underneath a rock nearly six feet
deep. With painstaking slowness, I worked from above with a knife
to loosen the frozen soil. The temperature plummeted as the evening
light faded and my fingers became numb. The minutes stretched into
more than an hour. Finally I felt the statue loosen. As I turned it in
my hand, I stared into the face of a female deity. For a moment I shivered. I felt I had gone back in time. With a feeling of deep respect, I
held the statue aloft in my hands. I was experiencing an emotion that
archaeologists are lucky to feel even a few times in their lives.

We spent a total of 12 days on the summit and devoted 200
man-hours of work to excavating a platform that was only 6 feet deep
and roughly 26x13 feet. Never before had such a platform been excavated in its entirety. Looters had already disturbed so many that we
might not find another one so pristine. For the first time we saw how

different objects related to each other, and we established the process by which the platform was constructed. We would have a model with which to compare similar structures elsewhere in the Andes. This was of more value than the statues we had found.

The Incas built up the platform in stages, albeit over a short period of time. Minor offerings, such as pieces of hair, cords, and grass, would be made during the work, while more important items were offered, sometimes burned, as the day's work was completed. Once finished, outlines of stones formed crude circles that may have been used to indicate where the statues had been buried.

Other puzzles confronted us: Why were feathers, nuts, human hair, and even dragonfly wings distributed throughout the platform? Their positions in the site and ethnohistorical accounts led us to interpret all of them as offerings.

The logistics involved in building such sites are staggering. Any climber soon realizes that the Incas invariably chose the best routes, demonstrating that they used men with a solid knowledge of mountaineering. They also solved many of the most important problems of high-altitude ascents. They built base camps and additional camps in stages up the mountain, normally within visual contact of one another. Deep deposits of ashes show that large quantities of wood were burned. The trails to the summit connecting the ruins demonstrate that repeated ascents were made and loads ferried. At one site at 20,739 feet, walls enclosed an artificial filling of rocks and gravel brought from 300 feet below. An estimated 4,000 carries would have been necessary to complete the structure.[23]

The summit sites usually are not large, often consisting of no more than a few simple buildings for housing the priests, a few symbolic walls made of rows of stones, and a platform with walls to hold in gravel filling. As Bernabé Cobo wrote in 1663, "Not all the shrines were temples and houses with living quarters. The ones that were hills, ravines, cliffs, springs, and other things of this sort had no house or building; at the most there might have been a buhio or hut where the attendants and guards of the guacas lived."[24]

However, the simplicity of the summit ruins belies their importance. For example, the site on the summit of Huanacauri, considered the second most important ritual place in the Inca Empire, did not impress the Spaniards. Its most important object of worship was a stone so insignificant in appearance that it was ignored when the Spaniards destroyed the shrine.[25]

To provide an idea of the tremendous effort the Incas expended in constructing high-altitude sites, take the mountain Llullaillaco. To reach it they had to carry wood and supplies across more than a hundred miles of barren desert, then build way stations on its slopes until they reached an altitude nearly 8,000 feet higher than the summit of Mount Rainier or almost 2,000 feet higher than Mount McKinley. For us, just reaching the various sites on and near the summit was difficult enough. The thought of constructing them made our efforts pale in comparison.

If the site on the summit of Llullaillaco is impressive for its altitude, the complex of ruins at 13,222 feet near the base of Coropuna (21,079 feet) is spectacular for its size and location. The volcano is depicted receiving a child sacrifice in one of Guaman Poma's drawings of 1613. Cieza de León wrote in 1553 that the "temple" at this mountain was the fifth most important in the Inca Empire.[26] Yet the temple had never been described, and its location was one of the mysteries of Andean archaeology. José Antonio Chávez and I had long planned an expedition to search around Coropuna's slopes. In the early 1980s he visited ruins while traveling in the area, and in 1989 we returned to investigate them further.[27]

While I took photographs, José oversaw the team surveying the maze of ruins. We found more than 200 structures, some with the best Inca stonework we had seen in the region. This had to be the temple noted by Cieza de León. The ushnu (ceremonial platform) on the plaza was nearly intact. Only a few ushnus escaped destruction by the Spaniards. Situated at the foot of Coropuna off the main trails, this massive complex of ruins had passed unnoticed.

The author examines penitentes on the slope of Llullaillaco. Formed by wind erosion and melting, fields of penitentes present a nightmare for climbers.

Later we followed an Inca trail and canal—surely the world's highest—to nearly 18,000 feet, where they disappeared in the snow and ice of Coropuna. Once again the Incas had accomplished feats in the mountains that left us in awe.

I'VE OFTEN BEEN ASKED HOW I KNOW WHICH MOUNTAINS TO CLIMB. A series of factors plays a role. Sometimes I read accounts of modern-day climbers who describe seeing ruins. In the Peruvian Andes the early Spanish writers sometimes noted certain mountains as being especially sacred, urging priests to destroy any sites of worship connected with them. I compare their accounts with maps to see any possible association with lower-lying archaeological sites and how they fit within the region's ecological system.

Some peaks are difficult to climb even with technical equipment, and I do not expect to find sites on their summits (although I might search lower areas on their slopes or on nearby hilltops). For example, no one would expect to find pre-Hispanic sites on the permanently snow-capped peaks in the Cordillera Blanca of Peru or the Cordillera Real of Bolivia. On the other hand, if an easily climbed mountain was at the head of an important river system, it might contain ruins—and almost certainly would if it were noted in historical and ethnographic accounts.

I am inclined to search first on the highest point of a summit, but if it is too steep and narrow to build a structure there, ritual sites were often situated elsewhere. Sometimes ease of access appears to have played a role, and at other times a place was chosen because of its location relative to a major population center below or because of its association with some other part of a sacred landscape, such as a lake.

A GOOD EXAMPLE OF THE VAGARIES IN SEARCHING FOR MOUNTAIN sites is my expedition to Ausangate. This took place only two months before we climbed Ampato in 1995 and found the Ice Maiden. I hoped to solve a mystery that had long intrigued me. Why did one of the most important and dramatic of the traditional festivals in the Andes, Qoyllur Riti, take place in an isolated area far to the east of Cuzco?[28]

I suspected that I would find an Inca mountain sanctuary in the general area of the festival. If I did, it might explain why the festival takes place where it does. Ausangate is located a few miles south of the site of Qoyllur Riti, and I had already unsuccessfully searched for nearby Inca ruins during the 1980s. At 20,905 feet Ausangate is the highest mountain in the region of Cuzco. Its distinctive layered and pyramidal shape stands out on the eastern horizon 60 miles from the city. Indeed, it is the only permanently snow-capped peak visible from Cuzco.

I knew from historical sources that Ausangate figured prominently in Inca religion. Writing in the early 1600s, the famed chronicler of Inca customs Guaman Poma noted that Ausangate was one of the most important sacred places (*huacas*) of all of Collasuyu, one of the four quarters of the Inca Empire. He reported that the priests dedicated to its service were equivalent in stature to that of canons in the Catholic church and that "the Inca emperor personally supported them."[29]

Ausangate is still the most powerful traditional deity in the Cuzco region today. One legend even has it that once its snows recede the world will end. Ausangate bestows health and prosperity on the people who worship him, while also increasing the fertility of crops and animals, especially through his control of weather. He is considered the owner of all alpacas and llamas, which in the remote past originated from lakes near the mountain. Because he is the owner of the wild animals, they are supposed to do his bidding. For example, the vicuña and vizcacha (a rabbit-like rodent) help him transport things, and the condor is perceived as his "chicken." It was a vision of Andean society writ large in nature.[30]

Not surprisingly, Ausangate is the deity most associated with ritual specialists in the Cuzco region, being responsible for the selection of many of them—sometimes by striking them with his lightning bolts. The 3,000 traditional curers in and around the city of Cuzco consider him the most powerful of the deities they invoke for help. It was this assemblage of powers attributed to him that led me to study Qoyllur Riti.

The festival currently encompasses a complex series of sites and beliefs, many of Catholic origin, which unite traditional Andean religious concepts into a single ritual system. Each year prior to Corpus Christi thousands of people make the pilgrimage to a shrine 15,747 feet high at the base of the mountain Sinakara. Many people believe that Sinakara is a part of Ausangate and that worship at Qoyllur Riti really appeases that mountain.

I had participated in Qoyllur Riti during the mid-1980s. For some people the festival provides the emotional peak of a lifetime. It certainly was one of the most spiritually moving experiences of mine. During the years to follow, I collected everything I could find that was written about it.

Cieza de León published the earliest account of Ausangate in the mid-1500s. He wrote that in "ancient times" there was a "great temple"

In this night time exposure, a person walks with a flashlight over lines at Nazca with the city's lights in the background. The author interpreted the enigmatic Nazca lines and figures in terms of sacred landscape and Andean beliefs relating to water and fertility.

called Ausangate.[1] After not finding anything near the peak in the 1980s, I suspected that the "great temple" might actually refer to the mountain itself. However, that still did not rule out a possible Inca pilgrimage site being located closer to the location of the Qoyllur Riti festival.

Once again I explored the region north of Ausangate for an Inca ceremonial site. This time I focused my search farther away from the mountain. I soon heard of a group of ruins situated on the crest of a ridge on the other side of a river, not far to the southwest of the Qoyllur Riti festival. While examining the ridge, I saw remains of a building and several artificial platforms along it at 13,160 feet. Just below the ridge was a classic group of Inca structures. It had clearly been located here to house participants for rituals, which would have taken place at the platforms on the ridge above.

The lower complex, built on the hillside opposite Ausangate, had been deliberately placed for a view of it; the mountain can be seen through a low point of the ridge. The site is situated between a confluence of rivers that in turn were fed by the sacred waters of Ausangate. It also dominates the area where agriculture can first be undertaken in earnest. The platforms on the ridge top provide a 360° panoramic view of all of the snow peaks of the region, including Sinakara and Ausangate. It was a perfect spot for worshipping the region's sacred peaks.

The site, which had been an Inca pilgrimage center, was abandoned after the Spanish conquest and never reoccupied. Unlike many hill-top ritual centers, the Spanish priests did not destroy it—at least not totally. Nonetheless, the indigenous people could not have reestablished a pagan center at the same place, since it could be seen clearly from Spanish settlements in the valley below. This would help explain why the Qoyllur Riti festival came to be held on the opposite side of the river and higher up. It would be blocked from view, and mountain wor-ship could be continued under a thin veneer of Catholicism.

I thought that whatever else happened during the summer of 1995, I had at least helped provide a reasonable explanation for the mystery of Qoyllur Riti's location and the underlying reason that it existed at all.[32]

THAT MOST SCHOLARS PAID LITTLE ATTENTION TO THE SACRED ASPECTS of the physical environment in their studies and analyses of ancient sites in the Andes is not surprising. Little historical, or even ethno-graphical, information was available, and even that was usually buried in obscure publications. Above all, scholars were unaware of just how and why geographical features might have played roles at the sites. Before I began my research, I was guilty of this myself. Now when I visit a complex, my eyes focus first on the surrounding terrain and only then on the ruins.

Despite the importance of the high-altitude sites, I would never have remained so long in the Andes if my investigations hadn't led me beyond their study. At the same time that I was researching them, I gathered historical and ethnographic information over a vast region and began to see patterns that led me to new interpretations of some of the most important sites in South American archaeology. These included Inca ruins such as Machu Picchu and, perhaps more important, the ceremonial centers of three major pre-Inca cultures that dominated Andean cultural development during nearly three millennia: Chavín, Tiahuanaco, and Nazca.[33]

Chavín de Huantar is one of the most important sites in Peruvian prehistory. It arose nearly a millennium before the time of Christ and was the center for the first culture to unify a large area of the Andes. The Chavín culture's dominating role in the development of Peru lasted until 200 B.C.

The monumental complex of structures at Tiahuanaco, Bolivia, constitutes one of the most impressive archaeological sites in South America. Large monoliths were used in making religious structures nearly 1,700 years ago. This urban-ceremonial complex was the center for a civilization that lasted more than 700 years— longer than the Roman Empire.

One of the best-known archaeological sites in South America consists of large figures and lines drawn on the desert's surface (geoglyphs) by the Nazca culture in southern Peru. Most of the largest figures were constructed between 300 B.C. and A.D. 700, and some measure more than 300 feet in length. The geoglyphs can only be seen without distortion from the air. The lack of a satisfactory explanation as to why they were built has led to the complex being called "one of the most baffling enigmas of archaeology."[34]

I was convinced that the study of Andean people's beliefs about the natural environment, particularly as they related to mountains, would dramatically increase our understanding of the meanings of these ancient ceremonial complexes. I published books and articles about them, but new discoveries are constantly being made.[35] This has made for a heady mix—one that has continued to occupy my life for a quarter of a century.

Doctors at Johns Hopkins Hospital examine computerized images of the CT scan as they are being taken of the Ice Maiden (in the background).

CHAPTER SIX

JUANITA'S JOURNEY

It is a paradox that as death becomes personalized,
a life force becomes energized.
—GAIL SHEEHEY

They bring out the mummified bodies of their ancestors . . .
and it looks like the living and the dead come to judgment.
—JOSEPH DE ARRIAGA, 1621

ONCE THE HOLIDAY SEASON ENDED, SO DID THE RELATIVE QUIET surrounding the Ice Maiden. I had agreed to present preliminary results of our research to the scientific community at a meeting in early January. One of the worst snowfalls in history trapped me in my home in the mountains of West Virginia, forcing me to cancel—and causing some amusement among the participants. They appreciated the irony.

Bill Conklin was able to attend, however, and his slides and information about the textiles fascinated many of those present. Anyone working in archaeology is aware that there exists a group of people fanatically devoted to textiles. Although I don't share this enthusiasm, I understand it. We had not only found textiles in excellent condition, they had been excavated in their original context.[1]

In mid-January NATIONAL GEOGRAPHIC notified me that they intended to devote only 14 pages to the Ampato finds in the June issue. The relatively few pages concerned me, because the Society, Catholic University, and I personally had been heavily criticized due to the magazine's exclusive rights for the story. Peruvians in the government and press had been assured that a benefit of the exclusivity would be the prominent coverage the story would receive. The magazine had nearly 10 million subscribers and reached the eyes of more than 40 million people.

I anxiously awaited the "wall walk" held on January 17. In this meeting key representatives of the different departments of the magazine examine a rough layout of the story as presented on a wall. Usually included are the people who will be most closely working on the article, such as those involved in text editing, illustrations, layout, captions, fact checking, and cartography. Decisions made at this stage are difficult to change, and it can be a writer's and photographer's worst nightmare. People do not hold back their opinions—after all, they will be stuck with the results, and they are all professionals at one of the world's most prestigious magazines.

Bill Allen, the editor in chief, and I had known each other since I began preparing a story for the magazine in 1987. Although he never told me so, I heard that he had been influenced by one of the illustration editors that the photographic coverage was not good enough to justify more than 14 pages. Fortunately, the comments at the meeting were supportive. Bill quizzed each person present concerning what he or she felt about the story. One by one, each said, "More." One long-time staffer told me afterward, "I have never heard such unanimous agreement for a story needing more space." Much to my relief, the number of pages rose to 22. Even then, I knew this would seem short to some Peruvian officials, given all that had happened.

WHILE IN THE U.S., I HAD A CRITICAL TASK TO ACCOMPLISH. I HAD been aware all along that the Peruvian public wanted to see the Ice Maiden on display. Mummies are extremely popular, and they are exhibited in museums throughout Peru. Even the bones of a human sacrifice found on nearby Mount Pichu Pichu had been exhibited for decades in a museum at Arequipa's National University.

However, the Ice Maiden could not be exhibited until a display unit had been constructed that controlled the temperature and humidity. Specifically, we required a machine that would supply a high relative humidity at below-freezing temperatures, without the glass fogging up. Even if this type of unit could not be built, we needed a freezer unit in which the mummy could be trans-ported—at least if it was to have a stereolithographic (3-D) CT scan. Several scientists, including members of the Iceman team, had recommended such a scan before work continued with the mummy. But no stereolithographic CT scan existed in Peru.

While I was in the U.S., José took the Ice Maiden for a regular, two-dimensional CT scan at the Hospital Nacional del Sur in Arequipa. I was relieved when he told me over the phone, "The organs and bones are well preserved. The doctors also recommended that a three-dimensional scan be done, especially of the cranium to better clar-ify the presence of fractures and to determine more precisely the possible presence of a hematoma."

Hematoma? I knew it was a mass of clotted blood formed when blood vessels that surrounded the brain broke. The blood can't escape through the skull, so it collects inside it. If a hematoma existed, then it must have occurred while the girl was still alive. This raised the question as to what would have caused it—and the answer might explain how the girl died. As a result we were keener than ever to have a 3-D CT scan done.

In addition to the public's clamor to see the mummy, José also had to deal with various governmental and military VIPs who came to Arequipa and asked to view her. It was extremely difficult for him to single-handedly refuse showing the mummy, although he tried his best. By late April he estimated that small groups totaling more than 200 people had seen the Ice Maiden. Once the NATIONAL GEOGRAPHIC article and film were out, the pressure to show her would be overwhelming.

In the meantime, we could not find any organization willing to invest the money to build the custom-made (hence expensive) unit the mummy needed, either inside or outside Peru. It did not help that such a unit had never been successfully manufactured before. The possible liability concerns were enough to scare off most companies. "We could get sued for millions if something went wrong," was one response.

The Italian conservation company Syremont had already contacted me in November about making a special facility. At the time, Syremont was in the process of constructing an environmental control system for the Iceman for its eventual exhibition in Italy. They had researched the subject extensively and provided me with a detailed report. However, the $1.2 million they quoted me for the facility was far beyond our means.

I had discussed the problems we faced with Dale Petroskey, a senior vice president at the National Geographic. One night Dale was watching a basketball game played by his alma mater, Syracuse University, when an idea struck him: The Carrier Corporation, based in Syracuse, was the world's largest manufacturer of air conditioners. They had even created the environmental control system for the Sistine Chapel. There could hardly be a better company anywhere in the world to build the unit. Would they be interested in the challenge of making it? Maybe, he thought, if they were able to reap benefits from the publicity. They might even offer to do it at a reduced cost.

I knew something was afoot when Dale invited me to his office one day and greeted me with a big smile on his face. "I have talked with the Carrier Corporation," he said, "and they have agreed to build the kind of unit you need. Not only that, they will make two units, one of which will be a backup, and they will donate them to Catholic University at no cost." They estimated that the value of the labor and parts would be $250,000. In return, they asked that the unit be built in their plant and that the mummy be exhibited in the United States for a few days. That way they could both give the unit a final test and gain some well-merited publicity for their work.

Dale had also made contact with Johns Hopkins University, and they agreed to run a stereolithographic CT scan for free. That saved us an estimated $10,000. Now we had to find a way to pay for the transportation.

A few days later Dale called me and said, "If we can arrange a short exhibition at National Geographic in May when the magazine appears, we would pay the expenses involved in transporting her to and from the U.S., including those of a Peruvian scientific team to accompany her at all times."

This seemed like an exceptional opportunity. The worldwide publicity would emphasize to Peruvians the importance of preserving their cultural patrimony and could help raise funds for conservation. Looting of tombs was endemic, although it was by no means restricted to Peru. (For example, it was once estimated that 220,000 tombs had been looted in China over a five-year period.)[2] Anything that drove home to the public a deeper realization of the loss this involved would be helpful. Furthermore, the Ice Maiden was already being shown to VIPs. The pressure was such that she was bound to be displayed to the public eventually, irrespective of our concerns.

But such a trip raised a critical question: How would the Peruvian public react if an exhibition of the mummy were held in the U.S. before one had been arranged in Peru? This would surely be a sore point with many Peruvians, but I saw no other option. It was a Catch-22. In order for a specialized unit to be built for future display in Peru, she had to travel to the U.S., where one could be obtained at no cost.

Fortunately, Peruvian government officials soon realized the unique opportunity this presented. Aside from Peru obtaining conservation units for no cost, the government had another perspective on the benefits of the trip. After years of adverse publicity because of the Shining Path guerillas, this trip would advertise Peru impressive cultural heritage and help increase tourism. Unbeknownst to us, President Fujimori had been planning to attend a meeting in New York in May, where he would have the opportunity to call yet more attention to the find.

The government asked that the National Cultural Institute (INC) undertake a study of the possible risks and problems that might occur with the transportation of the mummy outside of Peru. The INC established four committees to deal with key issues, ranging from the archaeological and human biological to the legal. After debating the issues and clarifying precautions to be followed, they gave their approval. President Fujimori signed the final document just as time was about to run out for scheduling the trip.

What I had not foreseen was the reaction of Sonia and members of the Iceman team. They had stressed in December that a stereolithographic CT scan should be carried out before work continued on the mummy. Drs. Seidler and Spindler had said they would seek funding for transporting the Ice Maiden to Innsbruck, but nothing had come of this.

Even though Sonia had chosen to distance herself from the project in December, I respected her opinion and discussed the possible trip to the U.S. with her in a telephone call on March 3. I was surprised at how upset she became at the news, since she knew the advantages of having a display unit and a CT scan.

Some members of the Iceman team (including Dr. Seidler and Dr. Spindler) went to Peru later that month. They invited José and Catholic University's rector, Dr. Carpio, to join them for a lunch in Lima on March 21 with the Austrian ambassador and the new director of the INC. That evening I called José, and he said, "The Iceman team launched into a diatribe against the U.S. trip, emphasizing the risks of 'contamination' of the mummy. A key complaint was that the climate of the U.S. would expose the mummy to a different microbiological environment."

Both José and the rector were surprised by the intensity of the attacks. In response, the rector asked the Iceman team what they were doing for the project. Since they were planning to go on to Arequipa to view the mummy, José innocently noted that if they were so concerned about contamination, then the Ice Maiden should not be brought out of the freezer for them to study her. This elicited the reply that they were scientists. Of course, so were many of those who would see the mummy in the U.S., and José's point was made.

In our opinion the contamination issue made little sense, especially since the microbiological environment in Arequipa was hardly the same as on the summit of Ampato. Also, how could the mummy be contaminated if it were in a sealed unit and kept well below freezing? When brought out for the CT scan, the mummy would be in a hospital setting. Only a rare microbiological contaminant could remain active when the mummy was returned to the low temperatures of the freezer unit.

The Iceman team also brought up the possibility that the mummy might be lost in a plane crash. There was, after all, no way to replace the Ice Maiden. This was certainly a concern, but if that was the case for a trip to the U.S., why hadn't it been raised for the proposed trip to Austria?

They also argued that the exhibition of a mummy in the U.S. would violate Native American beliefs against the display of the dead. We were sensitive to these concerns as well. We had discussed the issue as soon as the possibility of an exhibition had been raised. However, the Native American Graves Protection and Repatriation Act (NAG-PRA) states that the customs and desires of the ethnic group with which a mummy was affiliated should be respected. In Peru mummies were on display in museums throughout the country. Even the indigenous people who lived in the area where she had been found wanted her to be exhibited. Indeed, a mummy was on display in the local school in Cabanaconde, and we knew the villagers there hoped to eventually display the Ice Maiden.

To us a large dose of hypocrisy was involved in the issues the Iceman team had raised. For example, the Iceman was to be permanently exhibited in a museum in Italy. Their arguments appeared to have been presented mainly to block the trip to the U.S. Equally irritating, they had made their opinions known to public officials without bothering to consult with José and me first.

The timing of the Iceman team's meeting in Lima seemed deliberate. They knew that I would arrive in Peru on March 25, and it appeared as if they hoped to block the Ice Maiden's trip before I had an opportunity to talk over their concerns with them. They visited the rector of Catholic University on March 23 and bombarded him once again with arguments against the trip. This time he told them that, while he respected their opinions, he would not be taking instructions from them. They left Arequipa for Sonia's museum in Ilo the day before I arrived.

Just as I reached Arequipa, a newspaper published an interview with Miki and he appeared on Panamericana TV as well. He also objected to the U.S. trip, stating the same arguments as the Iceman team but adding the erroneous claim that the National Geographic had paid $200,000 for the exhibition and promised an additional million dollars! (Nothing was paid except, of course, for expenses.) It appeared to us that Miki was being misinformed and manipulated in yet another attempt to prevent the trip.

AMID ALL THE DRAMA IN PERU, THE TEMPO OF WORK INCREASED to finish construction of the freezer unit. The Carrier Corporation decided that the heart of the mummy conservation/display unit would be a packaged terminal air conditioner (PTAC) that had already proven its worth in thousands of installations throughout the world.[3] The unit's cooling capacity was being applied to a relatively small space (44 cubic feet) while maintaining a temperature of 15° F.

Dr. Charles Bullock, engineering fellow of Carrier's Corporate Advanced Systems, was the team's project leader. They considered several options, but rejected them all for a variety of reasons. For example, thermoelectric cooling was attractive because it had no moving parts. But they determined a thermoelectric system as large as they needed for the display case would be too expensive. In the end, they decided on a PTAC because it already existed, it was reliable, and it was easy to maintain in any part of the world.

At one time Carrier had a total of 85 people working on the unit,

including technicians, engineers, and craftspeople. They constructed
the first case and began tests on it. Dr. Bullock said to me later, "We
have designed some technically complex systems for a variety of purposes, including the Sistine Chapel, but this was a first even for us."

They also began the construction of a unit that was to be used solely
for transporting the Ice Maiden to the U.S. It consisted of a well-insu-
lated metal box weighing 700 pounds that would hold a Plexiglas
mummy enclosure. No electrical power was required, since there were
internal sheet metal pockets that could contain 50 pounds of dry ice,
enough to provide refrigeration for at least two days. The top could
be taken off to allow filling of the dry ice pockets, and removable wheels
meant the case could be rolled when necessary.

Carrier modified the PTAC unit by adding a larger cooling coil
that contained internally grooved copper tubes to improve heat
transfer. Computer-based digital electronic controls were added to
allow the monitoring of temperature and relative humidity inside the
case. These were adapted from controls originally meant for a much
larger commercial air conditioning system. "It was kind of like
putting satellite navigation and radar on a canoe," noted Eric Johnson,
a Carrier team member, later. A larger capacity rotary compressor and
a special coil-defrosting method to automatically remove frost from
the cooling coil were also added. Both audio and visual alarms would
be activated if the temperature in the unit rose above 25° F.

Cold air was produced in the bottom part of the unit, which had
an outer shield of stainless steel. The air was directed into the upper
section and around the interior chamber containing the mummy. The
exterior case was made of triple-paned, thermally insulated glass
that was filled with argon, an inert gas with little ability to transfer
heat. The mummy was placed in a Plexiglas-covered unit that could
slide out to allow the mummy to be examined. The electronic control unit could also be slid out in case it needed to be quickly replaced.
A bolted door protected the removable tray. A built-in battery pack
automatically supplied electricity in case of a power failure. In total

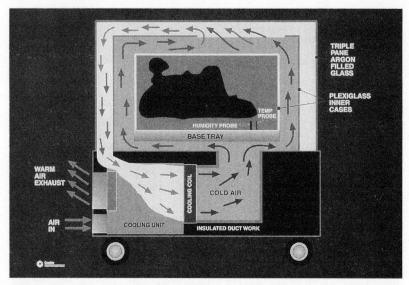

The freezer unit to conserve the Ice Maiden was custom built by the Carrier Corporation.

the unit's weight was 900 pounds—not light, but a far cry from the permanent installation we originally thought would be necessary. We were impressed. It was much more than we could have hoped for only two months previously.

Once the first case and transport unit were completed, they were sent to Arequipa, where a Carrier team consisting of Charles Bullock, John Ferguson, and Steve Stopyra assembled them. They monitored conditions to ensure that they functioned properly and pronounced them ready to go.

The second case had remained in the U.S., and the transport unit would serve as a backup in case of any emergency. Following the exhibition, they would both be available as backups in Arequipa. In addition, Carrier supplied extra refrigeration and electronic control units, along with a gasoline engine–powered electric generator in case of extended power outages. All in all, they had not only managed to build units that met all the specifications, they had also thought out virtually every eventuality that could go wrong and provided backup systems. It was an amazing accomplishment under any circumstances, and Carrier managed to pull it off in only a couple of months.

Unaware (or unappreciative) of these achievements, the project's detractors fired other salvos. Sonia had a petition circulated that tried to stop the trip to the U.S. Misinformed both as to precautions being taken and the purpose of the trip, some Peruvian scholars were urged to quickly sign it in protest. Meanwhile, a colleague informed me that Sonia had called him and others asking for the names of Native Americans who would protest the exhibition. It was hardly the kind of action one would expect from a specialist whose life was devoted to investigating mummies—work contrary to the beliefs of many Native Americans.

Initially, I could not fathom why Sonia and some Iceman team members had reacted so negatively, since the trip to the U.S. would, at most, mean that a CT scan in Austria would not be necessary. Based on emails I received from Dr. Seidler and our conversations, though, the reason became clear. Once scientists in the U.S. were involved, they thought they would lose out on the research potential that the Ice Maiden represented. Dr. Seidler and Dr. Spindler wanted to have a CT scan done using the equipment in Innsbruck. Among other things, this would demonstrate its continued value for mummy research, since its role in the Iceman research had long since been completed. Both Seidler and Spindler had told us of their hope that the Andean mummies' research would eventually bring in many of the specialists who had worked with the Iceman. I understood their interest to remain involved in the research, but they appeared convinced that the best way for this was for the Ice Maiden be removed from Catholic University and placed in the custody of another institution. If this occurred, one of the obvious candidates would be Sonia's mummy laboratory, the Centro Mallqui, which they continued to support.

Thus I was not surprised that some individuals also used the petition as a rationale for transferring the Ice Maiden to the custody of the INC. All of this maneuvering was what Sonia would later refer to as "mummy politics." My main concern was that if this happened, it could eventually lead to the mummy's destruction. What might seem fine in the short run could easily cause irreversible damage over the long term. Even if the INC had the best equipment and all the money necessary—and we knew they did not—and there were well-intentioned and trained personnel on hand one year, they could be gone the next. Being political appointees, the people in control might eventually be inexperienced and untrained, with disastrous results. We had not forgotten the loss of dozens of mummies when the Arequipa INC staff was changed only a few years before.

POLITICS, MUMMY OR OTHERWISE, DID NOT PREVENT JUANITA'S journey or dampen the excitement that surrounded it. On the day she was to leave, two bands played in the plaza, creating a cacophonic rivalry as she was driven off under guard. A police motorcade accompanied her to the Arequipa airport. It was a send-off worthy of a princess—and that seemed only appropriate. She was going on a far longer journey than that which took her to the icy summit of Mount Ampato.

The Ice Maiden was wheeled in her case onto a Peruvian Air Force plane and flown to Lima, accompanied by José and an INC representative, physical anthropologist Hilda Vidal. The Carrier team of John Ferguson and Steve Stopyra followed them on a commercial flight a few hours later. They found the military waiting for them, as they were the only ones authorized to open the unit and replenish it with dry ice. John and Steve were escorted into the air force conference room where the mummy had spent the night. Steve let out a whistle—military policemen carrying submachine guns with fixed bayonets were guarding the unit.

Customs officials held up the Ice Maiden's departure, while José anxiously tried to cut through the red tape so that she would be in time for the commercial flight. After a last-minute flurry of calls and paper signing, she was on her way, transported with special care by American Airlines to the capital of another country.

In the U.S. other members of the Carrier team had built a second unit, taken it apart, driven with it to Washington, and reassembled it in time for the Ice Maiden's arrival. José landed with the Ice Maiden the afternoon of May 13, 1996. By coincidence, it was also Mother's Day, leaving wags to deem it "mummy's day." As the plane touched down, a thunderstorm passed over the airport and gave off dramatic flashes of lightning. Given my theory about the role the Ice Maiden played in controlling weather, it seemed somehow appropriate. It was as if she had announced her arrival.

Once she had been cleared by bemused customs officials, she was taken in an armored van with armed guards to the Department of Radiology at Johns Hopkins University Hospital. She would be examined in one of the world's most advanced stereolithographic CT scan units.

We rolled the unit into the entrance and found to our surprise that the man at the reception desk had not been told of our arrival! At first he was taken aback by the armed guards, but then he listened politely as we explained that the unit contained the body of a 500-year-old Inca mummy, and after a call to the Radiology Department, he permitted us to go on our way. An entire assemblage—Johns Hopkins doctors, Peruvian archaeologists and government representatives, and National Geographic personnel—was waiting expectantly in the radiology section. The Ice Maiden was brought out of her travel case and entered the high-tech world of modern medicine. I felt a strange mixture of anticipation, accomplishment, and wonder. Images of finding her lying on a field of ice were fused with a white operating room with white-robed, masked doctors working in front of computer screens.

Technicians from the Carrier Corporation opened first the outer, then the inner case. Although not surprised, we could not help but be relieved to see that the Ice Maiden had arrived in perfect condition. She showed no sign of even the minutest movement having disturbed her during her journey.

After all the hurdles in bringing her to the U.S., it seemed anti-climactic to watch her pass in only a matter of minutes through the

CT scanner. Unlike an x-ray machine, which uses a beam of radiation to penetrate through a body in order to create a two-dimensional image, a CT scan machine shoots radiation beams from several locations around the body as the source of the radiation rotates around it. An attached device receives the images and transmits them to a computer. The computer's software organizes the data into narrow "slices," which are combined into a three-dimensional image.

We were soon to see the results—the images literally seemed to leap out at us. Wearing glasses adapted for 3-D viewing, we could observe the clothes being removed by computer from the Ice Maiden and even examine the condition of her bones and soft tissues. This technological breakthrough allows doctors to study internal organs and bones without touching them.

We had arrived in the evening, after CT scans had been completed on patients, and by the time we began watching the results it was 2:00 a.m. Dr. Elliot Fishman, director of the Division of Diagnostic Imaging, was still receiving data from the CT scan on his state-of-art computer program—the same kind used for making the movie *Jurassic Park*. Despite being tired, for more than an hour we did not take our eyes from the computer screen. Images kept being compiled, taking on new forms. In some of them it appeared as if the ribs would poke us in the eyes. We were even able to peer out from inside the skull.[4]

"Look at the fracture by the right eye," said Dr. Fishman as he enlarged it on the screen. "Clearly she had been hit with a sharp blow to the head. It looks like she suffered a hematoma," he said, pointing to an image of the brain pressed up to the side of her cranium.

"Could the fracture have happened when she fell?" I asked.

"The lack of any healing indicates that a blow probably caused her death. The intracranial bleeding must have been severe and death virtually instantaneous," he replied. "Also, there is a difference between the edges of a fracture formed at the time of death and those formed long after death when the skull has become more brittle."

Then he pointed out another factor. "See the orbit of the right eye where the fracture begins?" he asked. "If she had been frozen, it wouldn't explain why her orbit has sunk. A sunken orbit takes time to happen," he said. In short, it was highly unlikely the injury was caused by a fall after she was dead and frozen.

Everyone present grew silent as the stark reality of the girl's death sank in. José was the only one not taken by surprise, for he had examined the right eye socket a few weeks before and seen that the right eye had been damaged. He felt that this probably was due to a blow to the head. As for me, I had not expected a fracture to be the cause of death, since most reports of Inca human sacrifice stated that the child was buried alive or suffocated. Scholars had assumed this was done so the body remained undamaged for the child's stay among the gods.

One more mystery about the Ice Maiden appeared to have been solved. When I later reviewed historical sources, I found that three Spanish writers in the 1500s and 1600s reported that a blow to the head was sometimes used to kill a human sacrifice.[5] In 1652 Bernabé Cobo wrote in his well-researched history of the Incas that, instead of being buried alive, children might be "killed by strangulation with a cord or by a blow with a club, and then they were buried." We had found the first case that substantiated that report.

The girl probably was dazed due to exhaustion and the altitude, and a blow to the head would have meant a quick and relatively painless death. Indeed, it could have been performed as an act of compassion. In Cedric Mims's book When We Die, a Canadian Jesuit missionary of the 1600s said that for the seriously ill the natives would "hasten death by a blow from a club . . . and do this through compassion."[6] From personal experience, I knew that when knocked unconscious, you do not know that you have been hit until you wake up. It was Juanita's fate that she never did.

The CT scan established that the girl was four feet ten inches tall, had normal skeletal growth, and showed no signs of malnutrition. "She probably has the best set of teeth I've seen in many years," said Dr. Fishman.

Microbiological studies had been conducted prior to the Ice Maiden's journey, and we would not be undertaking intrusive examinations. Dr. Edward McCarthy and Dr. Patricia Charache of the Department of Pathology at Johns Hopkins did perform needle biopsies, using a 14-inch-long bone marrow aspiration needle. Although we knew the mummy was frozen, we didn't realize how solidly until Dr. McCarthy tried to insert the needle. Considerable pressure had to be applied to penetrate deep enough to obtain the samples we had hoped for. The first two attempts, in the sternum area, reached less than an inch deep. On the third try the needle penetrated three inches—we had a sample. Then attempts were made in the left side of the rib cage and, just as with the sternum, the first two tries penetrated only one inch. The third time once again proved the proverbial charm, and 3 ½ inches was reached. Amazingly, this pattern was repeated when biopsies were taken of the distal femur: only on the third one did the needle penetrate to 2 ½ inches. A final biopsy went three inches into the abdomen. With these samples, Dr. McCarthy had sufficient material to undertake a detailed analysis. With luck, he might be able to discover what the Ice Maiden had eaten for her last meal.

Some of the tissue samples were frozen using liquid nitrogen (–323°F/–196°C) for later genetic analysis, while the remainder were placed in formaldehyde for routine tissue processing. The Ice Maiden was returned to the transport case and driven in the armored van to the National Geographic, where the main freezer unit awaited her. It was after 3:00 a.m. when the rest of us finally left for Washington, tired but aware that we had experienced something unforgettable.

One of the advantages of having an exhibition in the U.S., however brief, was that scientists could view the Ice Maiden and the conditions in which she was being kept. Robin Siegel, conservator of photographs and cultural materials at the National Geographic Society, had been in contact with several specialists in the field of frozen tissue and mummy conservation. They had offered their opinions as to how to best conserve the Ice Maiden. Naturally, given how new this field was, they had different opinions on specific points. Nonetheless, they found general lines of agreement, such as when one of the scientists stated, "The Iceman team's recommendation of 20°F is too warm, because at that temperature chemical processes still take place to cause eventual decomposition of organic material. Just put a hamburger in a freezer for a year at 20°F and see what happens." Chemical processes do not entirely stop until –323°F— the temperature of liquid nitrogen—but this is so low that it is difficult, not to mention expensive, to maintain over decades.

On the other hand, some scientists were concerned about possible cell breakdown at such low temperatures. Fortunately, the chemical processes are considerably slowed down long before such levels are reached. A few thought that –22°F would be an ideal temperature. Not everyone agreed, however. For example, I later attended a lecture where Dr. Platzer of the Iceman team said that cell breakdown could be extensive at temperatures lower than 0°F. Several scientists advocated 0° to –5°F. A temperature within this range, they argued, would slow down chemical activity without risking extensive cell breakage.

Our original decision to use 14°F was based both on recommendations we received from specialists and on our own hard-earned knowledge that this was a common nighttime temperature on Ampato's summit. Most scientists, including the Iceman team, agreed that 14°F was a good compromise. Yet we were committed to taking a long-term view of preservation that was calculated in centuries. In the end, we decided to lower the temperature to 0°F. There did not seem to be a great urgency for this, since the chemical processes had already been slowed down considerably. In the relatively short time period of a year or two, no damage would occur to the body, the scientists agreed. This meant that another unit would have to be built, since the original one was not constructed to maintain the lower temperature we wanted. Carrier generously agreed to build the unit, and a year later it was installed in Arequipa.

The relative humidity in the chamber also had to be considered. José became concerned when he thought he could see a slight color change in the skin. Members of the Iceman team, along with some

American scientists, had told us that this might occur. The Ice Maiden's outer skin layer would undergo a natural process of adapting to the conditions inside the unit in order to reach its own level of stability. The mummy had clearly gone through a variety of temperature changes while on the surface of the glacier and would need to adjust itself to one set of conditions that was constantly maintained. In particular, we expected a difference to occur with regard to the head, since it was desiccated, whereas the rest of the body was not.

Although there was no indication of any change having occurred below the surface of the outer skin, José decided to err on the side of caution. He was in a delicate position. If anything went wrong with the mummy, his future career in archaeology in Peru would be in jeopardy.

José decided to put three trays filled with water into the unit to "bump up" the relative humidity even higher than the 80 percent we had requested of Carrier. He also began a routine of lightly spraying distilled water over the exposed part of the Ice Maiden's skin each time the unit was opened. Some specialists thought this made sense, because the skin had obviously been frozen and a fine layer of ice would provide yet one more protective cover over it. (Independently, the same decision would be reached years later with regard to the Iceman. A fine spray is now being periodically applied to his body and ice is kept inside his chamber to prevent dehydration.) Other scientists were less certain, feeling that this was defeating the idea of the body reaching its own level of stability within the unit.

The Carrier engineers agreed with this latter opinion, especially for the short time of the exhibition. Placing water trays in the unit was a particular concern, because the water quickly froze and in the process tended to frost up the unit's viewing panes. This left the impression that the unit was not functioning, when in fact it was operating exactly as planned. José felt that impressions were less important than doing what he believed was best for the mummy.

Specialists also observed fogging up from another source. The original unit appeared to have a variation in temperature caused by the adjacent airflow in the outer part of the case. There was a difference between the temperature of the air being supplied from outside and its temperature when it exited. The slight difference was enough to cause light condensation to form on the front pane of the unit, which was cooler.

This looked worse than it actually was, since condensation is water vapor that has turned into a liquid and formed on a colder surface. With such a low temperature inside the unit as a whole, this did not affect the body, but it did obstruct the view of the mummy. The problem was quickly solved by the Carrier engineers, who placed another Plexiglas case inside the main case, thereby adding an additional thermal barrier. A later version of the unit would make the airflow and its temperature uniform.

Our concerns about the exhibit did not end with the unit. We knew that artificial lighting could affect the textiles, and it was controlled as well. One lux is the amount of light given off by a candle, and more than 30 lux were believed to be harmful to textiles over time. I thought that half that amount would safeguard the textiles, while supplying enough light for viewing the mummy and artifacts. José decided to be much more conservative and opted for 6 lux. "That is barely enough light to see by," I groused. This decision was to lead some people to think the condition of the mummy had worsened, because her body was not as visible as it had been when photographed with lights. To this day the light is kept this low and is turned off as soon as visitors leave the room. The majority of the time, the Ice Maiden rests undisturbed in the dark.

ON MAY 21 WE GATHERED IN THE NATIONAL GEOGRAPHIC'S auditorium for a press conference. The five speakers included Reg Murphy (president of the National Geographic Society), Jane Pratt (CEO of the Mountain Institute, which had been supporting my research since 1992), José Antonio Chávez, Elliot Fishman (a Johns Hopkins radiologist), and me.

Because I had not lectured in more than a year, I was anxious about appearing in front of a crowd of reporters at a press conference, not to mention the millions of viewers who would see extracts of it on the news. Showing slides helped and, with great relief, I was soon finished. A few minutes later Barbara Moffet, of the Society's public affairs office, pulled me aside and whispered, "The president of Peru and the First Lady have arrived. They are on their way to see the Ice Maiden in the Society's Explorers Hall." José and I hurried off to meet them while Dr. Fishman was still making his presentation. The press was soon alerted and the audiovisual operators had to cut him off to tell the media crews to go over to the exhibition.

José and I struggled through a crowd of U.S. and Peruvian government officials, Secret Service agents, media representatives, and National Geographic personnel to reach President Fujimori and the First Lady of Peru, waiting with yet another First Lady, Hillary Clinton. I described details of the finds to them, and after Mrs. Clinton had left, President Fujimori more formally inaugurated the exhibition. He jokingly referred to this as a meeting of three "First Ladies"—two being from Peru. He used the occasion to score political points by noting the gains Peru had made since he took power six years ago.

However, the core of his speech contained elegant words that resonated with the audience:

> On behalf of the people of Peru, I am proud to be here to introduce Juanita, the Princess of Ampato. Hers is a tale told across half a millennium, one that might have remained buried forever, but has emerged suddenly to astound the world. The story of her discovery is known to you—her long journey from the top of Mount Ampato to Cabanaconde, on to Baltimore, and then here today. The lessons we, and all the world, may learn from her are beyond today's calculations. We are proud to share with you, our neighbors and friends to the north, this

> great and precious treasure—lifted by nature herself from the
> very depths of the ground atop one of the highest peaks on earth.
> Juanita's awakening—and her long journey to this time and
> place—leave us mindful of the great distance the world has trav-
> eled in these centuries. The Princess could not have known that
> one unimaginable day fate would give her a new and con-
> spicuous place on the global stage of the future. May she teach
> us lessons, bring us to look into our hearts, our history, and our
> conscience. And may the soul of Juanita rest in peace.

The Peruvian press corps proceeded to photograph President
Fujimori with the mummy. The display area was so small that it had
to be restricted to only a few journalists/photographers at a time. Before
opening the exhibition to the crowd waiting outside, we were able to
welcome a group of more than a dozen people who had been born
in Cabanaconde. The majority of them showed up in traditional
dress for the inauguration, and they were proud to have the Ice
Maiden as a representative from their homeland.

The exhibition was a modest one. Besides the Ice Maiden and some
illustrations, it included only her shawl, a pair of sandals, a feather-covered bag, a few statues, wooden utensils, and pottery pieces. Visitors
were provided with handouts in various languages, which placed the
mummy within her cultural context and stressed the need for a
respectful atmosphere. Later a video clip was shown on monitors before
the visitors entered the room where the exhibition was held.

I had been particularly anxious about the reaction of children to
the Ice Maiden. Not having had any children of my own, I was unprepared for their fascination with this link to the past. "Mummies and
dinosaurs. You can't miss with either one for getting kids excited,"
someone said to me. The Ice Maiden became even more interesting
for children once they realized that she was close to their own age.

The exhibition was held for less than a month at the National
Geographic Society's Explorers Hall. Lines sometimes stretched for

blocks, and people often had to wait for hours to spend the allotted six minutes in the room with the Ice Maiden. The amount of time had been restricted so that the line could be kept moving. It was one of the most successful exhibitions in the history of the National Geographic and even in Washington, D.C., what else can match the power of viewing a person from ancient times? There is a tangible sense of stepping back in time. As the naturalist Stephen Jay Gould wrote, "Authenticity stirs the human soul."[8]

MANY PEOPLE, ESPECIALLY NATIVE AMERICANS, ARE CONCERNED about the public display of mummies and the excavation of sacred sites.[9] I should make it clear at the outset that I do not support either of these activities—as long as the sites are protected and the people culturally affiliated with them oppose their excavation and the display of their contents. Why then do I believe that the excavations are necessary at the high-altitude sites?

At present, these Andean sites cannot be protected, and they will—sooner or later—be looted. That is not a guess—it is a fact, one underlined by the looting that already has taken place at many of them, not to mention at thousands of tombs throughout the coastal region and highlands of western South America. Of the several dozen high-altitude sites I have seen, only a few have not been at least partially looted already—in the sense of items having been taken from the surface and holes dug. It is impossible to post guards on the summits or even around the mountains, which are, after all, several miles in circumference. Furthermore, mountains can be climbed from many sides, and if situated on a border between countries, they are even harder to protect.

Several factors have combined in recent years to increase the likelihood of the sites being looted. Access has become easier as roads have penetrated throughout the Andes, in large part due to mining. Poverty and the displacement of people has increased, while at the same time the amount of money being paid on the black market for artifacts has multiplied. The number of mountain climbers has increased, gear (and its availability) has improved, and guidebooks now provide descriptions of routes up most of the mountains. Furthermore, all this is taking place within the larger context of global warming. Throughout the Andes, the permanent snowline is receding, exposing ruins previously hidden from sight. In 2001 the glaciologist Bernard Francou wrote, "In ten to fifteen years' time, the small glaciers of the Andes, which constitute 80 percent of all the glaciers in the tropical regions of that mountain chain, are likely to have vanished."[10]

It is not a matter of *if* the mountain sites will be looted, but *when*. As for the ease of destroying one of them, a single person with a stick of dynamite could be on and off the summit in less than an hour. Dynamite has already been used on several peaks, such as Quehuar, Chachani, Chuscha, and Chañi.[11]

The policy of not excavating these sites can be justified if they are protected. Otherwise it indirectly assists the destruction of cultural patrimony and supports looters. Often, when I have been criticized by someone for excavating sites, I have asked him to provide a better solution. I have yet to be offered one.

If an indigenous group with direct ties to a site did not want it disturbed and guaranteed its protection, I would be delighted. So many sites have been partly destroyed—or are about to be destroyed—that it would be wonderful if groups would organize to protect them. In fact, many Native American tribes have agreed that excavations can be warranted in emergency situations, such as when sites are under the threat of certain destruction. As the Native American Joe Watkins noted in Indigenous Archaeology, "American Indian groups and archaeologists share a desire to protect the cultural heritage . . . from the unnecessary or unwarranted destruction from all sources."[12]

Once it becomes clear that no direct cultural affiliation can be traced between ancient human remains and living descendents, the question arises: Who "owns" them? Clearly, some group or institution has to have authority in such cases. Presumably, this responsibility would involve an institution representing the people of the country in which the remains were found. It seems logical to me that unaffiliated ancient human remains need to be preserved, if for no other reason than their indeterminate status. This allows for the possibility that an affiliation might be established at a later date as technology improves, and thus the remains could receive special treatment by their true descendents, if so desired.

Some people have made the argument that culturally unaffiliated ancient human remains belong to humanity as a whole, especially if they are so old—several millennia in some cases—that their genes would have been passed on to numerous ethnic groups. Why, they ask, should a particular ethnic group, with no proven affiliation with the remains, have the right to destroy them? Wouldn't this just be mirroring the situation where non-Indians made decisions about how to handle the dead of the tribes they encountered? Therefore, in cases of unaffiliated ancient human remains, I would advocate establishing special places to hold and protect them, ensure their conservation, and maintain control over their access.

Turning to the case of Inca mummies on mountain summits, it might appear easier to decide who should "own" them, because only 500 years have passed since they were buried. However, Inca ceremonies involving human sacrifice were not of local origin. Such mountaintop sacrifices were an Inca custom that was imported into regions when they conquered new areas. In the cases where we have DNA, there has been no direct correlation to local inhabitants, and historical documents state that this was the normal pattern.

So who should claim ownership of a body that was sacrificed? The descendents of the Incas, who were responsible for it? Not only is it unclear who would represent the Incas, but often the dead person would have come from a different ethnic group. If the victim's ethnic group should have ownership, then who in that group (which could have hundreds of villages and be spread out over thousands of square miles) should obtain the mummy?

I do not have answers to all these questions, although obviously practical considerations will play a role. For example, usually the country (as represented by its government) where the human remains were discovered will retain "ownership." I have placed quotation marks around the word "ownership" because ultimately it may be best to think of this instead as "custodianship."[13] Within the country, the actual custody of a mummy would seem best determined by the cultural arm of the government. This ideally should be given to whichever institution or organization can best guarantee the long-term conservation and integrity of the mummy and the objects associated with it.

Several Native American tribes have agreed with this position, stating that the preservation of human remains is the critical issue. After all, there will be no cultural patrimony to talk about if a mummy (or other sacred object) is destroyed. The loss of human remains also means they are lost to the indigenous groups—and to their future descendents, who may want to learn from them.

The display of dead bodies is a separate issue from the excavation of them. The same people who approve of the excavation of a burial could strongly oppose the display of human remains. A person's attitude toward display is founded in his or her cultural and personal background. Native Americans generally do not approve of the display of the dead, albeit many would also disapprove of the ways other tribes handled their corpses in the past. Nor have all tribes acted uniformly in modern times as to how to treat the graves of other Native Americans.[14] In one recent case a tribe had bones disinterred from a hillside burial ground in order to make way for a road to be built to the reservation's casino. Another tribe put grave goods on display in its museum, even making them its main focus. To believe that one set of beliefs and practices governs all Indian tribes is to ignore reality—both past and present.

Treatment of the dead varies considerably in other parts of the world.[15] Are the Tibetans who carve up bodies and leave the pieces out in the open to be eaten by vultures showing disrespect to the dead? Are the New Guinea natives who use their ancestors' skulls as head rests showing disrespect? Clearly, it depends on the beliefs of the people performing the rituals, and rarely is there any intention of showing disrespect—rather the contrary. By performing these acts they are actually demonstrating their high regard for the dead.

An article about the exhibition of the Ice Maiden was published in the June 3, 1996, issue of *Native American News*.[16] It presented a balanced view, noting that indigenous Peruvians were mostly in favor of the display. This was a key point to be made to the Native American community, since it established that the spirit of NAGPRA was not being violated, even if the law itself did not exist in South America.

Since the Incas are the ones that made the sacrifices at the mountaintop sites, it is helpful to have a better understanding of how they treated the display of the dead. Among the Incas, mummies were brought out to be shown during major ceremonies.[17] This was the case with Inca emperors, but it also occurred with naturally mummified bodies in some Andean communities up until recent times. Usually, these were the more honored dead who had played important roles in the communities while alive. In many cases the "normal" dead received attention from their descendents for a generation or two and then were no longer attended to. Taken together, this helps explain why many indigenous peoples in the Andes have no problem with a display of the dead, especially if this is done in a way that shows respect.

While the Ice Maiden was on exhibition at the National Geographic Society, more than 80,000 people actually viewed the mummy. I was told that not one complaint had been received at the front desk by people who passed by on their way to and from the exhibit. The overwhelming majority of the reactions we received by other means (email, letter, etc.) were supportive. Since then, nearly a million visitors have viewed the Ice Maiden in Peru and in Japan with few complaints. What complaints we did receive were almost entirely from people who never saw the exhibition.

Whereas thousands of people personally viewed the Ice Maiden, millions saw her on television. The National Geographic TV program *Mystery of the Inca Mummy* aired concurrently with the exhibit, and television news coverage of it was extensive, including in other countries. Being so much in the public eye, she was soon appearing in all sorts of forms, including some we could never have foreseen. For example, the Japanese developed a Jeopardy!-like game show around Juanita, and the cult TV favorite *Buffy the Vampire Slayer* had an Inca frozen maiden (named Ampata) come back to life, feeding on victims for sustenance!

No subject receiving so much press coverage had any chance of escaping the attention of conspiracy theorists and tabloids—in short, new myths were being created. One such myth was that we had taken the mummy to the U.S. so that American scientists could obtain her DNA—in order to help create a new race for the third millennium![18]

For conspiracy theorists and tabloids alike, the Ice Maiden had truly arrived.

AFTER THE EXHIBITION IN THE U.S. ENDED IN JUNE 1996, THE ICE Maiden was flown back to Arequipa, where bands and a full escort awaited her arrival. While an exhibition was being arranged for the Peruvian public in the case provided by the Carrier Corporation, we already had begun to receive the results of studies undertaken by scientists in several countries.

The needle biopsy established that the Ice Maiden's stomach was filled with vegetable matter at the time of her death. "She must have eaten a meal of vegetables within six to eight hours before dying," said Dr. McCarthy. Given the difficulty of climbing to Ampato's summit, she probably had eaten her last meal at the grass site (Punta Ichu) at 20,300 feet—within view of the place where she was to die.

The next finding of the needle biopsy would capture the attention of the scientific world—her DNA.[19] Inside a cell's nucleus are thread-like structures called chromosomes. Humans have 46 chromosomes in pairs, 23 inherited from our mothers and 23 from our fathers. Each chromosome is largely made up of units of DNA (genes) and proteins. Each gene has DNA (short for deoxyribonucleic acid), which in turn consists of thousands of chemical units that are bonded together chemically in such a way that a chainlike molecule is formed, resembling a twisted ladder (a double helix).

Two complete sets of the human genome can be found inside most cells. Because nuclear DNA is inherited half from the mother and half from the father, scientists can trace both descent lines. Unfortunately, it is difficult to use it in tracing relationships over long periods because it is scrambled each generation. It is also quickly destroyed at death.

However, mitochondrial DNA is inherited independently of nuclear DNA, and it appears inside the cell in units (mitochondria) that are located outside the nucleus. A human cell has an average of 1,700 mitochondria and about eight DNA molecules in each of them. This arrangement makes it easier for some to survive the damage that can occur to a cell when an organism dies.

Unlike nuclear DNA, mitochondrial DNA is transmitted intact solely from mother to daughter. The result is that normally a mother, grand-mother, great-grandmother, and so on, will share the same genetic code. Sons will have mitochondrial DNA from their mothers, but they are unable to pass it on to their sons and daughters. Although it is passed on relatively unchanged from generation to generation, certain changes eventually will take place due to occasional mutations and the pressure of natural selection. This makes it easier for scientists to estab-lish genetic links between people along maternal lines, even though they have been separated through the centuries. Aside from this advantage, mitochondrial DNA is much more common than nuclear DNA, and it is less expensive and less difficult to isolate. Thus it is the DNA most archaeologists and paleogeneticists study.

With the mitochondrial DNA in hand, geneticists could begin the laborious process of tracing back the Ice Maiden's ancestors and comparing her with other mummies. Even though many so-called mummies in South America are often no more than skeletons, their teeth can provide the DNA required. Obtaining DNA from living people is much easier—only hair roots or cotton swabs from inside cheeks are necessary.

Dr. Craig Venter, later renowned in the race to be the first to complete the sequencing of the human genome, was CEO of the Institute for Genomic Research in 1996, and he agreed to undertake analysis of the Ice Maiden's DNA at no cost. Dr. Keith McKenney was put in charge of the project, using a sample of the needle biopsy for analysis.

There was a hitch, however. "The tissues are very well preserved and there is no decomposition, but the lack of cell nuclei makes it likely that the body underwent a slow freeze-drying process," said Dr. McCarthy. Although this meant that DNA could not be recovered from the cell nuclei, the mitochondrial DNA was another matter. "In the field of ancient DNA, this is probably some of the best ever extracted," Dr. McKenney told me. He and his colleague Tracy Spriggs were able to isolate and sequence two relatively large regions of the Ice Maiden's mitochondrial DNA. They compared these sequences with thousands of entries in scientific databases.

Dr. McKenney (by then at George Mason University) was later able to obtain DNA samples from 19 people who had been born in Cabanaconde. "The Ice Maiden did not have a relationship with any of them," he said. Then came the surprise: "The closest relatives we could find in the databases were the Ngobe Indians of Panama."

A comparative study of this kind is always limited by the amount of data that has been collected—and made public. In the case of DNA, the collecting of samples from different ethnic groups had just begun, and much of that had not been published. Too few samples had been taken of Quechua and Aymara peoples, the main original inhabitants of the highlands of Peru. And other, lesser-known ethnic groups had inhabited areas near Arequipa, but their DNA had not been published and thus could not be compared to Juanita's. On the other hand, due to special circumstances, certain ethnic groups were particularly well represented in the sample. The Ngobe tribe was one such group.

A question often asked by reporters was "Do you have any results from the Ice Maiden's DNA?" I would note the lack of a solid DNA database for the Andes, but add the fact that no relationship had been found between her and the 19 people sampled from Cabanaconde. "Of course, other samples might later prove that one exists," I would stress. Eventually, I mentioned that the closest known relatives thus far identified were the Ngobe Indians. The reaction was not long in coming.

The news went around the world, and before long we heard that Panamanian government authorities had contacted the Peruvians about the possibility of Juanita being exhibited there—after all, they thought, it was her homeland! Some villagers in Cabanaconde were upset at what they saw as an attempt by the government, Catholic University, or both to usurp their rights to Juanita. I learned my lesson as to how factual DNA information could be taken out of context and reinterpreted according to the hopes or fears of distinct groups.

In another field of scientific research, we sent pollen found with the Ice Maiden to Dr. Alex Chepstow-Lusty, working at the Department of Plant Sciences at Cambridge University in England. In the cloth that was used to carry some of her personal items, he found the pollen of 17 plants. These included maize, beans, tubers, two cereals (quinoa and *canihua*), and several species of trees, shrubs, and grasses adapted to the highlands of Peru. In a sense we are able to hold in our hands plants that were familiar to the Ice Maiden and even the kinds of vegetables that she may have eaten at her last meal.

Even a nuclear reactor was to play a role in the work with the Ampato artifacts. Drs. Tamara Bray and Leah Minc sent samples of the pastes from several of the Ampato shards for neutron activation analysis (NAA) at the University of Michigan's Ford Nuclear Reactor.[20] This is expensive and not easy to arrange—only a few hundred such tests are carried out each year. The NAA method analyzes a ceramic's paste composition by bombarding the nuclei of the object's various elements with neutrons. Radioactive isotopes are produced that can be examined to determine trace elements specific to a pottery source, thereby creating a chemical "fingerprint" of ceramics.

Based on a comparison of the trace elements, some of the finest Inca pottery was found to come not just from Cuzco, capital of the Inca Empire, but from the southern basin of Lake Titicaca, as well. Lake Titicaca was a legendary place of origin for the Incas, and it was a logical place for prestigious pottery to be made.[21] What we didn't know was that it would reach the summit of Ampato.

"The very small amounts of pastes necessary for the analysis were only taken from vessels with preexisting breaks. That way no pottery was damaged," explained Dr. Bray. Ironically, we had such well-preserved ceramics that this meant samples could only be obtained from part of the collection. Nonetheless, the results established that the Ampato girl with the headdress had aribalos from both Cuzco and Lake Titicaca buried with her. There was much less pottery with the other girl, and the single piece analyzed turned out to be from Cuzco. Only one statue was found with the second girl and her textiles were not equal in quality to those of the first girl. "I think that it is reasonable to assume that the second girl was of a lower status and that Lake Titicaca pottery is associated with especially high ritual status," said Dr. Bray. In short, both the quantity and the origin of pottery appear to vary according to the status of the children sacrificed.

One of the most common methods used by archaeologists to date an object is using radiocarbon.[22] Carbon, one of the building blocks of life, occurs in three forms, or isotopes. The two labeled carbon 12 and 13 are stable, but carbon 14 is radioactive, and half of it is constantly decaying every 5,560 years into stable nitrogen 14. This is termed a "half-life," and the process of decay enables scientists to obtain relative percentages, which provide a close approximation of an object's age.

Dr. Irv Taylor of the Radiocarbon Laboratory of the University of California, Riverside, obtained a date by examining the carbon 14 in the Ice Maiden's hair. This showed that she lived 530 years ago (with a margin of error of plus or minus 50 years). I realized that she might have already been born when the Incas entered the area around A.D. 1460. Since the Spanish arrived in A.D. 1532, we could narrow the likely period of the sacrifice to some time between these two dates. We found an ash layer under the platform on Ampato, and a volcanic eruption reportedly occurred around 1460–70. If the ash came from the same eruption, then the Ice Maiden may have been sacrificed not long after the Incas conquered the region—only a generation before Columbus landed in the New World.

A fairly close approximation of the age of a skeleton can be made based on bone development, but especially useful are the teeth.[23] Charts have been established showing the ages when different teeth appear (or disappear). Even though these may vary between cultures and time periods, they still can help pinpoint an age to within a couple of years. For example, the back molar appears at age 18, whereas the first incisor appears at ages 7 to 8.

Dr. John Verano of Tulane University examined the x-rays of the three Ampato mummies. Based on the crown development of the Ice Maiden's third molars, he estimated that she was 13 to 15 years old. The boy was a skeleton and thus his teeth could be directly examined. Dr. Verano felt that the boy was 9 to 10 years old when he died. His study of the second girl was complicated because the radiographs were less clear than those for the other mummies. (The outer textiles were frozen and had not been removed.) Since both her first and second permanent molars appeared to be in occlusion, he thought that she was probably 12 to 14 years old. These ages agree with reports that the Incas sacrificed only children in the capacocha ceremonies.

The high quality of the boy's x-rays enabled Dr. Verano to observe so-called Harris Lines in a femur and a tibia. Although the lines cannot be linked to specific diseases or nutritional deficiencies, they

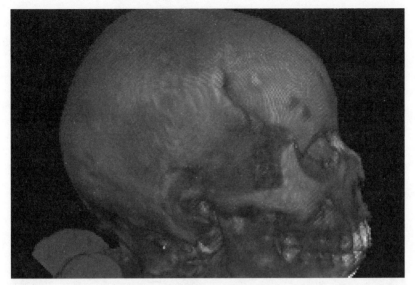

The fracture that caused the Ice Maiden's death can be seen leading from her right eye in this CT scan taken at Johns Hopkins Hospital.

indicate that the boy had experienced several periods of nutritional stress or childhood illness.[24]

Many studies remain to be done with the Ice Maiden, not least because we have not allowed truly intrusive work to be undertaken. For example, we have refused to allow an autopsy, since the body would have to be unfrozen and the organs removed. Technology will continue to improve, and as it does, less intrusive means will likely be found to obtain the same information—and much more that we can only begin to imagine.

Two team members examine the highest point of Pichu Pichu's summit, while the man below stands on the Inca ceremonial platform where human sacrifices were later found.

CHAPTER SEVEN

PEAKS, STORMS, and SARITA

Opportunities multiply as they are seized.
—SUN TZU

The principal [deities] . . . were, and still are, the high snow mountains.
—JUAN DE ULLOA MOGOLLÓN,
DESCRIBING RELIGIOUS BELIEFS OF COLCA VALLEY
INHABITANTS IN 1586

TWO WEEKS AFTER THE EXHIBITION OF THE ICE MAIDEN AT THE
National Geographic Society ended, I was on my way back to Peru.
No matter how many times I go on expeditions, I always seem to end
up in a last-minute rush, but this one was worse than usual. I was
undertaking a series of climbs in Peru, which I would follow almost
immediately with expeditions to the Nepalese and Indian Himalayas.
I would not return to the U.S. for five months.

I was looking forward to this summer's trip more than most
because my companion, Jackie, was going with me. For the first time
I would have the company of a lady friend while I was doing high-
altitude archaeology. For years I had regretted not being able to
share the joys of the discoveries with someone special in my life.

Although Jackie had no climbing experience, she enjoyed trekking
and had worked on an archaeological excavation in Syria. We had met
while she was researching a book that Time/Life was publishing on
South American archaeology. A professional artist, she was planning
to make sketches of the pottery and the mountain landscape.

We landed in Arequipa, where the city gave us first-class treatment. Our Ampato team was to be honored, and the mayor put us up in a luxurious hotel. We ate meals that cost as much as a week's worth of food in the mountains.

As for the Ice Maiden, when she went on display in August, Peruvians were lined up to see her. In the first two days more than 5,000 people passed by her display case. For the next two months she was exhibited within a cloister of the church of San Francisco, one of the oldest in the city.

Initially, many thought that the Christian setting was an odd place to display a mummy. The contrast was made even stranger because the Ice Maiden had been placed facing a large mural of the Last Supper. Yet the sacred atmosphere that permeated the chamber seemed appropriate. She had, after all, become a revered symbol for Arequipa, and even for all Peru. "The Ampato Maiden has helped Peruvians unite and feel that we have inherited the heroism of the Incas," proclaimed the newspaper El Pueblo.

The long line of people waiting to view the mummy included some who believed that she might cure their illnesses if they prayed to her and made offerings. Few saw a contradiction between believing in Juanita and Catholicism. After all, similar worship was bestowed on the Virgin Mary at various places in Latin America and Europe. For many Andean peoples, each place had its own Virgin Mary (often seen as "sisters"), and Juanita was regarded as a dramatic manifestation of the sacred sent by God.[1] "I overheard a woman tell her friend that she knew that Juanita was an angel because she had wings. She pointed to the ice attached to her mantle," Ruth Salas told me. Nor was this kind of belief to be found only in the Andes. In Washington, D.C., women were overheard discussing the Ice Maiden while they sat in a hair salon. "She is an angel sent by God to announce the Second Coming," said one.

The food offerings and flowers that were left behind became a nuisance for the staff, because they would decompose and attract insects.

The area needed to be kept as free as possible from possible contaminants, so José had to prohibit people from leaving offerings of anything organic. We began to wonder if we were witnessing the birth of a "Juanita cult."

However, we heard rumors that, if true, were of much greater concern. The effects of the many eruptions of Sabancaya had caused considerable destruction in the village of Maca, located close by. Indeed, some villagers call Sabancaya the "navel" of Maca. Sources told of a child having been sacrificed to Sabancaya to placate its anger.[2] The report was probably nothing more than people mistaking stories of ancient human sacrifices for modern accounts, but it was hard to be certain. We could only hope that an ancient practice hadn't been revived because of Sabancaya's eruptions.

Of course, I had not returned to Peru only for the awards ceremony or the exhibition—I had other mountains to climb. Three volcanoes lie close to Arequipa, and two of them, Misti and Chachani, are especially prominent. Few tourists notice the third volcano, Pichu Pichu. It actually forms a longer massif than either Chachani or Misti, but its greater distance and lower height make it appear less significant. The name *pichu* simply means "peak," and its repetition is a way of denoting its multiple summits. The highest of these is 18,578 feet, which is several hundred feet lower than Chachani and Misti.

We know that the Incas considered Pichu Pichu important, because in 1963 Inca artifacts and remains of a human sacrifice were found on its summit.[3] This site became the scene of archaeological investigations I undertook with teams in the 1980s and in 1991.

If offerings were no longer made on the summit of Pichu Pichu, they nonetheless were still being made to it from lower-lying places. José had been doing archaeological research near Pichu Pichu for years, and he had found that people living on the northern side of Pichu Pichu still worshipped the mountain, making offerings of alcohol and coca leaves during the months of August and November. They did so to protect their animals and to receive items they desired.

His findings confirmed those published by the anthropologist Horst Nachtigall in the 1960s.[4] Nachtigall wrote that people living to the north of Pichu Pichu viewed it as a protector of the people, fulfilling their requests and helping the ritual specialists. This was in contrast to Misti, which was believed to cause people harm, mainly through illnesses, eruptions, and earthquakes.

I FIRST CLIMBED PICHU PICHU IN 1982. I HAD WANTED TO investigate one of the few high-altitude sites in Peru where remains of a *capacocha* sacrifice had been found. I interviewed one of men who had participated in the 1963 expedition, Miki's father, Carlos. "We completely excavated the area where we found the offerings. At the deepest point we found a cranium and other bones," he told me. As far as he could recall, the other items had been found distributed above the bones.

On that first expedition in 1982 we merely surveyed the site. Miki and I took a bus that passed to the west of the mountain and hiked several miles to its base. Once on the summit, Miki showed me where the men had uncovered Inca artifacts a few yards down slope from an artificial platform. Besides a few tiny fragments of bone, nothing else remained.

The principal structure is an oval-shaped platform located 90 yards away and 100 feet lower than the highest point. We found remains of a small retaining wall for a trail leading out from the platform toward the high point, where it ended at the foot of a ten-foot-high wall. The terrain fell off steeply from a narrow section of bedrock, and it looked like another platform had collapsed due to natural causes.

On our 1989 expedition to Pichu Pichu, José and I led a team that stayed a week on the summit.[5] This time we uncovered the rest of the skeleton of the young woman found in 1963. We found a few other artifacts with it, including two wooden vases, a wooden spoon, a ball of yarn, some beads, and both a large and a miniature shawl pin. The latter was of gold and must have fastened the clothes of a female statue, presumably one of those found in 1963. If Miki's father was right about where they had discovered the items in 1963, the upper part of the offerings must have slid down the slope a few yards. Powerful earthquakes have shaken Arequipa in the past and may have caused this displacement. In any event, we found the bottom part of the skeleton located higher up, buried against the outside of the wall of the platform.

The girl's age had been estimated as between 16 and 18 years, relatively old for a human sacrifice. A medical report noted that death was likely caused by a blow to the head and also added that blood was present near the fracture. Even though a rock may have fallen on the girl's head after it was exposed, this seems too coincidental. The girl had been sacrificed and blood was even reported at the point of a fracture—one located at a logical place for a blow. (Interestingly, we later found a bronze star-shaped club head interred on Mount Huarancante, not far from Pichu Pichu.)

The location of the girl's burial outside the platform raised a question in my mind: Was she the only sacrificial victim? Could she have been sacrificed to serve as a companion to a more important sacrifice inside the platform?

We returned to Pichu Pichu twice in 1991. First we camped on the summit in November and extended our excavations of 1989. The frozen soil of the platform still made excavating difficult, and after a ten-day period we ran out of food. Rather than sending for additional supplies, we decided to postpone work a few weeks. Although we realized it would likely make only a slight difference, we hoped that the onset of the South American summer might unfreeze the earthen fill enough to allow us to penetrate into a drier layer of earth beneath the permafrost.

When we returned in December, conditions hadn't improved. We used the time instead to search for sites on other peaks of the massif and to survey the tambo (way station) at the foot of the mountain. The archaeologist Eloy Linares had published a rough sketch of it in 1966, and we wanted not only to have a better idea of the complex but also to finally establish the route used by the Incas between it and the summit.

Pichu Pichu's tambo had not attracted much attention in modern times because it is partly buried under volcanic ash and not very impressive. The size of tambos varied considerably, but they shared basic architectural features that were characteristically Inca, such as a rectangular layout and trapezoidal niches. The tambo at Pichu Pichu could have housed several dozen people, and it had a central plaza where public ceremonies probably were held. Due to the difficulty of keeping it supplied, the tambo was unlikely to have been occupied year-round. With continuous occupation we would have expected to find refuse areas and more than one occupational layer, but this has not yet been the case either here or at other tambos that have been investigated.

Sometimes we found a few structures at tambos that were better constructed than the others and isolated from them. They usually contained finely made ceramics, and we felt certain that these buildings indicated that a division existed between the priests and sacrificial victim and the participants of a lower status. We found a separate group of ruins like this at Pichu Pichu's tambo, and the summit platform was in plain view. "The sacrificial girl probably stayed here with the priests," mused José. We tried to imagine what she would have been thinking when she looked up at the place where she knew she would die.

Now in August 1996 we were back to make one more attempt to excavate the site. The National Geographic did not want to support work on yet another peak so soon after Ampato, but I had funding from the G. L. Bruno Foundation and the American Museum of Natural History. The documentary filmmaker Brando Quilici had also organized a crew to shoot footage for a movie for Discovery TV titled Andes: Life in the Sky.

José brought his students Walter Diaz, Orlando Jaen, Ruddy Perea, and Jimmy Bouroncle to make up the archaeology team.

Carlos Zárate brought two men to help out with loads, and Arcadio and his brother Ignacio filled out the climbing team, which was mainly to assist the TV crew. Brando came with Celia, his assistant, and John, a cinematographer. They had contacted an agency in Cuzco that sent a cook, Zoilo Carrion, and his assistant, Genaro Alaca, to prepare their meals on the mountain. This would be our first experience with a full-time cook, and we were all looking forward to it.

The expedition started poorly. On the first day a late departure left us searching for the faint dirt track through the desert after the sun had gone down. Unable to follow it in the dark, we ended up returning to the hamlet of Chilitia at 14,200 feet and setting up camp using the headlights of the vehicles.

Walter had been responsible for organizing transportation with his relatives who owned a bus and a van. We were not pleased to discover that they were both in sad need of repair. This led to one difficulty after another, wasting the entire day. I returned from a solo trip to our base camp at 16,300 feet to be told the bad news. "The bus got stuck in the sand. We will have to ferry loads from it and make a cache at the end of the trail," José said. It meant another day's delay and thus loss of supplies. All in all, it was not an auspicious beginning. But I had a superstition: the worse the start, the better the end. You had to earn what you discovered. It made for optimism during difficult times, if not much sense logically.

The next day the men were able to round up several llamas, a burro, and even a few humans to help us ferry loads to base camp. Luckily, two policemen happened to stop by Chilitia in a pickup, and they used it to ferry loads up from the trapped bus to the cache. Our fortunes seemed to be changing, and soon we were all positioned for a climb to the summit.

We took it easy carrying loads to the summit the next day. Eating an orange and a chocolate bar seemed a sure-fire thirst quencher and energy booster, but the mix left me feeling queasy. I had also forgotten how crumbly the rock was, especially the final few hundred feet to the summit ridge, and we decided to place a rope to help men carrying heavy loads. Brando filmed us with a long lens from below as we crossed to the ceremonial platform. I was relieved that it seemed unchanged from our last visit in 1991.

The next morning we set off to the summit, this time to stay. Jackie, along with others who had never climbed so high, would be put to the test. I helped by carrying some of her things over the most difficult part, but she arrived in tears nonetheless. There was limited space on the ridge, so Brando's team descended a few hundred feet to a level area with more room. We had some soup and then relaxed in our tents—such as we could. I'd forgotten how crowded my summit tent could be with two people in it, and I recalled too late the saying, "The best two-man tent is a four-man tent." The altitude was 18,600 feet, and I could only hope that Jackie would have a decent night's rest and feel better in the morning.

Since we pitched our tents on the east-facing side of the ridge, we were relieved when the first rays of the sun struck our tents at 6:00 a.m. Although I had had coughing fits during the night, Jackie felt fine, as did most of the rest of the team. We started up the stove for a morning tea. While adjusting the outside of the tent, my hand accidentally poked a hole through it. I had used it so much over the years, the sun had weakened the fabric. Jackie was not amused, and after covering the tear with duct tape, I wondered if the tent would hold up for the remainder of the expedition.

We were anxious to start work, and after eating a light meal I went ahead of Jackie in order to help direct the excavation. When she arrived, she had been badly shaken by her walk over from our camp. I had failed to take into account how terrifying a part of the ridge could be for an inexperienced person. In one section the ridge narrowed to a foot wide, with a vertical drop on one side and a steep ice slope on the other. Since the footing was solid and the section was short, most climbers barely noticed the exposure. From her perspective she had come close to perishing. She was having a tough introduction to high-altitude archaeology.

Ropes were fixed on Sara Sara to make the route easier for carrying heavy loads.

As we began excavating the platform, it proved to be the same rock-hard mixture of earth and ice that we remembered all too well. The stoves were fired up to make boiling water to pour on it, but even the water had little impact. The work proceeded slowly, with plenty of rest breaks, since we were still acclimatizing.

A little canvas chair had been carried up for Jackie, and this became a much sought-after piece of property, whenever she made the mistake of leaving it unoccupied. I had originally thought the chair was something that only an artist sitting for long periods might need. But it was truly a pleasure to sit on something comfortable for the first time on a mountain's summit.

After Ignacio arrived with a load from base camp the next day, he took a turn with the pick. "Come take a look," he said after his first swing of it had moved a little soil. I strolled over and looked down at the upper part of a female spondylus statue, complete with miniature gold shawl pins. "During all our work on the platform in 1989 and 1991, we didn't find a thing, and you uncover a statue with one swing," I said in wonderment.

The find galvanized us all, and we proceeded carefully, removing more of the fill. Within a few hours Walter had uncovered a silver male figurine. It was sobering to think that when we left in 1991, we had been only inches away from making a major discovery.

Our third day on the summit brought an unusual find. As we were digging at the edge of the platform, a gold female statue appeared. It had been placed within a protective "box" made of flat stones. At the statue's feet was white powder—borax the Inca must have brought up from Laguna Salinas, the salt lake below. "Maybe the statue represents the goddess of the lake," José suggested. He knew that workers extracting borax and salt from the area still venerate the lake today.

More digging exposed the top of a skull, then other exposed parts of a skeleton. We left it intact in the frozen sand and gravel. Shawl pins indicated that this, too, was a young female. We continued working our way around the skeleton, and four more female statues emerged. Only the wall separated this burial from the skeleton we'd found outside the platform in 1989.

Later, when José examined the girl's skull in his lab, he was surprised by what he saw. "As I cleared away the soil, I couldn't seem to reach the level of the eyes. Eventually I realized that the entire cranium had a conical shape, and in front of her eye sockets I found a small tube of gold."

"Maybe this was a child from the Colca Canyon," I said, when he told me. Various groups practiced head deformation in the Andes before the Spanish arrived. In 1653 Bernabé Cobo wrote, "When a child was born, it was customary among some nations to mold the child's head into different shapes. Since they were not satisfied with the heads given them by God, they wanted to improve on the natural human body and give their heads the shape that was most pleasing to them. They would squeeze their heads by securely tying on small boards to [them]." I recalled Juan de Ulloa Mogollón's report in 1586 that the Collagua people, who lived in the Colca Canyon, had their heads conically shaped to represent Collaguata, a volcano from which they believed they were descended.[6] Whatever the child's origin, this was the first example of head deformation we knew of from an Inca human sacrifice.

We began excavating the opposite side of the platform, where the ground was shallower. The earth wasn't as frozen there, and soon fragments of burnt textiles were uncovered. Beneath them lay another skeleton, accompanied by a bag of coca leaves, a male statue, and more textile fragments. Further signs of burning emerged, and we thought that, like the burial uncovered in 1989, a volcanic eruption probably caused the damage. Given the male figurine and the lack of shawl pins, we assumed that this was the burial of a boy. Early Spanish writers had observed that the Inca sometimes sacrificed a girl and boy together, as if they were married.[7] We thought we might have found another example of this practice to match what we had uncovered on the Ampato plateau the previous fall.

"I doubt that the girl found in 1963 was a 'companion' to one of the children buried in the platform," I said to José, comparing notes. "She had an exceptionally rich artifact assemblage with her, and it seems to me more likely that she was sacrificed after the platform was built. Once the fill was placed inside the retaining walls, it probably froze hard, stopping the Incas, just like us."

Pablo made the ascent on August 12 and spent a few hours examining our excavation. August 13 marked the last day for most of the team. Brando, having filmed the removal of the block containing the female skeleton, was ready to leave. John, Celia, and Jackie were feeling ill after so many days at altitude, and they also wanted to go down. José was told his son was sick, and he needed to return to check on him. Walter and Orlando went along to drive them to Arequipa, and the TV crew's support climbers were needed to make carries down to the cache. As a result, Jimmy and I were the only ones remaining on the summit that afternoon. We didn't find anything else, and I wondered if I should have wrapped up the excavation and gone with everyone else.

That gloom was dispelled the next day. Arcadio and Ignacio climbed up in the morning to help us. By two o'clock, we had found spondylus statues representing a male and a female. Digging deeper, I uncovered a silver disk. It seemed to belong to a necklace. I slowly brushed aside some earth and more disks appeared. "You won't believe this," I called out to the others. After a moment of shock, I realized that the disks were all tied by threads to what seemed to be a single piece of cloth that had been folded over. It was very fragile, and we didn't dare open it. But we could see that the disks were arranged in rows of decreasing size. I suspected it was one large piece of cloth decorated with at least 50 disks. They turned out to be attached to a male tunic, likely worn by an Inca noble or a priest.

I had seen only a couple of pieces similar to this in museums, and they belonged to pre-Inca cultures. If this textile proved to be as old, it would be the first time an artifact predating the Incas had been found at a high-altitude site. It clearly conferred high status on the wearer, and I read later that a man named Colque Guarache described in 1575 shirts with silver "sheets" being sent as special gifts from the Inca emperor to local rulers. The chronicler Arriaga noted that shirts overlaid with silver were offered to the huacas (sacred places or objects) or worn by priests when making the offerings.[8] Craig Morris, an Inca expert at the American Museum of Natural History, later confirmed that nothing like this textile had been found before among the Incas. They may have borrowed the style from the Chimu culture, located on the coast of northern Peru. Contemporaneous with the Incas, they were noted for their fine metal work. Whatever its origin, it was one of the most unusual artifacts we had ever found.

Thinking the textile might be the top portion of a mummy bundle, we carefully cleared the soil around it. Finding the cloth to be a single piece, we removed it in one block. I had hardly started removing earth from the area beneath when I was stunned to find myself looking into the face of a large silver male figurine. It was facing east, toward the rising sun.

A foot tall, it was one of the biggest Inca statues I'd seen. The vast majority of Inca statues are less than four inches tall. Looking more closely at it, I saw that its crown was made of pieces of spondylus shell. "This statue must have represented a deity, a high priest, or possibly even the Inca emperor himself," I said to Arcadio as he helped remove it.

Next to the silver figurine lay a small male statue made of spondylus shell and three llama figurines, two of spondylus and one of silver. To have greater sensitivity in my fingers, I had not worn gloves. Now the tips of my fingers were bleeding from the work as I tried to carefully clear around the statues. It had suddenly grown cold, as darkness followed the setting sun. This, together with fear that blood might contaminate the finds, led me to call a halt for the day.

We returned to our tents in the dark, tired but elated, not only by these last finds, but by one of the most spectacular sunsets any of us had ever seen. From my tent I gazed in the direction of the platform, now out of sight in the shadow formed by the high crag that dominated it to the west. The sky turned from orange to a brilliant red until half the sun's ball looked like a bubble floating on the horizon. Then it disappeared instantly, as if pricked by a pin. It seemed like a good sign. "Tomorrow we will find a mummy," predicted Arcadio.

Nearly out of food and fuel, we had only a little soup for breakfast the next morning. Orlando appeared, but despite the five of us working hard, we found nothing more by noon. Since we had not detected the slightest indication (no change of soil texture, no piece of straw or wood, etc.) that something more might be uncovered, I decided we should quit. As if to underline that judgment, it began snowing while we took the tents down. We descended in the dark to the waiting bus, and by 1:00 a.m. we had returned to Arequipa.

VILLAGERS ASSOCIATE LIGHTNING WITH MOUNTAIN GODS, AND WHILE we were excavating on Pichu Pichu this belief surfaced in a modern form. Or so the more sensational news accounts said. On the same night we watched the spectacular sunset on Pichu Pichu, a tragic accident occurred in Arequipa. A fireworks display was held, watched by hundreds of people from vantage points along a bridge, the Puente Grau. Unfortunately, the people in charge of the fireworks were inexperienced and they overloaded the explosive charges. As a result, some of the rockets hit a power line above the bridge. It fell, electrocuting 35 people gathered below. Before long, a rumor spread attributing this accident to the wrath of Juanita.

The major news reports made clear where the responsibility lay. The lack of controls over how the fireworks had been fired was to blame, not an avenging mummy. Nonetheless, the idea of a "mummy's curse" was too juicy a story for the tabloids to pass up. The notion had first been raised when a Fawcett airplane had crashed near Arequipa earlier in the year, but at the time had not gained much currency. It stemmed from a curse similar to one that supposedly afflicted those who had removed the mummy of the Egyptian pharaoh Tutankhamun from his tomb. (Most of them were reported to have met early deaths. In fact, that was not the case, and the legend has been debunked.)

I was soon interviewed and asked the inevitable question, "Do you believe that there is a curse associated with Juanita?" I said I did not and explained the circumstances of the discovery. "Add up the positive benefits that Juanita can be shown to have brought to Arequipa

and compare them with the negative effects that can clearly be associated with her. Then judge for yourself. Certainly none of us associated with the discovery of mummies has suffered in any perceivable
way, beyond the usual kinds of problems that come with finding a
frozen mummy—which include having to deal with rumors like
this. If there is a curse, then that is it."

The accident on the bridge coincided with gatherings of *curanderos*
(traditional healers) that were taking place in Arequipa and in the city
of Juliaca, during its annual festival. There was also a Feria de la
Integración Andina (festival of Andean integration). Several curanderos
arrived in Arequipa from the coast of northern Peru and some even
from Bolivia, which has its border not far from Juliaca. Although
they did not overplay the "curse" aspect, they did feel that Ampato had
been unhappy because he had not received sufficient offerings. An
element of theater was involved. A few of them walked around with
land iguanas on their shoulders, advertising their services while
bringing considerable attention to themselves—a publicity tactic
local curanderos took care to avoid.

Before an assemblage of curious onlookers and journalists, the
healers first performed rituals near the bridge. They did not plan to climb
Ampato, but they did take a bus closer to its base. They left so late in the
day that they weren't able to find the road in the dark and ended up
having to make the offerings from a distant hill in view of the volcano. Since
then similar rituals have become a regular event. People now venture to
places from which they can view Ampato and make offerings. A new kind
of pilgrimage has begun based upon an ancient one—one that had been
revived after the discovery of the Ice Maiden.

Their offerings stem from an age-old tradition. The human
sacrifices found on some mountains obscure a salient truth about
the Incas—they rarely made them. Usually they offered less important objects—some similar to those still made in the Andes today.
In 1985 I met Cirilo Pumayalhi at his home in the town of Chinchero.
He examined coca leaves to see if my offerings would be accepted

The team uncovers the mummy of a girl sacrificed by the Incas on Sara Sara.

by the mountain gods. "Yes, the signs are good," he said. "Notice how the leaves fell with the shiny side up. The ritual will be successful." On a moonless night we walked to the base of a large outcrop above the town. After the surrounding mountains had been called and their blessing of my journey requested, the offerings of food-stuffs, metallic figurines, seashells, and llama fat were carefully wrapped up and burned. As we walked quickly away, Cirilo said, "Don't turn around. The mountain gods will harm anyone who sees them eating."

I had met Cirilo during my research into Andean beliefs about mountain worship in the region of Cuzco, center of the Inca Empire. He made no claim to be a powerful curer. "I am only a lower-level ritual specialist [paqo] and am not able to talk directly to the mountains like the high-level ones," he explained. In this region the ritual specialists are part of a hierarchy from simple curers at the bottom to the select few at the top who directly communicate with the major mountain deities, especially Ausangate and Salcantay. [9]

I have heard several stories of people encountering mountain gods during their journeys, but more often they appear in dreams. Although they can take the form of animals and especially condors, they can also appear as people. That includes every type from young children to old men and not infrequently Westerners, even to the extent of being blond haired with blue eyes. After I came down alone from a mountain, one man said, looking at me with undisguised curiosity, "The *apus* [mountain gods] can sometimes look just like you."

According to villagers, traditional place spirits have feelings. Mountains are, after all, only human. "They get hungry, have wives and children [the smaller mountains], and fight among themselves," said a villager near Cuzco.

Legends about mountains are common in the Andes. Unusual features of the terrain are invariably explained in terms of some bygone event. For example, the mountain Tata Sabaya has a notch between its two summits. "You see that hole? His tooth was knocked out during a battle with the mountain Sajama," said a villager of Isluga.[10]

The word *tata* means "father" among the Aymara people of the Bolivian highlands and expresses one of the most common beliefs about mountains, namely that they are like fathers to the people. In some cases they are perceived to be their actual ancestors.[11] Combined with the belief that they are the most powerful of local gods and control such weapons as lightning, it is no wonder that mountains are thought to be the war gods and protectors of the people who live in their realms. This is not just ancient history. Only a little over a hundred years ago Ausangate is thought to have defeated the Chilean soldiers when they entered the region of Cuzco.[12]

"The replication of the mountain metaphor across the Andean chain provides insight into the cultures of all Andeans; it lets the Andeans understand themselves and lets us understand them," wrote the anthropologist Joseph Bastien in his ground-breaking monograph *Mountain of the Condor* about the Callawayas of Bolivia.[13] Even today in traditional communities virtually every prominent feature of the landscape—and not just the mountains—is named and has a meaning for the local people.[14] As I was walking with a villager in northern Chile, he turned to me and said, "You must understand. For us the mountains are alive."

WE HAD LEFT AMPATO IN THE FALL OF 1995 WITHOUT HAVING TIME to conduct a thorough search of its summit area. One of my goals for the 1996 season was to return as soon as possible in order to fore-stall any looters, who by now were well aware of the discoveries we had made. Also, I had not forgotten the original plan to climb the west-ernmost summit of Hualca Hualca, which I had dubbed La Centinela (the Sentinel).

According to a document of 1586, the native inhabitants of the upper part of the Colca Valley, the Collagua, believed they had originated from a volcano called Collaguata, about 70 miles to the north. The Cavana people thought their ancestors also had descended from a volcano, but it was one that dominates the Colca Valley to the south—Hualca Hualca. They founded the village of Cabanaconde (Cavana-conde) after they conquered the original inhabitants of the area.[15]

The document notes that the principal sacred places of the region were the snow-capped peaks, including Hualca Hualca, worshipped because they provided water. Llamas, guinea pigs, and small gold and silver objects were offered, but if a mountain deity became particularly angry and the Inca emperor wanted an important offering made, a human being would be sacrificed. Today the most important moun-tain deities (aukis) near Cabanaconde are Ampato, Hualca Hualca, and Sabancaya. Of these, Hualca Hualca is considered the most important.[16]

One day in 1982 I was talking with a man in the village of Pinchollo, located higher up the valley from Cabanaconde. Miki and I had been arranging for a burro to help carry supplies to climb Hualca Hualca. The man told me that they still made offerings to the mountain in August prior to cleaning the irrigation canals. "There is a legend that long ago children used to be especially raised to be sacrificed to the mountain at that time. The child being offered would simply disappear into the spring where the river originated. Later llamas were sacrificed in their place, and now only simple offerings of grain foods, coca, and alcohol are made." He noted that the ceremony takes place at the foot of Hualca Hualca, where the river that flows to Pinchollo has its source. Villagers make the offerings to ensure a stable water supply.

Miki and I had continued on to climb Hualca Hualca's eastern-most summit, and during the ascent we found the skin of a puma amid rocks at 19,000 feet. This was the highest point where one could climb without entering the permanent snow cover and needing technical equipment. We saw that the puma's claws had been sewn on and that coca seeds were stuck in the folds of the skin—a clear sign that it had been used in a ritual. Holes had been symmetrically punched around the skin, and it had a specially sewn opening and patches. Presumably the leather had been used to form a bag.[17]

We don't know the date of the puma skin, and we will never know it, since it was lost while being kept in storage by the INC in Arequipa. However, someone who climbed to the spot must have left it as an offering to Hualca Hualca. Although not as commonly cited as coca leaves, coca seeds still figure as offerings to Pachamama (the Earth Mother) and the mountain gods in the regions of Cuzco and Lake Titicaca.[18]

Puma claws are also used in offerings to bring good luck and riches. Pumas are widely perceived to be the "cats" of the mountain deities that guard herds for them. People told of the nearby volcano Sabancaya having turned himself into a puma when he became angry. In Inca times leather bags containing coca were used in the worship of the mountain Pariacaca, one of the powerful deities of central Peru. The use of a puma skin bag for this purpose on Hualca Hualca indicates that the offering must have been of special importance.[19]

For our 1996 expedition, I had decided to attempt a climb of the Sentinel's 19,767-foot summit before we went to Ampato. I wanted to be sure not to miss it this time. The trip could then be combined with a more thorough exploration of a route to Ampato that passed Hualca Hualca's western base. It was a natural route that led directly up the valley from the Inca settlement of Kallimarca, though we did not know if the Incas had actually used it.

Kallimarca is one of the sites that Pablo de la Vera Cruz described in his article about the Inca presence in the region of present-day Cabanaconde.[20] Clearly, it was one of the most important Inca sites in the Colca Canyon. José and I visited the ridge-top site to see its artificial ceremonial platform (ushnu), one of the few to escape complete destruction by the Spanish.[21] Not surprisingly, the ushnu is in full view of Hualca Hualca. It was easy to imagine the Inca priests making offerings here before leaving to perform rituals high on Hualca Hualca itself. The Ice Maiden could well have stood at this very spot before she left on the last stage of her pilgrimage to Ampato.

According to Paul Gelles, people from Cabanaconde used to make annual pilgrimages to the base of Hualca Hualca using a route that passed by Kallimarca. Hualca Hualca's importance is closely linked to water, since a river comes from its slopes ten miles away to help irrigate fields near Cabanaconde 8,000 feet below. Because the Majes canal close by Cabanaconde opened in 1983, the annual pilgrimages have been discontinued.[22]

Busy with his university responsibilities, José was unable to participate in this expedition. Walter Diaz, Orlando Jaen, Jimmy Bouroncle, Arcadio, and his brother Ignacio made up the climbing team. Jackie also joined us. After her stay on Pichu Pichu, she was looking forward to a more relaxing time drawing at base camp.

As in the year before, people in Cabanaconde were occupied sowing fields, and thanks to his not owning land, Henri once again joined us with his burros. Two days later we were winding our way toward Ampato with burros trailing behind. This time, however, we passed the Inca ruins of Kallimarca and continued up a narrow gorge leading toward Hualca Hualca.

We trekked alongside streams and through rocky canyons with a variety of vegetation, including a fine forest of queñoa (not to be confused with the food grain quinoa) whose gnarled trunks and limbs created a visual feast of shapes. This was not the exposed dry flatness of our previous approaches to Ampato. Vizcachas (wild rodents that resemble rabbits) ran between the boulders. Once we watched a herd of vicuñas running off in the distance as we passed a hot spring. I thought this would make a fine trekking route for adventurous tourists, albeit with a rather high (ca. 17,000-foot) pass. They could continue over the pass and down again into the Colca Canyon, thus creating a loop without backtracking.

The next afternoon we set up camp at 16,360 feet, close to a spring. While we were cooking supper, a dozen wild horses appeared on a nearby ridge, spooking our burros. A condor flew overhead, doubtless surprised to see so many living creatures in such a remote spot.

The next morning, while Arcadio prepared breakfast, he told me of a dream he'd had. "We met an Inca princess, and she had recently helped an elderly lady find her way in the mountains." He thought this was a sign that we were going to make an important discovery.

As we approached the Sentinel from the north, it looked every bit as impregnable as it had when we had viewed it from Ampato. Its steepness, coupled with the lack of ruins on the approach, made me think that the likelihood of our finding anything on the summit was close to zero—assuming we could climb it at all.

We weaved our way up along the north ridge. Just below the start of the cliffs, we started coming across pieces of wood. "What are these doing here?" I wondered aloud. They were miles from where they could have grown. I did not want to spend too much time on an ascent that promised so little success, so I decided we should split up and try to climb the cliffs from different sides. At least we could verify that no easy route existed to the summit.

I continued up the ridge and came across a 15-foot hunk of straight, unworked wood near where the ridge met the summit cliffs. To my right was a sheer drop-off and in front of me was a vertical wall. I couldn't continue without a rope and a climbing partner, not to mention technical climbing gear. The Incas could not have come this way.

In the meantime Arcadio and Jimmy had veered off to the left and ascended up a gully. I shouted over to them not to try it unless they could be fairly certain of avoiding falling rocks, and they yelled back that it wasn't as bad as it looked. Soon I heard some shouts as they dodged a small avalanche of stones and gravel. They were out of earshot by then, and I could only keep my fingers crossed that all was well. We were now more than 19,000 feet high. If they suffered any major injuries, we would be hard pressed to get them back down the mountain.

To my surprise, Arcadio and Jimmy reappeared not far below the last bulwark of the summit cliff. They had traversed on a diagonal through boulders and scree, and had spotted large pieces of wood strewn about. The Incas presumably had taken that route, since no modern climbers would have brought wood this high. It was too late in the day for Arcadio and Jimmy to attempt the last couple of hundred feet to the summit, so we all descended and reached base camp in the moonlight.

Their finding the route left me in a quandary. I did not want to use up the supplies we needed for Ampato to spend another day attempting Hualca Hualca's summit. However, Arcadio and Jimmy had seen a way off the mountain that I hadn't. From their high point they saw a way to traverse the western slope and intersect the route we were going to take with the burros to Ampato. "We could make an ascent and come down the other side, meeting you at your camp," said Arcadio.

I hated missing out on the climb, but I needed to ensure that the burros and the rest of the team reached the campsite I had in mind. So the next morning our little band split up and headed off in different directions. Arcadio made an offering to the mountain gods before he and Jimmy started up the ridge. We reached the campsite without any mishaps that afternoon. We were not far from where Paul Gelles had said the villagers made their offerings. If the Incas had taken this route to Ampato, they would have had to ascend to the pass using the same route we did. We made a quick search for ruins, but did not have the time to investigate the entire basin area. Unfortunately, we did not find anything to indicate the Incas had passed this way.

Night fell without any sign of Arcadio and Jimmy, and we became concerned. I had visions of having to start a rescue attempt. We used ichu grass to make fires to help guide them to our campsite. Darkness had long settled around us when we spotted headlamps slowly descending the slope toward camp.

They had accomplished the ascent and made an astounding find in the process. The Incas had used long wood poles to negotiate a chimney formed where two rock walls met. Arcadio related, "We scrambled up without a rope, but had to pass our packs at a couple of narrow spots. While we climbed, we went by places where the Incas had put ichu grass and pieces of ropes made of ichu into niches. It looked like they used this to help them gain better footing."

Although they had found no well-built structures on the summit, they did spy some pieces of wood, a mortar stone, a few pieces of bones, and a rough alignment of stones. They had no doubt that the Incas had reached it. Five hundred years ago, the Incas had undertaken a difficult climb using "aids" at 20,000 feet! This is the world's oldest known case of true high-altitude "technical" mountaineering. It was a spectacular achievement that left us in awe.

THE NEXT DAY WE REACHED OUR OLD BASE CAMP AT 16,000 FEET ON Ampato. To my relief I saw nothing to indicate anyone had been there since we had left last October. Yet soon I discovered I had been overly optimistic. After we had carried up loads to the plateau at 19,200 feet, we found that looters had visited the site. Although the tools I'd hidden hadn't been used, some holes had been dug recently. Worse, the holes were located in places that we had previously identified as potential sites. This left us with the uneasy feeling that whoever made them had accompanied us the year before.

Jackie remained in base camp, but her tent was in plain sight, and we were able to talk at prearranged times using walkie-talkies. This turned out to be fortunate, because a blizzard struck the next day and buried us under a blanket of snow. Although it was daytime, I peeked out of my tent to find a blackened sky and freezing blasts that reminded me of the worst days I had spent in Antarctica.

We waited a few hours for the storm to ease up, then decided to do whatever we could, since the wind had lessened only slightly in intensity. Once back at work, my body tensed as I heard a roar increase in volume as if a train were approaching at high speed. I knew that within seconds a blast of wind would hit and leave me gasping. I turned my face away from the wind, as it literally sucked the breath out of me. I couldn't believe that not one member of the team asked to stop, and I finally called an end to the digging in the afternoon.

To talk with Jackie, I had to walk into the brunt of a wind that was so strong, pieces of ice were sent flying horizontally across the land-scape—some smacking me in the face. Much to my relief, she was not only fine, but rather enjoying the show that, to be sure, provided inter-esting scenes for an artist.

We crowded into one of the tents, listening to the wind howl and the tent walls flapping frantically. "We knew things were really bad," commented one of the men, "when you said three 'diablos.'" Puzzled, I asked him to explain. "Well, when you just say one 'diablo,' it's nothing serious. Two in a row means it's bad, and three means it's time to head for cover!"

Although the wind was still blowing the next morning, it was sunny, and clearly the worst was over. However, we could see the clouds speed-ing over the summit of Ampato, and knew it would be impossible to work on it in such windy conditions. We did not have the supplies to wait for the weather to improve, so reluctantly I decided to forgo the summit and spend the little time we had working on the plateau. We had already excavated the obvious alignments of stones the previous season, so we set up a metric grid system that extended out from them. This covered terrain that looked undisturbed, and none of us thought the excavations would lead to anything.

Systematically excavating open terrain proved richer than any of us had expected. A few statues came to light, and then a striking plumed llama figurine. It was the first of its kind we had seen.

The others stayed to work as long as they could, but I started down before them. Jackie had insisted that she was fine, but she had been patiently sitting alone in base camp the past few days, and I wanted to spend a little time alone with her before I was caught up with expedition concerns again.

Not long after I reached camp, I talked by walkie-talkie with Orlando. "It looks like we've found the top of another mummy!" he said excitedly. I was getting ready to climb back up when he called to say they had uncovered only a lump of blue cloth, and nothing else had been found with it. Satisfied that nothing further would be uncovered, the team descended to base camp.

After the excitement generated by another apparent mummy, I felt a distinct letdown when I saw the rather unimpressive frozen lump they had found. We wrapped it in ice and insulation and continued back to Cabanaconde. Clearly, the Incas had buried offerings without leaving any sign on the surface. Only a systematic excavation of the entire area using a grid system would reveal if there were more offerings. "Well, there is always next year," I thought. And it took another year before we learned how close we had been to making another major discovery.

Two years would pass before the blue lump was finally opened and restored by the textile specialist Dr. Vuka Roussakis of the American Museum of Natural History. It turned out to be a male tunic that looked brand new. It has a deep blue coloring that she had never seen before in Inca textiles. The tunic has a reddish decorative band with *tucapus* (abstract signs) about two-thirds of the way down, but then changes back to blue. Some scholars believe that blue was especially associated with Inca nobility, and that only the Incas had the privilege of using tucapu designs on tunics.[23] That meant we could be looking at a tunic made for one of the Inca's relatives or even for the emperor himself.

Wrapped inside the tunic was a bright red-and-white set of woolen cords bound together at one end. Attached to it was a clothed female spondylus statue. Since the cords were tied together, it superficially looked like a knotted cord (*quipu*), which the Incas used for counting. However, unlike a quipu, there were no knots, and the cords were too thick for it to have been used this way. It clearly had played some role in religious ceremonies, but there was no obvious explanation for it. What we did know was that it was unique among the finds of Inca textiles.[24]

ONE VOLCANO HAD PIQUED MY INTEREST EVER SINCE I FIRST CAME across a reference to it in 1980. I had been reading a document written by a Spanish priest in A.D. 1583 when I noticed that Sara Sara was listed as one of the most important deities in southern Peru. This little-known volcano was located in an isolated area of the Andes, yet the document mentioned an Inca emperor who had "reestablished the origin place [of the people] called Sara Sara, which is a snow mountain."[25]

The passage refers to the belief that the original inhabitants of the region had their origin from inside the mountain, that is, it was their ancestor. The Incas would sometimes "reestablish" such places by building places of worship or by adding to those that already existed. In this way they would gain greater control over them—and thus the deities and the people under their protection.

Another legend held that the Chankas people were descendants of Sara Sara and the lake of Choclococha. The Chankas were the legendary archenemies of the Incas. Indeed, the expansion of the Inca Empire is said to date from the time the Chankas were defeated by the great Inca emperor Pachacuti. This may explain why the emperor reportedly sent 2,000 colonists to "serve" Sara Sara. If this number is correct, it equals the number ordered to serve the deities associated with the Island of the Sun in Lake Titicaca—one of the most important religious sites in the Inca Empire.

At 18,060 feet, Sara Sara is not high by Andean standards, but its huge summit massif dominates the surrounding landscape, including the Parinacochas Lake basin. The lake figures prominently in local legends. According to one of them, the lake's drying up would be a sure sign that a major world upheaval (pachacuti) was about to occur. It would signal the end of exploitation by the Spaniards and their descendants and a return to the golden age of Andean culture.[26]

A rebellion took place in the 1560s in the Parinacochas basin against the religion of the Spaniards, that is, Christianity. The movement came to be called Taqui Onqoy (the "dancing sickness") after its priests, who were observed to dance around when possessed by traditional Andean deities. The most important of these gods were Lake Titicaca and Pachacamac, along with local mountain deities and ancestor spirits.[27]

In a modern-day myth, Sara Sara gave its riches (ranging from abundant water to gold) to the great peak of Coropuna, located not far to the south. Sara Sara has suffered a lack of these ever since. The name sara means "maize" in Quechua and repetition of the word refers to an abundance of it. This suggests that the mountain was perceived, at least originally, as playing a role in the fertility of this important crop.

As interesting as these stories were, I only began to seriously consider climbing the mountain after I read an article about it published in 1950. A local man had told the writer Dionisio Salas that some years before he had seen a cerco con muro de piedras, an enclosure with a stone wall, on the northern summit. One of his companions found a fragment of a *lámina* (flat metal piece) made of an alloy of silver and copper on the slope nearby.[28]

What especially caught my attention was his description of ruins at the foot of the volcano, which fit that of an Inca tambo. The site, called Naupallacta ("ancient town") by locals, featured buildings surrounding a plaza that contained a "table" (*mesa*) within it. This "table" sounded like an artificial raised platform. If so, it might be the remains of an ushnu, an Inca ceremonial structure. Reinforcing this possibility was the discovery of a large rectangular structure with five doorways that faced toward the plaza. Salas also found a pre-Hispanic cemetery behind the plaza. Taken together, I was confident that these clues indicated the Incas had used it as a base from which to climb to Sara Sara's summit and make offerings.

In 1983 I had headed alone to Sara Sara, after an all-night bus ride over a bumpy road that left me raw-eyed from lack of sleep. The mountain was in a region largely controlled by the communist Sendero Luminoso (Shining Path) guerillas, who had begun fighting the government three years before. I was the only gringo on the bus, and, from what I was told, the only one to have ridden here on a bus in years. I could hardly have stood out more, but my strategy was to use the element of surprise—I planned to be gone before Shining Path knew I had arrived.

I had the driver stop the bus when it reached a point on the road closest to the mountain. It was also in the middle of nowhere and no other passenger had indicated he would get off. Thus I knew no one would be following me, at least not for some time. To make tracking me more difficult, I stepped on stones while heading to the base of the mountain. I spent the night out of sight amid boulders and lit no fire.

To my unpleasant surprise, the next morning I could not find an easy way up the western side of the mountain. I finally scrambled up steep, frozen terrain before I eventually reached the southern, highest point. The summit stretched in a three-mile-long series of volcanic hills and valleys, and only after searching for hours did I find an Inca site on the lower, northern tip of it. The main section consisted of several artificial platforms with retaining walls up to six feet high. On one of the platforms lay a seashell and an Inca woman's silver shawl pin. No Inca woman would have come here unless she was to be sacrificed, I thought. I vowed to return one day to excavate the site.

Thirteen years had passed since then, and finally I had the wherewithal to conduct an encore expedition. When NOVA contacted me about filming one of my expeditions, I suggested Sara Sara.[29] They organized a joint project with the BBC and sent a film crew consisting of producer Tim Haines, climber Matt Wells, cameraman Edgar Boyles, assistant cameraman Kent Harvey, and sound recordist James Brundige, who had accompanied us on the expedition to Ampato the year before.

At the last minute NOVA decided to send Liesl Clark, who was to transmit images and daily reports about our expedition via satellite phone "live" over the Internet. The idea of live coverage concerned me at first, since we never knew how a climb would turn out. We might not find anything, and that futility would be displayed to anyone in the world who was watching the Internet site. As events would prove, Liesl did an excellent job under difficult conditions.[30]

I had the same team from the previous climbs that summer, and fortunately this time José was also able to join us. As on Pichu Pichu, he would oversee the archaeology students. This allowed me more time to investigate the summit, take photographs, and participate in the filming. Jackie had decided that three mountains were enough and had returned to the U.S.

To support the film crew, we had a larger team, including Zoilo, Carlos's younger brother Juan Carlos, and two climbers he knew, Michel and Pancho. Jim Underwood, an old friend from my hometown of Franklin, West Virginia, also joined us. In addition to being an experienced climber, he was a trained emergency medical technician—always an asset on an expedition. No less important, he was a hard worker, with an easygoing manner that was coupled with a problem-solving mind. This combination endeared him to the Peruvians despite the language barrier.

Before leaving Arequipa, we had arranged to meet with the local authorities in Quilcata, the village closest to Sara Sara. We were well received and promised full support. I hired three additional men, including the town judge, Dario, and its deputy mayor (teniente alcalde), José Luis. Both of them had climbed to the summit of Sara Sara previously in order to bring down ice, which they had then used to make Popsicles—a novel idea, to be sure.

During our climb toward the mountain, we investigated a complex of ruins on a hilltop at 14,977 feet that local people called Incatiana ("the Incas' resting place"). Although reused in recent times, portions of the architecture indicated that the Incas had once occupied it. Yet we found no ritual structures, and as we continued up the mountain, we saw no evidence that the Incas had proceeded to the summit from it.

We set up our base camp at 15,100 feet in an open area at the bottom of a slope that led steeply up to the summit. Although we had plenty of room for our tents, it had one major disadvantage—there was no water. Fortunately, we were able to arrange for a man from Quilcata to stay with burros in order to fetch water from a spring an hour away. We were ready to begin ferries to the summit.

While climbing with loads, we came across another archaeological site—one unlike anything we had expected. A cave was spotted in a cliffside at 16,400 feet, and from a brief look we could see that it had been used in pre-Hispanic times. We continued on to leave our loads in a place we selected for our high camp, set in a protected gully 350 feet below the summit. We would be able to camp on dry ground, and snow was nearby for making water.

We returned to investigate the cave, which turned out to penetrate more than 70 feet into the mountain and broaden to as wide as 35 feet. Inside we found human bones, pieces of wood, metal fragments, and pottery shards. None of the latter appeared to be of Inca origin, and this site apparently had been used for "common" burials in pre-Inca times. We were later told that locals referred to it, aptly, as Yanapunku ("black door").

Placing the dead in caves was a common practice in the Andes. There is a widespread belief that caves are doors into the spirit world.[31] The ancestors of indigenous peoples came out of the mountains, and some people believe their souls return to the mountains when they die. Indeed, I knew that this was the case with the nearby peak of Coropuna in Inca times. That belief even continues to this day, albeit somewhat transformed. In one version Saint Peter holds the key, not to heaven, but to open the door into Coropuna.

A burial cave, and a pre-Inca one at that, so high on a mountain was an unusual find. "Since they made normal burials so close to the summit, they might have done this on the summit as well," said José. If true, this would be the first time a pre-Inca site had been found over 17,000 feet. Even if we found nothing else of significance, this discovery alone would justify the expedition.

The next morning we made a ritual offering. We chewed coca leaves, while Arcadio let a few fall into a fire on a flat stone. He then added incense, invoking the mountain spirits. He lifted the stone and gestured with it toward the cardinal directions and the mountain. We sprinkled wine with our fingers on the ground for the Earth Mother, Pachamama, and in the same directions as Arcadio. "This will put us in harmony with nature and the mountain," he said.

I had asked Arcadio to perform this simple offering in the presence of the cameras so that it could be documented. As on the other mountains, the actual burning of an assortment of offerings (a pago, or payment) to Sara Sara and the burial of llama fetuses would take place at night, without a film crew present. Ironically, due to the ritual not being filmed, we had been criticized by one group in the U.S. for not respecting Andean customs while on Ampato in 1995. In fact, the ceremony had been conducted at night without any photographers present, precisely because of our respect for local customs.

Unfortunately, we could not locate level ground to establish our high camp at about 17,600 feet, so we dug out platforms for the tents. Nonetheless, the camp was relatively luxurious, and a couple of days later we even had a mess tent with a table and stools—a first for us so close to a summit.

I became worried when I took stock as the team installed the camp. Several people were ill, and we had not even begun work at the ruins. Jimmy and Liesl had been vomiting yesterday, and José was sick today. Tim, Jim, Edgar, and Pancho had not been feeling well, and the ailments ranged from sore throats and intestinal problems to sore ribs and blisters—often in combination.

These concerns were somewhat offset by the discovery of several silver shawl pins. José and Jimmy had gone ahead the day before and spent the night at the high camp in order to get an early start searching the summit area. That afternoon we followed their tracks through the snow and came upon them clearing away boulders that covered one of the platforms. They had found the shawl pins on the surface and begun a small excavation. After they uncovered a silver shawl pin just beneath the surface, nothing else appeared deeper down. José said grimly, "I'm afraid that the pins might be the leftovers from looting." The site might not be as undisturbed as we had hoped.

The next morning we shoveled aside snow from the highest platform and began the laborious chore of digging through the frozen soil. I had hoped that the deep sand and gravel fill of the platforms would be easier to penetrate, but it was frozen hard, just as on Pichu Pichu. Often these lower sites were more difficult to work than higher ones, because over time the snow melts and penetrates deep into the soil. It then refreezes, creating a rock-solid mass that rarely, if ever, completely unfreezes again.

Once the upper layer is uncovered, however, the sun will help unfreeze the soil, but this is a very slow process. I set up two Primus and two MSR stoves surrounded by screens under an overhang to protect them from the wind. They were used nonstop making water that we could use to loosen the frozen soil. Unfortunately, the kerosene fuel was so polluted that one man had to constantly monitor the stoves to keep them burning. In addition, the wind would whip around the rocks and blow out a flame, no matter how well protected it was.

A poignant chord was struck later as Edgar Boyles left a Tibetan prayer flag near the cross on the summit. He had brought it to leave in memory of his friend, Jonathan Wright. Edgar didn't know that Jonathan had also been a friend of mine. He was a mountaineering photographer who had died in an avalanche on a sacred mountain in China. He had participated in our Everest climb in 1976, and we had shared an interest in Buddhism. We had been planning an expedition to Tierra del Fuego just before his tragic death in 1980. He was an exceptionally talented and decent man, and I was pleased that a prayer flag was being left on the mountain to honor his memory.[32]

Despite the difficulties we encountered, this turned out to be one of the most enjoyable climbs I'd been on. Each morning Zoilo, who called himself "the Inca cook," and Genaro would be the first ones up. At five o'clock, in the bitter cold and dark, the sound of roaring kerosene burners could be heard. They would start the never-ending chore of melting snow to make water.

No one else rose until the sun had illuminated his tent and the worst of the morning chill had abated. As people filed into the mess tent, they would be greeted with mugs of tea or hot chocolate, followed by bread and jam, cheese, oatmeal, the previous evening's leftovers, and occasionally eggs or pancakes. "Now, this is the way to run an expedition," I said to José with a smile. Bringing a film crew along had its advantages.

Three days passed without finding anything. Hopes of a major discovery began to evaporate as more time passed, and the film crew wasn't alone in feeling apprehensive. Then it happened: "Johan! Aquí!" Walter shouted. This cry was repeated several times in the hours to come, as first one and then another of seven Inca statues was uncovered.

Walter had been excavating a small niche in the side of the cliff that dropped off from the main platform. He had seen some burnt material and bits of textile on the surface and soon found a silver female statue wrapped in miniature clothes. A smaller silver male statue, a gold llama, a female figurine made of spondylus, and then a spondylus and a silver llama were uncovered. (Early the next morning a gold female figurine was also found.) The shape of the gold "llama" looked more like that of a vicuña, and, if so, this would be one of only a rare few.

The artifacts ensured that the filmmaking efforts were rewarded. As producer Tim Haines said, "These discoveries have certainly given us all a boost." For José and me the finds were not only important in their own right. The textiles of some were in good condition, and that gave us hope that any mummy we uncovered might be as well.

Here the hot water technique again proved valuable, since some of the statues still wore their fragile clothing, yet were frozen into gravel. One was frozen against the side of a boulder. Although a couple of the statues got wet, this method kept them from suffering damage by exposure to the sun. Once freed, we refroze the statues to conserve them until they could be examined in a laboratory setting.

Our excitement and good humor lasted into the evening meal. At any time, there are disadvantages to gathering a group of people in one tent at high altitude, and at the top of the list are odoriferous smells. Air gets trapped in the intestines, and as air pressure drops the higher you ascend, it expands and eventually escapes to produce some extraordinary sound effects. This evening they caused more wisecracks than usual. But what really set the team to laughing was when José asked, "Hey, Zoilo, how come my supper is under my dessert?" Zoilo hadn't cleaned off the plate after José finished his spaghetti meal and instead returned it to him with pudding piled on top.

Despite days of work, we had barely made a dent in the plat-forms—indeed two picks had been broken. So while some men continued excavating them, small test pits were dug at other locations around the summit. While snow was cleared from a corner of the outer platform, a beautifully preserved silver llama figurine was found suspended in the ice. Straw and pieces of wood lay above it, but none of the items had actually been buried.

José studied the area carefully. "The figurine appears to have been either accidentally dropped or, more likely, been thrown over the side mixed with refuse when looters dug out the platform," he said. Nothing was found when we excavated the site, and the soil appeared to have been worked over. But this looting must have happened many years ago, perhaps not long after the Spanish conquest. The Spanish apparently had taken to heart Cristóbal de Albornoz's instruction of 1583 to destroy Sara Sara's site.

To help lighten the mood, I buried something in a niche and called José over. "I'm worn out. Could you continue excavating here? I think there might be something." His students were much amused when he uncovered a rubber doll. "There must have been some really lonely looters here," someone wisecracked.

While searching for sites on the eastern edge of the summit, I used binoculars to see if I could spot any ruins below. I was excited to spy the typical rectangular shape of an Inca tambo below and realized that it must be the site of Naupallacta, the site described in the 1950 publication. Unfortunately, it would have to wait for a future expedition.

I had begun to lose all hope of finding an intact burial when, after more than a week on the summit, I detected the distinct musky, pungent odor of a dead body. "Get ready," I warned the film crew. In temperate climates an unpleasant smell is usually given off four to six days after death. This is primarily caused by the release of the gases methane and hydrogen sulfide. As Cedric Mims wrote, "The smell of a decomposing corpse is remarkably persistent and penetrating."[33] We had discovered that this was true of the smell of some mummies even centuries after death.

A few hours later, someone shouted, "José Luis found it!" I walked over and looked down at the exposed top of a mummy bundle. It seemed appropriate that the first person to uncover a mummy on Sara Sara was the mayor of a village at its base.

The mummy lay in a simply constructed earth platform on the sunny, east-facing slope. A shawl pin on the mummy's outer garment indicated that it was a female, and inside the burial with her were four statues. A male gold statue and a female silver statue had been placed above her head, and two female statues, along with a bundle of coca leaves, were found by her knees. Exposure of the soil to the sun had long since reduced most of the girl's body to a skeleton. Her legs were crossed, but one aspect of the burial struck us as distinctly odd—her knees were pressed all the way to her shoulders.

"Maybe it was done to represent female fertility," suggested José. "The legs are positioned apart as if she were giving birth." I thought it unlikely that a woman would give birth in that position, and I suspected instead that the legs were placed that way to fit her into the relatively narrow space where she was buried. But whatever the reason, this was a feature we hadn't seen before in an Inca human sacrifice.

When we returned to camp that night, Liesl had some interesting news for us. "Yahoo and the *Journal of Higher Education* have just selected our Web site as one of the best on the Web," she said. "And that was *before* we found the mummy," she added.

Discovering the mummy when we did was fortunate, because our supplies were running low, and we had only a few more days left on the summit. As if to underscore this fact, a storm struck. Our hair was electrified, and I had had too many close calls in the past to stay anywhere near a high point. Liesl, Matt, and I descended a few hundred feet and hunkered by a boulder under ponchos while a heavy snow fell for nearly an hour. The others took refuge just below the summit. Once the storm had passed, we returned to transport the mummy to a more protected place under an overhang, where we covered it with snow.

I had taken pictures of the various excavations and decided not to have them backfilled. I thought that I had learned my lesson on Ampato the month before. We expected to return the next season and deepen many of the excavations. Why cause ourselves the back-breaking effort to excavate a site all over again? The ground would quickly refreeze, so that took away one reason for backfilling, that is, to protect the sites. I also hoped that seeing the holes might convince any looters that there was nothing left. The decision not to backfill the excavations was one I was later to regret.

The final morning we set off with heavy loads down the mountain. Among them, Dario shouldered a huge bag of ice to use for making Popsicles in the village. Jim and Carlos had set up fixed ropes in one steep section to make the descent shorter. As we rappelled down, I remembered the joy of true mountaineering.

Once in base camp, we transferred the loads onto burros, and they carried the burdens the rest of the way to Quilcata. Soon we felt the warmth of the lower altitude and experienced the pleasure of drinking cool water from the foot of a small waterfall. I was sad to see the expedition end, but I also was relieved that the Andean climbing season was over for me. I had obtained funding for José to lead a team to search for ruins on Mount Coropuna, while I was to continue on to join an expedition into the mountains east of Everest.

That evening José and I discussed the finds before 200 assembled villagers. A spirited discussion ensued when we asked them what to call the mummy. A sizable number were in favor of naming her after a well-known female ritual specialist who had died a few years before. However, the decision of the majority was to call her Sarita ("little Sara").

Before we left, José helped establish with local leaders a Committee for the Protection of Cultural Patrimony. Nonetheless, I felt uneasy.

Involving locals at all stages of work seemed ideal in theory, but it also meant putting at risk the very sites that we hoped to keep protected. Not everyone in a community felt the same way, and while some respected the ancient burial sites, many regarded them as resources that they had a right to exploit, just like a mine.

After Liesl returned to the U.S., she called to say that the NOVA Sara Sara Web site had averaged more than 30,000 hits a day. On October 2 it had 140,000 hits. This news was especially gratifying because there had been no publicity and many of the hits were made by schoolchildren going online. To put the numbers into perspective for us, Liesl compared them to those obtained during another expedition she had been on. She was in charge of the NOVA online site during the spring 1996 expedition to Mount Everest, when the worst tragedy in its history occurred. "There were 130,000 hits when the story about the disaster broke on network TV, but the site actually averaged 18,000 hits a day—less than Sara Sara."

"That fits well with the interest generated by the Ampato expedition part of the National Geographic Web site," I said. Initially, it had averaged 175,000 hits a day, drawing in people of all ages. An unexpected pleasure from our work was to hear of the excitement it caused among school kids and the learning that it generated.

Back in Arequipa, José examined the mummy's skull in the laboratory. The girl had died from a devastating blow to the left side of her head. Later a CT scan of the bones established that she had been about 15 years old. Once again details provided by the chroniclers had proven chillingly accurate.

We had made some extraordinary finds that summer, including two mummies on Pichu Pichu and one on Sara Sara, yet I wasn't satisfied.[34] An idea had been increasingly gnawing at me. Frozen mummies are invaluable sources of information about the past for scientists and indigenous groups alike. However, none had been found without imperfections in its preservation—including the Ice Maiden. Her desiccated face had haunted me since the moment I first saw it. Despite having spent 17 years working in the Andes, I had still not recovered a completely frozen mummy. I had learned from experience that goals, when actively pursued, have power. One of my overall goals remained the same: rescue Inca artifacts and mummies before they were lost forever. But a more specific goal took shape in my mind. I would keep searching until I found a perfect Inca mummy.

Jimmy Bouroncle, right, holds Orlando Jaen while he examines the slope near where the Ice Maiden had been buried on the summit of Ampato.

CHAPTER EIGHT

EARTH MOTHER, MOUNTAIN FATHER

Adversity introduces a man to himself.
—Anonymous

They see him [the devil] in the volcanoes of Arequipa.
—Juan de Betanzos, 1551

THE ICE MAIDEN'S FAME WAS SPREADING. WHILE I WAS IN NEPAL, *Life* magazine's 1996 Year in Review issue featured a double-page spread devoted to her. It was a stunning counterpoint to the immediately preceding spread of John Kennedy, Jr.'s wedding. She appeared in the 1997 *Guinness Book of Records*. *Esquire* had a little fun with her, including the mummy in its annual issue devoted to "Women We Love." She was even the subject of a presidential joke.

During the 1996 presidential campaign, President Clinton attended a Democratic National Committee fund-raiser. One of the speakers at the gathering, Senator Joe Lieberman of Connecticut, said about Bob Dole, "He is so old, he dated that Inca mummy in high school." After President Clinton heard this, he made a light-hearted comment, "I don't know if you've seen that mummy, but you know, if I were a single man, I might ask that mummy out. That's a good-looking mummy! That mummy looks better than I do on my worst days."

The AP reported his joke, and it appeared on the evening news.

Even the normally imperturbable Tom Brokaw of NBC looked bewildered after he noted the comment. Some people referred to it as "Mummygate," and comedians couldn't pass up what one of them called "manna from weird-news heaven." President Clinton's joke was revisited in *People* magazine's year-end edition and in the book *Spin Cycle* about the Clinton presidency.[1]

The Ice Maiden had generated interest at all levels.[2] To be sure, not all presidents have the curiosity of Bill Clinton, but he was not alone in the political realm. Senator Diane Feinstein, Ethel Kennedy, Lady Bird Johnson, and Supreme Court Justice Sandra Day O'Connor were among many well-known personalities who were fascinated by the Ice Maiden.

One of Latin America's most renowned authors, Mario Vargas Llosa, personally came to see Juanita and vividly described part of the reason for this attraction in his book El Lenguaje de la Pasión (The Language of Passion):

> She was the age of Shakespeare's Juliet—fourteen years—and, like her, she had a romantic and tragic history. . . . I detest mummies, and all of those I have seen in museums, tombs, or private collections, have always produced in me an infinite loathing. I have never felt the emotion that they inspire in so many human beings. . . . I was convinced that the spectacle of the puerile and centuries-old skull would turn my stomach. It was not like that. It takes nothing else than to see her. . . . Her exotic, lengthened face, with high cheekbones and large, somewhat slanted eyes, suggest a remote oriental influence. She has her mouth open, as if challenging the world with the whiteness of her perfect teeth that purse her upper lip in a coquettish expression. . . . I was moved, captivated by Juanita's beauty, and, if it were not for what people would say, I would have stolen her and installed her in my home as owner and woman of my life. [my translation][3]

The Ice Maiden's fame rubbed off on me, helping me gain a salaried position for the first time in years. The National Geographic hired me as an explorer-in-residence (EIR) for the year 1997, and by early February I was installed at the Society. Because of the extensive coverage the Ice Maiden received, many people wrongly assumed that I had been employed full time at the National Geographic. In fact, I did not become a regular staff employee until 2000.

The Arctic explorer Will Steger was the first person named an EIR in 1996. What the National Geographic meant by the position was that a recognized explorer was associated directly with the Society and based out of its headquarters.

The next year (1998) the oceanographer Dr. Sylvia Earle became an EIR. In 2004 eight EIRs were serving simultaneously: the ocean explorer Robert Ballard, Sylvia Earle, Paul Sereno (dinosaur expert), Louis and Mauve Leakey (paleontologists), Wade Davis (writer and ethnologist), Zahi Hawass (Egyptologist), and me. Until 2003 Jane Goodall (primatologist) was one, as was (until his recent death) historian Stephen Ambrose. The group includes specialists in widely varying fields. Thus we were surprised to discover that we shared similar views on the future of exploration and positive and negative aspects of the times we are living in.

Many people have asked us variations of the same question: is there any place left to explore? They feel that nothing remains, since either we have been to every part of the world or we can see every feature of it thanks to satellites. In a review of books on exploration, Steve Hendrix noted that much of the popular literature about the topic actually involved "contrived exploits." Instead of, say, the first ascent of a mountain, it is the first time it has been skied or snowboarded (and so on). Others have retraced famous journeys—interesting, but also adding to the impression that nothing new remains to be explored.

Yet all the EIRs felt that we were living in one of the great eras of exploration. In their conversations and lectures Sylvia and Bob would stress how the oceans were only now becoming accessible to man. "We've only looked at about 5 percent of the world's oceans," said Sylvia. Most of our planet is under water, yet only a fraction of the seven seas has ever been seen, let alone investigated. Wade would note how little we know about the variety of human cultures. Zahi would point to the exciting discoveries being made in Egyptology. Paul would discuss the great finds that were changing our understanding of dinosaurs. For my part, archaeology has yet to find a world of sites, since many of them still lie hidden in the earth or underwater.

There is a widespread feeling that today's exploration requires high-tech specialists from a variety of scientific disciplines. Certainly they have their roles, but dedicated individuals still are making profound discoveries. The fact that geography can be observed in detail from space means that such physical things as the origins of rivers are no longer mysteries. But this focus on geographical features has obscured how little we understand the customs and beliefs of the peoples found in these plots of geography. That kind of exploration still requires people who are willing to immerse themselves in a foreign language and culture—often for years. The fact that people have Coca-Cola signs in their villages and wear T-shirts does not mean they think and act the same as we do.

On the other hand, all of us agreed on one overwhelming negative element in our research. The coming decades are critical to the very existence of what we are studying. The oceans are being polluted; environments necessary for the survival of primates are being destroyed; archaeological sites are being looted or wiped out by development—the list goes on and on. These processes have been occurring for some time, but today the scale and rapidity has escalated dramatically. This lends a special urgency not only to our research but also to the development of strategies to avoid the destruction of much of the variety that makes our world such a fascinating and unique place. Once lost, it can never be regained.

TOP: (1) Peruvian villagers combine worship of the cross with that of sacred mountains during the festival of Qoyllur Riti near Cuzco, the center of the Inca Empire. BOTTOM: (2) Team members approach the summit of Sara Sara.

(3) We found the Ice Maiden's mummy bundle lying in the open amidst ice pinnacles, after it had fallen down from Ampato's summit. Once freed from the ice, we saw her face for the first time.

TOP: (4) While excavating an Inca burial site at 19,200 feet on Ampato, the team observes an eruption of Sabancaya.

BOTTOM: (5) The reconstruction of a girl's burial at 19,200 feet on Ampato demonstrates the way the Incas organized offerings around her and manipulated her headdress to fit into the limited space available.

(6) The highest point (20,700 feet) of Ampato's summit had steep gullies leading down from it. The Ice Maiden was swept down one of the gullies when a part of the summit ridge collapsed.

TOP: (7) The Ice Maiden was sacrificed to the gods on Ampato more than 500 years ago. Her frozen body evokes her humanity, while also being a time capsule, providing unprecedentd information about one of the ancient world's most important civilizations.

BOTTOM: (8) The Ice Maiden's hand clutches her dress tightly against her side and vividly demonstrates the excellent preservation of her body.

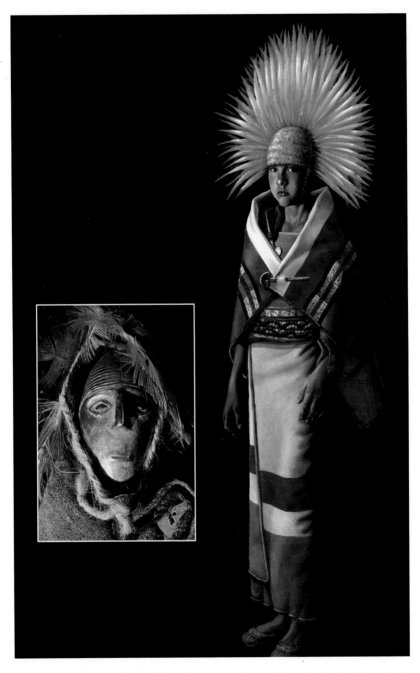

(9) This reconstruction illustrates how the Ice Maiden would have looked with her shawl, but wearing the headdress found on one of the other female mummies.

INSET: (10) Looking like new, the face of a rare Inca gold female statue looks out from underneath a feather headdress.

TOP: (11) We camped 12 days near the summit of Mount Copiapo (19,855 feet) in order to scientifically excavate an Inca ceremonial platform in 1986.
BOTTOM: (12) For the first time, an archaeological team was photographed from the air while it was working at a high-altitude site. To the right of the snow on Mount Copiapo's summit is an Inca ceremonial platform, and three team members stand inside it, while two look on from the ridge.

TOP: (13) Jimmy Bouroncle, left, Orlando Jaen, and José Antonio Chávez excavate the site of the Ice Maiden's burial on Ampato's summit. Hualca Hualca is in the background. BOTTOM: (14) Orlando Jaen returns after completing a rappel from the highest point of Ampato's summit, while others wait their turn.

TOP: (15) Vicuñas cross in front of Misti, a 19,101-foot-high volcano, where our team found the remains of six human sacrifices in 1998.

BOTTOM: (16) Inca offerings were found buried near the rim of Misti's inner crater. The massif of Pichu Pichu can be seen in the distant background.

TOP: (17) Team members survey a site on Llullaillaco's summit.
BOTTOM: (18) From the highest point of Llullaillaco's summit, we could look out over the "priests' house" (lower center) and the ceremonial platform beyond. Inca ruins have been found on many of the snow-capped volcanoes in the distance, and our high camp is visible in the lower right corner.

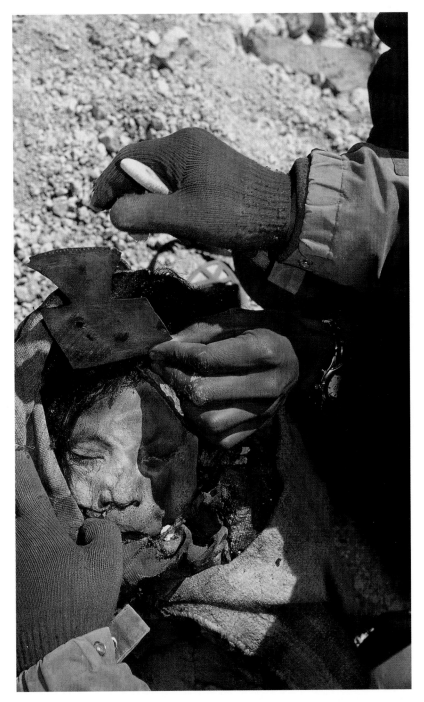

(19) To our surprise the head cloth worn by the younger female on Llullaillaco had been partially burned due to a lightning strike and revealed a silver plaque on her forehead.

TOP: (20) The team excavates the summit platform of Llullaillaco.
BOTTOM: (21) A team member descends to our high camp from the summit of Llullaillaco.

TOP: (22) A tunic with the Inca key pattern looks like new. It was found draped over the older girl's shoulder on Llullaillaco.

BOTTOM: (23) A blue Inca tunic was found buried close to one of the female burials at 19,200 feet on Ampato.

TOP: (24) A female silver statue from Llullaillaco wears a striking gold and green headdress.
BOTTOM: (25) Llamas (two of spondylus and one of silver) and two male statues (of spondylus and gold/silver) were found placed in a row, as if forming a symbolic caravan.

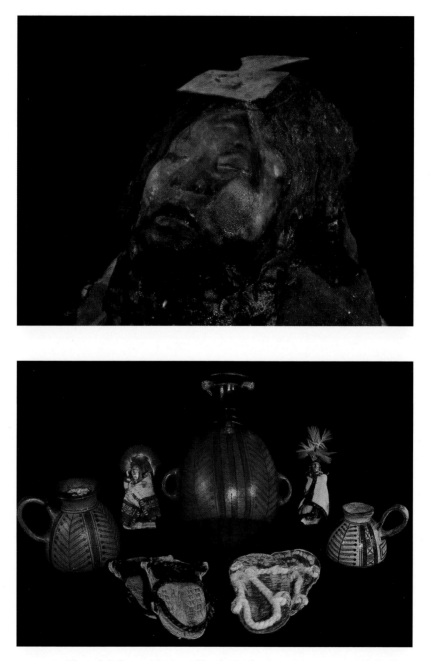

TOP: (26) Although lightning damaged her body, the face of the younger Llullaillaco female appears untouched.

BOTTOM: (27) Two stirrup pots, two pairs of sandals, an aribalo, a female statue with a red headdress, and a male statue adorned with yellow feathers illustrate the variety of artifacts found in the burials on Llullaillaco.

TOP: (28) The Llullaillaco boy was found wearing a silver bracelet and with his headdress held in place by a sling.

BOTTOM: (29) The older Llullaillaco female seems alive, as if she is only asleep in eternity.

One way to confront the problem is by educating others. All the EIRs have been involved with educational initiatives, and some projects, like Bob Ballard's Jason Project, have taken them in totally new directions. In my case I was surprised by how much interest children showed in the Ice Maiden. I decided to gather material for a book that would appeal to them. I could use material that had been developed for other popular articles and present it in a way that would be accessible to kids age ten and up.

My writing a children's book provided no end of amusement to my friends. I had no children of my own, and thanks to my lifestyle, I hardly knew any. I did not have a clue how to interact with them. No one could have been more surprised than I when the Junior Library Guild selected my book Discovering the Inca Ice Maiden as an Outstanding Book of the Year.[4] Now I was the one amused—and I still can't resist ribbing my friends about it whenever the opportunity arises.

Other publications about the Ice Maiden were designed for all but the youngest of readers. A novel about her life was written, and a board game was developed based on our Sara Sara expedition—including every major event that occurred ("Slow going, carrying Sarita down mountain–miss a turn"). The National Geographic compiled a Read and Explore Kit, which brought together my book with visual aids and an instruction manual for teachers. I found several courses developed, some on the Web, about the finds and their importance.[5] Clearly, the mummies had sparked an unusual degree of interest that was being used by teachers as a starting point for studying a vast array of subjects. The following letter is an example of many similar ones I received: "I am a teacher of grades 3-4-5. We are reading Frozen Girl as a class. After a chapter or two, I showed them the beautiful photos from your book. They are thrilled and so anxious to learn more. Kids who have never been particularly interested in reading any information or learning about history are hanging on every word. You make learning fun!"

At the same time, I was engaged in a whirlwind of other activities, including putting together a geography education project for the National Geographic, preparing reports for the INC in Peru, meeting with conservation and other specialists, giving interviews, and presenting a series of lectures in cities across the U.S. Since I had lived for nearly 30 years outside the U.S., I hardly knew the country—and what I did know seemed from another time. I presented talks in Berkeley, Los Angeles, New York, Binghamton, Hartford, Palo Alto, Santa Barbara, Palm Beach, and Chicago, not to mention various venues in the Washington, D.C., area. I finally began to feel like I was no longer a stranger in my own land.

One trip proved especially fruitful. At the beginning of 1997, I was asked to be a cultural consultant for a trip to South America being undertaken by members of the Young Presidents Organization, which had been founded years before by a man who saw the need for an organization to bring together young, creative business leaders. Since many were interested in learning and traveling, the organization had members from around the world meet annually in different countries. They could combine traveling and learning more about other cultures with spending a few days in an "academy," which involved a more traditional educational environment.

In the spring of 1997 they chose to visit sites in Peru before attending an academy in Buenos Aires. Some of the members make donations that helped finance two expeditions in Peru that fall, and one of the men, Doug Tipple, became instrumental in updating my antiquated communications equipment—such as it was.

Doug persuaded the Canadian company he worked for, Bell Sygma (at the time a subsidiary of Bell Canada), to supply me with items I badly needed. He couldn't believe that I was still using a computer that accepted only floppy disks, that I had no video camera, no up-to-date communications equipment—indeed, I was feeling rather embarrassed by the time we had listed all the things I lacked. I explained that I couldn't afford them, and that was all it

A blizzard caught us while we were climbing near the summit of Ampato in 1997.

took for Doug to take the initiative. Before I left the U.S., he out-
fitted me with an assortment of sophisticated equipment. More
important, he perceived a key lack that I had never even considered
before—a Web site.

In late July I met with Bell Canada employees Daniel Jones
and Stanley Wu at the National Geographic Society. Dan had been
assigned the task of setting up a Web site for me, and just
before leaving for Peru, I delivered to him an eclectic collection
of papers and images, which he was somehow to assemble into
a coherent whole.[6]

Stanley was a computer specialist who had obtained a variety of
specialized equipment the company had donated, including a state-
of-the-art Panasonic laptop. With infinite patience he taught me
how to use it to coordinate a satellite telephone, digital cameras,
and power sources for sending "live" images from mountain summits. I began planning to create a scaled-down version of NOVA's
online broadcast during our expedition to Sara Sara.

Bell Sygma wasn't the only institution helping to improve our
equipment. In the spring of 1997 the Carrier Corporation engineers

brought to Peru a modified version of the refrigerated display unit. They had broken new ground in designing these cases. No one had ever before been successful in simultaneously preserving and displaying frozen mummified remains. Archaeologists, anthropologists, conservation experts—all had little experience to build on. During the month the Ampato maiden was on display in the U.S., Carrier saw ways in which the case could be improved, given the luxury of time.

Engineers and technicians from Carrier's Advanced Systems Group added a larger compressor to the cooling unit and rerouted the internal cold air flow, which maintained the temperature in the 44-cubic-foot case at between 0° and –8°F. The altered airflow path within the display case also ensured even temperatures throughout the case and the elimination of any "cold spots." A highly accurate "chilled mirror"-type dew point sensor was added, along with a precision temperature sensor, to provide precise monitoring of relative humidity. If relative humidity was maintained at 90 percent or higher, scientists thought the mummy would not slowly desiccate over time. Several modifications helped eliminate the buildup of ice in the refrigeration unit, which in turn reduced the need for maintenance. The unit's computer-based electronic controls, powerful enough to control the air-conditioning in a large building, were reprogrammed so that technicians in Peru could more easily and more accurately monitor and adjust conditions within the display case.

The original case had been operating nearly full time since the previous July with no problems. The modified case, along with three modified refrigeration units, would give Peruvian scientists added confidence that this rare glimpse of a past culture could be preserved well into the future for more scientific study and also for viewing by the Peruvian public. In the years since then, including the Ice Maiden's trip to Japan, that viewing public now numbers more than a million.

Such corporate generosity was much appreciated. The publicity the mummies garnered led many people to wrongly assume that the

Ice Maiden's conservation was well funded. Ironically, they think my expeditions cost a fortune, when it is the conservation of the finds that is most expensive. Expedition costs are relatively easy to calculate. Salaries make up a major part of them, and these vary depending on a person's experience—and the budget available. Usually, if a grant is obtained, an average per diem falls in the $30 to $50 range.

Thus, the cost of a ten-person team totals about $500 a day. Allotting $10 per day per person for food adds up to $100 a day. Transportation usually costs $1,000 to $2,000 for an expedition, plus the same for burros, if needed. I now have most of the basic equipment (tents, stoves, backpacks, sleeping bags, walkie-talkies, archaeological tools, etc.), so less than $1,000 usually covers any additional supplies, medicines, and miscellaneous costs (such as those relating to permits, telephone calls, and photocopying). Most expeditions do not exceed 20 days in the field, so a normal one should not cost more than $15,000—and thus far, never has.

We have made do with far less, especially if the mountain is relatively easy to climb and team members live in the region, as in the case of mountains near Arequipa. I have never been paid a salary for field research projects (although I have been paid for participating in the filming of a few) and my round-trip airfare and pre- and post-expedition expenses usually do not exceed $3,000 total. Compared to the amount of money budgeted for almost any other kind of expedition of equivalent size and difficulty, the total sum we need for an expedition is quite modest.

Modest, but not easily acquired. When I was undertaking high-altitude archeological research from 1980 to 1995, I was never able to obtain a grant of $15,000 for an entire year's research, let alone a single expedition. Not until 2002 was I able to obtain a vehicle for our research, and that was a welcome donation by Toyota of a Land Cruiser.

After the discovery of the Ice Maiden, the funding of an expedition became easier. Financing the less "sexy" aspects of the work, such as conservation and lab research, is far more difficult. Yet they are vital to the overall project. Indeed, without them there would be little justification for the expeditions in the first place. We have been fortunate that universities have provided support in this regard, both in Peru and Argentina (and also the provincial government in the latter country). Nonetheless, a serious gap remains between available funds and conservation and research needs.

WHILE READING ABOUT THE CONSERVATION OF FROZEN BODIES, one subject kept being brought up—cryogenics, a branch of physics that deals with very low temperatures.[7] Absolute zero is −459.67°F (−273.15°C), the temperature at which all molecular and atomic activity ceases. Although it is technically possible to reach extremely close to absolute zero, the practical use of cryogenics tends to focus more on "warmer" temperatures, such as that of liquid nitrogen. Why liquid nitrogen? Because its temperature is low enough for metabolic and biochemical activity to be suspended.

In cryogenics, living tissues have been stored at the temperature of liquid nitrogen (−323°F), and when thawed, many of the cells were still alive. This technique has been applied to preserving sperm, eye corneas, embryos, blood, and recently entire human bodies. And a new field has evolved—cryonics.

"Cryonics, simply stated, is the rapid cooling of a person's body, usually in liquid nitrogen, in order to preserve the tissue, cellular and molecular structure in the hopes that future advancements in science and technology will be developed to allow the scientific means to repair the ravages of diseases . . . or the effects of aging, thereby potentially restoring the individual back to good health," wrote Michael Darwin and Brian Wowk in their 1992 article "Cryonics: Reaching for Tomorrow."[8] In short, as some wags saw it, the frozen body becomes a "corpsicle."

However, there are still seemingly insurmountable hurdles to overcome (cost being the least of them) to preserve bodies cryogenically over time, not to mention bringing them back to life. How would this be possible, even if only in theory? Some scientists point to the new field of nanotechnology. This has been defined as the act of purposefully manipulating matter at the atomic and molecular scale—the "nanoscale." To provide an idea of the size being considered, a freckle the size of a pinhead is some one million nanometers wide.

The idea is that eventually scientists will be able to send huge numbers of tiny, bacteria-size "machines" (nanocomputers) into the body to repair cells. In addition, new cells could be fabricated to replace any that had been lost. Over the course of time, cells in a body could be fully restored. Such is the hope.

Many scientists find such hope misplaced. They have noted that it is far easier to repair simple cells than to bring a thinking human being back to life. This, they believe, will remain impossible because of the complexity of one indispensable organ—the brain.

As I read more about the brain, I was surprised at how little we still know about it. "The human brain is . . . truly an internal cosmos. . . . [It is] the most elaborate structure in the known universe. No galaxy cluster, no star, no planet, no other living creature we know of, comes even close to the brain in complexity," wrote Joel Davis in *Mapping the Mind*.[9] No wonder then that scientists have only just begun to understand how the brain functions.

There are two main types of cells in the brain, and about 100 billion of these cells are neurons—information-carrying nerve cells. Each one of them is connected to other neurons through tens of thousands of connections. In some areas of the brain there are as many as several hundred thousand of these connections, which means your brain as a whole has approximately 100 trillion connections. When a person dies, so do an awful lot of brain cells.

Scientists discovered that simple cells might be restored to life after freezing, but complex cells, not to mention entire organs, would be very difficult, if not impossible, to reanimate.[10] Since thawing conditions can vary depending on the types of cells, different thawing techniques might have to be used with cells that could even be next to each other.

The team searches the slope beneath Ampato's summit near the spot where the Ice Maiden was found.

Another problem remains to be solved. Dr. Angelique Corthals, a specialist in frozen tissues at the American Museum of Natural History, wrote me that a cryoprotectant, a kind of antifreeze, would have to be added to freeze and revive cells. None currently exists capable of preserving an organism with a multitude of different cell types.[11]

Obviously, the key requirement for any future technology to successfully bring a person back to life is for the brain to be well frozen. However, although nanotechnology, or some other future technology, might succeed in restoring some cells, it is difficult to imagine it ever being able to fully restore the extremely complex connections between neurons—and these are what give rise to the cognitive functions of a person. Even if the brain started functioning at some level, the person would never have his original personality and memory, no matter how well preserved his body might outwardly appear. Nonetheless, much can be learned from a body without the person coming back to life.

What does this have to do with our discoveries of frozen mummies? After all, the extremely low temperatures, such as of liquid nitrogen, do not occur naturally on earth and no mummy had ever been found with its brain frozen in its original state. Still, I thought that if we ever uncovered a body that had been rapidly frozen at death and remained basically unchanged—the "perfect" mummy—we needed to know what alternatives existed to best preserve it. And precisely because of its complexity, special precautions needed to be taken to insure the brain's preservation. However, for the time being, this remained just a theoretical concern—we still had not found such a mummy.

WHEN I LEFT FOR PERU IN THE SUMMER OF 1997, I WAS CARRYING equipment that I had previously only dreamed about. A Panasonic CF-25 laptop computer (made especially for rough conditions), weather-resistant solar panels, a Nera satellite phone, six Motorola walkie-talkies, a small gas generator, a wind-powered generator, several North Face tents, two digital video cameras, two digital still cameras, a 35-mm Nikon camera—I felt like I'd celebrated several years worth of Christmases. Doug had procured more gear in a few months than I'd been able to afford in 17 years.

Because I began the expeditions relatively late in the fall of 1997, I wanted to first test the equipment on a mountain close to Arequipa, and I decided that Pichu Pichu was the best candidate. Although we had excavated much of the platform, we hadn't completed the excavation the previous year, and I wanted to find out if anything was buried deeper beneath the large silver statue.

The choice of the mountain was also influenced by other factors. Members of Bell Sygma would be joining us, and some had no experience in mountaineering. Pichu Pichu was not too high, and climbing it would give my Peruvian team a chance to acclimatize before we moved on to higher peaks. The National Geographic decided to send an Internet specialist, Yancey Hall, to send "live" reports and images via satellite phone to its Web site. Although more fit than most of us, he also had no climbing background. I had never led an expedition with so many people lacking mountaineering experience, and if any problems arose, Pichu Pichu would be close to Arequipa.

After I landed in Peru on October 10, I met with José to finalize preparations for the expedition. The Canadian group, consisting of six people, would not arrive for another week. José had rounded up the usual suspects from last year to fill out the team. Jim Underwood also joined us, and Carlos had arranged for another climber, Marco, to help with tasks lower on the mountain. Altogether 21 people would ascend the mountain.

Four men at a time took turns carrying to base camp a 100-pound gas generator that the National Geographic had supplied. The only way to do this was by supporting it as it hung from poles on their shoulders. I was reminded of the scene in *Raiders of the Lost Ark* when the Ark of the Covenant was taken up a mountain. The generator would be used to charge the batteries of a rock drill, which we hoped would be able to penetrate the frozen soil. (Once we encountered cultural material, we would switch back to using more traditional methods.) If the drill worked on Pichu Pichu, we planned to use it on Sara Sara.

Jim had calculated how much power each piece of electronic equipment would use per hour and the output of each power source. Of course, this could only be approximate, especially since the cold affects batteries. For example, the computer needed roughly 2.5 Ah to run three hours and the satellite phone 2.5 Ah every two hours. As for the power sources, a fully charged solar panel could produce 6 Ah a day, and with 6 panels we had 36 Ah available. The solar panels would charge a marine battery in order to keep an even and continuous energy flow. If a storm struck or the day clouded over, we could switch to a wind-powered generator. In a worst-case scenario, we could send equipment down to base camp to be charged. The power needs for the drill's battery were so high that it could be charged only with the gas generator.

By October 15 we had set up a base camp at the foot of Pichu Pichu. We conducted a thorough survey of the lower ruins of the tambo and checked the summit site as well. It was covered in snow, but the area where we planned to camp was suitable. We left part of the team behind to make carries to the summit while we returned to Arequipa to meet the Canadians.

After a few days to let them acclimatize in Arequipa, we camped at Chilitea on October 20, and two days later moved to the base camp at 16,250 feet. One of the most useful items the Bell Sygma team had brought turned out to be a huge North Face dome tent. For the first time we could gather a dozen team members in one tent, work on artifacts, cook out of the wind, and so on. "You could hold a square dance in it," said one of the Canadians, and he was exaggerating only slightly. I felt like I left the mountain behind when I entered the tent. We could stand up or lie around and joke with teammates, even while a storm raged outside.

The Canadians had come solely to climb to the summit. They did not plan to stay camped on it while we worked there. By October 23 they felt acclimatized enough to make the attempt. A poignant aspect of the expedition was the ascent by Alyssa, Doug and Laura Tipple's 12-year-old daughter. "You are almost the same age as one of the girls sacrificed here," I said to her when we stood on the platform. "I'll bet you are the first girl your age to reach the summit in 500 years." In fact, she had made one of the highest ascents by a girl her age in modern times.

After the Canadians celebrated reaching the summit, we descended to base camp. John Lochow and Peggy Foster had so much enjoyed the experience that they were already planning expeditions to other mountains. The Canadians were driven back to Arequipa, while the rest of us returned to the summit to focus on the excavation.

The drill did poorly in the soil, barely making a dent and quickly losing power. The mixture of cold and altitude seemed to have had its effect. Despite exhausting work over the next few days, we found nothing significant to add to what we had uncovered in 1996. However, notwithstanding the drill, the new equipment performed well. We were able to maintain constant communication via satellite phone throughout the expedition and send out emails and digital images. Our work appeared "live" online at the National Geographic's Web site, and I felt ready to use the phone for such transmissions on expeditions to come.

We had also finished one of the few complete excavations of a high-altitude ceremonial platform. We now had information to compare with other ritual sites—and not only on mountains. Few Inca religious sites of any kind had been thoroughly excavated, so Pichu Pichu provided a model to compare them with as well. Usually, we would have left a section of a site untouched in order for future archaeologists to be able to excavate it with improved technology. We agreed with this strategy in principle, but it required that the site be protected—an impossible task on high mountain summits.

We decided to make a quick excursion to climb the 18,455-foot volcano Ubinas before returning to Arequipa. We could do this only if we were able to load the vehicles, drive to Ubinas, climb it, and get back down in time to return to Arequipa the same night. Only motivated climbers eager for exercise could think of this as a "fun" trip, but everyone was looking forward to the challenge with glee after having spent several discouraging days on Pichu Pichu.

Like the other volcanoes in the region, Ubinas has figured both in historical accounts and in local legends as a powerful deity.[12] But, unlike the others, no ruins had been located on it. We did not have time for more than a quick search of part of the crater rim and a brief look at the smoldering fumaroles below. We couldn't help but wonder if there might be ruins somewhere else on the volcano and planned a return visit.

As we descended to the waiting vehicles, we watched a brilliant red sun set behind Pichu Pichu, silhouetting it against the western horizon. By amazing coincidence, a darker ray of light shot into the sky from directly behind the location of the sacrificial platform. "The mountain god is saying goodbye," someone whispered as we stood looking on in humbled silence. We drove off to Arequipa in high spirits. We might not have found anything, but that special day made the whole expedition feel worthwhile.

THE WEATHER WAS STILL HOLDING, AND WE DECIDED TO FINISH excavating a site that I had last visited in 1991. Huarancante is a 17,585-foot-high peak located on the southern edge of the Colca Canyon. The anthropologists Ricardo Valderrama and Carmen Escalante have described the role it still plays in rituals today.[13] Streams lead from the mountain north to the town of Chivay and south to large areas of pasturage. The people of Yanque in the Colca Valley consider Huarancante (also called Chucura) one of the most important deities of the region. The volcano is regarded as the older brother of Mount Mismi, which also receives considerable ritual attention. (Climbers found an Inca statue on its summit in 1977.) People still climb Huarancante's slope to the beginning of a ten-mile canal, where they make offerings to the Earth Mother, Pachamama, and the deity believed to reside in the mountain. Like many Andean peoples, they show respect to the peak by using the term *tata*—father.

When Miki and I had climbed Huarancante in 1982, we found more than a dozen river stones strewn about the summit, and a few of them had red crosses marked on them. Mountain climbers had also used several stones to build a cairn to mark the spot. I was not surprised, because I knew that an Australian climber, Peter Ross, had reported seeing river stones and remains of ashes when he reached the summit in 1977.

Since the highest section of the summit was flat, it looked like a natural platform, but we had seen nothing that indicated a structure had been built there. While Miki was sitting on a boulder, he idly swung his ice ax into the sand a few times. Suddenly he said, "Hey, this looks like a shell." He had uncovered a llama figurine that had been carved out of spondylus shell in typical Inca style.[14]

The figurine was found under only an inch of sand, and I suspected that it had been left behind by looters. We soon discovered that there were two distinct areas of charcoal just beneath the sand as well. Only a half-yard square, the first had a layer of charcoal six inches deep. The second area, three times that size, had a charcoal layer five inches deep. Flat stones had been used to cover the charcoal. We saw a small burnt corncob and part of the jawbone of a camelid buried amid the charcoal in one place. A tremendous amount of wood would have been needed to make such a large and deep area of ashes. Clearly this had been an important place for burning offerings, but were the ashes, river stones, bone, and corncob ancient or recent?

I had found river stones used in current-day ceremonies on mountain summits before, but they also were reported in rituals in 1631. The Huanca (Wanka) people living in the mountains to the east of Lima used flat stones as plates when they made offerings to a mountain deity.[15] Llamas were commonly sacrificed at both Inca and modern-day ceremonies, and the chronicler Joseph de Arriaga wrote in the early 1600s of ears of corn being burned at a harvest ceremony.[16]

A similar tradition has continued to the present. The people of Yanque use flat river stones as plates on which to make offerings at ceremonies for obtaining water from Huarancante. Called *enqaychus* of the water, they are taken from different rivers and kept where offerings are made near the sources of irrigation canals. The term *enqaychu* is used for objects possessing the vital force of the element it represents, and thus the river stones are used to invoke water.[17]

In 1991 I had returned with a small team: Miki, his brother Juan, and archaeology student Walter Diaz. On this expedition we initially spotted a few shards on the surface. A couple of them were decorated and clearly of Inca origin. I decided to focus our excavation near the cairn where the llama figurine had been uncovered in 1982. With this

A team member crosses an ice field on Ampato en route to our high camp at 20,000 feet.

grid we uncovered a spondylus shell 12 inches deep in the soil. Another eight inches down, a gold Inca statue, complete with well-preserved miniature clothing, materialized amid some boulders.

Throughout the summit area the terrain had been overturned a long time ago, and I suspected that the site had been looted soon after the Spanish conquest five centuries before. The mountain was close to a road used by the Spaniards and relatively accessible. As I took photographs, I said to the team, "It does not look like any special care was taken in the placement of the statue, so I'll bet that looters simply overlooked it."

Near an outcrop 30 yards lower down from the main summit, we excavated a two-meter square area and found it too had been looted. However, we did uncover the bronze club head of an Inca mace (champi), which looks like a six-pointed star with a hole in the center. Originally, a straight wooden handle would have extended through the hole and made it a lethal weapon in the hands of skilled warriors—and the Incas were famous for being just that. Since it was made of bronze (and not stone as commoners used), this had likely been carried by someone who had a prominent role in Inca society, presumably a captain or noble of some kind.

"This could have played a role in a human sacrifice," I said, thinking of the fractured skull found in 1963 on Pichu Pichu. However, I knew that mountains were also believed to be war gods and that club heads had been found in ceremonial contexts at other Inca sites.[18] In a document written in the late 1500s, Inca captains were reported to have worshipped their war clubs. Perhaps the club head was used in battles in the area and subsequently buried as a votive offering. Still, since the discoveries of the Ice Maiden and the victim on Sara Sara, my first hypothesis remains a possibility.

After we returned from Pichu Pichu on the current expedition, I sent Marco, a student of José's, to Pausa to arrange burros for our expedition to Sara Sara. That would take almost a week round-trip, so we decided to use the time to complete the excavation on Huarancante.

In early November, José, Jimmy, Arcadio, Ignacio, and I trekked to the foot of Huarancante after having been dropped off along the road. Orlando won a coin toss and stayed to watch equipment that we left behind for a carry the next day. We reached a good spot for a campsite just before dark at 16,500 feet. We were attracted by a trickle of water that ran nearby—at least until it froze after night fell.

The next morning José and I climbed to the summit while the others returned to transport the remaining loads. Little had changed in six years. We selected areas to excavate and estimated that we would be able to finish the work in a few days. For that reason we would not need to establish a higher camp. Although we would have farther to climb to reach the site each day, we could forgo the carries up and down the mountain necessary to establish a summit camp.

The others took up the archaeological tools the following day, while I stayed in camp. I set up solar panels to charge the marine battery, and then caught up on emails and calls. For lunch Arcadio had left a sandwich for me nicely wrapped in toilet paper.

Via satellite phone I called Jackie, who had been planning to join me. "I'm thinking of not coming," she said, "since it wouldn't be for that much time." She sounded sad, and I suspected it stemmed from more than her plan to cancel the trip to Peru. We had separated temporarily during the summer, and she briefly dated someone else. Even though we had reconciled before I left, the other man lived near her and I had been gone for more than a month. Only the week before, she had talked enthusiastically about coming. Alarms were going off, and so I almost instinctively asked, "Have you been seeing someone?" I knew full well who it would be if she said yes.

"Yes. But he has left," she replied. "I love him, but I love you, too."

The hardest breakups are the ones where one of the partners isn't certain what he or she wants. She went on, "I can't see how I fit into your life." I knew how difficult it was to maintain a relationship with my being gone for such long periods after we began dating in 1994. This had been further complicated after the discovery of the Ice Maiden, since I had become involved with myriad events associated with the mummy. She felt she was losing her identity, not just as an artist but as a sailor as well. The other man Jackie was interested in was a sailor with his own boat. He was preparing to go long-distance ocean sailing, which had long been Jackie's dream. How could I leave for months to follow my interests and not be willing to allow her the same opportunity? Of course, her going sailing for months with another man she loved meant that there was little chance we would ever be together again.

After I hung up, I felt physically ill and called José to tell him I would not be climbing up that day. I had no interest at all in archaeology—or anything else, for that matter.

When the team returned from the summit that afternoon, José was convinced that the site had been completely looted. They had not found anything, not even the ash layer of Huayna Putina, which had erupted in 1600, leaving a telltale marker for archaeologists. For that reason he thought the site had been looted after then. "You were lucky to have found the statue," he told me, downcast, "since little of this site was left untouched."

I was still depressed the next day, as we wrapped up the expedition and carried down the equipment. By November 16 we were back in Arequipa.

I HAD ORIGINALLY PLANNED TO GO TO SARA SARA BECAUSE I thought the higher summit of Ampato would be covered in snow this late in the year. Upon our return, though, I was surprised to see that it was completely snow free. El Niño had caused a drought in the region, providing what could well be the last opportunity to work on its summit for years to come. In addition, the dry spell meant that a route up the opposite, eastern, side was an option. Not only was this more direct, we could also check for Inca ruins on that side of the peak. Thanks to financial support provided by some members of the Young Presidents Organization, Ampato became the third mountain we worked on that year. It would once again provide us with an unforgettable experience.

The seven of us heading to Ampato in late November had all been working on mountains at altitudes over 18,000 feet since the middle of October. José, Jimmy, Orlando, and I made up the archaeology component, and Arcadio, his brother Ignacio, and Carlos Zárate joined us. We knew the weather was highly unstable at this time of year, and we expected bad weather while on the summit. So we were glad to have a team of experienced climbers who had all worked together before.

The day we drove to Ampato we could not even see the mountain—hail was falling and clouds obscured it. We made carries amid snow flurries and thunderclaps to a cache at more than 16,000 feet, and then established Camp 1 at 18,000 feet. From there we set off through increasingly towering seracs to set up our high camp at 20,250 feet.

By the afternoon of November 26 we were assembled just below Punta Ichu (the grass summit), kicking out flat spots for our tents. We had been lucky to find a ledge in the slope wide enough for us to be able to pitch them in single file. We couldn't place stakes in the frozen soil, so we scoured the slope looking for stones to use in tying down the tents. The view was spectacular, and we did not mind the steep drop just a few feet away. We were out of danger from avalanches and lightning strikes. In the middle of a sunny day, a small waterfall even gushed out from the snowfield close to our camp. "Anyone for a shower?" someone quipped.

I began to transmit digital images and text via my satellite phone, and they were then posted on my Web site by Dan Jones of Bell Sygma. For me, the interest generated among schoolteachers and students had been one of the most satisfying results of my work. The only drawback to the arrangement was how long it took to transmit images, thus using up battery power.

The electronic gear caused other problems as well. Ignacio had carried up the marine battery to charge the satellite phone and computer. As soon as he took the pack with it off his back and set it down, he yelled, "My pants! It's burned holes in my pants!" The battery acid had leaked out, much to the amusement of the others. I gave him a spare pair of ski pants that I had brought, and then we patched up holes in other items that had been affected, including my sleeping bag. Now it no longer seemed so funny.

While at high camp, I was interviewed "live" by Alex Chadwick of National Public Radio. Since NPR replayed the broadcasts, they eventually reached eight million people. To my surprise, I ended up receiving more feedback from that program than any shown on TV, despite TV's reaching more than double that number.

Before long I was on the phone with a variety of government authorities, such as Peru's minister of education, who normally would be difficult to reach. After all, who could turn down taking a call from 20,000 feet? I couldn't resist calling friends, despite the cost. I especially relished making a call to Yvon Chouinard, owner of Patagonia and one of America's most renowned climbers. Yvon and I had been on an expedition together in eastern Nepal in 1977, and I had been in awe of his effortless combination of climbing ability and grace on ice. His ascent up a frozen waterfall reminded me of watching a ballet dancer. Despite having become a millionaire, Yvon did not forget his own impecunious background or that of his friends. Once I wrote him asking if I could have a discount on some articles of clothing his company sold, and he replied: "No, you cannot. But you *can* have anything you want for free."

A purist, he rebelled at the inclusion of satellite communications systems while mountaineering. The mere idea of climbers calling friends with their cell phones while in the middle of a climb could set him off on a rant decrying the decadence of modern expeditions. That's exactly why I couldn't resist.

"Hi, Yvon, I've got some free time and thought I'd say hello. I'm at over 20,000 feet—ain't technology wonderful?"

Sounds of soft groaning gave way to exasperation. "What the hell are you doing with a phone on the summit?"

"Well, I'm actually a bit below the summit, lying here in a warm sleeping bag, munching chocolate," I replied.

"That's what you called to tell me, you bastard?" he exclaimed, but with a chuckle. By now he realized he was being put on. No doubt about it, if nothing else, technology made for some amusing distractions.

But I understood all too well what bothered Yvon about this kind of technology. While it served a useful purpose on a scientific expedition, you missed the sense of being totally out of touch with the rest of world, wholly dependent on your own skill and knowledge. On your own, you felt more a part of nature, more alive to its nuances and to its beauty. Even if I never used the phone, simply having it with me took away a part of this magic.

One day, as we were traversing under the summit's final cliffs, two climbers suddenly materialized on top, having ascended the peak from the southwest. They were just as surprised to see us as we were to see them, and one of them called out, "Who are you?" José shouted back, "An archaeological expedition from Catholic University." With that, they vanished from the summit, descending before we could find who they were. They left no card at the summit cairn, as most climbers do, and we wondered if they had come solely for the climb. Very few people had ascended the mountain before then; perhaps we had missed, by mere minutes, meeting looters.

Once on the summit, we quickly excavated what little remained of the stone platform that had served as Juanita's tomb. We rigged fixed ropes to help climb to it via the steep northern cliff side that Miki and I had tried, and failed, to ascend in 1995. Thanks to the ropes, we avoided the time-consuming ascent up the southern-facing slope, but we found nothing more on the summit ridge.

We then began to systematically search the slope down which the Ice Maiden had fallen. Artifacts were not all we were hoping to find. We had kept quiet, throughout all the interviews and publicity, about our hope of finding a second mummy. From the beginning, we had considered the possibility that the torn cloth Miki and I found above the Ice Maiden might have belonged to a separate mummy bundle. Although two human sacrifices had been found together at only one site on a low summit in Chile, I knew that some chroniclers had referred to their having taken place in pairs. Our discovery of the two mummies at the plateau site in 1995 had whetted our desire to make a more careful search in the area where Juanita had fallen.

In a repeat of my technique two years before, José threw stones down the gullies that led down from the summit platform. We watched from below to see where they landed. It appeared that Juanita had not fallen down the gully that began where we had found the summit statues, but rather one a little farther north. After searching its slopes, we recovered two wooden spoons, several potsherds, maize kernels, llama bones, and still more pieces of cloth torn from the outer wrap of the Ice Maiden's mummy bundle. But we found no sign of a second mummy. Instead, we saw evidence that looters had been searching the area before us.

Once we were satisfied that we had fully inspected the area, we moved on to carry out test excavations at the 20,400-foot Punta Ichu. The Incas had brought the grass up from thousands of feet below, and we soon discovered how it had kept from being swept off the mountain. The grass had been tied together with ropes and was separated by ice into at least two tiers. "This indicates that the site was used during different years and that the grass had served as insulation from the ice and frozen soil," said José, confirming what we had previously assumed—the Incas had used the summit for ceremonies more than once.

Of special interest was a textile we uncovered that bore designs similar to those of the Chancay, a culture of northern coastal Peru. It was rare to find a non-Inca artifact at one of these sites, and it suggested that the Chancay might have been involved in some way with the rituals. Could Juanita have originated from there? A series of test excavations revealed little of interest, and we wondered if further work on the mountain was worth the effort.

Since we had enough supplies to remain for several more days, we decided to continue excavations on the plateau at 19,200 feet, the same place we had found the two mummies in 1995 and the blue tunic in 1996. Because we had established our camp at 20,300 feet and it was located along our return route, we decided to keep our camp where it was. That put us in the curious situation of having to climb a thousand vertical feet down to the plateau and then back up every day.

We had already excavated most of the stone-marked sites on the plateau, so we decided to work out from them, using a standard two-meter grid pattern. José descended with the team to set up the grids, while I remained at the high camp sending out images and fielding emails. At a transmission speed of 2.8 kbps (even the slowest phone line was ten times faster), it was time-consuming and tedious work. I was beginning to eat my words to Yvon about the joys of having a satellite phone.

After two days, I dropped down to see how the team was faring. Nothing had yet been uncovered, not even in the 50-foot-long platform, oriented in the direction of the June solstice sunrise. "Maybe it was built after the original burials, perhaps as a place to make invocations to the gods," I said to José. If food and liquid offerings had been made on its surface, they wouldn't have left much of a trace.

The next day I stayed in camp "working the phone." I first transmitted a series of emails to the National Geographic about an upcoming article that would update my work, including the discoveries of the Sara Sara and Pichu Pichu mummies. I called the team on the plateau at lunchtime and was told that they had just uncovered the top of an Inca jar. We kept the walkie-talkies open, and soon I heard my name called—and with an unusual urgency. "Johan, Johan. Do you hear me?" I quickly confirmed the call and Orlando said excitedly, "We have found more pottery and the top of a mummy bundle!"

At long last, after two months in the mountains without finding anything of significance, we had found the intact burial of a mummy. For the first time since that terrible conversation with Jackie weeks before, I felt animated again. We all knew it was not only the last mountain we would likely investigate this season but also the last time we planned to work on Ampato.

Before ascending to our camp in the afternoon, the team cleared a space around the top of the mummy and lightly covered it. We did most of the digging the next day. The mummy emerged still wrapped in textiles and thus was one of only a half dozen human sacrifices ever recovered in situ. Fine pottery and a spondylus female statue were cached with the bundle, and the shawl pins proved that it was another female. We now had two females and a male sacrificed on the plateau site. The theory of a symbolic "marriage" no longer looked tenable. Whatever the reason for the sacrifices, never before had four human sacrifices been found on a single volcano. This further underscored Ampato's exceptional importance to the Incas.

I was able to quickly solve one problem the discovery caused. We were nearly out of food and only had one more day's worth stored at Camp 1. The satellite phone now proved its value by allowing me to call Arequipa and arrange for climbers to bring additional supplies.

A few days later two more of the Zárate brothers, Juan Carlos and Carlitos, reached us. It was fortunate that they arrived when they did. In addition to needing the food, we now had the unenviable task of carrying a 100-pound mummy bundle up to our camp at 20,300 feet and then higher still to cross back over the summit ridge and down the eastern side of the volcano to our base camp. Once again Arcadio did the lion's share, carrying the bundle strapped to a special frame we had brought along just for this purpose.

Heavy snowfall and, worse, lightning strikes on the summit ridge close above kept us trapped in our tents for a couple of days. Food was running low again when there was a short break in the weather. We decided to risk being caught out in a storm and quickly broke camp. Sure enough, we were nearing the summit ridge when the storm started again, and we worked our way down through the ice and rock to the site of Camp 1. Snow flurries reduced visibility, and we straggled into camp just as the evening light faded to black.

The morning after we reached base camp, two vehicles arrived from Arequipa to take us back. As we watched clouds form around the volcanoes, we knew that we had been lucky to stay on their summits as long as we had. Only two weeks remained before Christmas, and everyone wanted to be home with his family. The expeditions were over for the year.[19]

José and I spent the next few days examining the finds in the laboratory. An x-ray showed that, just like the other two mummies we had recovered from the plateau, this one had also been badly damaged by lightning. Although we had found four mummies on Ampato (and four on other volcanoes), we had still not found a perfectly preserved mummy. Even if we found another human sacrifice on the mountain, I doubted it would be well preserved. Indeed, given what we knew of other possible sites, such as Sara Sara, I began to wonder if we would ever be able to find well-preserved mummies in Peru. But if not in Peru, then where?

As I prepared to return to the U.S., I began to think of mountains in Chile and Argentina that had the potential for such finds. Although he knew he might not be able to participate, José understood when I said to him, "It's time I started organizing expeditions to mountains in other countries."

Orlando Jaen excavates around one of the human sacrifices on Misti.

CHAPTER NINE

MISTI'S CHILDREN

I am a great believer in luck, and I find the harder
I work the more I have of it.
—THOMAS JEFFERSON

There is another mountain above Arequipa. It is the volcano
of the city, where the Inca placed many colonists for its service.
—CRISTÓBAL DE ALBORNOZ, 1583

BACK IN THE U.S., I DEBATED WHICH MOUNTAINS TO INVESTIGATE
next. Sara Sara still figured in my plans, and I thought another
mountain in southern Peru should be included—to help with
acclimatization, if nothing else. So I added Misti, Peru's most famous
volcano, to the list. It towers behind the city of Arequipa, providing
one of the most photographed backdrops in all Peru. Its conical shape
is reminiscent of Mount Fuji, and when it is covered in snow, it
provides a striking contrast with the surrounding desert terrain.
With good reason many of Arequipa's inhabitants call themselves
Mistianos—the "children of Misti."

Despite being 19,111 feet high, Misti is one of Peru's most-climbed
volcanoes.[1] A meteorological observatory was constructed on its
summit in 1893, and in 1900 men erected a 30-foot iron cross with
the aid of 30 mules. Races to the summit have been run since the 1970s,
and people have reached it riding bicycles. A marriage, billed as the
world's highest, was held on the summit in 1974. The first paraglider
flew off from it in the early 1990s. There was no mystery left to

Misti—or so we thought. But it was to yield one of the most important finds ever made in the Andes.

Of the mountains in Chile and Argentina, Llullaillaco had been number one on my excavation "wish list" for 20 years. East of it was Quehuar, and I selected this peak mainly as a training climb before tackling the higher and more isolated Llullaillaco. I submitted a proposal to the National Geographic's Expedition Council and it approved funding expeditions to these four volcanoes during 1998–99.

As much as I wanted to complete the work on Sara Sara, the looting that the site had undergone tempered my enthusiasm. Llullaillaco, on the other hand, held out significant promise. At 22,100 feet it had the world's highest archaeological site and thus presented a good opportunity for finding perfectly preserved artifacts—and mummies. I had been to the mountain three times in the 1980s, reaching the summit twice, and knew it well.

That expedition would have to wait, though. Good weather would not return to Llullaillaco until late 1998. As we had learned, the weather in southern Peru could be fine through November. What with work in the U.S. keeping me tied up until mid-August and other obligations during October–November, the only window for the Peruvian expeditions opened during August–September. I would have six weeks free to dedicate to excavations on Misti and Sara Sara. Although usually too short a time period for working on two volcanoes, I thought that there was little chance of finding anything on Misti and our exploration of it would be over quickly.

Misti is also one of the few volcanoes in the Andes that still has active fumaroles. The Incas told the Spanish that Misti had erupted in the 15th century, wiping out the entire population.[2] For five days ashes spewed upward and winds carried them more than 500 miles distant. The eruption reportedly occurred during the reign of the Inca emperor Pachacuti, considered the founder of the Inca Empire and responsible for the construction of many of its most famous sites, including Machu Picchu. He is also said to have come personally to

Arequipa to make offerings to placate Misti's ire. The only original inhabitants who survived the eruption were those who had been fulfilling their work obligations for the Incas elsewhere.

After the eruption, the Incas repopulated the region with these survivors and with colonists. Many of the colonists were specifically designated to serve Misti, and their descendents settled in several villages not far from the volcano (including Arequipa). According to one tradition, Yumina was occupied by Inca nobles from Cuzco. They not only administered the Arequipa valley but also played a key role in the worship of Misti. In 1583 the Spanish priest Cristóbal de Albornoz listed Misti (using its original name of Putina) as one of the region's most important deities—and one that needed to be destroyed.[3]

Geologists have confirmed that a massive eruption took place 2,000 years ago, and subsequent ones have been comparatively smaller. In the 35,000 years prior to that, however, several enormous eruptions occurred. Evidence of them can be seen in the layers of volcanic material forming the foothills of Misti.[4] The volcano leaves the impression that it could blow again, because of the smoke emitted by the fumaroles. At times this can be quite impressive, as in 1985, when smoke rose 3,000 feet in the air.

José demonstrated in his 1993 book *La Erupción del Volcán Misti* how vulnerable Arequipa would be in the event of a major eruption. His findings were supported by those of the French volcanologist Jean-Claude Thouret. In 2001 Thouret said the potential impact of an eruption of Misti "is as worrisome as that of Vesuvius near Naples."[5]

Misti has a reputation of being ill tempered, causing people harm through illness, eruptions, and earthquakes. Some believe that Misti helps witches, and human sacrifices are rumored to have taken place on its slopes in recent times. Over the centuries Arequipeños have never stopped fearing Misti, even as they view it with great pride.[6]

Misti was the first volcano I climbed in Peru. In the summer of 1980 I joined a team of Argentine climbers led by one of the pioneers of high-altitude archaeology, Antonio Beorchia. Antonio had tried to obtain Carlos Zárate, Sr., as a guide, since his team included members with little climbing experience. Carlos was not available, however, so he sent his young son, Miki, to assist the group. It was the first time we had met and Misti would be the first of several climbs we were to make together.

As the group had wound its way slowly up the slope, I went on ahead and stopped at the foot of the gigantic cross that marks the highest point of the summit ridge. Misti has two concentric craters, the diameter of the outer one spanning a thousand yards and the lower, inner one 1,800 feet. But neither the statistics nor the pictures I had seen of the crater prepared me for the view. A hundred years ago Solon Bailey, a Harvard astronomer, described his feelings when he first saw it: "We did not come to the crater; the crater came to us. The whole view was spread out before us in an instant as if a curtain had been drawn. The great altitude, the enormous craters, the sulphurous vapors, the drifting clouds, the deep shadows cast by the setting sun . . . combined to produce the profoundest sense of awe."[7]

I, too, had stood in awe of the spectacular panorama spread out before me. Not seeing anyone approaching, I wondered if I had gone to the wrong place. I decided to make a quick exploration of the area between the two crater rims, figuring that I would be visible inside the crater from anyplace Antonio's team reached.

The lower depression between the outer and inner rims is called today El Callejón del Diablo (Devil's Alley) by climbers. I measured some crude shelters that had been made by piling stones between boulders, but these appeared to have been built in recent times. As soon as I saw members of the team begin reaching the cross, I climbed back up to it. We descended as a group and surveyed ruins close to the rim of the interior crater.

In July 1980 I had seen sites only on the summits of Licancabur and Paniri in Chile. Although those had been modest, consisting of a few structures and outlines of stones, they were well built compared to the ones on Misti. Simple lines of stones had been laid out to form the crude outlines of two oval and two rectangular-shaped "structures."[8] Even more disillusioning, many of the stones had been moved some distance away and used to spell out a climbing club's name, Grupo Puma.

The Spanish priest José de Acosta reported in the late 1500s that the remains of pre-Hispanic sacrifices had been seen on Misti. (He did not specifically name the volcano, but his description fits only Misti.) Although we inferred that they were located on the summit, we had no idea where. In 1677 a Spanish priest, Alvaro Melendez, climbed Misti to "exorcize the crater" after it had grown especially active and alarmed the population. He reported finding vestiges of a small stone structure and pieces of wood in the same area where we surveyed ruins. He thought this was where local inhabitants had made sacrifices before the Spanish conquered the Incas. Although others reported seeing ruins, not until 1937 did Enrique Rondón publish rough sketches of them.[9]

However, I did not feel certain that the ruins we surveyed predated the Spanish. In the late 1500s they had begun extracting sulfur (a practice continued into the 20th century) from the crater bottom, and the ruins were located at the sole point of access into it. Only by excavating the ruins could we establish their provenance. Antonio pointed out another strike against the site being Inca. "These are the first ruins I have seen on a mountain summit that has no view." They simply did not fit the pattern of other Inca ceremonial sites.

In August 1998 my small five-member team was now to go to the summit, mainly to acclimatize ourselves for Sara Sara. We would search for sites that might have been missed in the past, but on such a popular mountain I doubted that we would find anything of interest.

I was able to gather three of my old teammates—Orlando, Ruddy, and Arcadio. José was unable to join us, but we gained a new addition to the team. Constanza Ceruti, a 25-year-old archaeologist, had come from Argentina. She had written me a few times previously, asking to join one of my expeditions. I had been hesitant to encourage a young woman I did not know to come from so far away. Expeditions were always iffy due to many factors, such as weather, and I couldn't in good conscience ask her to pay all her expenses out of her own pocket. On the other hand, my funds were also limited, and I thought they should go to Peruvians. Finally, I was concerned that she might have only a passing interest in this rather extreme kind of work.

However, by 1998 she had amply demonstrated that she had a serious interest in high-altitude archaeology. Since her first mountaineering ascent in 1996, she had climbed more than 40 peaks in her search for high-altitude ruins and published several articles about them. She had not yet conducted excavations on any of the summits, though, and she wanted to learn more about equipment and techniques that she might be able to apply to her work in Argentina. She also hoped that this would count as graduate course work for her university.

Until now she had focused on climbing volcanoes in northwest Argentina, which is where Llullaillaco is located. Although she had not scaled it, she had climbed Quehuar, the volcano I planned to use as a training climb before attempting Llullaillaco. It seemed to me an ideal opportunity to work together on a peak in Peru before I continued with research in Argentina.

Constanza had followed my career and even repeated dozens of my climbs. She recalled that as a nine-year-old she had seen a film about the Andes, which showed archaeology in the mountains and diving in Lake Titicaca. She did not remember that I had been part of that film, but she had been fascinated by it. In 1987 she saw a photograph next to an announcement of my winning the Rolex Award for my work in the Andes. Beneath the photo was the caption "Would you dare to follow in his footsteps?" "In that moment I knew the question was for me," she later wrote. "This mixture of vocation and challenge disturbed my sleep at the time."

My 1992 NATIONAL GEOGRAPHIC article "Sacred Peaks of the Andes" had an especially powerful impact on her.[10] She read it just as she was entering the university, and she began searching for everything she could find on the subject. Although raised in the city and know-ing nothing about mountains, she already thought about becoming a high-altitude archaeologist. Once at the University of Buenos Aires, she set out with a single-minded determination to do just that. After she had climbed her first mountain in 1996, she knew that she had made the right career choice.

It was a pleasure to have on the team a person who so completely shared my passion for the topic—certainly it was rare enough in high-altitude archaeology. Although José and Dr. Schobinger (Constanza's thesis supervisor) had made important contributions to the field, both had other specialties, and the number of "full-time" high-altitude archaeologists numbered, thanks now to Constanza, precisely two. I hoped that after her experience on Misti, she would begin undertaking excavations at mountain sites in Argentina. More archaeologists had to become involved if the finds at these unique sites were to be saved from permanent destruction by looters.

On August 25 we left Arequipa and drove to the reservoir of Aguada Blanca, where guards protecting Arequipa's water supply checked our papers. Once allowed through the gate, we continued on a dirt road until it dead-ended at 13,000 feet. From there we trekked a few hours and set up a temporary base camp on the northern slope of Misti. We camped near a trail used by climbers that had become the standard climbing route. The next day we carried and cached supplies near the summit, and by August 27 we were camped inside the crater.

At the bottom of Misti's central crater is a lava dome pockmarked with fumaroles, vents that emit small clouds of sulfurous gas. We set up our camp in Devil's Alley, the depression between the outer and inner rims. Although less exposed than the summit, wind still swept along it, and we had to place our tents behind boulders for protection. We were relieved to see some ice on a nearby slope that we could use to make water.

The stone alignments that we had surveyed 18 years before were located close to the edge of the inner crater rim. Looters had left open holes in a few places, but other areas appeared undisturbed. I decided to make two small test excavations to see if there was anything that might help us identify who built the site.

Almost immediately we uncovered fragments of spondylus llama figurines, presumably broken when the site was looted. At first I was disappointed, since it looked as if treasure hunters might have dug up even the "untouched" areas. However, soon we uncovered intact miniature llamas of gold and silver. There was now no doubt that the site had been built by the Incas.

We had not brought much food, since we expected to return to the city the next day, August 29. No matter what happened, I had to return by August 31 for the inauguration of the museum. Catholic University had built a new one to exhibit the Ice Maiden and our other finds. Although we only had a little pasta, some bread, and one hot dog for the five of us, that would be enough for us to stay for one more day.

I tested the walkie-talkie and found that I could communicate with José at Catholic University more than 12 miles away—at least as long as we remained in line of sight. As a result, I was able to have him change the day we were to be picked up.

The sun lit our tents at 7:45 the next morning, but by the time ice had been melted for water and we had eaten, it was ten o'clock. Constanza and Ruddy completed making a plan of the site, while Arcadio, Orlando, and I continued with the previous day's excavation. First, more llama figurines were uncovered, then a quartz projectile point and a few round stones. They must have been used for bolas, I surmised. Similar ones were found on the summit of a peak in Chile. I thought that they were offerings to increase success in hunting. Such items were rarely recovered from high-altitude sites, and I started to think that we were at the beginning of an excavation that would rank as one of our most interesting to date.

As if to underscore my thoughts, gold and silver statues, a shawl pin, and a couple of ceramic plates were uncovered in rapid succession. "There has to be a mummy here," Arcadio said, expressing a certainty that by now we all felt.

"Here it is!" he shouted only minutes later, as he removed volcanic ash from the top of a cranium. Amazingly, we had found a human sacrifice in situ on one of Peru's most visited volcanoes.

The dry, acidic soil meant that little would remain of the textiles and body tissue, but nonetheless we had made an important discovery. However, we were unprepared for conducting a full excavation and conserving the material, so I immediately stopped work. We put a protective cover over the finds and filled in the excavation. We had to return as quickly as possible with everything we needed.

When we began our ascent out of the inner crater the next day, we were surprised to observe a large number of climbers standing near the summit cross. "It looks like some club must have just made the climb," Arcadio said. Only after we drew nearer did we realize a Catholic mass was being held!

We happened to be there the one time of the year that a local priest climbs up with several of his parishioners to perform a ceremony on the summit. By a strange coincidence, we had found the remains of a sacred Inca ritual on the very day that they had started climbing the volcano. We joined the group to give our silent thanks.

Once we reached the base of Misti, we hid some tools we intended to use on our return. Our friend Gustavo Casos was waiting for us at the road with his van, and two hours later we were driving through the bustling city of Arequipa.

José and Ruth were in the midst of frantic preparations for the inauguration of the museum, aptly called the Museo Santuarios Andinos (Andean Sanctuaries Museum). Many of the artifacts were not placed into their display cases until just hours before the opening. The main attraction was, of course, the Ice Maiden, but also featured were several rare artifacts, including the statues and the blue tunic that had been beautifully restored by the textile specialist Vuka Roussakis. Unbeknownst to the dignitaries gathered on the evening of the opening, we were already imagining a special room devoted to the finds we hoped to make on Misti.

We decided to keep the discovery of the burial quiet, in order to prevent treasure hunters from reaching it ahead of us and to avoid, as much as possible, local climbers from bothering us while we were excavating. We had no idea how extensive the site would prove to be, and we did not know how much work we would be able to complete this season.

We returned to Misti September 5 with a full, well-equipped team. In addition to the five from the first climb, José, Walter Diaz, Ignacio, and Edgar joined us. We reached the base camp called Monte Blanco (15,699 feet) with heavy loads in less than three hours from the road. We wanted the least acclimatized team members to spend the night at the road and bring up supplies the next day. Those of us already acclimatized would stay the first night at the base camp. Constanza and I would then ascend to the ruins and remain there to remove the backfill, while Ruddy and Orlando would make a carry, returning that night to the camp. That way we could accomplish work at all levels on the mountain while at the same time acclimatizing the different team members.

We had been assailed by strong winds when we trekked up to base camp, and they grew worse the next day as we climbed to the summit. When we reached the exposed ridge, I was afraid that Constanza, with her small size and weight, might literally be blown off. The wind was blowing steadily about 50 mph, and it gusted to much more. The wind chill made it bitterly cold, and the wind sucked the air from our lungs, making it difficult to breathe. I began having coughing fits that I would not shake for the rest of my stay on Misti.

Orlando and Ruddy were carrying the tents, and they had left after us. Originally, Constanza and I had planned to meet them on the summit and carry their loads down into the Devil's Alley to make our camp. But after waiting a half hour exposed to the wind, we decided we had better go down inside the crater before we froze. Devil's Alley turned out to have a strong wind swirling through it as well. We prepared a bivouac behind a boulder in case Orlando and Ruddy were driven back.

When they still had not arrived by six o'clock, we began to think they must have turned around. Just as darkness fell, they appeared, and we were able to set up two tents in the dark. Ruddy wanted to stay, but we did not have enough water, nor did they have insulated pads or sleeping bags. Although the descent would be unpleasant, they could return to base camp in an hour. There they would have water, a decent meal, and a good night's sleep—none of which they would get if they stayed. So once the full moon had risen high enough, they started back without even needing to use their headlamps.

The wind had died down only slightly when Constanza and I began removing the dirt fill the next morning. Little whirlwinds kept spraying us with dust. In the afternoon some of the team literally dropped in. They had found a more direct route and rappelled off the crater rim, thus avoiding the summit entirely. To our relief, they also brought water, and we added to it by melting snow.

Once the backfill had been removed, we began finding more llama figurines made of gold, silver, and spondylus shell. "This is a regular llama zoo," said José. Over the next few days we excavated around the human sacrifice. The bones were fragile, and we decided to take them back in a block. However, the volcanic soil was soft, so how would we be able to pull this off?

"We can re-create the conditions we've found at other mountaintop sites," reasoned José. "If we pour water on the soil around the bones when it's cold during the night, that should freeze them into a block. We can cover it during the day when the sun is out."

Once the block was freed, we placed it amid boulders where the sun never shone and covered it with snow. Normally our problem was to ensure that a mummy remained frozen after we had uncovered it. The irony of having to cause a human sacrifice to be frozen at more than 19,000 feet was not lost on us.

Conditions were special inside Misti's crater. The average annual temperature on Misti is listed as 18°F. However, that disguises the fact that it can get quite warm inside the crater, especially when the sun is high. Misti is dominated by a freeze-thaw regime that occurs most days of the year. In this type of weather, sometimes called "perpetual spring," the sun daily melts the previous night's frost.[11]

Arcadio was interested in traditional beliefs, and especially those of the Incas. After all, he had been raised in a culture that shared many of the same concepts and even customs with them. One concept concerned their beliefs in the stars. In the thin atmosphere they lit up the sky, a familiar sight when in the mountains. However, from inside a crater, its sides seem to frame the sky, drawing special attention to it.

One night we were talking outside the tents, and someone commented on the clarity of the stars. I knew a smattering of traditional Andean beliefs, thanks to a friend's ground-breaking research on Inca and Quechua astronomy.[12] "Were you taught anything about the constellations when you were growing up?" I asked Arcadio.

"Not much. I know the Milky Way is believed to be a celestial river and that some of the constellations represent animals, but I've forgotten a lot of what I heard as a child." He gave me a quizzical look. "Tell me what you have learned about Inca beliefs."

I told him my friend Gary Urton had found that villagers near Cuzco distinguish between two types of constellations, which he called Star-to-Star and Dark Cloud constellations. The Dark Cloud constellations are the black areas that show up in the part of the Milky Way where there is the densest clustering of stars. These constellations were believed to mainly represent animals.

"I know about the llama," Arcadio said. He was referring to the Dark Cloud constellation of the Llama, whose "eyes" are the stars Alpha and Beta Centaurus next to the Southern Cross. He had heard that the celestial llama assists in the circulation of the earth's waters and the fertility of llamas.

Arcadio knew that the Star-to-Star constellations are like the ones in Western astrology. Among the Quechua, they link stars to form zoomorphic, geometrical, and even "architectural" figures along or near the main path of the Milky Way. For example, Gary described a star constellation called "the Serpent that is changing into the Condor." Serpents are, as they were in Inca times, associated with water in Andean beliefs. They can transform themselves into rivers and lightning, which are controlled by mountain deities. Condors, which soar around the highest slopes of the mountains, are widely thought to be the representations of the mountain gods.

"The Incas were very wise: for them everything in nature fit together, everything was in harmony," said Arcadio.

The high camp was luxurious by our normal standards. We had our mess tent set up in a protected place. For the first time we had relative accessibility to the outside world. We established specific times to talk using walkie-talkies, and we ordered supplies sent out in Gustavo's van. These were then picked up and carried to the summit. Since driving to the base of the mountain took only a couple of hours, the supplies—cookies, donuts, chocolates, fried chicken— could reach our summit camp the same day. Before long we had stacked a pile of pizza boxes off to one side of the mess tent.

Our eating so well on a mountain was mainly thanks to the efforts of Edgar. He enjoyed spending the night at the lower altitude of the Monte Blanco base camp, so named because it is nearly the same altitude as Mount Blanc in the Alps. Edgar started from it to climb the mountain on an almost daily basis. He even did it twice on some days, and he routinely hung around until nearly dark to help out with the excavations. By the end, he had climbed Misti 19 times in 23 days! Given how hard the other Mamanis, Arcadio and Ignacio, also worked, I began to call them collectively "the Mamani Machine."

We were not without entertainment (aside from the nightly joke sessions). Commercial jets sometimes flew directly over us, and a couple of times tipped their wings or blinked their lights to signal hello. We also had radios and, being so close to Arequipa, could listen to FM stereo and keep up on the news and music. Newspapers came with the pizza. The Starr Report, Mark McGuire hitting his 62nd home run, even news reports of ourselves supposedly suffering from the weather—we missed nothing. Well, almost nothing.

All the luxury could not mask one major problem—water. The snow had a markedly sulfurous taste, and filtering had little effect on it. José had brought up pH strips to test the acidity of the water, and the results made some of the team resist drinking it as much as possible. "The pH reading is 2.5," he said with a grin, as if I knew what that meant.

"Why is that important?" I asked.

"Well, 7.0 is pure water and 0 is pure acid," he replied.

Sulfur pervaded the atmosphere inside the crater. In the early mornings, tiny fumaroles gave off clouds on the crater rim above us, accompanied by the strong rotten-egg smell of sulfurous gas. It fulfilled our images of hell, lacking only heat to complete the picture. The team began calling the campsite "Concentration Camp Reinhard," humorously providing scenarios of me having men thrown into the lava dome for minor infractions.

A source of some amusement (then anger when it ate our salami) was a mouse. "It must hold the high-altitude climbing record among its kin," joked Orlando. Now we knew that not all the dead mice we had found at mountain sites had been offerings, such as some scholars had thought. They must have followed up the Incas (and later modern-day climbers) in search for food.

We continued to excavate a large number of artifacts. Most spectacular among them was a ten-inch male statue. It was nearly the same size as the one we had found on Pichu Pichu, becoming another of the largest Inca statutes to have survived the Spanish conquest. More important finds remained to be uncovered, however.

The breakthrough came when José called me over and said, "Look at the change in the coloring of the soil. This burial must extend farther down."

He and his team continued digging before finally reaching the bottom of the burial 12 feet down. Clearly, the Incas intended to place the capacochas as deeply as conditions permitted. After the men had worked for a couple of hours another skeleton was uncovered. José carefully whisked away the soil and revealed the bones of what appeared to be a small child lying next to it. "This is probably a baby," he said. Based on the absence of female shawl pins and only masculine statues having been found in the burial, we thought the skeletons were of males. They must have sacrificed the child and older person, covered them and then made a third sacrifice above them later.

While the excavation continued at this spot, others were undertaken nearby, and soon Orlando uncovered the burial of a female. This sacrifice featured a greater variety of pottery than the male burials, but what most distinguished it were the shawl pins, the female statutes, and the lack of llama figurines—unlike the male burials. Before long the skeletal remains of another adult and baby were uncovered.

This pattern of human sacrifices had never been described before. I knew of only a local legend of a man, a woman, and a baby being sacrificed in ancient times in the Colca Canyon. Yet here on Misti the Incas had dug down 12 feet to fashion two symmetrical burials of what we felt certain were three males and three females, including the babies, along with offering assemblages distinctive to each gender. We could not be certain if they had all been buried at the same time, although it seemed to make more sense for the lower burials to have been made at one time and the upper ones later.

Could the females all have been related, especially the babies and adults with whom they were buried? For that matter, could the males and females have been related, perhaps even members of the same family? Unfortunately, acidic soil is especially damaging to DNA, and we might not be able to obtain results that would help establish relationships between the victims. Bone contains a calcium-based mineral, hydroxyapatite, which helps protect the DNA from decaying by keeping out the bacteria and fungi.[3] However, calcium is alkaline and does not survive well in acidic soils. Ironically, both dry volcanic soils and wet bogs are poor sources of bones with DNA because of their acidity.

Heat adds to the problem, by helping organic molecules break down. Furthermore, Misti's fluctuations between warm and cold could have caused more damage than heat alone. Thus any DNA recovered from the skeletons would likely be damaged, if not largely destroyed.

The discovery of a large number of llama figurines suggested that the fertility of herds was an important reason for the capacocha offerings. The eruption of a volcano was known to destroy pasturage, and this fits with the hypothesis that the offerings had been made following such an event. "The offerings are either on top of a layer of dark ash, which is a marker of an eruption, or intrude through it," José pointed out.

"The placement of the structures inside the crater supports volcano worship," I said. "They are directly above the lava dome, rather than on the highest point of the summit. They also don't align with the cardinal directions or solstices, which you would expect if they were made for the Sun."

The description by the Spanish priest Martin de Murúa in 1590 is also suggestive: He noted that the Inca emperor offered a large quantity of llamas to Misti to forestall its eruptions. Although in and of themselves the finds with the females did not support this observation, the parallels between the two burial assemblages indicate that they had been paired offerings.

The location of the site, the importance of the offerings, the numerous llama figurines, and the evidence of a volcanic eruption give credence to the legend described by Murúa.[14] He wrote that when the Incas could go no farther due to the heat and the quantity of ash, the Inca emperor stood on his litter and used a sling to throw offerings. These were clay balls saturated with the blood from sacrificial animals, meant to break open when they hit. If the story has a factual basis, the best place from which to throw offerings into the lava dome would have been from the edge of the crater rim adjacent to the structures in which the Incas had buried the most important of all their offerings—human sacrifices.

José had to leave the expedition for a few days to tend to business in Arequipa, so we arranged for a vehicle to transport him, along with one of the mummy "blocks." He would organize the freezers that we would need when we returned with the other remains. Although the block did not include the weight of a frozen body, it was heavy from the mix of ice and dirt. Once again the Mamani Machine took over the job of carrying it down. I liked the symbolism involved. These men were not only indigenous to the region, but also respectful of local traditions. When the mummy was removed, Arcadio made an offering that included a llama's fetus.

The team worked extremely well under the circumstances. People experienced occasional illness, but nothing that didn't clear up after a few days. Walter, a great joker, would do a wicked impersonation of my coughing fits, much to the amusement of all. However, as days turned into weeks, tempers began to fray. Walter argued with Ruddy and later with Constanza over insignificant work issues, and even José became unusually upset once with Orlando when he made a mistake in shoring up the walls in one of the excavations.

We had been working without a break for weeks, and I was actually relieved when new excavations we undertook proved less productive than the original ones. For example, we spent a considerable amount of effort digging a site on top of the crater rim within view of Arequipa but found only a few pieces of straw, wood, hair, and carbon. We also excavated some of the holes made by looters to see if they might have missed anything. They hadn't.

We had seen climbers reach the summit cross on a few occasions, but none had visited us during the first two weeks we were camped in the crater. One day we spotted a lone climber on the rim not far above us. To reach this position, he would have had to go far out of his way. Some of the team expressed concerns about a band of climber-thieves holding us up and stealing our finds. I strongly doubted it, but the possibility could not be dismissed out of hand. We knew that rumors were spreading about us having found "treasure," and our situation made us vulnerable.

On September 19 our isolation came to an end. Climbers who worked at the borax mine near Pichu Pichu dropped into the crater to meet us. Having been fairly isolated for weeks as well, they hadn't even heard about our expedition. "We were surprised when we looked down from the summit cross and saw the large group of tents below," one of them told us.

The very next day four more climbers reached us. This group had deliberately come to see us after reading about us in the papers. Then four Peruvian volcanologists came to study the fumaroles and stayed a night. Although we enjoyed the chance to talk with new people, it also felt somehow like an intrusion. José firmly discouraged the visitors from taking photos of our work.

Arnaldo Ramos, an archaeological supervisor sent by the INC, arrived on September 20. He had acclimatized well and proved to be a welcome addition to the team. He assisted with the excavations and served as an independent witness to our work and finds. His only failing was in bringing an air mattress, not realizing that it provided no insulation against the cold—rather the reverse. Fortunately, José had a spare insulated pad.

The satellite phone wasn't working well, so newspaper correspondents in Arequipa interviewed us using our walkie-talkies. Once again we had to walk the tightrope of not divulging too much information before the news conference that we had planned.

After two hard days of backfilling the excavations and burning and burying garbage, the team wanted a farewell treat. To most people a descent into an active crater would not seem like a "treat," but these clearly were not ordinary people. I stayed above filming them—praying nothing would happen—while they descended to the smoking lava dome 600 feet below. I was initially concerned about the fumes, since people have been known to pass out while investigating fumaroles.

My concern increased when I watched some of the men make their way out among the fumaroles in the center of the lava dome. I remembered what had happened to a friend of mine who had once been walking among geysers in northern Chile. The ground gave way and the skin of his legs had been instantly burned off. Yet the wind and distance prevented them from hearing me when I shouted a warning. I was able to relax again only when they started back up.

By the next day we had carried everything off the mountain. Someone had brought a scale, prompting much wisecracking while they weighed their immense loads. At 60 pounds I was carrying the lightest pack. That same night we reached Arequipa and had the unusual experience of sleeping in comfortable beds. For some reason, I thought I could still smell sulfur.

The expedition resulted in the discovery of six Inca human sacrifices and 47 statues—the most ever found at a single site. These finds were made during nearly a month's stay at 19,000 feet.[15] As extraordinary as this discovery was, however, it was destined to serve merely as a prelude to the wonders that awaited us later that season. On the remote mountain of Llullaillaco, we were to find more than I had ever dreamed of.

Constanza Ceruti, left, and Arcadio Mamani clear the soil around the headless
mummy found on Quehuar.

CHAPTER TEN

QUEHUAR'S HEADLESS MUMMY

*An adventure is simply physical and emotional discomfort
recollected in tranquility.*
—TIM CAHILL

*In this cordillera are many of these huacas [sacred objects]
placed in volcanoes and snow mountains.*
—CRISTÓBAL DE ALBORNOZ, DESCRIBING IN 1583
HUACAS NEEDING TO BE DESTROYED IN THE SOUTHERN ANDES

THE MISTI EXPEDITION HAD SUCCEEDED BEYOND ALL EXPECTATIONS,
but it is was only one of the four mountains I had included in my proposal to the National Geographic. I had originally expected that our
work on Misti and Sara Sara would be finished by early October, but
our long stay on Misti had thrown off that schedule. Now I had
other commitments that kept me occupied until the rainy season
began in Peru. Sara Sara would have to wait until next year. However,
the climbing season in Argentina came later, and we could excavate
sites on the two remaining peaks on my list—Quehuar and Llullaillaco.
Experienced climbers would be essential if we were to successfully
excavate ruins at 22,100 feet on Llullaillaco. I began thinking we had
a good chance only when seven members of the Peru team agreed to
join the expedition. José, Jimmy, Orlando, Ruddy, and the three
Mamanis—Arcadio, Ignacio, and Edgar—made the core of a strong
team. Unfortunately, José knew he could not remain for the entire
period because of his responsibilities in Peru. He had to help prepare
the Ice Maiden's upcoming exhibition in Lima, and immediately

after that he had to leave for a year's stay with her while she was exhibited in Japan.

José and I had been in touch with the director of Salta's Cultural Patrimony Department, Mario Lazarovich, for several months. Mario's office issued permits for archaeological work in the Argentine province, and he kindly offered to assist us in obtaining one. Mario and Salta archaeology student Christian Vitry had established a group devoted to researching and protecting high-altitude archaeological sites. They named it the Center for the Conservation of High-Altitude Patrimony (Centro para la Conservación del Patrimonio de Alta Montaña, or CECOPAM), and one of its members was Constanza Ceruti. Since so few people had conducted high-altitude research, the Center was naturally a small one. Nonetheless, it was organizing the first conference dedicated solely to high-altitude archaeology and they invited me to attend. By coincidence, the conference was scheduled for early April 1999—when I estimated that we would be finishing our expeditions to Quehuar and Llullaillaco.

Since José was co-director of the expedition, he was able to obtain leave from his university to work in a different country. I hesitated at first to name a non-Argentine as a co-director, but Mario was receptive to the notion. Indeed, he seemed to like the idea of an international expedition: part Argentine, Peruvian, and American. At the same time, the National Geographic was debating how much to be involved. It eventually decided not to incur the expense of a film crew for a project so unsure of success, but they did send one of America's top mountaineering photographers, Gordon Wiltsie, who was to accompany us for the Llullaillaco part of the expedition. Although I did not know Gordon personally, we had mutual friends, and I had heard glowing reports about him.

After having worked so well on Misti, Constanza Ceruti was a natural choice for the team. That gave us an experienced core of nine, and I hoped to find other Argentine climbers and archaeologists to participate. This did not prove to be easy. Few men or women could devote the two months that I had estimated for both of the expeditions. Two potential team members, Christian Vitry and Adriana Escobar, decided to allot their two weeks of free time for the more challenging of the mountains, Llullaillaco.

Thanks to the National Geographic's support, I had just enough funding to cover the expenses of everyone participating on the expedition and salaries for those who stayed to work on the summits. This meant mainly the Peruvians, but that seemed to me only fair given their experience and their willingness to leave their families to come nearly a thousand miles to Salta. As usual, I received no salary, and Constanza also refused one, because she had a grant from Argentina's National Counsel of Scientific and Technological Investigations (Consejo Nacional de Investigaciones Científicas y Técnicas, or CONICET).

Nonetheless, little money would be left over for conservation of any materials we might find, and this was one reason I wanted to find a local institution willing to shoulder this responsibility before we left for the mountains. Salta is home to two major universities: the National University of Salta (Universidad Nacional de Salta or UNSA), a public one, and Catholic University, which is private. As might be expected, an intense rivalry exists between them. I had heard that if the expedition were conducted under the auspices of one university, members of the other would not participate. But one of my goals was to build the core of a team, similar to the one in Arequipa, that could continue research on high altitude sites after I was gone. Constanza was closely allied to Catholic University and lobbied for the expedition to be affiliated with it, but Mario and Christian were associated with UNSA. In the end I decided to keep the expedition independent of both universities so that students from either university would be free to participate. This was to prove a major mistake.

Salta has been called the best-preserved colonial city in Argentina. In a way it parallels Arequipa's position in Peru, having one of South America's most picturesque plazas, while serving as a base for visitors to see volcanoes, scenic canyons, and pre-Hispanic ruins. Its situation in the lush Lerma Valley at 4,000 feet allowed the Spaniards to grow crops and pasture animals here that helped maintain the mining industry located in the cold and barren highlands. Although the great mule trains no longer head out to the mountains as in the past, agriculture still plays an important role in the province's economy. The region was well populated in pre-Hispanic times and even has one of the densest collections of Inca sites to be found outside of Peru.

When I reached Salta on January 31, it was the heart of the South American summer and the weather was hot and humid. My previous visits had left me with the impression that it had a more temperate climate. I especially felt the heat because I was loaded down with equipment—so much that I wondered what the reaction of Argentine customs officials would be. In addition to bringing more camping and climbing equipment (donated by North Face) than I could possibly use personally, I had two digital video cameras, two satellite phones, four walkie-talkies, three cameras, and two high-tech computers. In short, I looked more like a marketing representative than a mountain climber. Much to my relief, I was waved through customs without a hitch.

I met with Constanza and the Peruvian team at the Residencial San Jorge, a pleasant hostel run by Constanza's friends Nené and Jorge. José and Arcadio had done a terrific job of organizing the gear and having everything carefully labeled and transported by bus to Argentina.

After the Peruvians left to buy supplies, Constanza and I went over a number of issues, including her designation as co-director. Mario had said that I did not need to name an Argentine co-director and this would also help avoid potential problems between the universities. However, Constanza was the only full-time high-altitude archaeologist in Argentina, and Salta province had been a central area of her research. As long as the expedition could remain independent, it made sense for her to be named as a co-director, so I revised the proposal and resubmitted it to Mario the next day.

I also wanted to meet with officials from the two universities. Unfortunately, this was vacation time, and Mario had been unable to reach archaeologists at UNSA. Although the university did have an archaeology department, it had only two full-time staff archaeologists and neither was interested in high-altitude archaeology. With no one available to meet at UNSA, José, Constanza, and I visited one of the heads of Catholic University, Dr. Miguel Escudero, who assured us of his university's support.

Meanwhile, we assembled the Argentine members of the expedition. Alejandro Lewis, a student in tourism and anthropology, had been on an expedition with Constanza, where he had proven to be a strong climber. Mario asked that we take Antonio Mercado and Federico Viveros, archaeology students at UNSA. Neither Tony nor Federico had ever climbed a mountain, and none of the three had excavated a mountaintop site. But they were all eager to participate, and I hoped that they would eventually form part of a permanent high-altitude archaeology team in Salta.

Their inexperience reinforced my desire to climb a lesser mountain as a warm up for Llullaillaco. To get in shape, acclimatize, test gear, and have the team accustomed to working together, I had selected Quehuar (20,111 feet) in my original proposal. It is located in northwest Argentina in the same general region (hence climate) as Llullaillaco. I did not feel we would find anything of importance, but I was interested in the volcano because it had a rare structure on its summit. The ruin contained the only example of a classic Inca ceremonial platform (ushnu) at high altitude that I knew of—one of the few to have escaped destruction following the Spanish conquest.

Antonio Beorchia had led a team that made the first survey of the ruins in 1974. Buried inside in a large oval structure near the ushnu, they uncovered part of a mummy bundle containing the body of a child completely encased in ice. They could see only the upper part, but it was enough for them to see, with a shock, that the body had no head. They discovered that looters had used dynamite to loosen the frozen ground and in the process blown off part of the mummy's torso.

Antonio was unable to free the rest of the body from the ice in the short time they were on the summit.

In 1981 Antonio had organized another expedition to recover the mummy bundle, and he invited me to join it.[1] Unfortunately, a storm covered the ruins in five feet of snow. While clearing it away, I found fragments of the cranium and even a piece of flesh embedded in the bottom of the wall close to where the body had last been seen.

"They must have been blasted into the wall by dynamite," I said to Antonio. "It looks like looters returned after you reported seeing the mummy in 1974." It began snowing and we stopped shoveling snow to examine the piece of flesh.

"That's an earlobe!" exclaimed Antonio. "The body must have originally been perfectly preserved." Treasure hunters had blown up one of the most valuable finds in the southern Andes. We left the mountain convinced that little, if anything, of importance remained to be found.

Before finalizing the expeditions in 1999, I had asked Mario if he knew of any indigenous groups in the city that I should talk with about our excavating sites on Quehuar and Llullaillaco. "Relatively few descendents of the province's original inhabitants live in Salta, and they haven't organized institutions to represent them," Mario explained. "Indigenous groups here have never raised objections to archaeological work," he added. He should know, I thought, as he is the director of cultural patrimony and oversees the issuing of permits for excavations. This would prove to be another mistake.

In any event, the city of Salta lies far distant from both mountains, and it seemed to me that the key thing was to have the support of indigenous communities located closer to them. In such a desolate region, these were few, indeed. Mario had contacted the authorities in San Antonio de los Cobres, the center of the region in which the peaks were located, and the authorities there had offered to help us in any way they could. He had also sent word to men in Santa Rosa de los Pastos Grandes, the closest village to Quehuar. They agreed to have burros ready for us to help carry supplies to a base camp. It appeared that all the preparations had been made.

Only one small problem remained: We had no vehicles to take us to Pastos Grandes. Mario had been trying to obtain support from the army in the form of a couple of Unimogs, powerful all-terrain trucks. The military option proved a chimera, however, and we decided to simply take a regular bus to the town of San Antonio de los Cobres. It lay along our route to the mountain, and we were assured that we could rent trucks there to transport us the rest of the way. Since we would have to pass through this town on the way to Llullaillaco, we also hoped to leave some equipment stored there for later use.

David Roberts, one of America's premier writers on mountaineering, joined us in Salta. He had been assigned to do a story for *National Geographic Adventure*, a magazine that the Society had only recently started publishing. Some readers enjoyed this magazine even more than its parent one because it featured in-depth stories, placed less emphasis on photography, and, of course, focused on adventurous topics.

David and I had met in Banff at one of the annual Mountain Film Festivals. He took pride in being a writer who did not mince words. At the festival he had announced, "I know I have not done a good job if the person I am writing about is pleased with the result." Hmm, this could get interesting, I thought.

As luck would have it, David had been held up by a canceled flight, so Constanza and I stayed behind to accompany him. We would catch up with the team the next day.

The drive from Salta to San Antonio de los Cobres takes only about three hours, but the change of scenery could hardly be more dramatic. The road winds through a canyon called Quebrada del Toro, which provides a superb lesson in geology—a mini Grand Canyon with the advantage that you can drive through its center. Along the way is the important archaeological site of Tastil, a pre-Inca complex with ruins sprawled over several hillocks. Soon you emerge on the highlands with views of snow-capped volcanoes, including several higher than 20,000 feet. Running through the region is a tourist train, aptly named Tren de las Nubes (Train of the Clouds).

When we reached San Antonio de los Cobres, we met with Cosme Damián, the intendente, or local authority, of the region. He effusively offered to help and arranged for a vehicle to pick us up when we returned from the mountain. The team had already rented a truck and departed for Pastos Grandes. We continued on to the village, arriving amid a light rain in the afternoon. The village is 13,000 feet high, and spending the night there was an important step in acclimatization. One of the villagers, who had been our burro driver 18 years before, helped arrange the 16 burros we estimated we would need. By nightfall, we were ready to go.

Before we left the next morning, I gave a little speech about the importance of working as a team and focusing on a common goal. Our expedition included people of different nationalities who had never worked together, and I felt like a football coach giving a pep talk before the big game. I ended it by saying, "This is the first time in Argentina that a team will remain camped on a high mountain summit, and even if we find nothing, we can at least demonstrate that serious archaeology is possible." Corny, certainly, but it established a basic theme that I would draw upon frequently during the coming months.

The 16 burros were not assembled until 11 o'clock, and due to the lengthy process of loading 2,600 pounds of gear, we did not depart until 12:30. The late start did not concern me, because we would reach 15,000 feet in a few hours, and we did not want to exceed that altitude on the first day.

It rained during the first night, and it kept up in an on-off pattern the next day while we weaved our way to Quehuar. We followed a narrow valley toward the mountain and did not have a glimpse of Quehuar until two o'clock. Since I had been filming the expedition, Orlando and I climbed up a hillside and waited for the team to pass.

"I want to shoot the burros in a scene together with Quehuar," I told Orlando as I took the camcorder out of his pack.

A half hour later I had finished, and we started walking quickly to catch up with the others. We saw that the burros had stopped, and as we approached closer I realized to my horror that the men had begun to unload them. We had the burros for only the two days, and we had agreed that they would return after dropping off loads at a suitable site for a base camp. Both the burro driver and Constanza had estimated 2 ½ hours to reach one, so we had not been in a hurry. However, this place was too far from the mountain and too low to serve for a base camp.

Kicking myself for not having stuck closer with the team, I hurried forward to stop the unloading process. Once completed, we would be stuck there for the remainder of the expedition. "Damn it," I muttered to Orlando. "We will lose at least two days just ferrying loads closer to the mountain, and that will mean two days' fewer provisions." In all our discussions, I had stressed the need to set up base camp close to the mountain. We could always send men either up for snow or down for water, but it was much harder to ferry all the loads up to another site.

"Why are you unloading the burros here?" I asked the burro driver as I arrived, gasping for breath.

"Arcadio and Constanza thought this would be a good place because there is water," he said. "They have gone to see if there is another place higher up, but they thought the burros should remain here with the loads in case they couldn't find anything." He added, by way of explanation, "The burros are getting cold standing around. We have to head back today anyway, so we began unloading them."

I ordered them to load up again. As the weather began to deteriorate, I had the burro caravan start up a ridge. Eventually Arcadio appeared. He was apologetic once he realized what had happened, and reiterated what the burro driver had told me.

"But they would have been able to drop the loads off higher up and return here in any event," I said, exasperated with myself as well as him. My focus on filming had been partly responsible for what happened. I went ahead with the burros, afraid the burro drivers would stop if they were left on their own. As we neared the foot of the mountain, snow began to fall, limiting visibility and leaving me wondering how much longer we would be able to keep advancing.

Eventually we found a flat area that had a small spring nearby. It was ideal for a campsite. Once the burros were unloaded, they quickly headed back down the mountain—they knew they were heading back to pasturage and flowing water. As for us, we soon had the tents pitched and huddled inside them, out of the snowfall. At 16,500 feet we were now excellently positioned for carrying supplies up the mountain.

When we awoke the next morning, the usually barren rock was covered with a white blanket of snow. The team made carries to a cache at 17,700 feet, while I remained in camp to get things organized. That afternoon David was keen to interview me, as there had been little time before. Although he had made a carry and was tired, he joined me in my tent and started asking questions. I began by explaining my background and what had led me to become a high-altitude archaeologist.

After hearing about some of the experiences I had gone through over the years, he said, "This must be the toughest job in archaeology." I hadn't thought of it that way before, and visions of excavations in the Sahara and underwater ran through my mind. I had no idea that in less than two days we would live through an experience that would dramatically demonstrate his point.

The next day we ferried up equipment to leave on the summit. I filmed the team's progress, even capturing a rare corona, which I can only describe as a double upside-down rainbow. This occurs when a thin layer of cirriform clouds forms between the sun and the viewer. Because the ice crystals in such clouds are six-sided prisms, when the sun shines through a cirriform cloud, a colored ring is formed due to the diffraction of the light through the crystals.[2]

I knew this logically, but at a deeper level I felt as if I was walking under God's umbrella. The awe was only slightly marred by the realization that coronas usually foretell a change of weather, in this case an approaching snowstorm. But for now the sun was out, and we were actually hot from its reflection off the snow as we climbed. It had been a beautiful day, and the team descended to base camp in high spirits.

As expected, the good weather did not last. We arose to threatening clouds the next morning. Federico had injured his ankle and would not be able to climb that day. Tony's knee was bothering him and Ignacio had slight snow blindness, so they too decided to remain in camp. The rest of us set off with especially heavy loads, because we did not plan to return.

The weather worsened as we ascended, with occasional lightning and thunder in the distance, and it began to snow. We were unable to find a flat place to set up a high camp until we emerged on a little plateau just below the summit. We would be exposed to storms and lightning, but we had no alternative. In the end, we placed our tents in a large depression off to one side. David said to me, amid what had turned into a blizzard, "This is the hardest day that I have had in the last ten years."

Before we left Salta, I had had Arcadio search for metal poles and copper wire to make a lightning rod, which I had planned to place on a nearby high point above camp. I especially was worried about Llullaillaco, because I could not recall any flat area high on the volcano until on the summit itself—right where lightning would be most likely to strike. The concept of a lighting rod is simple enough: Mount a metal rod on a high point, attach a wire to it, and lead it down to another rod buried in the ground. That was a feasible plan for Llullaillaco, but I did not think there would be anyplace close enough on Quehuar for it to be of any use.

So we had decided to leave the rods and wire behind for the Quehuar expedition. Of course, no sooner did we start setting up the tents than the blizzard turned into a severe thunderstorm.

Sound travels a mile every five seconds, so by counting the seconds between a flash and thunderclap you know how close lightning has struck. Soon, no time at all separated the flashes and thunderclaps, which meant the strikes were hitting places less than a few hundred feet away. The sound was deafening. "It's like being in the middle of a bombing raid," I heard someone shout between booms.

Everyone threw their ice axes and other metallic gear into a pile at a slightly higher point, hoping that if any lightning came close, it would be attracted to the metal. We knew that if lightning actually struck the little pile, it would probably shoot electricity out into our tents. But it was psychologically important to do something. As it was, the electricity in the air caused a buzzing sound and our hair was charged. This was the worst lightning storm any of us had ever seen. The lightning strikes were so close that at times we thought they had actually hit somewhere in our camp. Sitting inside our tents, we could not see anything and could only wait—and hope. To our relief, the storm finally diminished until only a light snow was falling.

It was sunny and windless the next day, and we ended up suffering from the reflected heat while we organized camp. Several of us had badly burned lips because our sweat had washed off the sun block. I always have had a problem breathing through my nose in the mountains, but breathing with my mouth open had its disadvantages. I managed to get sunburned on my tongue, caused by the glare off the snow.

Some of the men dropped down to the supply cache and returned with more food. I tried to get the Nera Worldphone operating and receive emails, but there was some problem with it. Fortunately, Motorola had provided me with an Iridium satellite phone, though it could be used only for talking—not sending and receiving data. A part of me was relieved, since I had been dreading the time-consuming task of uploading images. At the incredibly slow rate of 2.8 kbps, it would take an hour to send only a few photos. Plus, not being able to receive emails had its advantages.

On February 11 we were ready to begin work at the summit ruins. David had not been sleeping well due to a cough, headache, and indigestion. We had known all along that he had other obligations and would have to cut short his stay. Now the time had come. He said, "This is one of the best assignments that I have been on in the past couple of decades." We were both disappointed that he had to leave just as we were to begin excavating the site.

Initially, the effort involved no more than removing snow, and gradually the ruins began to appear in their totality. I was happy to see that they had suffered no major damage since my last trip in 1981. I took compass bearings and noted to Constanza, "The ushnu platform is aligned to 114°. That's close to the December solstice sunrise."

"Yes, and that means it coincides with the best time to climb the mountain," she added, since the weather would be too severe for the Incas to hold a ceremony here at the June solstice, the other important date in the Inca religious calendar.

The day was warm, but after the sun went down we were quickly reminded that we were camped on snow at nearly 20,000 feet. The temperatures would plummet during the night, often reaching 0°F. Tony's boots froze solid one night, so I loaned him a spare pair that I had brought along for just such an emergency. David had kindly left his boots in base camp, and these also came in handy.

We cleared the circular ruin and began to excavate inside it to see if anything remained of the mummy that had been dynamited. Soon we were recovering pieces of a textile, blackened shards, fragments of wood and llama bones, maize grains, and so on strewn about due to the dynamite blast. We were excited to uncover a triangle of stones, but found nothing inside it. It appeared that looters had taken the mummy bundle, just as we had suspected in 1981.

Although they sometimes took turns, Tony, Arcadio, and Ruddy generally took measurements, while Constanza and José wrote them down. I had decided that all the measurements should be duplicated. Thus both the Peruvians and the Argentines would have a complete record of the excavation. This not only meant that if one set of data was lost, there would be another available but also meant that there was a check on the quality of the data being recorded.

Ignacio, Edgar, and Alejandro excavated in the circular structure, while Orlando and Jimmy began excavating a section of the ushnu platform. José, Constanza, and I oversaw the work, and I was especially occupied with photography and taking video footage of the excavation.

When we began work the next day, José said, "If we are going to find anything, we should soon, as we are close to reaching bedrock." The team excavating in the ushnu platform found remains of a sardine can and scraps of dynamite. I began to fear that the ruins had been so badly looted that no Inca artifacts remained.

Then the team uncovered a spondylus female statue with its textiles somewhat mangled, but still intact. "It looks like it got mixed up in the refuse the looters tossed aside," José observed. Although the statue turned out to be the only find of importance within the platform, we soon had more luck inside the circular structure.

I had noticed the distinctive musky, pungent smell of a mummy the day before, but I had thought that it was the remaining pieces of the one dynamited years before. Today, however, we found the cloth wrapping of a mummy bundle. We hoped it might belong to a second mummy, but we soon realized this was the bundle Antonio had seen in 1974. "We only missed it by inches in 1981," I said, recalling our disappointment at the time. José crouched down and closely examined the bundle. Finally he stood up and said, "Unfortunately, Beorchia was right about its head having been blown off. Worse, most of the upper torso was blown off as well."

A sad reminder of its fate was a tooth lying on top of the bundle and a torn and badly preserved plain cloth full of dirt—probably part of an outer covering that looters had not considered important enough to take. Despite the missing torso, the remainder of the mummy bundle looked intact. "Let's hope that when it was exposed to the sun on past occasions that the heat did not penetrate far into the body and cause it to decompose," I said. We would not know until we had a CT scan done. For now, we could only remove soil to free the mummy so we could get it to a laboratory.

Arcadio was digging around it, when suddenly he exclaimed, "It looks like there is another mummy!" Soon a second, smaller bundle was uncovered next to the main one. "Maybe it's a mummy of a baby," said Arcadio. Since it was slightly lower and to the side of the headless mummy, there was a good chance that it might be perfectly preserved, unlike the two baby skeletons we had found on Misti. "If this is a frozen Inca baby, it will be a first," said José, stating aloud the thought that had run through our minds the moment it was revealed.

Since the combined weight and bulk of the two bundles together would have been too much even for Arcadio, we spent the next few hours carefully using water to open a space between them.

In the meantime, Edgar and Alejandro descended to base camp to bring up more supplies. One of the burro drivers had brought us some meat from Pastos Grandes, and we were looking forward to a real meal for a change. For obvious reasons it is rare to have any fresh meat on expeditions. Soups, stews, bread, chocolate, and cheese constituted our usual fare. These suited the Mamanis, who were vegetarians and carried up heavy loads of vegetables to add to the fare. I could hardly believe they could keep up their energy over weeks spent in the mountains.

One morning Constanza came to my tent visibly upset. She had asked to copy some of the measurement data Tony had written down, and he had loaned her his notebook. He had used part of it as a diary, and Constanza had stumbled on what he had written about her. His words were so full of venom as to be truly disturbing. This created a dilemma, because Constanza did not want me to discuss this with him, since they were in the diary section of his notebook. Still, it was difficult to miss. "How could he give me this and not expect that I would see what he wrote?" she asked.

Tony had gotten along well with the rest of the team, and he had proven himself a hard worker and knowledgeable about archaeology.

However, he did have a chip on his shoulder, possibly due to his rough upbringing, and he still had a problem with authority, as he himself admitted. He had managed to overcome many obstacles to reach a point where he had nearly finished his university studies. On the other hand, Constanza came from a family of professionals in Buenos Aires, and from the beginning he saw her as having enjoyed a privileged upbringing. Worse, he was convinced that she had been acting in a brusque and authoritarian way toward him. (I couldn't help but notice that the faults he saw in Constanza were ones commonly attributed by Argentines to people from their capital city. There is a saying in Argentina: "God is everywhere, but he receives you in Buenos Aires.") It did not help that she was a more experienced mountaineer than he was, and, unlike him, she had already published extensively on archaeology. But I also realized that Tony's attitude was itself founded in the male-dominated society of northwestern Argentina. He was not alone in being sensitive toward women with strong personalities.[3]

We did not find anything else in the two structures, and we continued on with test excavations at the highest point of the summit. Yet we hit bedrock there without finding anything, and so it was time to wrap up things and leave.[4] I used the Iridium satellite phone to report our finds to Mario in Salta. "I've arranged for vehicles to meet you in Pastos Grandes, and we'll bring dry ice to help keep the mummy frozen during the return to Salta," he said. Then he added, "I think the mummy should go to UNSA."

So far Catholic University was the only institution willing to take on such a responsibility. "We should first have a meeting in Salta to see which university would best be able to care for it," I replied cautiously.

Tony went ahead to arrange for the burros to meet us at base camp. Once the equipment was loaded on them, we trekked back in the rain to Pastos Grandes. The people were celebrating Carnival and barely noticed the bedraggled people wearily walking through town.

Mario met us with military men driving a Unimog. He had

brought with him Christian Vitry and Dr. Juan Schobinger, who happened to be in Salta at the time. Juan had been at the forefront of high-altitude archaeology in Argentina since the mid-1960s. He had participated in the excavations of the mummies found on El Toro and Aconcagua, and it seemed only fitting that he be present for the recovery of the Quehuar mummy. We drove off amid rain and sleet, and on the afternoon of February 21 we reached Salta—and hot showers, good meals, and soft beds.

The next day Dr. Schobinger, Christian, Mario, José, Constanza, and I went to see Dr. Colombo, the rector of Catholic University. He repeated the university's offer to take over responsibility for the mummy. He completely agreed that a committee, including government and UNSA representatives, should be established to oversee conservation. Research would, of course, be open to all qualified scientists. We could not have asked for more.

Mario had a CT scan conducted at the hospital the evening of the 23rd. As at Johns Hopkins, we were scheduled after the doctors had finished with their patients. The CT scan was performed first on the smaller bundle, and we anxiously awaited the results. Would it contain a perfectly preserved mummy?

The data began materializing on the computer screen, and we strained our necks to look closer. It did not take long for the shapes to form. "It looks like there is a pot and something like a maize cob," one of the radiologists said. Other items appeared that we couldn't identify, but clearly the bundle did not contain a mummy.

"I confess I'm disappointed," I said. "But at least we can take some consolation from the fact that we found something unique. We have an untouched bundle with offerings, and they will provide valuable information of their own."

The bundle with the mummy was next placed on the CT scan, and now we would see if what remained of it was as well preserved as we hoped. On the one hand, the piece of flesh I had found in 1981 indicated that the mummy had been in exceptionally good condition at the time it was dynamited. But could its exposure have led to it becoming desiccated?

Once again we closely watched the computer screen while the mummy passed through the scanner. I couldn't distinguish much in the images of the body, and I waited expectantly for the radiologist to start pointing things out to us. Unfortunately, he wasn't able to make out much more than we could. He thought he could identify some of the internal organs, but said, "The sand and gravel must be mixed into the outer wrapping of textiles, making it difficult to decipher details."

Fortunately, enough was visible to show that the body was well preserved. However, we could not see any shawl pins, and this, together with Antonio Beorchia's description of a male tunic, led us to think that the mummy was a male. It would be several months before we had proof that it was a female.

Since the Quehuar mummy was frozen rock-hard inside an equally frozen layer of textiles, we knew that doing a needle biopsy would be extremely difficult. I decided to take a small piece of one of the vertebrae that had been left barely attached and exposed by the dynamite blast. Bone is not as good for obtaining DNA as tissue, but it can be used if well enough preserved.

Much later, on July 21, 2001, the offering bundle was carefully unwrapped by textile specialists Clara Abal and Luis Massa, assisted by Constanza.[5] The items recovered included two pairs of sandals, two small cloth bags, a pedestal pot (still containing the remains of cooked vegetables), one small jar, a pair of ceramic plates, one wooden plate and spoon, a comb, some charcoal, and food items (maize and chili). The girl had been buried with the basic provisions that she would need in the afterlife. Once we trace back the plants' DNA, we'll eventually be able to find out where the food came from.

We now had to determine which institution would take custody of the mummy. Christian arranged for a meeting at UNSA the next day, and he, Mario, Constanza, and I met with Dr. Graciela Lesino, jefe de investigaciones (chief of research), and the heads of the departments of geology and chemistry. Almost as soon as the introductions had been made, Dr. Lesino said, "We do not have the funds to take responsibility for the mummy." She reiterated this in different forms, making clear that UNSA could not assume the costs involved and did not have the facilities for storing one mummy, let alone any others that might be discovered. Nonetheless, she added, "We would like for our scientists to be involved in the research." We assured her that any qualified scientist was welcome. We left the meeting convinced that the basis for future collaboration had been established.[6]

Mario and Christian were silent as we drove back, since Catholic University now remained the only option. Mario himself had opposed a third alternative, the Anthropology Museum, both because of a lack of funds and the structural problems it had that resulted in it having high humidity. I thought that it was time to finalize the arrangement with Catholic University. We were leaving soon for Llullaillaco and might return with even more mummies. We had not even seen the military base where Mario said the Quehuar mummy was temporarily stored. Mario assured me that the mummy was being kept well frozen in a freezer, but I was concerned at its long-term conservation, and everyone agreed that its home could not be a military base. Yet Mario still did not make a final decision.

On February 24 I sent a letter to the governor, Dr. Juan Carlos Romero, expressing my support for the establishment of an independent foundation that would include representatives from the government and both universities. The idea was to ensure that conservation of the Quehuar mummy (along with any other mummies that might be found) would be shared between scientists and political appointees in coming years, since the latter would lack the necessary experience.

Having arranged matters as best I could, I turned my attention to Llullaillaco. Most of the team was in good condition, except for ailments such as swollen lips, sore fingers, and the like. Jimmy had a toothache and saw a dentist, while Constanza complained of her toes having suffered frost nip. A doctor examined them and thought they were fit enough for Llullaillaco. Ruddy had a potentially very serious problem—arrhythmia, or alteration in the rhythm of the heartbeat. It can be caused by several factors, and one of them is altitude. However, he was experiencing this condition at the low elevation of Salta. Fortunately, a cardiologist could not find anything wrong with his heart. The apparent cause of the arrhythmia was an infection in Ruddy's lungs, and he had to start a course of antibiotics.

With the exception of Francisco, we retained the same group that had explored Quehuar. Gordon Wiltsie, the photographer for the NATIONAL GEOGRAPHIC story, had arrived, while Christian Vitry and two other Salteños were also joining us. Adriana Escobar, an archaeology student at UNSA, had climbed with Constanza in the past. Mario's brother, Sergio Lazarovich, also had climbing experience.

Unfortunately, Christian, Sergio, and Adriana could not stay away from their jobs long enough to assist us on the summit. Even so, I thought that at least we were adding two Salta archaeologists who could form the core of a team in the future. They could work at the lower ruins while they were acclimatizing and other members of the team ferried loads up the mountain.

I was especially pleased that Adriana could participate. Besides helping with the archaeology, her presence would provide some support for Constanza, who would no longer be the lone female—at least for two weeks.

"We will need every experienced person we can get," I explained to the team when we met to finalize our preparations for our departure. José had returned to Peru, and no one had been added to the team who could work on the summit. Gordon would be doing photography for the magazine, while I hoped to concentrate on filming and photography. That left eight people to do most of the excavating, and Ruddy's arrhythmia made his participation doubtful.

I had learned that, as a general rule, at any one time a quarter of the team would be unable to work because of health problems. Over a lengthy period at 22,000 feet, I expected the percentage to be higher. While in the Himalayas, I had once spent 31 consecutive days at 22,000 feet, so I knew that it was possible to remain so long at this altitude. But I also knew that I had been lucky and couldn't count on that happening a second time. Most likely, only six people would be excavating the site, and that was a minimal number for work at that altitude. People would be taking turns, leaving only three active at any one time. The weather on Quehuar had not been good either, yet we would be more isolated and less able to get quickly off Llullaillaco in an emergency. I was especially concerned that at 22,000 feet the ground would be frozen, making the already difficult work even harder.

I explained all these factors to the assembled team and ended by telling them somberly, "This will be the most difficult expedition we have ever undertaken." Before I could say anything more, Arcadio interjected: "We just want to get out of the city and back on a mountain." And everyone laughed.

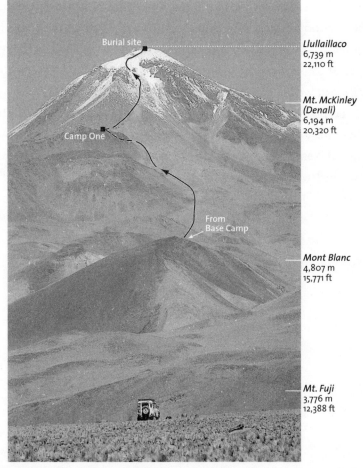

Burial site

Camp One

From
Base Camp

Llullaillaco
6,739 m
22,110 ft

**Mt. McKinley
(Denali)**
6,194 m
20,320 ft

Mont Blanc
4,807 m
15,771 ft

Mt. Fuji
3,776 m
12,388 ft

Our route to the summit of Llullaillaco is indicated on the photo, along with the altitudes of well-known mountains in the world to provide a sense of scale for the Incas' achievement.

CHAPTER ELEVEN

MOUNTAIN of DREAMS

*We shall not cease from exploration and the end of our exploring will be to
arrive where we started and know the place for the first time.*
—T. S. Eliot

*And it will be known that the things that the dead wore were as follows:
The women wore jewels and carried small jars full of chicha, bags with
coca, and pots full of roasted and cooked maize as well as plates, bowls,
jars, and tumblers of service.*
—Juan de Betanzos, 1551

During our expeditions to Llullaillaco in the early 1980s,
we had passed several well-built Inca structures at 17,000 feet and surveyed buildings with walls more than six feet high at a daunting 21,400
feet. As we struggled higher, one question kept repeating itself over
and over in my mind: had the Incas buried anything on the summit?
At 22,109 feet Llullaillaco has the world's highest archaeological site.
Five hundred years ago the Incas had built a road and way stations
for hundreds of miles through the world's most arid desert and
then constructed buildings at an altitude that would not even be reached
by others until 400 years later.[1]

If a human sacrifice had occurred at this altitude, it should be perfectly preserved, I reasoned. The discovery of such a mummy would
be of incalculable value to science—and to Argentina's cultural patrimony as well. It would be a powerful argument for the protection
of pre-Hispanic archaeological sites, an issue Argentine scientists
felt the government did not take seriously enough. The country's
archaeological heritage has been destroyed at an alarming rate due to

economic development and the looting of sites. We had seen in Peru how the discovery of a single frozen mummy had ramifications that went far beyond its inherent value. It had increased awareness among people throughout the country about the importance of preserving their cultural heritage.

Llullaillaco (pronounced yu-yai-YA-ko) is the seventh highest peak in the Americas and one of the world's highest volcanoes. Because it is so isolated, its first modern-day ascent was not made until 1952. The Chilean climbers Bión Gonzalez and Juan Harseim reached the summit only to discover, much to their surprise, that the Incas had been there centuries before them.

The volcano's name is probably derived from the Quechua words for "water" (llaco) and "lie" or "a thing that deceives" (llulla). This seemed an odd name until I looked at a map and realized that, despite its huge massif and permanent snow, no rivers extend far out from it. Men crossing the barren Atacama Desert must have indeed felt deceived when they passed the mountain and did not find flowing water. While crossing through this barren region, early Spanish explorers were told of a river named Ancha-llullac ("great liar") for much the same reason.[2] It would stop flowing during the night and only later did they realize this was caused by the river freezing higher in the mountains. As it turned out, we had to bring water to Llullaillaco with us as well.

Llullaillaco played tricks on us in other ways, especially due to its size and the clear desert air causing us to constantly underestimate distances. I still vividly recall an experience I had during my first expedition to Llullaillaco in 1983. I had been examining the interior of a building for several minutes, and my mind had adjusted to thinking I was in just another typical Inca ruin. When I squeezed through the doorway and stood up outside, however, I looked around me, and the magnificence of their achievement hit me in a way it never had before. I was standing at 22,000 feet and visibility extended more than 100 miles. The terrain swept down thousands of feet below. A sense of power swept over me simultaneously with a feeling of oneness with nature. At that moment I was convinced the Inca priests had experienced exactly the same emotion. I felt like I had walked through a warp in the time-space continuum. From that time on, I always thought of Llullaillaco as the mountain of my dreams.

In 1983 I had trekked to the volcano with three experienced mountaineers. One of them, Rob Blatherwick, was a much-decorated Vietnam Special Forces veteran and one of North America's strongest climbers. We had climbed together on a dozen peaks in 1982 and 1983, including expeditions to Paniri and Licancabur, where Rob and I had even scuba dived in lakes more than 19,000 feet high. Louis Glauser had joined me on several earlier mountaineering trips, and he had invited along Martin Erb, a Swiss climbing friend.

We had approached Llullaillaco from its western side, which lay over the border in Chile. Pat Burns, then director of the Escondida Mining Company, had helped us find our way through the maze of mining roads in the region, including a Chilean mine field that had been built at a time of tension between Chile and Argentina.

Antonio Beorchia had discovered a pre-Hispanic cemetery at the foot of the volcano. Although not Inca, it was still important because such sites are rare on high mountains. I wanted to see how it might fit into the broader picture I was putting together about high-altitude ruins. We spent a day searching for it without success. Eventually we made our way up the boulder-strewn northwestern slope to the summit. If the Incas had ever gone this way, no trace remained of their ascent.

No plan existed of the summit ruins, so our first goal was to survey them. Based on the borderline on the Chilean military's 1:50,000 map, most of the ruins were on the Argentine side, albeit only by a few dozen meters. The ruins leading up the mountain were also in Argentina, and this finding would affect my future expeditions.

On the summit was a metal box containing a notebook in which climbers recorded their names. To our amazement, after years without any ascents, a team had reached the summit only the day before—and we hadn't seen a sign of them.

Louis and I returned to Llullaillaco in 1984 to search for the cemetery, but this time we approached the volcano from the northeast. We drove south from Peru in Louis's old, much-abused Land Cruiser, aiming for a dirt track that led to the Socompa Pass between Chile and Argentina. The vehicle broke down when we were halfway there. Our prospects looked bleak. We were stranded in the middle of the world's driest desert, had not seen another vehicle the entire way, nor did we have any way to communicate with anyone. I began to estimate how long it would take us to walk more than 50 miles to the nearest settlement. "This road isn't traveled much, because no one, except for some bandit or homicidal fugitive, will go to so much trouble," wrote Reginaldo de Lizárraga in 1607.[3] Add climbers, and some things never change.

I am hopeless as an auto mechanic, but having had so many problems with his car over the years, Louis had almost turned into a pro. He took a section of the engine apart, and after several hours he had fixed the problem. As it became dark, we spotted an old mining camp. It was Christmas Eve, and we ended up sleeping on the floor of an empty building. We were grateful for the luxury of being out of the wind that had begun howling outside.

We obtained permission from the Argentine military post at Socompa Pass to enter Argentina. However, since it was not an official border crossing, we had to promise not to visit any town and to remain within a few miles of the border. As it turned out, military units were practicing maneuvers in the area. So we used the border post's radio to call the military commander in San Antonio de los Cobres and obtain his permission to climb the peak from the Argentine side. Unbeknownst to us, he neglected to inform his men in the field.

We navigated a way to the base of the mountain, and, after several false leads, we were able to drive to 16,000 feet. The next morning an Argentine military helicopter flew low over us. I assumed that they did not want to land at this altitude, and it was obvious they were not amused by our friendly waves. "What could be wrong?" I asked Louis. "They must know we have permission to be here."

We began our climb, and after reaching 18,000 feet, we stopped to watch as a Unimog materialized from one of the gorges below. They must have followed our car tracks. I peered through my binoculars and watched as armed soldiers gathered around our tent. Then two of them, still carrying rifles, started up after us. We waited awhile, until we realized that they were going too slow to reach us before nightfall. "Do you think we should go down to talk with them?" asked Louis. He was understandably concerned about what they might do to his vehicle, especially if they became convinced that we were Chilean spies. Tension still lingered along the border between the two countries. "If they decide to take anything, they will be long gone by the time we get there," I replied, all the while thinking it could be worse if they stayed. "We may as well keep going."

We started up again, and later we saw that the soldiers had turned back. By late afternoon, the Unimog was gone. We camped that night out of the wind amid rocks at more than 19,000 feet. The next day we surveyed a site at 21,600 feet that had been excavated by the renowned Austrian climber Mathias Rebitsch in 1958 and 1961. Finding a rusted pick near one of the ruins, I hid it out of sight from potential looters.

As we continued on to the summit ruins, we were surprised to see part of a retaining wall for a trail leading to them. We could hardly believe our eyes. We were looking at the world's highest road.

After checking the summit for any structures we might have missed in 1983, we descended toward base camp, wondering what the soldiers had done in our absence. On the way I noticed a trail leading off to the left, and we followed it to a dozen Inca structures at 17,200 feet. This was an untouched complex of ruins, clearly a tambo, located on the route the Incas had taken up the mountain. We had come across what had been the Incas' "base camp." We followed the trail for a ways below the tambo. Louis continued on along it, while I searched (unsuccessfully) for a possible connecting trail between the tambo and the cemetery.

Having taken a shorter route than Louis, I reached our base camp before him. I was relieved to see that nothing was missing from our tent, although the soldiers had certainly rifled through everything. More importantly, the Land Cruiser was fine.

Then I noticed their footprints leading off toward the mountain in a direction I knew we hadn't gone. Curious, I followed them until I came to the cemetery that we had been searching for. By chance, we had parked within a few minutes' walk of it. Unfortunately, looters had sacked the site and bones were strewn about everywhere.

A few months later Louis and I returned to search for the Inca trail we were convinced must lead to Llullaillaco from the north—the location of the closest Inca settlements. We found sections of the trail and surveyed ruins 15 miles distant from the volcano. I felt that I now knew where all the key sites were, both on the mountain and leading to it. I left Llullaillaco hoping to return within a couple of years and excavate the summit ruins. When funding failed to materialize, I began to doubt I would ever see the mountain again.

FOURTEEN YEARS AFTER I HAD LAST CLIMBED LLULLAILLACO, I WAS returning with a team to fulfill my dream. Given our numbers and the month's time we planned to remain in the field, we needed to transport more than a ton of supplies to the base of the mountain. This included fuel and even water, as none was available nearby.

We rented a Land Rover to have available in case of an emergency and to return Christian, Adriana, and Sergio to the city after their two-week stay with the expedition. Two Unimogs were supplied by the Argentine military. These vehicles proved to be a mixed blessing, as the cost of fuel was expensive and they were not in good condition. They averaged only 25 miles an hour on paved roads. We loaded them up and set off by noon. We had not even left the outskirts of Salta when one of the Unimogs had to return because of mechanical problems. A few team members went with it and hurriedly transferred the supplies to another Unimog. When it didn't show up, we called the military base, only to be informed that the replacement Unimog's oil pressure was low, and they had to transfer the supplies to yet another one! "At this rate, we'll go through all the army's Unimogs before we reach the mountain," Orlando wisecracked. At long last we made the three-hour drive to San Antonio de los Cobres, where we spent the night.

We drove through spectacular moonlike scenery the next day, but the Unimogs were so slow that we reached the railroad town of Tolar Grande only after seven o'clock that evening. We decided to stay the night there and start early the next day. While unloading the trucks, we discovered that gas had spilled from one of the barrels and soaked several people's personal items, including my sleeping bag and a large portion of the vegetables. "Just what I wanted—no vegetables and to go to sleep every night smelling gas," I grumbled, annoyed that no one had noticed the leak.

The next day we crossed a long stretch of flat salt desert—the Salar de Arizaro. At one place quite literally in the middle of nowhere, we passed crosses used to mark places where people had died. "Pretty hard to have an accident here," I said. "Maybe they died from boredom." Someone with a dark sense of humor had written on a board placed by the crosses: "*Que tengan un buen viaje, amigos* (have a good trip, friends)."

Those of us in the Land Cruiser went ahead to scout out the route. As we drove higher into the mountains, the engines of the Unimogs overheated on even gradual inclines. In order to save the water we would need at base camp to cool them, the drivers would park the vehicles crossways in the road to catch the breeze—a tactic that did not encourage forward progression. We should have reached base camp that afternoon; instead we found ourselves staying the night at the military post at Socompa Pass.

We couldn't blame the vehicles for causing slow progress the following morning. Although Christian, Sergio, and I had traveled to the mountain before, we all had a hard time finding the route through the labyrinth of similar-looking hills and gullies and barely visible tracks. An image nagged at my memory, and we finally found an indirect way in from its eastern side. But by then it was too late to reach base camp, and we ended up camping out in the open.

We had to push one of the Unimogs around for more than an hour before it would start the next morning. A few hours later we reached base camp, five days after having left Salta and three days more than it should have taken. We cheered when the last vehicle rolled in.

After base camp had been set up, I divided everyone into teams. Constanza and Adriana would survey the nearby ruins and cemetery, while Christian and Sergio searched for possible sites along the ridge above camp. Gordon was to stay to acclimatize and shoot photos of the location. The rest of us were already acclimatized, so we would make carries to 19,200 feet, where I planned to install our high camp.

During our ascent, I began losing my voice to a bad cough. I had suffered bad spells of coughing on climbs before, so I did not consider it much of a problem. I had had laryngitis on Everest in 1976, and on a mountain in Pakistan I had coughed out a hunk of something from the lining of my throat. Coughs were common while climbing at high altitudes, because of heavy breathing in dry air. A single laugh could set off a coughing fit. As someone once said during our Everest expedition, "You know you are on Everest when you tell a joke and everyone coughs."

By good luck, the place I had selected for Camp 1 at 19,200 feet had a large pool of water near it. Anyone who has had to heat ice to make water at high altitudes knows what a pleasure it is to have a large quantity of water at hand. The camp proved to be one of my most pleasant high-altitude sites ever.

Once back in base camp, we compared notes. Constanza thought there might be enough bones for three complete skeletons at the cemetery. Christian and Sergio had come across a few small sites, but nothing of special interest.

I wanted to keep up the momentum, and the next day most of the team made a carry to the high camp. Alejandro and Orlando planned to remain there and carry supplies to the summit the following day. Ruddy, Tony, Constanza, and I went to find the tambo. It took longer than I expected, but eventually we found ourselves gazing down over the ruins, and we scampered down the slope to them.

The site was located off the normal route used by climbers, and no one seemed to have visited it since we had in 1985. Indeed, it appeared not to have been occupied since it had been abandoned some 500 years ago. Many of the buildings were nearly intact and some of the roof beams were still even in rough alignment, albeit collapsed. Finding roof beams preserved in an Inca structure was rare. The wood must have been brought from more than 50 miles away. Shards lay strewn about on the surface. They were of utilitarian wares, pointing to the mainly nonreligious and supportive nature of the site. This was further supported when Drs. Tamara Bray and Leah Minc later sent samples of the shards for neutron activation analysis.[4] They were able to establish that several had come from the Inca administrative center of Catarpe, some eighty miles to the north near the present-day oasis of San Pedro de Atacama. None were of high-status imperial pottery sent from Cuzco and Lake Titicaca, such as we had found in ritual contexts on mountain summits.

"This must be one of the most untouched Inca sites in Argentina," said Tony in wonder, when we had finished looking over the ruins. Ruddy and Tony took measurements, while Constanza and I descended farther to search for the ruins that Louis had seen in 1984. We surveyed them and traversed our way around back to camp.

Constanza, Adriana, Tony, Christian, Ruddy, and Sergio set off the next morning to conduct a few test excavations at selected places inside and outside the tambo. I remained at base camp to fix the satellite phone and give my cough a rest. Since we could not keep in radio contact, I had to name someone with archaeological experience as supervisor. Neither of the two most likely candidates, Constanza and Christian, wanted to take on this responsibility. Due to his heart, Ruddy might not be able to remain there the entire day, so I designated Tony. There was still tension between Constanza and him, and I hoped they would be able to get along.

Unfortunately, the truce they had made earlier did not last. When they returned that afternoon, Constanza was furious with the way Tony had talked to her. Clearly, I would have to keep them apart in the future. Tony came to me later to apologize for arguing with her. "I will return to Salta with the others, if you want," he said. "I can't guarantee that I won't lose control again." "Can you at least make a serious effort?" I asked. I was relieved when he promised he would, as I did not want to lose a strong worker before we had even reached the summit.

The next day Ruddy, Jimmy, and Adriana returned to finish work at the tambo, while the rest of us made our final move to Camp 1. Gordon decided to rest another day to help his cough get better, and before long I wished I had stayed as well. I went slowly to keep my breathing less forced, and I chewed on caramels and sucked on candies to keep a steady flow of liquid going down my throat. It made no difference, and I hacked my way up the mountain. By the time I reached Camp 1, I had full-blown laryngitis. I wondered if I had bronchitis, and I began to feel better only after taking some powerful painkillers chased down by hot tea. Still, I was to be wracked with coughing fits throughout the night.

We devoted the next day to organizing loads for our stay on the summit, although a few dropped down to fetch supplies from base camp. By remaining in camp, I was able to rest my cough and recover from flu-like symptoms that had arisen during the night. Yet I was more concerned about Gordon. He had reached camp after dark, feeling beat.

The lack of climbing difficulties to Camp 1 did not mean it was easy. "I thought it wouldn't take long to reach the camp until I realized a speck barely visible above me was a person," Gordon said in frustration. We were all underestimating distances because of the combination of clear air and the vast scale of the mountain.

When I unzipped the tent door the following morning, I looked out on a beautiful sunrise. More importantly, there was no wind. This made a big difference psychologically—the mountain seemed friendlier, more welcoming. Although I still had trouble talking above a whisper, I felt much better, glad we were heading to the summit that day. Everyone appeared to be healthier and in good spirits as we gathered in the mess tent.

We were missing someone, though. While we were sipping the tea that Arcadio had prepared, I asked, "Has anyone seen Gordon?"

"He's in his tent. He said he was tired, but that he was OK," Arcadio replied.

After breakfast, I went to my tent and selected the items I had to take to the summit that day. We could leave behind some of the equipment for a later carry, but we never knew if the weather would change or some other problem arise that might cause a lengthy delay. Once I was ready, I went over to Gordon's tent to ask what his plans were for the day.

"I'm fine," he said. "I just don't have much energy. I think I'll stay in camp today." I suggested that he should go down, but he would hear none of it. One of the problems of having a professional photographer (or cinematographer) on an expedition is that he is determined not to miss anything. He is expected to record key events, and he will put up with a lot of suffering to stay in the midst of the action. This desire was accentuated, I suspected, because everyone was driven to do his best for the National Geographic.

I noticed that Gordon's speech was a bit slurred, but then again, he was drowsy. Alarms bells began to ring only as I rose to start off on my climb. I happened to ask, "How do you like the way your tent is facing?" We had moved it yesterday, because in the rush of setting it up in the dark it had been placed with the door into the wind.

"What are you talking about?" he asked. After I explained, he said, "That's impossible. If you moved it, you must have done it with me in it."

Then I knew—he had no recollection. I immediately asked more questions to test his memory. "It's interesting that you are questioning me, since I was meaning to ask you a question as well. Why were you in my tent last night?"

Now I was worried. I had not been near his tent at night, let alone inside it. After a few more bizarre comments, I realized he had been hallucinating.

I began checking for physical signs: Arrhythmia? No. Any retinal damage? None I could see. Problems moving a body part? No. Bubbles in the lungs? "Yes," he replied casually.

I was stunned. "Why didn't you mention this before?" He was an experienced climber. He had worked for years as a mountain guide. He should have known that bubbles in the lungs could mean he had pulmonary edema. To my horror I realized that he had classic symptoms of both cerebral and pulmonary edema. If he did not descend to a much lower altitude fast, he would die.

High-altitude cerebral edema (HACE) is less common than high-altitude pulmonary edema (HAPE), but it is usually deadlier.[5] It occurs when fluid leaks from blood vessels in the brain and causes it to swell. Mental acuity and motor skills quickly deteriorate—often in a matter of hours and sometimes even faster. Symptoms include loss of balance and a strong desire to do nothing (more than natural tiredness). People affected by HACE rarely realize it, and if they don't climb to a lower elevation within hours, they die. In the case of HAPE, the lungs become filled with fluid. Unfortunately, HACE and HAPE often occur together, making for a deadly combination.

Because of Gordon's considerable experience, I had mistakenly expected him to tell me if he had a problem. I had been deceived by the fact that he had remained so articulate, complaining merely of lethargy. Early at base camp he had headaches, but these had gone away.

I had failed to take into consideration that a person experiencing cerebral edema might talk normally, while also having hallucinations and losing the ability to recognize serious symptoms, such as bubbles in the lungs.

Even after I explained to him the seriousness of his condition, he did not want to leave Camp 1. I realized that he probably would not be able to return to work on the mountain, but I didn't want to argue with him—he needed to go down. So I told him we would not do any excavating until he felt better and could return to take photos. Even then, he wanted to stay longer to teach me a few photography techniques!

I hurried to the mess tent and talked with the others. "He has to go down no matter what he says," I emphasized. "There is no way he can stay another night here." At night barometric pressure usually drops, and the effect would be the same as if he had moved to a higher altitude. That was the reason most edemas took place during the night. "Under no circumstances is he to come back up until it is 100 percent clear he has recovered from the edemas."

It may sound strange that I even considered his return a possibility, but I had a friend who suffered similar symptoms on the first Chilean Mount Everest expedition. After some days of recuperating at base camp, he had soloed Everest's neighbor Changste without any complications.

I assigned Ignacio, one of our strongest men, to help Gordon down to base camp, where he would remain and keep a close watch on him. It was an easy descent, but if necessary, Ignacio was strong enough to carry him. I gave Ignacio a walkie-talkie so that we could remain in constant contact, and I would also monitor their progress by binoculars. If the need arose, we could make a quick run down the scree slope to help out. Ignacio did not know how to drive a car, but Sergio was returning to base camp that night. At the slightest sign of any problem they were to drive lower with Gordon and, if necessary, to continue on to Salta.

Gordon used my Iridium satellite phone to call his wife, Meredith, and explain his symptoms. She was surprisingly calm and supported my decision. The call swept away the last remnant of Gordon's resistance, and he and Ignacio soon began their descent.

Most of the team had already started up by the time Constanza and I left at noon. The slope steepened above Camp 1, and the loose scree made for an agonizing climb. These conditions could make for a wonderful run down, but the combination caused a "two steps up, one slip down" progression during the ascent. My cough returned in full force, and my chest was congested. I did not have the dreaded bubbles, but I couldn't help but wonder if I was making the same mistake as Gordon and refusing to recognize the symptoms in myself.

We caught up with Adriana and Sergio just below the place we planned to establish our high camp. Sergio was moving very slowly, and I was surprised that they were still heading to the summit despite the late hour. Sergio had originally planned to reach it and return to base camp, while Adriana had intended to remain at Camp 1. She was to climb up again the next day to stay a few days with us at the summit camp, and thus there was no sense in her pushing for the summit now. At their present pace they would both end up going down in the dark. Due to laryngitis, I asked Constanza to call out to Adriana to tell her they should turn back. Adriana shouted a defiant reply, "Down—no! I'm going to the summit." And they continued their slow climb.

By the time Constanza and I arrived, the team had begun to set up tents in a small snow bowl 200 feet below the summit. Adriana and Sergio did not reach our camp until eight o'clock amid a light snowfall. They had reached the summit, but now they were tired and wanted to spend the night with us. I couldn't believe it. They had continued on solely to be able to say that they had made the summit. We were camped at nearly 22,000 feet with limited supplies and uncertain weather. Neither of them was as acclimatized as the Quehuar crew was. Now they wanted to stay with us without sleeping bags and use our supplies, all the while running a serious risk of altitude sickness.

I immediately rejected their request, although I had to ask Arcadio and Edgar to help them down in the dark. Making matters worse, Sergio had promised to return to base camp that night in order to drive Gordon to a lower altitude if necessary. Fortunately, Gordon had reached base camp and was OK, but Sergio did not know this when he had decided to continue to the summit.

"They just don't get it," I complained to Arcadio. "They haven't enough experience to understand the snowball effect actions like theirs can have on an expedition." Summit fever is a common malady among climbers, who become focused on reaching the highest point of the mountain so they can claim an ascent. Thanks to hard-learned lessons, I knew that the accumulation of seemingly minor mistakes can quickly lead to disaster in the mountains. A slight change in the weather, exhaustion, an injury, or altitude sickness could force an emergency and the extra expenditure of men and supplies—and possibly the end of the expedition.

Fortunately, with Arcadio's and Edgar's help they made it to Camp 1. However, following so closely on Gordon's close call, I regarded these events as warnings, and I became more concerned than ever about what lay ahead.

The next morning, I talked by walkie-talkie with Gordon, who said he was fine, though still coughing and feeling lethargic. His thinking was still fuzzy as well. He called me David, and he couldn't remember Ignacio's name.

I also called Meredith to tell her about Gordon's condition. Although the phone worked perfectly, I could barely talk due to laryngitis, and she had difficulty understanding me. "You sound worse than Gordon!" she said. She had contacted Dr. David Shlimm, a specialist in high-altitude illness, for his opinion. He later said, "Given Gordon's condition, if he had remained at the high camp, I estimate he had about 12 hours left to live." It occurred to me that if I hadn't talked to Gordon—and I almost hadn't, because I did not want to disturb him—he would now be dead.

Meanwhile, the first night at 21,800 feet had not been kind to some of the team. Jimmy, Ruddy, and Tony had headaches. I thought everyone should rest and settle in, a decision made easier when it started snowing shortly after lunchtime.

Orange sunlight brightened our tents before eight the next morning, and we looked forward to finally starting work on the summit. When I checked on Gordon, he said he felt better, and he was more cognizant of how serious his condition was. He agreed that he should return to Salta and see a doctor before he tried climbing the mountain again.

Work on the summit proceeded slowly that day. At first we were above the clouds and working under a brilliant, clear sky, but as we began surveying the site, the weather deteriorated. By the time we took a lunch break at two o'clock, it was snowing. At 2:30 we headed back to camp in the middle of a heavy snowstorm. Soon we were hearing thunder and lightning striking simultaneously. We were grateful to be camping lower down, while hell broke loose above us.

We awoke to a light snow and limited visibility. I was concerned that snow at base camp might prevent those there from driving out, but they had escaped the worst of the storm. Orlando and Alejandro agreed to descend and drive Gordon to Socompa, along with Sergio, Adriana, and Christian, who were returning to Salta as planned.

Bad weather kept us from working on the summit, and instead a few of the men dropped down to the pass to pick up loads that had been left there. Rather than improving, the weather worsened. A blizzard moved in the next day, with winds gusting over 60 mph and lightning crashing on the cliffs around us. The clouds flying over the summit reached more than 80 miles an hour. Even when the storm passed, the wind remained, and we could not leave tent doors open for a second without spindrift blowing in, covering everything in a fine white blanket.

I grabbed my water bottle for a drink the next morning only to gag on a mouthful of urine. After years without making a mistake, I had finally done it. I had confused my pee and water bottles. There are good reasons to have a special bottle for urinating. One of the more unpleasant tasks in mountaineering is getting up in the night to relieve yourself. At a minimum this means putting on more clothes and boots and going out in the cold. And if the weather is bad, it can be downright miserable. More than once spindrift had blown in my tent when a tent mate or I had to go out during a storm. It is also difficult to sleep at high altitudes, and I was a firm believer in at least trying to get as much as possible. Obviously, people who are rested perform better than those who are not, and at altitude this could make a critical difference in how well a person can work. Getting up several times throughout the night was not conducive to being rested, but it was a Catch-22. In order to help acclimatize you have to drink as much as possible, since liquids help keep cerebral and pulmonary edemas from developing. In some situations climbers take the medicine Diamox for acclimatization, but it acts as a diuretic. Taken together, there were good reasons to use pee bottles. And one good reason not to.

As the weather stayed unstable, I was starting to get worried. Seven of us were camped here: Constanza, Tony, Ruddy, the three Mamanis, and me. By March 14, 17 days had passed since we left Salta and 5 days since we had pitched tents on the summit. Yet we had not even begun excavations. "We would usually be finished by now," I grumbled to Arcadio. Even though the sun came out that morning, it was still windy and bitterly cold.

We started zigzagging our way to the summit at 11:00. Making a trail through the fresh snow was slow and exhausting, but at least we were sheltered from the wind on this side of the mountain. The prevailing wind blew steadily from the west, which explains why the Incas built the structures the way they did. Although the platform was exposed, the walled structures had been constructed on the lower, eastern side of the summit ridge and their openings also faced east. Practicality combined with religion, as this was a sacred direction for the Incas. With the wind blowing at 30 mph, most of the team started excavations in one of the more protected buildings, while Ruddy and Tony finished taking measurements of some of the outlying ruins. Despite our acclimatization, any exertion at this altitude was enervating, and they were wielding picks and shovels.

The wind gradually began to die down, and I climbed to the highest point of the summit in order to better film the work. The view was even more spectacular than before. Snow covered the lower peaks as far as the eye could see. Clouds swirled around them, carried by the wind. I spied several of the volcanoes I had climbed in the 1980s, and I knew that almost all of them bore evidence that the Incas had reached their summits. When viewed as a whole, I was overwhelmed by what the Incas had accomplished. As Arcadio had said once in awe, "Los Incas fueron hombres (the Incas were men)."

The team did not find anything in an open-sided structure, so the excavation was backfilled. After a break for lunch, I had part of the team excavate one of the stone circles near the platform. It too yielded nothing, not even an indication that the earth had been touched.

Others had begun to work at the platform. They found a little ichu grass, but soon encountered bedrock in the center, directly under the outline of a double circle. In 1983 I had seen that looters had dug to a depth of at least 28 inches, and a few cloth fragments had been left strewn about. I had hoped that a deeper excavation would uncover more artifacts, but now that looked doubtful.

We kept working. Much to our surprise, the soil beneath the exposed part of the summit was largely unfrozen, and the digging was far easier than we had expected. The cold was so constant that the melting and refreezing of the soil that had so plagued us at lower sites never had taken place. The wind picked up again after 4:30, and an hour later it was so cold I called a halt. Arcadio had gone ahead to camp to heat water for our tea and prepare our supper of stew. It was a pleasure to reach the warmth of the mess tent before the sun set behind the ridge. Once the sun was gone, the temperature plummeted. After a day and a half without finding anything, the terrible feeling crept over me that all our efforts would be for nothing. "We have about two weeks of supplies," Arcadio said in reply to my question. I wondered if we would be leaving the mountain much sooner.

While we were working on the summit, Alejandro and Orlando had returned to the high camp. They brought newspapers they had obtained at Socompa. We had a brief escape to a world seemingly full of misfortune. The truly bad news for me, though, came from a different source. "I have been offered a job and am going back to Salta tomorrow," said Alejandro. We had barely begun the excavation, and already we were down one man.

The weather was much better when we reached the summit the next morning. I asked Ruddy and Tony to excavate another circle of stones, while the remainder of the team concentrated on the platform, and I filmed and photographed their progress.

The Mamanis worked together in one place, slowly making their way down around the sides of bedrock. They soon uncovered a spondylus llama figurine, followed by gold and spondylus male statues with perfectly preserved textiles. After a break for lunch, they continued the excavation and discovered an alignment of statues. There were three llama figurines, one made of silver and two of spondylus, and two male figurines, one of spondylus and one of silver, in front of them, as if they were leading them in a line. "It looks like a symbolic llama caravan, even better than the one we found on Misti," I said excitedly.

What most caught our attention was the necklace made of large, carved spondylus shell pendants that surrounded the statues. "It looks like the cord was made with human hair," Arcadio said with surprise.

"I've only seen one other necklace like this, and it was from a pre-Inca mummy bundle found on the coast of Peru," I told the team as they gathered around.

"There will be a mummy under it," Arcadio added with certainty, proceeding to brush away the soil around the necklace.

After filming and measuring the items, I thought that an explanation of the finds should be made on camera. Since I had laryngitis, Constanza narrated their significance in both English and Spanish. By the time she had finished, it was six o'clock and we needed to quit. After so much delay and the problems we had experienced, I was relieved to discover such an important cache of artifacts. "Even if we don't find anything else, this makes the expedition worthwhile," I said to Constanza as we started down to camp.

We were a happy crew in the mess tent that evening. It was astonishing the difference a few hours made. The discovery of artifacts proved once again to have a remarkable effect on team morale at high altitudes. On this mountain it could not have happened at a better time.

The next day the Mamanis continued excavating in their sector, while Tony, Orlando, and Ruddy began clearing topsoil in the northeast section of the platform. Jimmy and Constanza had been keeping track of the measurements in both areas, occasionally helping out with the excavations, while I was busy photographing and videoing the work.

This time it was the northeast corner team that found artifacts. A gold and a silver llama were recovered, but lightning had damaged both. The team continued on until they struck bedrock and then switched to excavating closer to the center. The irregular bedrock made it impossible to work in uniform depths throughout a quadrant, but at least the area containing soil was relatively easy to excavate.

The Mamanis had widened their hole so that they could excavate deeper without loose soil collapsing into it. We had brought masks in case we encountered dust. Wind often made mini-whirlwinds inside the excavation, covering everything with dust. It would be difficult for a human being to get filthier.

Most days the wind began rising around noon. It was an irritant to everyone, but especially so to Constanza, who was in charge of keeping notes. She had to tape down pages to keep them from being lashed about by the wind. Often she would take off her gloves to write measurements, only to have her fingers become numb and need to be warmed.

By this time all of us had our fingertips worn raw from working in the soil without gloves. We did so in order to be as careful as possible. As time went on, though, it became painful for us to even tie our shoelaces. They would return to normal only weeks later.

Throughout the cold and exhausting work, one man never faltered. Arcadio is one of the strongest men I have ever worked with at high altitudes—and that includes Nepalese Sherpas, who I never thought could be outdone. Just as important, he has developed a second sense about archaeological sites that sometimes is uncanny. He insisted on continuing excavating, even when the possibilities seemed to be exhausted. He pointed out to me where he had spotted a slight variation in ground color, indicating an intrusion into the natural soil. Eventually he found an Inca jar, which still had a plug attached to it.

Given how hard he had worked, it was appropriate that he was the first to shout the word that caused all of us to freeze: "Mummy!"

Five feet down, his digging revealed the top of a cloth-wrapped bundle. "There are white feathers of a headdress," exclaimed Arcadio. Although smaller and less elaborate than the one we had found on Ampato, the headdress was intact. "The feathers are in great shape," I said, relieved because this boded well for the preservation of the mummy. The artifacts we had found above it suggested that the mummy would be a male. "Maybe the headdress is different because it was made for a man," I said to Constanza.

Just as we began to carefully clean soil from around the bundle, Orlando called out from his own excavation. "Two statues! There are gold and spondylus female statues here!" While we gathered around Orlando, discussing how best to continue, the wind increased. The brutal cold penetrated even the thickest of our down clothing. I called a halt to work for the day, then stayed behind to film. My fingers nearly froze, but the effort was worth the pain. The scenes of the team descending to camp in the late afternoon were the most striking of the trip.

That evening I used the satellite phone to talk with Gordon in Salta. He sounded much better, and now he was concerned about how bad I sounded. I assured him I just had laryngitis, but I certainly did not sound in the best of health. He had spoken with Dr. Shlimm, who convinced Gordon that he should not go back up the mountain. "I am returning to the States tomorrow," he said. I felt guilty telling him of the mummy discovery, knowing how much he wanted to be with us. I asked him to get in touch with the National Geographic as soon as he could.

Arcadio reinforced the deepest part of their excavation with stones the next morning, and he and his team set out to expand it even more. Orlando continued clearing out the soil around the two female statues that he had begun uncovering yesterday. In the meantime, Tony began a separate excavation to the western side of the platform.

Work had settled back into a routine when Tony called out, "I've found feathers!" He cleared around them and soon the outline of a mummy bundle was revealed. Placed on top of it, as if it were being worn in life, was a white feathered headdress. It had been constructed much like the one we had found on Ampato, but this one was in perfect condition. "Can you tell if the mummy is OK?" I asked, remembering the charred mummy on Ampato. "No, but the clothing looks really well preserved," he replied. I leaned into the hole and examined the headdress. "This is the best Inca headdress ever found," I said, awed by its size and superb condition. "It could have been made yesterday."

The hole was so small that no one could join Tony, and he continued excavating around the mummy alone. He uncovered a silver female figurine with a miniature headdress exactly the same as the one on the mummy. Other items were gradually revealed, including pottery, wooden spoons, and a pair of wooden drinking vessels (keros). The keros were incised with geometric designs, and I knew that images had been painted on them only after the Spanish conquest. The pairing of keros and plates was related to the Andean etiquette of ritually sharing the food and drink, as described in the chronicles.

None of the artifacts showed signs of a lightning strike, and our hopes increased that the mummy had remained untouched.

Constanza was kept busy writing down the constant flow of measurements being called out to her. Once finished, Tony began carefully handing artifacts to waiting hands. We watched as statues, pottery, and even food items, including maize, peanuts, and jerky, accumulated on a tarp we had laid to one side.

Then came the moment we all had been waiting for. Tony lifted the mummy, and Orlando and Arcadio took it from him and gently placed it on the tarp. The finds all pointed to the mummy's being a female, but she was still wrapped up so we could not see how well preserved she was. "She should be perfect," said Orlando. "Maybe, but we won't know for sure until a CT scan is done," I replied, remembering too well my disappointment in the lab with the Ampato girl. She, too, had been found with a headdress and her clothing had been in excellent condition. When we saw the mummy in the open, I noticed an even more striking similarity between them. "There is a male tunic draped over her right shoulder," I said with surprise.

The team settled down to writing data cards to accompany each object as it was stored away in a box or bag. Meanwhile, only a few yards away the Mamanis continued clearing around the other mummy bundle. "It definitely is a boy," called out Arcadio, after establishing that the mummy was wearing a tunic. "Johan, come here!" he called and excitedly pointed out parts of the body not covered by the outer cloth.

"Amazing," I said as I looked at the visible parts of an arm, hand, and foot in excellent condition, almost as if he had died only days before. I tried to keep calm as I said to everyone as they gathered around. "Well, we did it. This looks like a perfect mummy." As I spoke these words, I could feel a great burden being lifted. "Whatever else happens, the expedition has been a tremendous success. And it's thanks to all of you," I said with deep gratitude, as we shook hands and hugged.

Soon the boy had joined the "maiden" on the tarp. His knees were drawn up in a fetal position, bound tightly with a thick cord. Sandals and a sling had been placed next to his left arm. He wore moccasins and white fur anklets, a detail I'd seen only in Guaman Poma's drawings of 1613.[6] A broad silver bracelet covered his right wrist. We would not learn any more about the boy until we could remove the mantle covering his body and examine him under better conditions back in a laboratory.

I tried to call the National Geographic before the offices closed that afternoon in the U.S., but I discovered that having a satellite phone did not mean you could talk to people. I was only able to reach voice mail and answering machines! I didn't leave a message, because my voice was so weak that they would have had difficulty hearing. I was worried that they might think I was calling about an emergency.

I had continued to have terrible coughing fits, bringing up hunks of sputum and sometimes almost vomiting due to the exertions. One time I caught Arcadio watching me with concern, and then quickly turning away when I looked up. I began worrying that the coughing might lead to a rib fracture, which had happened to me while on Mount Everest. Even a sneeze would cause extreme pain in my ribs. I couldn't do much about the cough except suck on cough drops, drink liquids, and occasionally take doses of our limited supply of expectorant.

My chest was sometimes so congested that I was not sure if the telltale bubbles of pulmonary edema were there or not. I realized that I was becoming obsessed. I was determined not to leave the summit while we were still unearthing mummies, whatever the risk. "At least I'm not hallucinating," I told myself. "If that starts, I'm finished."

That afternoon, after the measurements and photography had been completed, we wrapped the mummies in insulation and buried them in snow below the platform. The discoveries had come so fast, one upon the other, that we did not realize we had not eaten the entire day until I called an end to work as the sun began to set.

Back in the mess tent, we discussed the day's events. "There might be another mummy, making three, like we found on Ampato," I rasped to the team. But there was also the possibility that this had been a "paired" male/female burial like some chroniclers had described. If so, we might be mostly done here. Given the circumstances, I was impressed that everyone was fit enough to keep working. If another mummy existed, I was confident that we would find it.

Constanza kept working until 11 o'clock that night (late indeed at this altitude). She worked alone by flashlight in temperatures well below freezing, and then rose at six the next morning to catch up with her notes. It is hard to imagine the phenomenal willpower necessary to do this under those conditions. In some ways the cataloging was harder than any physical labor on the summit.

The next morning I tried the satellite phone again, but failed again to reach anyone. "How ironic," I said to Constanza, who stood by a tripod with the video camera ready. "We have the world's best preserved mummies, and I can't even tell anyone about it!" Only after dialing eight people did I finally get someone, Maryanne Culpepper at National Geographic Television & Film. Once she recovered from her surprise, she told me they would arrange for a film crew to come as soon as possible. They would not have time to acclimatize and climb the mountain, but at least they could film us at base camp.

That call seemed to break a jinx, as I quickly reached Bill Allen at the magazine and then Dale Petroskey, who was responsible for Society-funded expeditions like mine. Bill said another photographer would be sent down, and Dale began coordinating the effort at the Society.

I also reached Mario. We had kept him up to date on our progress during the days before, sometimes with Constanza speaking with him and sometimes by leaving messages at his office. I explained that we had found two mummies, and we would soon be returning to Salta. We had agreed before I left for Llullaillaco on Catholic University taking custody, and I now emphasized that this had to be confirmed. Arrangements had to be made in the few days that remained before the mummies would arrive. To keep searching for an alternative up to the last minute would put the conservation of the mummies at risk. He did not argue the point.

Meanwhile the team uncovered yet more statues. Tony began an excavation in another part of the platform. Close to the surface he found the remains of an offering, including fragments of a pot, which appeared to postdate the Incas. We continued working until the wind increased and it became so cold that I called off work at the relatively early hour of four o'clock. "Thank God we're filthy," I said to Orlando, who turned to look at me quizzically. "Dirt helps keep in body heat. I'd hate to think how cold we would be if we were clean."[7]

Arcadio and Ignacio left early the next morning to make an offering to the mountain gods, and Constanza soon joined them. When we were all back at the site, Tony and Jimmy excavated the third of the circles that lay outside the platform, while the Mamanis continued their excavation where the boy had been found. Soon they began to uncover more statues. Later I asked Tony and Edgar to begin an excavation inside the double-roomed structure that we had come to call "the priests' house."

The Incas had skillfully placed some of their offerings in naturally formed niches in the bedrock. Since such niches couldn't be expanded and reached as deep as 10 feet, there was barely room for one person to fit. Eventually we became aware of a pungent smell emanating from one of these niches. "It looks like we've found another mummy," I said in wonderment at our good fortune.

Orlando began to uncover some pottery, and then I heard him say, "This is unbelievable." We peered in to see the top of a telltale bundle that, to our dismay, had been partially burned. Lightning had once again struck a mummy while it was buried in its grave.

Yet to the side of the mummy was what appeared to be the top of an untouched multicolored feather headdress. More clearing revealed four female statues buried in a straight line next to each other, each with its own miniature headdress. Although a couple of the metal statues had been blasted by lightning, their textiles were in perfect condition. The colors of the feathers formed a rainbow, including brilliant reds, yellows, and greens.

Because of the bedrock, we did not have enough space to excavate around the artifacts—if we stood on top of them, we would break them. This was out of the question, but how else could we excavate and measure the artifacts while they were still in context?

"OK. Any volunteers to go headfirst into the hole?" I asked. I couldn't think of any alternative, even though I knew how difficult it would be. The rush of blood to the head, the disorientation, the difficulty breathing, and the unusual strain on the body added by working at 22,000 feet were made worse by the smell. That the men willingly kept taking turns upside down is a testament to their tremendous determination and grit. I was glad I had the excuse of filming and photographing the process. Several of the artifacts were measured by this method, with the team performing ever more gymnastic movements the deeper they excavated.

In the meantime, the wind increased, and at three o'clock I ended the workday. The weather was clearly turning worse as the South American winter moved closer. Luckily, I didn't think we had much more to excavate.

The next morning Tony and Edgar quickly finished excavating the first half of the double-roomed structure. Inside they found mats made of grass, apparently used as insulation for sleeping on the cold floor. Another possibility was that mats had been laid over wood poles to form a crude roof. The structure must have served as a shelter for the priests and the capacocha victims.

In the second room, they found more mats, but also some well-made, thick straw bags that looked like they had hardly been used. "Maybe they were used to hold some of the more fragile ritual items, like the statues," I said to Tony as we examined the bags.

Once the site had been constructed, the priests would likely have visited it only once a year unless unusual conditions, such as a drought, occurred. The ceremony would probably be held only during the

South American summer months when temperatures were higher and there was less snow. December would have been ideal, and this also was the month that Capac Raymi took place, one of the Incas' most important ceremonies.

Inca presence in the region is thought to have begun after A.D. 1471 and lasted until the Spanish conquest of 1532. Although an Inca road ran through the area to the north and west of Llullaillaco, the closest Inca administrative center was Catarpe, near the town of San Pedro de Atacama 120 miles to the north.[8] Yet the textiles, statues, and pottery indicated an origin in Cuzco, nearly 1,000 miles to the north. Did the children also come from there, as part of a pilgrimage procession that lasted for months? Even if the children had been born in the region, they would still have had to travel by foot more than a hundred miles across some of the most barren terrain on earth to reach Llullaillaco.

Once all the artifacts had been measured and removed from around the third mummy, we debated how best to extract it. With no artifacts left, a person could stand beside the mummy, but the hole was still too narrow for him to bend over and lift it up. We tried to place a net under it, but we abandoned the effort when I realized that we would risk rubbing the mummy's outer wrapping against the jagged bedrock as we hoisted it up.

I decided that the safest method was to once again lower someone into the hole by his ankles. Since his arms would surround the bundle, he could prevent the mummy from hitting the sides of the hole. Orlando agreed to try it and down he went. When he emerged, he lay on the ground gasping for breath with the mummy lying beside him. "This is the reason God gave us students," I quipped.

I examined the area where the textile had been burned. The odor of charred flesh was still strong. The burnt head cloth was loose, and as I moved it slightly aside, I was stunned. I was staring directly into the child's face. With the exception of Juanita, we had never seen the face of a mummy until it was exposed in the lab. The child was remarkably well preserved, looking up with a pensive expression.

Although not to scale, this plan provides a perspective of the mummies (and the artifacts adjacent to them) found buried in the summit platform of Llullaillaco.

After I recovered from my initial shock, I was overcome with a mixture of feelings. I was saddened by the face, yet I was also pleased that the mummy had not been totally destroyed by the lightning strike. Despite the female statues, I thought at first the mummy was a boy. The metal plaque on the child's head resembled ones I'd seen only on males. In the 1613 drawings of Guaman Poma, men were depicted wearing metal plaques similar to the ones we have found in miniature on the heads of statues.[9] Controlled by the state, the adornments on the head functioned as signs of ethnic and regional origin. Intentional misuse was punishable by death.

However, looking more closely, I saw the seared remains of silver shawl pins. "It's a girl," I told Constanza. Her left ear and shoulder and part of her chest had been badly damaged, but the rest of her body appeared to be intact. Constanza later said, "It was more than finding a mummy—it was like meeting someone."

At a personal level, a wish I'd had for years was fulfilled—I had looked into the face of an Inca. It seemed almost too perfect that this happened with the last mummy found on the summit of the world's highest archaeological site. If I were a believer in mountain gods, I would have thought this proved they were looking out for me.

One last section in the platform was excavated and more statues were found. Soon the team hit bedrock without finding another mummy, and we began backfilling the site. The long expedition, made in the most arduous conditions, was over.[10]

We were able to work until nearly seven o'clock. The sun began to set on the horizon, leaving the summit glowing. We were infected with sadness at leaving. We doubted that we would ever again have an experience to equal this one.

After gathering together our equipment, the men began descending from the site with massive loads. Most incongruous of all was Tony's. He carried a huge bundle of straw matting from the priests' house over his shoulder.

I lingered awhile on the summit. I sat on an Inca wall, letting my thoughts roam. We had found three frozen Inca mummies, two of which were female. Until now the only other well-preserved female Inca mummy was the Ampato Ice Maiden. In a single excavation we had tripled that number. All of the mummies were among the best preserved in the world. At the same time we had found more than 20 clothed statues, nearly doubling the number of those previously known. Llullaillaco had provided us with some of the most important Inca finds ever made.

However, the sense of accomplishment I felt stretched well beyond this expedition to Llullaillaco. I thought back over the 20 years I had spent in the Andes, including three previous expeditions to this very peak. Memories of storms, hunger, pain, and close calls were mixed with the joys of companionship and discoveries—mental as well as material.

And then a new truth dawned on me. Events had come so fast that only now did I realize my Andean research had not been the new stage in my life that I had once believed. While still in my teens, I had set out to acquire a variety of "tools" to help make my mark as an anthropologist and explorer—and to use in a lifelong pursuit of a deeper understanding of the world around me. In the Andes I had been able to combine such academic disciplines as archaeology and ethnography with everything from cinematography to mountaineering and scuba diving. Now I realized that my Andean project was the continuation of a course I had chosen while still a boy and stood as a metaphor for all that I had been trying to do with my life. I felt the powerful tug of destiny, not in the sense of being programmed since birth but as the culminating point in the life that had emerged while I followed my dreams.

I turned to look north to Licancabur, its snow-clad summit glowing in the evening light. It was the first volcano with Inca ruins that I had climbed 20 years before. So many climbs, so many people's lives changed—especially my own. I realized that, whatever else happened, this was the real end of my work in the Andes.

I took my hat off and turned to look toward the mountains that extended in an unlimited vista to the north. "Thanks," I whispered. And then I started down.

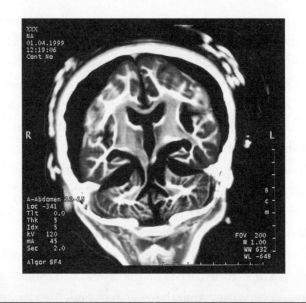

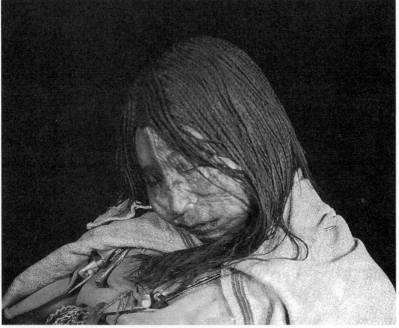

Top: A CT scan of the Llullaillaco boy's head taken at the Hospital of San Bernardo (Salta) shows his brain still intact.
Bottom: The peaceful face of the Llullaillaco maiden shows a piece of coca leaf beneath her nose and the impressions made by her braided hair.

CHAPTER TWELVE

PAST PERFECT

Mystery . . . pours energy into whoever seeks an answer to it.
—JOHN FOWLES

These maidens . . . could not have any blemish
or even a mole on their entire body.
—BERNABÉ COBO, 1653

BACK IN CAMP, MY THOUGHTS TURNED TO WHAT LAY AHEAD. WE HAD
already arranged via satellite phone for Mario to bring vehicles and
dry ice from Salta. Once we started down to base camp, we would be
in a race against time. Although we could carry a limited quantity of
ice down from the summit, there was none at base camp to replace
it, nor would we find any on the way to Salta. The trip would take two
days, assuming all went well. Dry ice quickly evaporates once it is
exposed, and we estimated that it would be nearly gone by the time
the mummies were placed in freezers in the city.

Constanza had talked via satellite phone with Dr. Colombo at Catholic
University, and he had arranged freezer units and storage facilities,
including an air-conditioned room to serve as a temporary laboratory. I
called Ruth Salas in Arequipa, asking for her help in setting up the laboratory. "I will come within the week," she said. Dr. Craig Morris, Inca
scholar and dean of science at the American Museum of Natural History,
thought that he could obtain support for the laboratory. Also, their textile conservation specialist Vuka Roussakis would be able to assist us.

Mario told us that the provincial education minister, Dr. Antonio Lovaglio, had offered us all the help we needed. We emphasized that Catholic University had prepared everything for our arrival—we only needed to transport the items there. Mario was planning to come with two Land Rovers and a truck to carry our equipment and the finds. The trip back seemed to be falling into place.

The weather held, and we were able to enjoy a lazy morning before taking down the tents and loading our packs for the carry to base camp. We had spent 13 days on the summit, but it seemed much longer. "Well, you can say we left our mark here," I said to Constanza. Looking at me quizzically, she asked what I meant. "Look at the hollows we made," I said, pointing to where the tents had been. Despite the insulated pads, our body heat had slowly melted the ice beneath the tent floors, leaving depressions formed in the shapes of our bodies. Visions of the pod people from the film *Invasion of the Body Snatchers* ran through my mind.

The descent was harder than I remembered, especially below the saddle. On a steep section with an unpleasant mix of gravel, stones, and ice, I had difficulty maintaining my balance with the heavy pack. I fell more than a half dozen times, bringing back vivid memories of my nightmarish descent with the Ice Maiden. By the time I reached Camp 1, my legs felt rubbery. I sank down next to a boulder, glorying in finally being able to rest. I was almost relieved to hear others straggle in complaining of the descent—I wasn't alone.

Camp 1 seemed luxurious, because we were camping on dry ground and had water readily available for the first time in two weeks. Everyone was set to go the next morning. Although we still were camped at 19,000 feet, the descent to base camp was easy from here and psychologically the ordeal was over. I felt guilty that most of the men had to return to the summit camp the next day to pick up loads and repeat the torturous climb down. Constanza and I remained in camp and made calls finalizing details for the expedition's return. We moved to base camp the following day, but left the mummies in rock crevices several hundred feet above it, wrapped in insulated pads and surrounded by clumps of snow. We would not bring them down until the vehicles arrived with dry ice.

The lower altitude of base camp had a soothing effect on me, because the next morning I was able to speak in a gravelly voice instead of a strained whisper. Unfortunately, I also found blood both in my sputum and in nasal secretions and felt constrictions in the muscles around my heart. "This might be my last climb for a long time to come," I said to Constanza.

The National Geographic crew arrived the next day. Mike Graber was one of the world's top mountaineering cinematographers, but Kevin Krug, the producer, and the photographer, Maria Stenzel, lacked climbing experience. Nonetheless, they all hoped that after taking the finds to Salta, we would return to Llullaillaco so that they could obtain additional climbing footage and photographs. For now, they would have to be satisfied with documenting our trip to the city.

Another day of carries from Camp 1 ensued, while other members of the team carefully packed the artifacts in boxes for the trip back. The National Geographic team filmed and photographed the mummies as they were brought down in the morning light. Mario arrived in the afternoon with two military jeeps, each with a wooden trunk containing dry ice. He had also obtained a truck from the municipality of Tolar Grande, which almost made it to base camp.

We were keen to pack up and reach Tolar Grande before dark. The thought of a shower and a bed to sleep in was on everyone's mind. Mario had other plans, however. He had come with the museum conservation specialist Pedro Santillán and said, "I need for all the boxes to be opened. We have to make an inventory before we leave."

I couldn't believe it. This had never happened in the past, and it made no sense now. "The items are already packed up, and the boxes will be in the vehicles under guard until we reach Salta," I explained. Even a limited documentation would take hours and we would not reach Tolar Grande until after dark.

"Why can't this be done in Tolar Grande?" I asked Mario.

"I was told I should make an inventory," he replied, but without any explanation as to why it had to be done here. They spent two hours documenting items, but as time dragged on they ended up simply taking note of the number of boxes and their contents without opening them. "They could have done this in the beginning," I said to Constanza in frustration.

Meanwhile a reporter and cameraman from Salta's El Tribuno newspaper arrived. They had by chance seen Mario's little caravan heading out from Tolar Grande and followed it. They became engaged in an argument with Mario, who tried to stop them from asking questions and taking pictures. We had not even returned to civilization, and already we were suffering the negative effects of the discovery. Thanks to the delay, we had to drive several hours in the dark and arrived at Tolar Grande at 10:30. It was after midnight before we finally had a meal.

None of the team could understand Mario's behavior, and the tension hadn't dissipated when we left town the next morning. I went ahead in a Land Rover and reached San Antonio de los Cobres at 2:15. When the jeeps still had not arrived over an hour later, we began to be concerned that one of them had broken down. After two hours had passed, Orlando and Constanza started to drive back to search for them. Just as they were leaving, the jeeps pulled in.

The film crew had the camera rolling when Mario walked over. "We had been going slowly and stopped at a military post at the edge of town so I could call the education minister," he said. "He told me that we should take the mummies to an ex-military facility that now belongs to the ministry," he added innocently.

This news struck me like a physical blow. In my opinion he was putting the mummies at incredible risk. How could a facility have been located so fast and be set up by the time we arrived in three hours? They had been unable to find one for more than a month!

These mummies had not been exposed and dynamited like the Quehuar mummy, and even in that case I'd been concerned about the conditions in which it was being kept. Mario knew these mummies were better preserved and that the most critical period for the mummies was the time between when they were taken out of the ground and put into freezers. The meaning of yesterday's events now seemed clear. I became convinced that they formed part of a deliberate attempt to keep the mummies out of the hands of Catholic University, despite Mario's promises to the contrary.

I was upset and let Mario know it in no uncertain terms. "If this is your idea of how to take care of cultural patrimony, you should quit your job," I said bitterly. "There is one basic principle that has to be followed at all times: Do what is best for the conservation of the mummies."

I asked Constanza to use the public phone to call the education minister, the governor, and the rector of Catholic University, but by that time offices were closed and no one was available. Deliberate or not, Mario's slowness prevented us from being able to contact anyone until we arrived in Salta, and probably not before the next morning—a Sunday morning, I realized, feeling yet more blindsided.

Mario calmly stated they would have lunch and continue on their way with the mummies when they had finished. Since there was nothing to be gained by waiting while they ate, we drove off, still carrying most of the artifacts. "At least we will be able to get them stored in a decent facility at the university," I said to the team.

At 7:20 p.m., while driving along a dusty road in the dark, we came up to a roadblock. Mario had called ahead and asked the gendarmería (national police) to detain us until he arrived. I demanded, and received, a signed document to that effect from the soldiers. I was not going to let this event become distorted later. Mike asked, "Is it OK if we film?"

"This needs to be documented, but it isn't meant for TV," I replied.

The gendarmería were embarrassed about the situation and were as helpful as they could be under the circumstances. We waited for more than two hours until Mario finally arrived.

"Why did you have us stopped?" I asked.

"I wanted us to reach Salta together," he replied.

"In that case, why did you take so long for a meal when you knew the dry ice was evaporating?" I asked. Without answering, he ordered that the boxes containing artifacts be removed from our vehicle. I said, "If you want to take them, then you will have to do a complete inventory before we leave." I recalled what had happened when artifacts had been stored in a military building in Arequipa—many ended up lost or destroyed. I had no illusions as to who would be held responsible if anything was found missing in Salta later.

"I am only doing my job," Mario said repeatedly, as if it was a magical mantra that explained all. But he realized an inventory would take hours, and he finally agreed that we could continue on. Nonetheless, there was another surprise in store for us. Several police cars were waiting when we reached the outskirts of Salta. We continued on in a convoy with flashing lights of police cars swirling in front and back of us. "It looks like he wants to create a show for the press," said one team member.[1] A light rain only added to a miserable night.

We were led to the Fragata Libertad, an unoccupied military building, where we were met by more officials, including Belisario Saravia, personal assistant to Salta's education minister. He was taken by surprise when I explained to him what had happened. "We weren't told anything about an agreement with Catholic University," he stressed.

We walked by a large abandoned kitchen, and they opened a small room that adjoined it. There was barely space for the large freezer they had arranged. The mummies were rolled in and their cases opened. The dry ice had mostly evaporated, but fortunately it had remained cold enough so that nothing had unfrozen. As for the freezer, by sheer luck the three mummies were able to fit inside it with hardly an inch to spare.

I was not the only member of our team who was upset. Everyone could see how poor the conditions were. When Orlando realized that most of the artifacts would not fit in the freezer and thus would have to stay in their boxes in the warm, humid room, he could no longer restrain his indignation. He faced a man, who he felt had been acting arrogantly ever since he arrived in base camp, and said, "Look at this place. It's dirty and humid, and you present yourself as a professional!"

"This whole thing is absurd," I said to Mario, but there was little that could be done—for now.

Outside were waiting the same El Tribuno writer and photographer who had been at base camp. They were not feeling particularly well disposed toward Mario either. It was already after two in the morning, so I arranged to give the paper an interview at 11 o'clock that morning to denounce what had occurred.

While on the mountain, I had imagined how relieved I would be once the mummies were safely in Salta. Now I was leaving the mummies and feeling more depressed than I had in years.

I was on the phone as soon as I awoke in the morning. Even though it was a Sunday, I called everyone I could think of, including friends at National Geographic and some internationally renowned mummy specialists. "Mario just doesn't understand," I explained in frustration. "If something isn't done, the mummies will be at risk not only because of the poor conditions at the military facility, but also because over time there won't be the kind of controls and care that would be provided in a scientific institution."

Constanza and I had breakfast with Dr. Colombo from Catholic University and described what had happened. We had been unable to reach him by phone until after reaching Salta, so he had been waiting for us through most of the night at the university. Rooms had been allocated for freezers and a laboratory. However, since he hadn't known how much space would be needed to house the mummies and all of the artifacts, he had had a freezer truck waiting for us with backup electric current to keep them below freezing.

That morning I also contacted the Salta correspondent of La Nación, one of Argentina's most respected national newspapers. By midday I had given interviews to both it and El Tribuno, denouncing what had happened.

Mr. Saravia came by and said, "A meeting is being arranged with the education minister and the governor later today, and they both think the issue will be quickly resolved." Kent Kobersteen of the National Geographic arrived and accompanied us when we went to the governor's mansion. Kent's avuncular presence helped ease the tension. The education minister, Dr. Antonio Lovaglio, drove us there, and on the way he said, "Mario never told me about the arrangement with Catholic University. He only said that mummies had been found and the government needed to arrange freezers for them."

We were met at the door by the governor, Dr. Juan Carlos Romero. He listened intently as I explained what we had found and the arrangements that had been made to conserve the mummies and conduct research. We soon discovered that he was a man of action. "I would like for you to be in charge of coordinating scientific work on the mummies and they will be transferred to Catholic University until the government has a facility to keep them," he said. Although he knew that this order would probably create problems for him with the national university, he was determined to see that the mummies received the best care possible.

This show of support was a tremendous relief. Calls were made to the newspapermen and the local story was revised in time to reflect the new developments. After several days of acute uncertainty, I could finally relax.

THE DAYS TO COME WHISKED BY IN A FLURRY OF ACTIVITIES. ON Monday we loaded the artifacts and the mummies, still contained in the freezer, into the freezer truck, and drove to Catholic University, where armed guards watched over them. An agreement was drawn up between the government, Catholic University, and myself that provided a legal basis for the conservation of the mummies. Simultaneously, arrangements were made to examine the mummies with CT scans.

The mummies were not the only ones in need of being examined—I had to see a doctor myself. After taking the mummies to the university, I had my lungs x-rayed and blood tests at a hospital. After waiting two anxious days, the results came in: To my surprise everything looked fine. All that coughing had barely left a trace. (Several months would pass before I learned that the coughing I had endured on mountains over the years was mainly due to asthma induced by exercise and cold.) As soon as the press conference was held, we would be heading back to climb Llullaillaco yet again—this time for National Geographic Television cameras.

The mummies were still well wrapped and kept below freezing, but the exact temperature and relative humidity necessary to conserve them depended on the condition of their body tissues. Five days after we reached Salta, the radiology facility was ready, and we took the mummies to San Bernardo Hospital for the CT scans.

We couldn't help being tense as we awaited the results of the first images to appear on the computer screen. Although we had expected good results, it was an unforgettable experience to see how well preserved the mummies were: Their organs, including brains, were intact with little, if any shrinkage. Dr. Previgliano pronounced, "These look like the bodies of people who were frozen only a short time ago."

The excellent condition of the mummies had not been a foregone conclusion. The upper left side of the youngest girl had been badly damaged by lightning, and we were surprised to see that most of her organs were still frozen at nearly their full size. This was in stark contrast to some of the mummies we had uncovered in Peru; while leaving their clothing virtually intact, lightning had turned those into charred skeletons.

The other two mummies were about as perfectly preserved as possible. "The muscle tissue is excellent and there has been very little shrinkage," noted Dr. Previgliano.[2] "The organs are not only intact, they look like they could still function," I said in awe after examining the images.

The CT scans did not provide us with the probable causes of death, unlike the case of the Ice Maiden. "I don't see any obvious fractures or other signs, nothing to indicate that they were killed by strangulation or blows to the head," said Dr Previgliano. This led us to suspect that they had died while semi- or totally unconscious, perhaps aided by ritual drinking of alcoholic beverages, common during Inca ceremonies. Certainly the extreme altitude would have abetted their deaths.

Dr. Previgliano then casually pointed out an explosive finding: "Look at the difference in density in the aorta and lungs. That can only be caused by blood—there is nothing else it could be." This was unheard of. Dried blood had been found in archaeological contexts before, such as in mummies and on some weapons. But liquid blood would enable tests to be done that would be impossible otherwise. "The presence of blood opens up a whole new window of research," said Dr. Arthur Aufderheide, one of the premier authorities in the pathology of ancient mummies, when I contacted him later. "If there is any blood at all in them, it usually is in very small quantities."

Blood not only is scarce in mummies, it is easily contaminated by similar molecules from other natural sources. As the chemist Joseph Lambert wrote, "The natural environment is constantly exposing ancient molecules to conditions that alter them chemically, such as oxidation and hydrolysis."[3] The former leads to the breakdown of organic molecules and the latter to water breaking up the links that form chains of molecules.

The frozen Llullaillaco mummies were the first to have a large quantity of uncontaminated blood inside their bodies. Blood contains a system of protein detection involving antibodies, which have the function of finding invasive organisms. "We can search for antibodies and they will indicate which diseases infected the children," said Dr. Aufderheide.[4] "This would increase our understanding of the way some diseases have developed over the centuries and may even help in combating them today." With current technology, one cubic centimeter of blood would be necessary for analysis. We decided to wait until technology improved to the point where only a very small amount would be necessary. Once scientists are able to complete a study of the blood, the results will represent a breakthrough in the field.

The CT scans had established what I had previously only dared hope. We had indeed found "perfectly" frozen mummies.

MOST OF THE TEAM RETURNED TO LLULLAILLACO IMMEDIATELY AFTER the CT scans were finished. They would establish base camp and start ferrying loads up to Camp 1, and the National Geographic team would have time to acclimatize. Constanza, Arcadio, and I remained behind to prepare for the press conference. We decided to hold it on Tuesday, April 6, because of the long Easter holiday. Monday would be the earliest that journalists and government employees would be returning to their jobs, and many would not be back until Tuesday.

"What do we exhibit and how much information do we provide?" was a question that cropped up frequently in the days leading up to the press conference. As with the Ice Maiden, this was a delicate matter, since the finds were the cultural patrimony of the government. The National Geographic Society had first rights only to publish a popular article and to use photos taken during the expedition itself. The government was interested in providing as much information as possible to the media. The trick was in having enough interesting material remaining so that it didn't ruin a future NATIONAL GEOGRAPHIC article and the publicity this would bring to Salta. As it turned out, besides our presentations at the press conference and the issuance of a press release, the Society provided the media with slides of the expedition and a video clip as well.

The mummy of the "lightning girl" was also put on display, temporarily placed in a glassed-in freezer and her face half-covered by her head cloth. We arranged a collection of artifacts on a table, where they could be viewed and photographed. All this was kept out of view of the public until the end of the press conference.

The room was packed as Constanza and I showed slides and related details of the expedition, conservation issues, and plans for future work. After Dr. Previgliano presented slides of the CT scans that dramatically portrayed the excellent preservation of the mummies, we took questions from the reporters. Before long I fielded one that I had been dreading.

"I understand there were problems during your return to Salta. Could you explain what happened?" a reporter asked.

"It was a misunderstanding that was cleared up in 24 hours, and there isn't any reason to discuss it further now," I replied, hoping to brush the question aside.

"He has become a politician," someone quipped in the audience, and with that the issue was laid to rest. The culminating moment soon arrived and the mummy and artifacts were unveiled. There was an immediate surge of people to the freezer, overwhelming anyone unfortunate enough to be in the way.

While this took place in Salta, some of my video footage was aired on network TV in the U.S. and on the Internet. An international media frenzy followed, and the discovery made front-page headlines around the world.

Despite concerns about my health, I was glad to leave all the hoopla behind and return to Llullaillaco the day after the press conference. We spent two days on the summit in cold that had by now become so intolerable that we couldn't sleep. But the film crew was able to shoot the footage that the National Geographic wanted, and we returned to Salta ten days later.

While we were on the mountain, Constanza oversaw the preparation of the laboratory at Catholic University. The timing of our discovery had been fortuitous, since some of the most experienced scientists associated with Andean frozen mummies had arrived in Salta. They were participating in the first international high-altitude archaeology symposium. Two of the pioneers in the field, Dr. Juan Schobinger and Antonio Beorchia, were in attendance, as were the physical anthropologist Silvia Quevedo and the archaeologist Ruth Salas. Silvia was one of the few people to have worked with both the El Plomo and Aconcagua mummies, and Ruth was to make an important contribution because of her experience with the Ice Maiden's conservation and the establishment of the lab in Arequipa.[5]

With government support, Constanza, Ruth, Silvia, and the conservationist Pedro Santillan set out to buy materials for the lab. They included such items as humidity and temperature sensors; surgical masks, robes, and gloves; acid-free cotton sheets; silica gel; and cards and tags for labeling. The group also monitored temperature and humidity controls for the rooms and freezers, oversaw the installation of alarms, sealed off rooms from exterior pollution, covered windows to control lighting, and prepared shelves for instruments and tables for use with the mummies—in short, they provided the basis for starting serious laboratory research.

On my first day back in Salta, I had one of the most moving experiences of my life. A group of us gathered at the lab to remove the outer cloths covering the mummies. Constanza, Ruth, Silvia, Pedro, Antonio Beorchia, and Juan Schobinger were all present.

As the older girl was taken from the freezer, I heard someone refer to her as la doncella (the maiden). I shivered as memories flooded back to me of the last time I had been in a laboratory with a doncella—Juanita. Suddenly I felt as if they were in some mysterious way inextricably linked. I had the irrational sense that she was the natural outcome of our discovery of Juanita, that she somehow completed her. And like Juanita, she would soon become the center of attention—Argentina's Ice Maiden.

A hush fell over the room as her head cloth was removed and we saw her face for the first time. Her hair was stylishly braided, and she appeared to be asleep. A reddish pigment had been applied on her cheeks, and the thought crossed my mind that she was blushing. The only lines visible on her face were those formed by the impressions in her skin left by her braids. We instinctively talked in low voices, as if we might wake her.

"Look under her nose," I heard Ruth say in a hushed voice. "There are pieces of coca leaves." Sacred to the Incas, the odor from these leaves may have been the last thing the girl smelled before she died. But I knew of another possible explanation for their presence, and it was unsettling. "When the hour of sacrifice came, they placed in the [child's] mouth a fistful of crushed coca leaves with which they smothered [the child]," wrote Alonso Ramos Gavilán in 1621.[6] A few pieces of the coca leaves were taken by tweezers and deposited in a bag for later analysis. Other tweezers were used to collect pieces of dirt stuck in the folds of her clothing.

We found some dampness where the girl's left foot pressed against the outer textile covering. "Lightning might have caused the tiny tear near it," said Silvia. She and Ruth recommended that absorbent cloth be placed next to the spot. They had already anticipated this kind of problem. "We think that disposable diapers best fit the bill," said Ruth to some amusement. She was right, and once they had been positioned, the mummy was wrapped up and carefully placed back in the freezer. Throughout the examination, conversation had been kept to a minimum—we were transfixed by what we were seeing.

We had removed the tunic from where it had been draped over the girl's right shoulder and now turned our attention to it. The tunic was one of a rare few to survive in perfect condition, and among the fewer still found in an archaeological context. The design on it, often referred to as the "Inca key," is well known from other Inca tunics. "These types of tunics were of high status and probably belonged to Inca nobles or had been given as gifts by the Incas to provincial leaders," said Ann Rowe of the Textile Museum in Washington when she examined photos later.[7] But why had it been draped over a girl who had been sacrificed?

One of the females we found on Ampato had also had a tunic laid beside her, albeit not one of such high status. As we hypothesized in her case, the tunic might have represented a kind of symbolic marriage between the girl and the deity. Another possibility is that the girl had been offered by her father, who wanted his ritual attire to accompany her into the realm of the gods. Both these customs were noted in the writings of chroniclers. However, we couldn't rule out the possibility that the tunic might be unrelated to the girl, offered instead by an Inca noble to accompany the other items in the funeral assemblage. I personally believe that the tunic was meant as an offering to the deity with whom the girl was perceived to reside—the mountain god Llullaillaco.

After returning the maiden to her freezer, we took out the boy. Wearing a red and blue tunic, he sat on a black one that was folded beneath him. A red and brown mantle or cloak covered his head and upper body, forming the exterior part of the mummy bundle. It looked like he was actually wearing a plain red tunic, with a separate red and blue tunic folded between his face and his knees. We removed the head cloth, but his face still was only partially visible. His knees were pressed so tightly against it, his nose was flattened.

Ruth quickly noticed a significant detail: "See the stain where his lips are pressed against the cloth?" she asked. "That looks like vomit. Maybe he had been drinking chicha as part of the ritual and couldn't keep it down."

That was possible, but vomiting didn't necessarily mean that the child had been drinking. It might have been an automatic reflex that can occur at the moment of death. Another possibility is that fear caused him to be nauseous or he had a reaction to the high altitude.[8] At this stage we couldn't say exactly what had caused it.

The legs were held tightly in place by a rope. "Maybe the boy died while being carried to the summit and his legs had to be tied to make for easier carrying, especially before rigor mortis set in," said Constanza. Rigor mortis normally starts one to four hours after death in small muscles, such as the fingers, and four to six hours for the larger muscles, such as the limbs, but this can be quicker in cold environments. It usually lasts between 24 to 48 hours, but the ambient temperature will affect this as well. The muscles eventually relax and the body becomes flexible again.[9] Constanza's theory made good sense, but I suspected that he had died on the summit, since the vomit suggested he was still alive when his legs had been tied.[10] Whatever had occurred, it certainly was unusual to see a human sacrifice bound in this way.

A woolen sling had been tied around the boy's head, and from it a small white-feathered headdress protruded above his forehead. Such headdresses were worn on special occasions, such as at major ceremonies. The use of a sling to hold it in place struck some of those present as odd, but I knew that slings had commonly been tied around a person's head in Inca times.[11] "Even an Inca emperor is reported to have worn one this way," I said.

Near his left arm were two *chuspas*, bags used to hold coca leaves. One was made of wool and the other was covered with white feathers. Two other bags appeared to have been made using llama scrotums. We thought they would likely contain hair and nail clippings from the boy— another common Inca practice.[12]

He had a silver bracelet on his right arm, similar to those worn by Inca nobles. It had probably been among items sent by the emperor as diplomatic gifts. Ruth noticed a small hole in the bracelet. "It must have been the result of a lightning strike while he was buried," she added. Fortunately, lightning had not caused the kind of damage as with the younger girl. Under the boy, the folded black tunic was probably intended as a spare one for his stay with the gods.

In symmetry with the white headdress, he wore white anklets, while his leather moccasins looked barely used. Both of these items were similar to those represented in Guaman Poma's renowned drawings of 1613.[13] "It is as if one of his sketches was made real," said Ruth.

Finally we examined the younger girl. We had already seen her face and charred shoulder while on the summit, and that blackened vision had remained engraved in our minds. Now we were able to focus on details we had missed in those emotional moments. The cord that had held the silver plaque on her forehead had been burned away, and so I placed it aside. We wondered if the metal had attracted the lightning that struck it. "Maybe the plaque served the same function as a headdress,"

I said, noting that each girl wore one of them, but not both. Then again, I knew that some ethnic groups were identified by the plaques they wore. Two braids were parted on each side of her face. Her mouth was slightly open and her teeth were visible.[14] Her hands and feet were tucked into her clothes, as if she had been cold. Under an outer mantle, now badly burned, she was wearing fine tapestry textiles.

We were all convinced that she had been struck by lightning after having been interred—not before. A section of the girl's upper chest had been virtually blasted away, and both the body and the clothes were otherwise burned in a way that indicated a powerful, fast, and highly focused source of heat—such as an electric charge. I also spotted the characteristic fulgurites, leaving little doubt that the damage had been caused by a lightning strike.

Although part of the girl's body had been badly burned by lightning, the artifacts surrounding her had largely escaped damage. She had been buried with a rich collection of items, including statues, coca bags, fine ritual pottery, and beautifully carved wooden beakers, befitting her high status. They provided archaeologists with a wealth of material to study.

A principal goal the first day was to prepare the mummies for long-term storage in the freezers. We had brought out each mummy for no more than 20 minutes. As each session ended, we wrapped the mummy inside a cotton cloth containing no chemicals that might be transferred to its body. Plastic was wrapped around each one, both for protection and to create a vapor barrier that would help the mummy to stabilize to its own requirements. We then placed the mummies in individual freezers at 10° F and at a relative humidity of 65 percent. We did not want to do anything further with them until we had developed a clear work program. Another ten days would pass before we next moved any of the textiles covering the mummies.

The Peruvian team members and the National Geographic TV crew left by April 22. The morning of May 1 Constanza and I met with Dr. Previgliano and Dr. Piloni, who were to take needle biopsies of the three mummies. The microbiologist Dr. Arroyo would check for any possible contamination on the surface of the bodies. As with the Ampato Ice Maiden, we were committed to a basic concept—no intrusive procedures would be done with the mummies that could not be done with a living human. Thus, for example, no autopsy would be performed, but a needle might be used to obtain a small tissue sample for analysis.

Rounding out our circle was Patricia Cornwell, the renowned writer of crime novels featuring forensic analysis. While on a business trip to Buenos Aires, she had contacted us. She had been fascinated by news about the mummies and flown to Salta to learn more about them. Although we normally would have been cautious about allowing a writer of fiction into the lab, she had credentials that made her unique. She had once worked in a morgue, and the descriptions of forensic evidence in her books were meticulously accurate. She had also helped establish one of the world's most advanced forensic laboratories in Richmond, Virginia. Her considerable background obtained through researching police investigations of dead bodies provided her with a perspective that the rest of us lacked.[15]

While examining the older girl, I moved aside the cloth covering her hands, and for a moment I froze—they looked perfectly lifelike, as if ready to move. For a brief instant my mind gave off an alarm that she was alive. Her hands showed not the slightest sign of desiccation—indeed, the texture of the skin on her hands was smoother than my own.

Initially, I was concerned that the bodies would be frozen as solid as the Ice Maiden, making it difficult to carry out needle biopsies. However, Dr. Previgliano soon discovered that he had no problem penetrating the tissue at all. How could this be, if the mummies were frozen and the organs had maintained their original shape?

The biopsies of the Llullaillaco mummies proceeded without a hitch. The Quehuar mummy, however, was covered in rock-hard frozen textiles, except where its upper torso had been blown off. Unfortunately, soil frozen in place covered this opening so that only a few broken bones stuck out. Rather than attempting a needle biopsy, we decided to use one of the small pieces of bone for DNA analysis.

Despite being frozen, the decomposition that had taken place after the mummy had been exposed by the dynamite still left the pungent smell of death. Once again we felt a mixture of anger with the looters and sadness for the dead child, whose body had been so badly mutilated.

Now that the lab had been established, and the mummies and artifacts safely stored and conserved, I felt that I could return to the U.S. I needed to catch up on personal matters that had been on standby for more than three months, not to mention beginning work on the NATIONAL GEOGRAPHIC article. I flew to Buenos Aires's domestic airport on May 5. With me I had brought samples of the needle biopsies in an insulated box with dry ice. Once the plane left the ground, I had a powerful sense of déjà vu—I felt I was reliving my 1995 flight home after finding the Ice Maiden.

DR. KEITH MCKENNEY MET ME AT THE AIRPORT AND IMMEDIATELY stored the biopsy samples in a freezer in his lab at –80°F. The idea was to slow down chemical processes as much as possible. "Even a few degrees of difference in temperature can make a major impact on the state of the biomolecules, because of how temperature affects chemical reactions," wrote Martin Jones.[16] The importance of maintaining samples in low temperatures had not been given much attention until biomolecules had been studied. Since then scientists have realized the significant advantages that frigid regions, as found in mountains and the Arctic, have to offer biomolecular archaeology. This was amply proven when the geneticists Paul Rasmussen and Juana Castaneda analyzed the Llullaillaco mummies' DNA under Keith's supervision. What they found was startling.

Keith called me in late May. "The mitochondrial DNA could not be better. It is the same as we find in DNA extracted from living humans." They had obtained every one of the 1,122 base pairs that make up the entire mitochondrial control region. Each of the three mummies' DNA sequences turned out to be unique, with new variants not found in the available databases. "This provides us with an excellent opportunity to find their modern-day relatives. What we know for now is that they were not siblings or closely related on the maternal side," said Dr. McKenney.

Dr. McKenney's team took the DNA of Constanza, Dr. Previgliano, and myself in addition to that of the geneticists who examined the DNA. This was done as a check against possible contamination. To the surprise and delight of Constanza, she was found to have Native American DNA—Haplogroup B, to be precise. Mine turned out to be the most common of all the European haplotypes, the one some scientists have called "Helena."[17]

The geneticists found that the DNA from the older girl almost exactly matched two samples from people born in the village of Cabanaconde in the Colca Canyon of southern Peru. "When they examined the entire control region, they discovered that she had only one base pair difference out of 1,122 with a living male from Cabanaconde. We took his DNA in 1996 to compare with that of the Ice Maiden," said Dr. McKenney, excitement rising in his voice. There had been no link at all with the 19 people to the Ampato Ice Maiden, but here was a close one with a girl sacrificed on a mountain nearly a thousand miles to the south!

"The Llullaillaco boy had only two base pair differences with mitochondrial DNA of the Mapuche tribe," he continued. I knew this tribe was originally found far to the south of Llullaillaco in modern-day Chile and Argentina. If it turns out that he is definitely of Mapuche origin, then Llullaillaco would provide a dramatic example of long-distance pilgrimages made to a single sacred site from opposite ends of the Inca Empire.

Not surprisingly, the Quehuar mummy's DNA was less well preserved than that of the Llullaillaco mummies, but they were still able to amplify 350 base pairs of mitochondrial DNA. "I've another surprise for you," said Dr. McKenney. "Juana Castaneda found that the mummy lacked the Y chromosome—the child you thought was a boy has turned out to be a girl."[18]

The DNA of the Llullaillaco mummies was so well preserved that Dr. McKenney decided to try for nuclear DNA. He reported finding the first perfectly preserved nuclear DNA ever from a mummified body. "We compared it with that of a man in prison in Texas, and it is impossible to tell which is that of a living human and which that of the mummy," he said. With nuclear DNA, eventually relatives on both the father's and the mother's side can be traced. One day we will be able to talk to the closest living relatives of each child sacrificed to the gods on Llullaillaco 500 years ago.

As THE MONTHS WENT BY, THE RESULTS OF OTHER STUDIES BEGAN to come in. The odontologists Facundo Arias, Josefina González, and Gonzálo Herrera carried out studies of the teeth of the Llullaillaco children and were able to narrow down their ages to 15 for the maiden, 7 for the boy, and 6 for the girl struck by lightning.[19]

Drs. Tamara Bray and Leah Minc sent samples of Llullaillaco pottery shards for neutron activation analysis using the University of Michigan's Ford Nuclear Reactor.[20] They found that the boy had an aribalo from the Lake Titicaca region and the lightning girl had two plates and a pedestal pot from there, in addition to fine Cuzco pottery. The older girl had imperial Cuzco pottery, but none of the samples were from Lake Titicaca. However, not all the ceramic pieces found with her could be tested. Of special interest for us was that the analysis established for the first time that classic Inca pottery not only was sent from Cuzco but also from Lake Titicaca—and that to a site more than 600 miles away.

Constanza helped Dr. Andrew Wilson in his study of the isotopic and DNA results obtained from samples of the mummies' hair—including that found in bags with each of the three children. Based on the reports of chroniclers, we assumed that the hair in the bags had been accumulated over the course of the children's lives, including from the time of their first hair cuttings. Thus, it did not come as a surprise when Dr. Wilson was able to prove the hair in the bags definitely belonged to each of the children, respectively. But then came findings that did surprise us and shed light on what happened to them in the months preceding their sacrifice.[21]

"About a year before the maiden [older girl] met her death, her diet changed dramatically to one rich in animal protein (likely meat) and plants such as maize," wrote Dr. Wilson. The increase in meat consumption continued until about $2 \frac{1}{2}$ months prior to her death, then began to drop, whereas the intake of maize continued. I wondered if the drop in animal protein might be attributable to the maiden being on pilgrimage to the mountain and thus with less access to meat. On the other hand, maize was kept stored in the tambos located along the Inca road and was considered a prestigious food item. It looked to me like we now had independent evidence, not only of the food preferences of the maiden during the pilgrimage but also of how long the procession took.

However, the other two children did not have such a dramatic change in diet. It seems reasonable to infer that a shift to a meat-enriched diet one year before death meant that the maiden was elevated to a higher social status. The differences between her diet and the other children's suggests she had the highest status of the three, perhaps related to her older age and her longer confinement in an acllawasi (house for chosen women).

The diet characteristics of the hair from the bags of the other two children turned out to closely parallel each of their diets. Like the maiden, their hair had been cut about six months before they had been sacrificed. Since all the hair was not tested, we do not know for certain if hair cut earlier (or later) was also in the bags. For example, Clara Abal had noted that the boy had a short haircut—was this hair in the bag as well? Short hair was a sign of nobility for Inca men. Could the boy's hair have been cut with this in mind?

Whatever the case, the results that Wilson and his team obtained point to all the children having undergone a hair cutting at a special event that occurred at a set time, and the Incas had deliberately kept this hair to be buried with them. Wilson's findings also support historical accounts of special treatment being given to the capacocha children beginning several months prior to their burial.

That wasn't all the children's hair was to reveal. Dr. Larry Cartmell examined it to see if it would test positive for cocaine. "All of the Llullaillaco mummies' hair tested positive. But more surprisingly, the amount ingested by the oldest girl proved to be three times as much as I've found in 350 samples I've previously examined. It takes about ten days before the ingestion of coca leaves for cocaine appears in hair shafts, so we don't know if coca was consumed immediately prior to the children's deaths," he wrote. Chewing coca leaves was an integral part of Inca rituals, and Dr. Cartmell's findings established that even the children had chewed them during their pilgrimage to the mountain. Once again, the maiden proved to have been specially singled out. But there was still much more to be learned.

Constanza and I contacted scientists at the Smithsonian Institution's Center for Materials Research and Education in 1999. They felt that the three mummies had not undergone a complete process of freeze-drying. In their opinion the mummies were quickly frozen ("flash frozen"), and then an extremely slow process of sublimation began which has not yet been completed. They objected to using the phrase "freeze-drying" for this process, because a fair amount of residual humidity still exists in the tissues.

After the chemist Dr. Charles Tumosa had finished looking at the CT scans, he said, "We need to understand the conditions under which the freezing process took place, since these bodies are better preserved than any we have ever seen. The conditions that occurred naturally must have been nearly perfect for the preservation of human body tissue."

We took the CT scans of the Llullaillaco mummies to show Dr. Gael Lonergan of the Armed Forces Institute of Pathology. She is a specialist in children's pathology and over the years has helped train hundreds of scientists in this specialty. "I can hardly believe I am looking at scans of children that have been dead for 500 years," she exclaimed.

She looked closely at the CT scans for several minutes, then turned and said, "It appears that a small amount of apidocere has formed." Apidocere is a soapy or waxy substance that has been found around skeletons under some circumstances. It is commonly referred to as "grave wax," and it occurs when the body's fat has transformed into glycerol and fatty acids. These can combine with alkalis in the soil to form the "soap" that is visible around some bodies.[22] It mainly develops in the fatty tissues, such as the cheeks and buttocks, but it can also form inside body cavities and help preserve internal organs— including the brain.

The brain, of all the body tissues, is especially difficult to find well preserved in mummies. "Look at the white and gray matter," said Dr. Lonergan, pointing to the CT scan of the boy's brain. "It is amazing that they are so well preserved. Even the brains of people who died recently rarely look this good." She paused as she saw the puzzled expression on my face and then continued, "White matter is underneath the cortex and fills the interior part of the brain. It has the 'wiring' that allows the signals to travel in your brain. But it is gray matter that is of most interest to us here. Gray matter is another name for the cortex, the relatively thin surface of the brain," she said, while she traced a line on the image. "The senses of touch, hearing, sight, taste, and balance are in the cortex."

The brains of the other two mummies were equally preserved, and her comments caused me to ponder the kinds of information that might someday be learned from them. I knew that brain cells start dying about five minutes after blood stops flowing to it. Indeed, the irreversible cessation of brain activity is one of the definitive signs that death has occurred.

However, not all dead bodies are equal. Corpses decompose at different rates depending on the conditions. Some bodies deteriorate to a point that only their bones remain, while others are in intermediate states of decomposition. Brain tissues (and parts of the brain cells) have been found intact in 8,000-year-old bodies recovered from the water-logged peat of a seasonal lake in Florida.[23] At the highest end of a "preservation scale" of the dead are frozen mummies—and especially those that froze at the time of death.

Since there was very little time between when Inca sacrificial victims died and were buried (some were even reportedly buried alive), a body could be frozen with little decomposition having occurred. Normally at death, cells start releasing their enzymes and contents and, if left unchecked by a process like freezing, this will have a domino effect that is extremely damaging. Unfortunately, freezing brings its own problems. Unless this occurs under per-fect conditions, when cells freeze they often burst the walls of surrounding cells.[24] It would be a difficult task indeed to restore a complete body if this occurred.

But restoring a body was not something we were concerned about, even if it had been theoretically possible. On the other hand, I had learned that researchers had begun examining the brain at the molecular level, studying, for example, how different genes are coded to create proteins in the brain. Scientists can now trace neural pathways and identify specific cell types. If the freezing of the mummies took place at a rate that was rapid enough to beat the natural process of cell breakdown at death, the possibilities would expand exponentially. What separates the Llullaillaco bodies from most other mummies (even other frozen ones) is not just the incredible preservation of their organs, but also of the cells in the organs.

We hardly understood the brain only a few decades ago (a split sec-ond in the time frame of human evolution). It is not out of bounds to consider it likely that decades from now some frozen and damaged brain cells will be repairable. Seen in a different light, the very com-plexity of the brain gives us reason to think that some parts of it, how-ever small, will eventually be capable of being restored. Just exactly what information we could gain may be difficult to imagine—but the possibilities are, well, mind-boggling.

WHILE CONSTANZA AND I WORKED ON PUBLICATIONS ABOUT the findings during the summer and fall of 1999, wild rumors began circulating in Salta. These ranged from our supposedly wanting to steal the mummies to the mummies having "thawed out."[25] The rumors were somewhat offset by the continuing international recognition the mummies received, for example, they were selected by Time magazine to constitute one of the ten most important scientific discoveries of the year. My NATIONAL GEOGRAPHIC article appeared in the fall, followed by the TV program about our expedition in November. Unfortunately, unbeknownst to me the program focused on the misunderstanding that arose during the transport of the mummies from Llullaillaco to Salta. I felt a need to return to Argentina to clear up any misunderstandings.

I arrived in Salta in December 1999 to present a lecture with Constanza and Dr. Previgliano organized by Catholic University. Open to the public, it would include our answering questions from the audience. The night of the lecture, we discovered that interest was greater than anyone had expected. The press also turned out in force, and we had to move from a conference room into an auditorium that seated more than 500. People still had to stand.

Constanza began with a presentation of our finds on Quehuar— a new topic for most in the audience. I discussed the expedition to Llullaillaco; Dr. Previgliano, the CT scans. Constanza described the artifacts, and I concluded with remarks about the DNA. We then opened the floor to questions and were not surprised at the ones that followed, which related to such issues as the condition of the mummies, the laboratory and museum, and plans for future work, especially relating to DNA and finding living relatives.

Most of the indigenous reactions to our discovery were favorable. One representative said, "After hearing your presentation, I have changed my mind and would like to thank you for the work you have done." Eventually, one of the representatives of a local indigenous organization criticized us for excavating a burial site. I explained that the alternative would have been to leave the site to eventual destruction by looters, and even he admitted that, without being able to protect the site, the mummies should not be reburied on the mountain.

The importance of the discovery for indigenous peoples was repeated many times in the years to come as they began to realize that it brought their culture—and the problems they faced—to the public's attention, whereas they had been largely ignored before. Over a relatively short period several indigenous groups of artisans had formed due to the interest generated by the Llullaillaco finds. Thanks to Constanza's efforts, an institute of mountain research was established at Catholic University, and indigenous people have been able to become more involved with the mummies and artifacts, gaining new insights into the past. The government of Salta built a museum devoted to the Llullaillaco finds, where indigenous artisans are able to sell their crafts.[26]

Traditional culture became revitalized in other ways. For example, in July 2003 several indigenous groups collaborated in organizing a fair held in honor of the Llullaillaco mummies. For the first time in Salta they allowed the public to attend a traditional ceremony complete with ritual specialists. During the two-day event they presented various aspects of their culture, including typical foods and crafts. Raúl Vilte, a representative of the Colla ethnic group, said, "We are convinced that there is a reason that the [Llullaillaco] children are in Salta. This is a message for all who inhabit the region that this is related to a rebirth of our ancestral culture."

The Third World Congress of the Quechua Language was held in Salta in late 2004 and brought together 300 representatives from Andean countries. The title of the congress was "Niños del Llullaillaco" (the children of Llullaillaco). At its conclusion the congress passed a resolution that included the following statement: "The congress approves supporting investigations of the Llullaillaco Children (Salta, Argentina) and the diffusion of such investigations for recognizing the greatness and the evolution of our ancestors from their origins to the present day."

THIS PROCESS OF USING THE DISCOVERY OF FROZEN MUMMIES as a means to highlight indigenous culture has gathered momentum in Peru as well. During the summer of 2000 I attended a ceremony at the museum in Arequipa to honor the Ice Maiden's return from Japan. A poster of her had been made to accompany her tour of 14 Japanese cities during 1999–2000. The painting depicted Japanese calligraphy surrounding a reconstruction of the Ice Maiden based on Chris Klein's painting of José's daughter—except that only her head was visible. Her eyes peered out in such a direct way that they seemed to never leave you.

Such is her power that perhaps it was inevitable that the static exhibition of the Ice Maiden evolved into a "live" performance. Seven years after her discovery, her life and her sacrifice were reenacted in Arequipa's National Stadium. This was the result of almost two years of work by Juana Carillo, who was so affected by her first experience of viewing Juanita that she had broken out crying. She decided to convey the Ice Maiden's importance to the world.

During the reenactment, over 500 costumed actors performed scenes for more than an hour. They began with Juanita's birth in a reconstructed village and then her selection by the Inca as an *aclla* (virgin of the sun). While loudspeakers blared the explosions of an earthquake, a huge artificially constructed volcano "erupted" with fireworks. A solemn reenactment of the girl's ascent of the mountain and sacrifice on behalf of her community followed, performed both in Spanish and in Quechua, language of the Incas. Katherine Concha, age 12, represented Juanita with a dignity befitting the ceremony, which concluded with the actors dancing to the music and lyrics of a song written especially for the event: "Juanita bajó del cielo" ("Juanita descended from the sky").

Our Peruvian finds had been kept since 1998 in a museum built in the confines of a pleasantly restored colonial building dating to the 1600s. The company Cervesur had generously loaned this to Catholic University at no cost for a ten-year period. However, the university could not make improvements to the building, since it would remain the property of the company. The university eventually bought its own building, and in September 2003 a new museum was inaugurated in Arequipa.[27]

Not all the news from Peru has been good, however. In November 2002 the Peruvian archaeologist Fernando Astete and I led a team to excavate a ceremonial complex on the summit of Pachatusan (15,886 feet), the highest mountain dominating the Cuzco Valley, and one of the Incas' most sacred peaks. We found evidence suggesting two human sacrifices, but the site had been extensively looted.[28] In December 2002 two climbers ascended Chachani from its rarely climbed northern side and found a cache left by treasure hunters. Picks, shovels, an old sleeping bag, canned goods, electrical cord used for detonating dynamite, and even a computer magazine were stuck among the rocks at a campsite that had recently been occupied. When the climbers reached the summit, they found several holes that had also been recently made. All the looters had to do was return to their cache and then climb on to the top to continue with their destruction of the site.

Similar problems exist throughout the Andes, of course, and Argentina is no exception. For example, in May 2000 Constanza, the three Mamanis, and I investigated the Inca site on the summit of Chañi at 19,882 feet. A mummy—now in poor condition—had been discovered there by treasure hunters in 1905, making it the first example known of a human sacrifice at a high altitude. Unfortunately, over the years looters had done a thorough job of destroying the site. We found small fragments of textiles, bones, and carbon, and tiny shards that had been strewn about, and once again it was obvious that looters had used dynamite. Only a rough outline of an artificial platform remained of what had once been an important sacrificial burial.[29] At least we felt confident we had established the precise place where the mummy had been found. It was small consolation.

Funds are desperately needed for fieldwork, laboratory research, conservation, and the training of local archaeologists in mountaineering. This would ensure the long-term continuation of studies and the conservation of the mummies and materials found with them. Not for the first time, I pondered the fact that millions of dollars are annually provided for the conservation and exhibition of works of art, but virtually no funds exist to search for, to conserve, and to investigate some of the world's most valuable inheritances from ancient times.

In my mind there is no conflict between having a scientific interest in the mummies and appreciating them as the dead deserving of respect. Both views can be held simultaneously, just as it is possible to be interested in a friend's medical chart when visiting a hospital, while still caring for him. I have received many letters that described the reaction of people at seeing the mummies. One person sounded a note I have heard in various ways from hundreds of people: "I read about your amazing discoveries of the three Incan children that were frozen.... I don't believe that I have ever seen anything so incredible in my life.... We now have the opportunity to look at a real Incan person. Not just an image or a drawing, but an actual 500-year-old person! I am so awestruck by the photos of these three children that I just stare at the photos and think about what the culture must be like, what these children must have been like."

WHETHER IN A MUSEUM, A LABORATORY, OR THE FIELD, RESEARCH on the mummies continues to add to scientific knowledge while at the same time helping protect the cultural patrimony of Andean peoples. Mummies and their associated artifacts also serve as means to help the economies of local communities through such avenues as arts and crafts, museum exhibitions, and focusing government attention on their needs.

Mummies provide information that can be used to educate the world about the unique history of a remarkable ancient civilization—and point the way to others. In the imaginations of children, mummies are second only to dinosaurs, and their educational potential appears to be unlimited. A mummy is a magnet and can be used as a teaching tool on many subjects, including archaeology, geography, human biology, conservation, and the environment.

True time capsules, these frozen bodies allow a view into the past that cannot be obtained through any other means, including that of the best preserved mummies found in other climates, such as in the deserts of Egypt and coastal South America. Due to their excellent preservation, finds made at high altitudes enable unique opportunities for studies ranging from the biological (perfect DNA, ancient diseases, nutrition, etc.) to the archaeological (e.g., extremely rare artifacts and the few remaining Inca ceremonial sites that have offerings in situ). Because of the Incas' practice of making human sacrifices at sites on high mountains, the Andes region is the only one in the world with a good chance of finding frozen mummies—assuming systematic work is conducted before they are destroyed and lost to mankind forever.

As I met more specialists from around the world, a question formed in my mind: Is there anything from the past that is more valuable than a frozen mummy? After all, the mummies never will stop adding to our knowledge, since technology is constantly evolving. New information will be obtained from them ten years from now, a hundred years from now—indeed, for as long as mankind exists. One day the mummies may no longer just be like time machines, they may become time machines, enabling us to recover living information from the past. There is nothing, however rare, that can begin to compare with the uniqueness, complexity, and unlimited knowledge provided by a frozen mummy.[30]

It seems ironic and yet just: 500 years ago the Ampato Ice Maiden was a young woman whose destiny was to be sacrificed to the gods. For centuries she lay forgotten. Then in 1995 she was found and once again has become renowned and honored. Now the Llullaillaco mummies are sharing a similar destiny—and one of them may have been born at the foot of Ampato.

By a strange twist of fate, these children have become better known and recognized than they were in the time of the Incas. For many people, mummies make the past become real by being individuals, sharing in our common humanity. Scientific research, rather than denying the mummies' humanity, makes it become much clearer as their personal stories unfold. Whatever the reasons for our fascination with them, they will always remain stunningly unique windows into the past.

Once a villager said to me, "The Incas are still alive. They are hiding inside the mountains, waiting for the right time to return." His expression turned somber. "For us they will never die."

I looked at him and smiled. "You are right. They never will."

ACKNOWLEDGMENTS

I am currently (2005) an explorer-in-residence of the National Geographic Society. I am also affiliated as a senior fellow of the Mountain Institute; as an honorary professor at Catholic University (Arequipa, Peru); and as a visiting professor at Catholic University (Salta, Argentina). I was a research associate at the Field Museum of Natural History (Chicago) and the National Institute of Archaeology (La Paz, Bolivia) during several of the years I undertook research in the Andes. I owe a debt of gratitude to all of these institutions for their support.

I would like to thank the Expeditions Council and the Committee for Research and Exploration of the National Geographic Society for grants to undertake research on mountains in Peru and Argentina during 1983, 1995, and 1998–2000. A National Endowment for the Humanities fellowship in 1992–93 made possible library research and the subsequent follow-up that led to the discovery of the Ampato Ice Maiden.

Since 2002, the Goldsbury Foundation has generously supported my research on sacred mountains in Latin America. Other organizations that have supplied financing for my Andean research since 1980 include: Rolex Montres, the Organization of American States, the Social Science Research Council,

Dumbarton Oaks, the American Museum of Natural History, the Fabricon Foundation, the G. L. Bruno Foundation, and the Kellner Foundation. Eagle Creek, Iridium, Mares, Motorola, North Face, Patagonia, and Tilley Endurables kindly made donations of clothing and equipment. I would like to especially thank Marmot for supplying an especially large amount of mountaineering gear, Toyota for the donation of a Land Cruiser, and the Carrier Corporation for making custom-built units for conserving the Ice Maiden.

The following individuals deserve my heartfelt gratitude for providing financial support that helped make possible my Andean research: Darlene Anderson, Dan Bennett, Larry and Cathy Bogolub, Mary Ann Bruni, Ben and Kim Chang, Kit and Angie Goldsbury, Will and Nancy Harte, George and Bicky Kellner, Bruce and Susan Levin, Terry Meehan, Bob and Nancy Merritt, Joseph and Sharon Richardson, Tom and Jean Rutherford, Steve and Marcy Sands, Doug and Laura Tipple, Moses and Angela Tsang, and Rob and Susan White.

Special thanks are due to José Antonio Chávez and Constanza Ceruti, who were my co-directors on several of the principal expeditions referred to in the text and responsible for overseeing much of the archaeological work relating to our excavations of Inca sacrificial sites, including the description and conservation of the mummies and artifacts. The reader will be aware of my debt to Arcadio Mamani for the many ways he helped make the expeditions successful. Antonio Beorchia and Juan Schobinger deserve to be singled out for their pioneering work in high-altitude archaeology and their unfailing support for my research over more than two decades. Robert Blatherwick and Louis Glauser were excellent climbing companions during dozens of ascents in the 1980s. Without the use of Louis's vehicle, many mountains would never have been attempted.

Constance Giddings-Parish (née Ayala) and Jacqueline Shafer provided invaluable assistance over periods lasting several years. Steve Allen and Sigrid Anderson made possible my writing in the congenial atmosphere of Arlington, Virginia. Brenda Simmons and Lee Ann Shreve provided administrative support far beyond the call of duty. While I was living in South America, Joanna Burkhardt kept me supplied from the U.S. with copies of publications that I could not have obtained otherwise. Charles Stanish and Catherine Cooke have been sources of constant support and sage advice over the years.

Others in North America who were especially helpful include the following: Ambassador Alexander and Judy Watson, Ambassador Bob and Alene Gelbard, Ambassador Dick Bowers, Ambassadors of Peru Roberto Dañino and Ricardo Luna, Marilyn Baker, Joe Bastien, Brian Bauer, Garth Bawden, Elizabeth Benson, Ed Bernbaum, Tom Besom, Priscilla Briggs, Peter Bruchhausen, Charles Bullock, Richard Burger, Alton Byers, Gabriel Campbell, John Carlson, Virginia Castagnola-Hunter, Juana Castaneda, Patricia Charache, Yvon Chouinard, Wade Davis, David Dearborn, Chris Donnan, Evelio Echeverría, Jim Enote, John Ferguson, Paul Gelles, Dieter and Murph Hoffmann, Bill Howe, John Hyslop, Bill Isbell, Joe Jehl, Robert von Kaupp, Vince Lee, Cindy Lipomanis, Tom Lynch, Margaret MacLean, Hervé and Pamela de Maigret, Gordon McEwan, Gerry and Carol Merfeld, Yvette Mimieux, Don Montague, Craig Morris, Amy Oakland, Dan O'Brien, Jane Pratt, John Rick, Mike Rodman, John Rowe, Betsy Royal, Howard Ruby, Jane Schnell, King Seegar, Lynn Sikkink, Helaine Silverman, Daniel Taylor, Patrick Tierney, John Topic, Richard Townsend, Jim and Janet Underwood, Gary Urton, John Verano, and Tom Zuidema.

With regard to this book, I would like to thank my agent Owen Laster at the William Morris Agency for his interest (and patience) and John Paine, who did an excellent job of editing a manuscript that originally was twice the length of the present work. Constanza Ceruti, José Antonio Chávez, Wade Davis, Rebecca Martin, Jane Seegar, and Charles Stanish provided valuable suggestions that helped improve the manuscript. Scientists sent sections of the manuscript and/or who replied to questions that referred to their specialties include: Tamara Bray, Dan Brooks, Larry Cartmell, Alex Chepstow-Lusty, Angelique Corthals, John Ferguson, Patrick Horne, Gael Lonergan, Edward McCarthy, Keith McKenney, Ann Rowe, Vuka Roussakis, Robin Siegel, Irv Taylor, Andrew Wilson, and John Verano.

Institutions in North America that provided assistance include: the American Alpine Club, Bell Sygma, the Explorers Club (NY), Geographic

Expeditions, the Institute for Genomic Research, Society Expeditions, the South American Explorers, and Wilderness Travel. My thanks to Starbucks in Arlington and McLean, Virginia, which provided environments conducive to writing.

There are many people at the National Geographic Society who have supported me over the years, and I would like to especially acknowledge the following: Eduardo Abreu, Bill Allen, Chuck Brady, Maryanne Culpepper, John Fahey, Cris Ghillani, Karen Gibbs, Yancey Hall, Chris Klein, Barbara Moffet, Oliver Payne, Mary Smith, George Stuart, and Mark Thiessen. I am particularly indebted to Terry Garcia, Dale Petroskey, and Rebecca Martin for ensuring the success of several of my projects over the years. I owe my appreciation to Neva Folk, Susan Reeve, Julie Rushing, and Annabelle Sbarbatti for going out of their way to be helpful. Ann Williams kindly made available her voluminous notes taken during a hectic week's lab work in Arequipa.

Numerous conservation and mummy specialists were consulted in the U.S. and Europe about the frozen mummies and I am especially grateful to: Arthur Aufderheide, Larry Bowers, Bob Brier, Julia Burke, Bill Conklin, Angelique Corthals, Eduard Egarter-Vigl, Toby Raphael, Horst Seidler, Katherine Singley, Konrad Spindler, and Steve Weintraub. Stefan Michalski, Judy Logan, and David Gratten of the Canadian Conservation Institute (CCI) were contacted by Robin Siegel with regard to the Ampato Ice Maiden, as was David Harrowfield, a Canadian frozen artifacts specialist. (We also benefited from the report of the CCI's Frozen Skin Project 1984 meeting about the conservation of the El Plomo mummy, which included eight specialists.) Members of the Smithsonian Institution's Conservation Analytical Laboratory who were consulted include: David Erhardt, Mark McCormick-Goodhart, and Charles Tomosa. I benefited from lengthy discussions with Miguel Corzo, Margaret MacLean, Shin Maekawa, and Alberto Tagle of the Getty Conservation Institute.

I would like to acknowledge the assistance and dedication of the following men who participated in several of the high-altitude archaeology expeditions in Peru: Jimmy Bouroncle, José Antonio Chávez, Walter Diaz, Orlando

Jaen, Dante Lucioni, Arcadio Mamani, Edgar Mamani, Ignacio Mamani, Ruddy Perea, Eduardo Saljero, Jim Underwood, José Antonio Zamalla, Carlos Zárate, and Miguel Zárate. I owe a debt of gratitude to Luis Carpio, the rector of Catholic University in Arequipa, for supporting my research over many years. Others in Peru who were most helpful to my research include: Trinidad Aguilar, Hernan Amat, Percy Ardiles, Fernando Astete, Stefan Austermuhle, Luis Barreda, Jim Bartle, Marilyn Bridges, Nilda Callanaupa, Reynaldo and Maria Casos, Jean-Jacques Decoster, Octavio Fernandez, Alfredo Ferreyros, Jorge Flores, Peter Frost, Peter Getzels, Martin van de Guchte, Sonia Guillen, Adriana von Hagen, Tom Hendrickson, Federico Kauffmann-Doig, Ann Kendall, José Koechlin, Margaret MacLean, Romero Matos, Max Milligan, Juan Victor Nuñez del Prado, Ruben Orellana, Jean-Pierre Protzen, Alicia Quirita, Robert Randall, Mauricio Romaña, Washington Rosas, Ruth Salas, Alfredo Valencia, Roger Valencia, Fernando Villiger, Doris Walter, and Wendy Weeks. Institutions in Peru that supported the research include: Catholic University (Arequipa), CERVESUR (Arequipa), Explorandes, the Fuerza Aérea de Peru, the Instituto Nacional de Cultura (Lima, Cuzco, and Arequipa, Peru), and Peruvian Andean Treks.

The expeditions to Quehuar and Llullaillaco in Argentina were made possible thanks to the following participants: Jimmy Bouroncle, Constanza Ceruti, Adriana Escobar, Orlando Jaen, Sergio Lazarovich, Alejandro Lewis, Edgar Mamani, Ignacio Mamani, Antonio Mercado, Ruddy Perea, Christian Vitry, and Federico Viveros. Other people whose support I would like to acknowledge include: Clara Abal de Russo, Arnaldo Arroyo, Dario Barboza, Fernando Bearzi, Christina Bianchetti, Jorge and Nené Dejean, Katia Gibaja, Pedro Lamas, and Luis Massa. I appreciate the interest shown in our work by the governor of Salta, Juan Carlos Romero; the minister of education, Juan José Fernández and the rector of Catholic University, Patricio Colombo. Several government authorities who assisted us in the course of our investigations include: Roberto Ibarguren, Mario Lazarovich, Antonio Lovaglio, Gabriel Miremont, José Neiburg, Eleonora Rabinowicz de Ferrar, and Belisario Saravia. My thanks also go out to those who collaborated in the conservation of the mummies, the microbiological, odontological, and radiological studies, and the needle biopsies: Facundo Arias, Arnaldo Arroyo, Mario Bernaski, Constanza Ceruti, Josefina González, Marcelina Matos, Jorge Pastrana, Gustavo Piloni, Carlos Previgliano, Silvia Quevedo, Ruth Salas, Pedro Santillán, Gerardo Vides, and Miguel Xamena. Argentine institutions that supported our research and laboratory work include: the Dirección de Patrimonio Cultural, the Ejército Argentino, Gendarmaría Nacional, the Institute of High Mountain Research of Catholic University of Salta, the Ministerio de Educación de Salta, and the municipalities of Santa Rosa de Pastos Grandes, San Antonio de los Cobres, and Tolar Grande.

In Bolivia the following people assisted my work: Simón Arias, Conrad von Bergen, Bernard Francou, John Janusek, Judi Johnson, Patrice Lecoq, Peter McFarren, Eduardo Pareja, Carlos Ponce, Miguel Reznicek, Oswaldo Rivera, and Wolfgang Schuler. Institutional support was provided by the Instituto Nacional de Arqueología (La Paz) and the Fuerza Naval de Bolivia.

During my research in Chile, I received support from the following: Ana María Barón, Patrick Burns, Angel Cabeza, Ralph Cané, Miguel Cervellino, General (R) Eduardo Iensen, Rodrigo Jordan, Agustin Llagostera, Patricio Lopez, Robert Lyall, Hans Niemeyer, Julie Palma, Silvia Quevedo, Julio Sanhueza, Calogero Santoro, George Serracino, Oswaldo Silva, and Betty Woodsend. The following institutions assisted our work: the Carbineros de Chile, the Corporación para el Desarollo de la Ciencia, the Corporación Nacional Forestal, the Fuerza Aérea de Chile, the Museo Chileno de Arte Precolombino (Santiago), the Museo Arqueológico de San Pedro de Atacama, and the Universidad del Norte (Antofagasta).

It would be impossible to name all the individuals who in one way or another contributed to my research in the Andes over a period of 25 years. This is even more the case if I were to include those who helped with the topics and sites only briefly referred to in this book, such as at Chavin, Nazca, Lake Titicaca, and Tiahuanaco, and the many villagers who welcomed me into their homes. I therefore apologize to those whom I have failed to acknowledge. Of course, none of the people named above are responsible for any of the factual errors that might occur in this book.

BIBLIOGRAPHY

ABAL DE RUSSO, CLARA
2001 Cerro Aconcagua: Descripción y Estudio del Material Textil. In El Santuario Incaico del Cerro Aconcagua,Juan Schobinger (ed.). Universidad Nacional de Cuyo, Mendoza, pp. 191-244.
2003 La Textilería en América Andina, con Especial Referencia a la Hallada en los Santuarios de Altura. Ph.D. thesis, Universidad Nacional de Cuyo, Mendoza.
2004 El Ajuar de la Momia del Nevado de Chuscha. In El Santuario Incaico del Nevado de Chuscha, Juan Schobinger (ed.). Fundación CEPPA, Buenos Aires, pp. 149-203.

ABERCROMBIE, THOMAS
1998 Pathways of Memory and Power: Ethnography and History among an Andean People. University of Wisconsin Press, Madison.

ACOSTA, JOSÉ DE
2002 Natural and Moral History of the Indies. Duke University Press, Durham.

ALLEN, CATHERINE
1988 The Hold Life Has: Coca and Cultural Identity in an Andean Community. Smithsonian Institution Press, Washington, D.C.

ARIAS, FACUNDO, JOSEFINA GONZÁLEZ, AND CONSTANZA CERUTI
2002 Estudios Odontológicos de las Momias del Llullaillaco. Boletín de la Asociación Argentina de Odontología para Niños 31(2/3): 3-10, Buenos Aires.

ARRIAGA, JOSÉ DE
1968 [1621] The Extirpation of Idolatry in Peru. University of Kentucky Press, Lexington.

ARRIAZA, BERNARDO
1995 Beyond Death: The Chinchorro Mummies of Ancient Chile. Smithsonian Institution, Washington, D.C.

ASHCROFT, FRANCES
2000 Life at the Extremes. University of California Press, Berkeley.

ASHMORE, WENDY, AND BERNARD KNAPP (EDS.)
1999 Archaeologies of Landscape. Blackwell Publishers, Oxford.

ATKINSON, WILLIAM
2003 Nanocosm. Viking Canada, Toronto.

ATWOOD, ROGER
2004 Stealing History: Tomb Raiders, Smugglers, and the Looting of the Ancient World. St. Martin's Press, New York.

AUFDERHEIDE, ARTHUR
2003 The Scientific Study of Mummies. Cambridge University Press, Cambridge.

AUFDERHEIDE, ARTHUR, AND ODIN LANGSJOEN
1998 Report on CT-scan of the Ice Maiden. ms. Dept. of Pathology, University of Minnesota, Duluth.

AUFDERHEIDE, ARTHUR, AND CONRADO RODRÍGUEZ-MARTÍN
1998   The Cambridge Encyclopedia of Human Paleopathology. Cambridge University Press, Cambridge.

BACKPACKER MAGAZINE
1999   Mountain Air. Backpacker Magazine (Special Pullout) 27(6) (August): between pp. 68-69.

BAHN, PAUL (ED.)
1996   Tombs, Graves, and Mummies. Weidenfeld and Nicholson, London.
2003   Written in Bones: How Human Remains Unlock Secrets of the Dead. Firefly Books, Buffalo.

BAILEY, SOLON
1899   Peruvian Meteorology, 1888-1890. Annals of the Astronomical Observatory of Harvard College 39(1): 1-39.

BAKER, MARILYN
2001   Technical Attributes as Cultural Choices: The Textiles Associated with an Inca Sacrifice at Cerro Esmeralda, Northern Chile. MS thesis, Trent University, Peterborough (Canada).

BÁRCENA, ROBERTO
2001   Los Objetos Metálicos de la Ofrenda Ritual del Cerro Aconcagua. In El Santuario Incaico del Cerro Aconcagua, Juan Schobinger (ed.). Universidad Nacional de Cuyo, Mendoza, pp. 281-301.

BARÓN, ANA MARÍA, AND JOHAN REINHARD
1981   Expedición Arqueológica al Volcan Licancabur. Revista de la Corporación para el Desarrollo de la Ciencia 1(4): 31-38, Santiago.

BASTIEN, JOSEPH
1978   Mountain of the Condor: Metaphor and Ritual in an Andean Ayllu. West Publishing Company, New York.

BAUER, BRIAN
1992   The Development of the Inca State. University of Texas Press, Austin.
1998   The Sacred Landscape of the Inca: The Cusco Ceque System. University of Texas Press, Austin.

BAUER, BRIAN, AND DAVID DEARBORN
1995   Astronomy and Empire in the Ancient Andes: The Cultural Origins of Inca Sky Watching. University of Texas Press, Austin.

BAUER, BRIAN, AND CHARLES STANISH
2001   Ritual and Pilgrimage in the Ancient Andes: The Islands of the Sun and the Moon. University of Texas Press, Austin.

BAUMANN, PETER
1986   Das letzte Geheimnis der Inka. Herder Verlag, Freiburg.

BEECH, HANNAH
2003   Stealing Beauty. Time, October 27 (Special Report).

BENFORD, GREGORY
2004   A Frozen Future? Cryonics as a Gamble. Skeptic 11(2): 28-31.

BENSON, ELIZABETH, AND ANITA COOK (EDS.)
2001   Ritual Sacrifice in Ancient Peru. University of Texas Press, Austin.

BEORCHIA, ANTONIO
1975a   El Nevado Quehuar. Revista del Centro de Investigaciones Arqueológicas de Alta Montaña 2: 29-35, San Juan.
1975b   El cementerio indígena del volcán Llullaillaco. Revista del Centro de Investigaciones Arqueológicas de Alta Montaña 2: 36-42, San Juan.

BEORCHIA, ANTONIO (COMPILER)
1985   El Enigma de los Santuarios Indígenas de Alta Montaña. Revista del Centro de Investigaciones Arqueológicas de Alta Montaña 5, San Juan.
2001   Revista del Centro de Investigaciones Arqueológicas de Alta Montaña 6 (1987-1999), San Juan.

BERG, HANS VAN DEN
1985   Diccionario Religioso Aymara. CETA, Iquitos.
1990   La Tierra No Da Así Nomás: Los Ritos Agrícolas en la Religión de los Aymara-Critstianos. Hisbol, La Paz.

BERNBAUM, EDWIN
1990   Sacred Mountains of the World. Sierra Club Books, San Francisco.

BERTONIO, LUDOVICO
1984 [1612] Vocabulario de la Lengua Aymara. CERES, Cochabamba.

BESOM, THOMAS
2000 Mummies, Mountains, and Immolations: Strategies for Unifying the Inka Empire's Southern Quarters. Ph.D. thesis, Binghamton University, Binghamton.
n.d. Of Mummies, Mountains, and Immolations: An Ethnohistoric Study of Human Sacrifice and Mountain Worship Among the Inkas. University of Texas Press, Austin. (in press)

BETANZOS, JUAN DE
1996 [1551-1557] Narratives of the Incas. University of Texas Press, Austin.

BIGGAR, JOHN
1996 The High Andes: A Guide for Climbers. Andes, Kirkcudbrightshire (Scotland).

BLOWER, DAVID
2000 The Many Facets of Mullu: More than Just a Spondylus Shell. Andean Past 6: 209-228.

BOLIN, INGE
1998 Rituals of Respect. University of Texas Press, Austin.

BOURGET, STEVE
1994 Los Sacerdotes a la Sombra del Cerro Blanco y del Arco Bicéfalo. Revista del Museo de Arqueología, Antropología e Historia 5: 81-123.

BOWMAN, ISAIAH
1924 Desert Trails of Atacama. American Geographical Society, New York.

BRADLEY, RICHARD
2000 An Archaeology of Natural Places. London: Routledge.

BRAY, TAMARA
2003 Inca pottery as culinary equipment: Food, feasting, and gender in imperial state design. Latin American Antiquity 14(1): 1-22.
2004 La Alfarería Imperial Incaica: Una Comparación entre la Cerámica Estatal del Área del Cuzco y la Cerámica de las Provincias. Revista Chungara 32(6).

BRAY, TAMARA, L. MINC, C. CERUTI, R. PEREA, J. REINHARD, AND J. CHÁVEZ
2005 A Compositional Analysis of Pottery Vessels Associated with the Inca Ritual of Capacocha. Journal of Anthropological Archaeology. (in press)

BRIER, BOB
1998 The Encyclopedia of Mummies. Checkmark Books, New York.

BRODA, JOHANNA, STANISLAW IWANISZEWSKI, AND ARTURO MONTERO
2001 La Montaña en el Paisaje Ritual. CONACULTA – INAH, México, D.F.

BROWN, MICHAEL
2003 Who Owns Native Culture? Harvard University Press, Cambridge.

BRUSH, CHARLES
1984 The Licancabur Expedition. Explorers Journal 62(1): 4-13.

BUELL, JANET
1997 Ice Maiden of the Andes. Twenty-First Century Books, New York.

BURKERT, WALTER
1983 Homo Necans: The Anthropology of Ancient Greek Sacrificial Ritual and Myth. University of California Press, Berkeley.

BURROUGHS, WILLIAM, B. CROWDER, T. ROBERTSON, E. VALLIER-TALBOT, AND R.WHITAKER
1996 A Guide to Weather. Fog City Press, San Francisco.

CARDONA, AUGUSTO
2002 Arqueología de Arequipa. Centro de Investigaciones Arqueológicas de Arequipa, Arequipa.

CAREY, CELIA
1999 Secrets of the Sacrificed. Discovering Archaeology 1(4), July/August: 46-53.

CARRIER CORPORATION
1996 Preserving Peru's Ampato Maiden. WeatherMakers, July/August, pp. 5-10.

CARTMELL, LARRY
2001 Hair Analysis in the Mummies of Mount Llullaillaco. Proceedings from the IV World Congress of Mummy Studies. In press.

CASTAÑEDA, JUANA MARÍA
2000   Molecular Genetic Analysis of Ancient Human Remains. MS thesis, George Washington University, Washington, D.C.

CERUTI, MARÍA CONSTANZA
1999   Cumbres Sagradas del Noroeste Argentino: Avances en Arqueología de alta Montaña y Etnoarqueología de Santuarios Andinos. Ediciones Universidad Católica de Salta, Salta.
2001a   Recientes Hallazgos en los Volcanes Quehuar (6130 m.) y Llullaillaco (6739 m.). Actas del XIII Congreso Nacional de Arqueología Argentina 1: 313-320, Cordoba.
2001b   La Capacocha del Nevado de Chañi: Una Aproximación Preliminar desde la Arqueología. Chungara 33 (2): 279-282, Arica.
2003   Llullaillaco: Sacrificios y Ofrendas en un Santuario Inca de Alta Montaña. Ediciones Universidad Católica de Salta, Salta.
n.d.   Excavaciones arqueológicas de alta montaña en el Nevado de Chañi (5.896 m.) y el Nevado de Acay (5.716 m.) (Provincia de Salta). Actas del XIV Congreso Nacional de Arqueología Argentina. (in press)

CHAMBERLAIN, ANDREW
1994   Human Remains. University of California Press, Berkeley.

CHAMBERLAIN, ANDREW, AND MICHAEL PEARSON
2001   Earthly Remains: The History and Science of Preserved Human Bodies. Oxford University Press, New York.

CHÁVEZ, JOSÉ ANTONIO
1993   La Erupción del Volcán Misti. Arequipa.
2000   Juanita: La Niña que bajó de los Cielos. PW Impresiones, Arequipa.

CHÁVEZ, JOSÉ ANTONIO, HORST SEIDLER, AND KURT IRGOLIOC
1996   Histological Examinations of Hair Samples: The Ampato Mummy I (Juanita). Preliminary Report. ms. Institute of Human Biology, University of Vienna.

CHEPSTOW-LUSTY, ALEX
1997   Preliminary Results of Pollen from Peruvian Mummy Samples. ms. Department of Plant Sciences, Cambridge University, Cambridge.

CIEZA DE LEÓN, PEDRO
1959 [1553]   The Incas of Pedro Cieza de León. Victor Wolfgang Von Hagen (ed.), University of Oklahoma Press, Norman.

CLARK, LEONARD
1953   The Rivers Ran East. Funk and Wagnalls, New York.

COBO, BERNABÉ
1983 [1653]   History of the Inca Empire. Ronald Hamilton (trans. and ed.), University of Texas Press, Austin.
1990 [1653]   Inca Religion and Customs. Ronald Hamilton (trans. and ed.), University of Texas Press, Austin.

COCKBURN, AIDAN, EVE COCKBURN, AND THEODORE REYMAN (EDS.)
1998   Mummies, Disease, and Ancient Cultures. Cambridge University Press, Cambridge. (2nd ed.)

COLEMAN, SIMON, AND JOHN ELSNER
1995   Pilgrimage: Past and Present in the World Religions. Harvard University Press, Cambridge.

CONKLIN, WILLIAM
1997   The Ampato Textile Offerings. In Sacred and Ceremonial Textiles, Textile Society of America, Minneapolis pp.104-110.

CORNWELL, PATRICIA
2001   Isle of Dogs. Berkley Books, New York.

CREWS, JOHN
2000   Phylogenetic and Molecular Analysis of 401 Human Mitochrondrial DNA Control Region Sequences. MS thesis, George Washington University, Washington, D.C.

CRONYN, J. M.
1990   The Elements of Archaeological Conservation. Routledge, London.

CURATOLA, MARCO
1977   Mito y Milenarismo en los Andes: Del Taki Onqoy a Inkarrí. Allpanchis 10: 65-92.

D'ALTROY, TERENCE
2002   The Incas. Blackwell Publishers, Oxford.

DARK, KEN
1995   Theoretical Archaeology. Cornell University Press, Ithaca.

DARWIN, CHARLES
1959   The Voyage of the Beagle. Everyman's Library, New York.

DARWIN, MICHAEL, AND BRIAN WOWK
1992   Cryonics: Reaching for Tomorrow. Skeptic 1(2): 32-43.

DAVIES, NIGEL
1995   The Incas. University Press of Colorado, Niwot.
1997   The Ancient kingdoms of Peru. Penguin Books, Harmondsworth.

DAVIS, JOEL
1997   Mapping the Mind: The Secrets of the Human Brain and How It Works. Birch Lane Press, Secaucus.

DENEVAN, W. ET AL (EDS.)
1987   Agricultural Terracing in the Colca Valley, Peru. British Archaeological Reports, Oxford.

DOYLE, ARTHUR CONAN
1963   The Lost World. Pyramid Books, New York.

DOYLE, MARY
1988   The Ancestor Cult and Burial Ritual in Seventeenth-and Eighteenth-Century Central Peru. Ph.D.
        thesis, University of California, Berkeley.

DRANSART, PENNY
1995   Elemental Meanings: Symbolic Expression in Inka Miniature Figurines. Research Papers 40,
        Institute of Latin American Studies, University of London.

DUVIOLS, PIERRE
1984   Albornoz y el espacio ritual andino prehispánico: Instrucción para descubrir todas las
        guacos del Pirú y sus camayos y haziendas. Revista Andina 2 (1): 169-222, Cuzco.
1986   Cultura Andina y Represión. Centro de Estudios Rurales Andinos, Cuzco.

ECHEVARRÍA, EVELIO
1977   Early Mountaineering in Peru. In Yuraq Yanka: Guide to the Peruvian Andes, John, Ricker
        American Alpine Club, New York, pp. 3-7.

EGARTER-VIGL, EDUARD
2003   Die Konservierung der Mumie des Mannes aus dem Eis im Südtiroler Archäologiemuseum.
        In Die Gletschermumies aus der Kupferzeit 2. Fleckinger, Angelika (ed.), Schriften des
        Südtiroler Archäologiemuseums, Bozen, pp. 35-40.

ELLIS, LINDA (ED.)
2000   Archaeological Method and Theory. Garland Publishing, New York.

ESTRADA BELTRÁN, FRANCISCO DE
1923 [1613] Idolatrías de los Indios Wankas. Inca 1(3): 651-667, Lima.

EVANS, W.
1963   The Chemistry of Death. Charles Thomas, Springfield.

FAVRE, HENRI
1967   Tayta Wamani: Le culte des montagnes dans le centre sud des Andes Peruviennes.
        Colloque d'études Péruviennes 61: 121-40.

FISHER, RICHARD, GRANT HEIKEN, AND JEFFREY HULEN
1997   Volcanoes: Crucibles of Change. Princeton University Press, Princeton.

FLANNERY, KENT, JOYCE MARCUS, AND ROBERT REYNOLDS
1989   The Flocks of the Wamani: A Study of Llama Herders on the Punas of Ayacucho, Peru. Academic Press, San Diego.

FLORES, CARLOS
1976   Enqa, Enqaychu, Illa y Khuya Rumi: Aspectos Mágico-religiosos entre Pastores. Journal of
        Latin American Lore 2(1): 115-136.
1997   El Taytacha Qoyllur Rit'i. Instituto de Pastoral Andina, Sicuani.

FOWLER, BRENDA
2000   Iceman: Uncovering the Life and Times of a Prehistoric Man Found in an Alpine Glacier.
        Random House, New York.

FRANCOU, BERNARD, E. RAMIREZ, B. CACERES, AND J. MENDOZA
2000   Glacier evolution in the Tropical Andes during the last decades of the 20th Century:
        Chacaltaya, Bolivia, and Antizana, Ecuador. Ambio 29(7).

FREIDEL, DAVID, LINDA SCHELE, AND JOY PARKER
1993   Maya Cosmos. William Morrow, New York.

FUNSTON, SYLVIA
2000   Mummies. Owl Books, Toronto.

GARCILASO DE LA VEGA, INCA
1966 [1609] The Royal Commentaries of the Inca and General History of Peru. Part One. University of
            Texas Press, Austin.

GASPARINI, GRAZIANO AND LUISE MARGOLIES
1980   Inca Architecture. Indiana University Press, Bloomington.

GELLES, PAUL
1990   Channels of Power, Fields of Contention. Ph.D. thesis, Harvard University, Cambridge.
2000   Water and Power in Highland Peru. Rutgers University Press, New Brunswick.

GENTILE, MARGARITA
1996   La Dimensión sociopolítica y religiosa de la Capacocha del Cerro Aconcagua. Bulletin de
            l'Institut Français d'Etudes Andines 25 (1): 43-90, Lima.

GETZ, DAVID
1998   Frozen Girl. Henry Holt and Company, New York.

GIRAULT, LUIS
1988   Rituales en las Regiones Andinas de Bolivia y Perú. CERES, La Paz.

GONZÁLEZ HOLGUÍN, DIEGO
1952 [1608] Vocabulario de la Lengua General de todo el Perú llamada Lengua
            Quichua del Inca. Universidad Nacional de San Marcos, Lima.

GOSE, PETER
1994   Deathly Waters and Hungry Mountains. University of Toronto Press, Toronto.

GOULD, STEPHEN JAY
1998   Leonardo's Mountain of Clams and the Diet of Worms. Jonathan Cape, London.

GOW, ROSALIND, AND BERNABÉ CONDORI
1982   Kay Pacha. Centro de Estudios Rurales Andinas, Cuzco. (2nd ed.)

GREEN, MIRANDA
2001   Dying for the Gods: Human Sacrifice in Iron Age and Roman Europe. Tempus Publishing, Charleston

GRIEK, SUSAN VANDE
1999   A Gift for Ampato. Groundwood Books, Toronto.

GUAMAN POMA DE AYALA, F.
1980 [1613] El Primer Nueva Coronica y Buen Gobierno. Siglo Veintiuno Editores, Mexico D.F.

GUTIERREZ DE SANTA CLARA, PEDRO
1963 [ca. 1603] Quinquenarios o Historia de las Guerras Civiles del Perú. Biblioteca de Autores
            Españoles, vol. 166. Ediciones Atlas, Madrid.

HALLIBURTON, RICHARD
1941   Richard Halliburton's Complete Book of Marvels. Bobbs-Merrill, Indianapolis.

HARRIS, STEVEN
2004   Vitrification Unjustly Vilified. Skeptic 11(2): 27.

HEMMING, JOHN
1970   The Conquest of the Incas. Harcourt Brace Jovanovich, New York.

HERNÁNDEZ PRÍNCIPE, RODRIGO
1923 [1622] Mitología Andina. Inca 1(1): 25-78, Lima.

HODDER, IAN
1999   The Archaeological Process. Blackwell Publishers, Oxford.

HORGAN, JOHN
1999   The Undiscovered Mind: How the Human Brain Defies Replication, Medication, and
            Explanation. Free Press, New York.

HOUSTON, CHARLES
1987   Going Higher: The Story of Man and Altitude. Little, Brown and Co., Boston.

HURLEY, WILLIAM
1978   Highland peasants and rural development in southern Peru. Ph.D. thesis. University of Oxford, Oxford.

HYSLOP, JOHN.
1984   The Inka Road System. Academic Press, New York.
1990   Inka Settlement Planning. University of Texas Press, Austin.

IENSEN F., EDUARDO
1979   Licancabur 1977. Instituto Geográfico Militar de Chile, Santiago.

ISBELL, WILLIAM
1997   Mummies and Mortuary Monuments: A Postprocessual Prehistory of Central Andean Social
       Organization. University of Texas Press, Austin.

ISERSON, K.
1994   Death to Dust: What Happens to Human Bodies. Galen Press, Tucson.

ISHERWOOD, DICK
1980   Buni Zom. Alpine Journal 85(329).

JOHNSON, CHRISTOPHER, AND MARSHA MCGEE (EDS.)
1998   How Different Religions View Death and the Afterlife. Charles Press, Philadelphia. (2nd ed.)

JOHNSON, MATTHEW
1999   Archaeological Theory. Blackwell Publishers, Oxford.

JONES, MARTIN
2001   The Molecule Hunt: Archaeology and the Search for Ancient DNA. Arcade Publishing, New York.

JOUKOWSKY, MARTHA
1980   A Complete Manual of Field Archaeology. Prentice Hall, Englewood Cliffs (NJ).

KAMLER, KENNETH
2004   Surviving the Extremes. St. Martin's Press, New York.

KRAHL, LUIS, AND OSCAR GONZÁLEZ
1966   Expediciones y Hallazgos en al Alta Cordillera de la Provincia de Coquimbo (Cerros Las
       Tórtolas y Doña Ana), 1956-1958. Anales de Arqueología y Etnología 21: 101-123.

KUBELIKA, WOLFGANG, ET AL.
1996   Identification and Chemical Analysis of Coca Leaves of the Offerings of the Ampato
       Mummy I "Juanita." Institute for Pharmacology, University of Vienna.

KUDALIS, ERIC
2003   Ice Mummies: Frozen in Time. Capstone Press, Mankato (MN).

KURTZ, HOWARD
1998   Spin Cycle. Free Press, New York.

LAMB, SIMON
2004   Devil in the Mountain: A Search for the Origin of the Andes. Princeton University Press, Princeton.

LAMBERT, JOSEPH
1997   Traces of the Past: Unraveling the Secrets of Archaeology through Chemistry. Perseus Books, Reading.

LEE, VINCE
2000   Forgotten Vilcabamba. Sixpac Manco Publications, Wilson (WY).

LEGROS, FRANCOIS
n.d.   The Active Volcanoes of Peru. (no publisher noted)

LINARES, ELOY
1966   Restos arqueológicos en el nevado de Pichu Pichu (Arequipa, Perú). Anales de
       Arqueología y Etnología 21: 7-47.

LIZÁRRAGA, REGINALDO DE
1999 [1607?] Descripción del Perú, Tucumán, Río de la Plata y Chile. Academia Nacional de la Historia,
       Buenos Aires.

LYLE, DOUGLAS
2004   Forensics. Wiley Publishing, Indianapolis.

LYNCH, THOMAS
1978   Tambo incaico Catarpe-este. Estudios Atacameños 5: 142-147.

LYNNERUP, NIELS, CLAUS ANDREASEN, AND JOEL BERGLUND (EDS.)
2002   Mummies in a New Millennium: Proceedings of the 4th World Congress on Mummy Studies.
       Greenland National Museum and Archives, Nuuk.

Lynnerup, Niels, Carlos Previgliano, Constanza Ceruti, and Johan Reinhard
n.d.   Imaging sans frontiéres: Exchanging and working with the digital imaging data of the Mount Llullaillaco mummies. (in press)

MacCormack, Sabine
1991   Religion in the Andes. Vision and Imagination in Early Colonial Peru. Princeton University Press, Princeton.
2000   Processions for the Inca: Andean and Christian ideas of human sacrifice, communion, and embodiment in early colonial Peru. Archive fur Religionsgeschichte 2(1): 110-140, Munich.

MacInnes, Hamish
1981   Look Behind the Ranges. Penguin Books, Harmondsworth.
1984   Beyond the Ranges. Victor Gollancz, London.

Masías, Pablo
1997   El Misti: Biografía de un Volcán. Edimaz Eril, Arequipa.

Mays, Simon
1998   The Archaeology of Human Bones. Routledge, New York.

Mazziotti, Gerardo, and Armando Vargas
2004   Estudio Médico-Tanatolico de la Momia del Cerro Nevado del Chuscha. In El Santuario Incaico del Nevado de Chuscha, Juan Schobinger (ed.). Fundación CEPPA, Buenos Aires, pp. 81-89.

McIntyre, Loren
1975   The Incredible Incas and Their Timeless Land. National Geographic Society, Washington, D.C.

McKenney, Keith
1999   Summary of Initial DNA Analysis of the Mount Llullaillaco Mummies. ms. George Mason University, Manassas (VA).

Menzel, Dorothy
1977   The Archaeology of Ancient Peru and the Work of Max Uhle. R. H. Lowie Museum of Anthropology, Berkeley.

Metcalf, Peter, and Richard Huntington
1991   Celebrations of Death: The Anthropology of Mortuary Ritual. Cambridge University Press, Cambridge.

Michieli, Catalina Teresa
1990   Textileria incaica en la provincia de San Juan: Los ajuares de los cerros Mercedario, Toro, y Tambillas. Instituto de Investigaciones Arqueológicas y Museo, Universidad Nacional de San Juan, San Juan (Argentina).

Miller, Kevin
2004   Cryonics Redux. Skeptic 11(1): 24-25.

Millones, Luis (compiler)
1990   El Retorno de las Huacas. Instituto de Estudio Peruanos, Lima.

Mims, Cedric
1999   When We Die: The Science, Culture, and Rituals of Death. St. Martin's Press, New York.

Molina, Cristóbal de
1959 [1575] Ritos y Fábulas de los Incas. Editorial Futuro, Buenos Aires.

Montgomery, David
2004   The Alfalfa Club Dinner Gets a Side Dish of Glam. Washington Post January 25: D1, D6, Washington, D.C.

Morris, Craig and Adriana von Hagen
1993   The Inka Empire and Its Andean Origins. Abbeville Press, New York.

Morrison, Tony
1972   Land Above the Clouds: Wildlife of the Andes. Universe Books, New York.

Moseley, Michael
1992   The Incas and Their Ancestors. Thames and Hudson, London.

Mostny, Grete (ed.)
1957   La Momia del Cerro El Plomo. Boletín del Museo Nacional de Historia Natural 27(1), Santiago.

Murúa, Martín de
2001 [1590] Historia General del Perú. Dastin, Madrid.

Nachtigall, Horst
1966   Indianische Fischer, Feldbauer, und Viehzuchter. Marburger Studien zur Völkerkunde 2, Berlin.

NEATE, JILL
1987   Mountaineering in the Andes: Expedition Advisory Center, London.

NICHOLS, DEBORAH, ANTHONY KLESERT, AND ROGER ANYON
1989   Ancestral Sites, Shrines, and Graves: Native American Perspectives on the Ethics of
       Collecting Cultural Properties. In The Ethics of Collecting Cultural Property, Phyllis
       Messenger (ed.). University of New Mexico Press, Albuquerque, pp. 27-38.

NILES, SUSAN
1992   Inca Architecture and the Sacred Landscape. In The Ancient Americas: Art from Sacred
       Landscapes, Richard Townsend (ed.). The Art Institute of Chicago, Chicago pp. 347-357.
1999   The Shape of Inca History: Narrative and Architecture in an Andean Empire. University of
       Iowa Press, Iowa City.

OLSON, STEVE
2002   Mapping Human History: Discovering the Past Through Our Genes. Houghton Mifflin, Boston.

O'NEILL, SEAN
2003   A Striking Mystery. Washington Post, July 29: F1, F5.

PARDO, LUIS
1941   Un hallazgo en la zona arqueológica del Ausangati (Cuzco). Revista del Museo Nacional
       10(1): 110-112, Lima.

PARSSINEN, MARTIN
1992   Tawantinsuyu: The Inca State and Its Political Organization. Socetas Historica Finlandae, Helsinki.

PAUSANIAS
1979   Guide to Greece (Vol. 2: Southern Greece). Penguin Books, London.

PAZ, PERCY
1988   Ceremonias y Pinturas Rupestres. In Lamichos y Paqocheros: Pastores de Llamas y Alpacas,
       Flores, Jorge (ed.). Centro de Estudios Andinos Cuzco, Cuzco, pp. 217-223.

PEARCE, FRED
2001   Volcanic Threat to Peruvian City Ignored. New Scientist, December 12.

PEARSON, MIKE
1999   The Archaeology of Death and Burial. Texas A & M University Press, College Station.

PEREA, RUDDY
2001   Análisis Morfológico y Comparativo del Contexto de la Cerámica en las Ofrendas de Alta
       Montaña. Facultad de Arqueología y Turismo, Universidad Católica de Santa María, Arequipa.

POLO DE ONDEGARDO, JUAN
1916 [1571] Informaciones Acerca de la Religión y Gobierno de los Incas. Sanmarti y Ca., Lima.

PREVIGLIANO, CARLOS, C. CERUTI, J. REINHARD, F. ARIAS, AND J. GONZÁLEZ
2003   Radiologic Evaluation of the Llullaillaco Mummies. American Journal of Roentgenology 181: 1473-1479.

PRICE, LARRY
1981   Mountains and Man. University of California Press, Berkeley.

PRINGLE, HEATHER
2001   The Mummy Congress. Hyperion, New York.

QUEVEDO, SILVIA, AND ELIANA DURAN
1992   Ofrendas a los dioses en las montañas: Santuarios de altura en la cultura Inka. Boletín del
       Museo Nacional de Historia Natural de Chile 43: 193-206, Santiago.

RACHOWIECKI, ROB, GREG CLAIRE, AND GRANT DIXON
2003   Trekking in the Central Andes. Lonely Planet, London.

RAFFINO, RODOLFO
1981   Los Incas del Kollasuyu. Editorial Ramos Americana, La Plata.

RAMOS, ALONSO
1976 [1621] Historia de Nuestra Señora de Copacabana. Editorial Universo, La Paz.

RANDALL, ROBERT
1982   Qoyllur Rit'i, An Inca Fiesta of the Pleiades. Boletín del Instituto Francés de Estudios Andinos
       11(1-2): 37-81, Lima.

REBITSCH, MATHIAS
1966   Santuarios en altas cumbres de la puna de Atacama. Anales de Arqueología y Etnología 21:51-80. Mendoza.

REID, HOWARD
1999   In Search of the Immortals: Mummies, Death, and the Afterlife. St. Martin's Press, New York.

REINDEL, MARKUS
1999   Montañas en el Desierto: La Arquitectura Monumental de la Costa Norte del Perú como Reflejo de Cambios Sociales de las Civilizaciones Prehispánicas. Schweizerische Amerikanisten-Gesellschaft Bulletin 63: 137-148.

REINHARD, JOHAN
1968   The Kusunda: Ethnographic Notes on a Hunting Tribe of Nepal. Bulletin of the International Committee on Urgent Anthropological and Ethnological Research 10: 95-110, Vienna.
1974a   The Raute: Notes on a Nomadic Hunting and Gathering Tribe of Nepal. Kailash, A Journal of Himalayan Studies 2(4): 233-271, Kathmandu.
1974b   Underwater Archaeology in Austria. International Journal of Nautical Archaeology and Underwater Exploration 3(2): 320, London.
1976a   Shamanism Among the Raji of Southwest Nepal. In Spirit Possession in the Nepal Himalayas, J. Hitchcock and R. Jones (eds.). Vikas Publishing, New Delhi, pp. 263-292.
1976b   The Ban Rajas: A Vanishing Tribe. Contributions to Nepalese Studies 4(1): 1-22, Kathmandu.
1978   Khembalung: The Hidden Valley. Kailash, A Journal of Himalayan Studies 6(1): 5-35, Kathmandu.
1981   The Chonos of the Chilean Archipelago. Bulletin of the International Committee on Urgent Anthropological and Ethnological Research 23: 89-98, Vienna.
1983   High-Altitude Archaeology and Andean Mountain Gods. American Alpine Journal 25: 54-67, New York.
1985a   Sacred Mountains: An Ethno-Archaeological Study of High Andean Ruins. Mountain Research and Development 5(4): 299-317, Boulder.
1985b   Chavin and Tiahuanaco: A New Look at Two Andean Ceremonial Centers. National Geographic Research 1(3): 395-422, Washington, D.C.
1987a   Chavín y Tiahuanaco. Boletín de Lima 50: 29-49, Lima.
1987b   The Sacred Himalaya. American Alpine Journal 29:123-132, New York.
1988   The Nazca Lines: A New Perspective on Their Origin and Meaning. Los Pinos, Lima (4th ed.).
1990a   Tiahuanaco, Sacred Center of the Andes. In An Insider's Guide to Bolivia, P. McFarren, et al. (eds.). La Paz pp. 151-181.
1990b   Heights of Interest. South American Explorer 24-29, Denver.
1992a   An Archaeological Investigation of Inca Ceremonial Platforms on the Volcano Copiapo, Central Chile. In Pre-Colombian Art and Archaeology, N. Saunders (ed.). Oxbow Books, Oxford, pp. 45-172.
1992b   Underwater Archaeological Research in Lake Titicaca, Bolivia. In Contributions to New World Archaeology, N. Saunders (ed.). Oxbow Books, Oxford, pp. 117-143.
1992c   Sacred Peaks of the Andes. National Geographic 181 (3) (March): 84-111.
1993   Llullaillaco: An Investigation of the World's Highest Archaeological Site. Latin American Indian Languages Journal 9(1): 31-54.
1995   House of the Sun: The Inca Temple of Vilcanota. Latin American Antiquity 6(4): 340-349.
1996   Peru's Ice Maidens. National Geographic 189 (6) (June): 62-81.
1997   Sharp Eyes of Science Probe the Mummies of Peru. National Geographic 191 (1) (January): 36-43.
1998a   Discovering the Inca Ice Maiden. National Geographic Society, Washington, D.C.
1998b   New Inca Mummies. National Geographic 194 (1) (July): 128-135.
1998c   The Temple of Blindness: An Investigation of the Inca Shrine of Ancocagua. Andean Past 5: 87-106.
1999a   Frozen in Time. National Geographic 196 (5) (November): 36-55.
1999b   Coropuna: Lost Mountain Temple of the Incas. South American Explorers Journal 58:5, 26-30.
2002a   Machu Picchu: The Sacred Center. Instituto Machu Pichu, Lima. (2nd ed)
2002b   Sacred Landscape and Prehistoric Cultures of the Andes. In Extreme Landscape: The Lure of Mountain Spaces, Bernadette MacDonald (ed.) National Geographic Society, Washington, D.C., pp. 207-225.
2002c   A High Altitude Archaeological Survey in Northern Chile. Revista Chungara 34(1): 85-99.
2003   Into the Hidden Crater. Explorers Journal 81(3): 16-23.
n.d.a   Ausangate, Mountain Sanctuaries, and the Festival of Qoyllur Riti: Ethnoarchaeology and Sacred Landscape Among the Incas. (in press)
n.d.b   Death of the Iceman: Reflections on Sacred Landscape and Ritual Practice in Neolithic Europe. (in press)

REINHARD, JOHAN, AND FERNANDO ASTETE
n.d.   Pachatusan: Investigaciones Arqueológicas en una Montaña Sagrada del Cuzco. ms. Proyecto Santuarios de Altura del Sur Andino, Arequipa.

REINHARD, JOHAN, AND CONSTANZA CERUTI
2000   Investigaciones Arqueológicas en el Volcán Llullaillaco. Ediciones Universidad Católica de Salta, Salta.
2005   Pilgrimage, Sacred Mountains, and Human Sacrifice Among the Inca. In Pilgrimage and Ritual Landscape in Pre-Columbian America, John Carlson (ed.). Dumbarton Oaks, Washington, D.C.
n.d.a   Investigaciones Arqueológicas de Alta Montaña en el Santuario de Altura del Nevado de Quehuar. ms. Institute of High Mountain Research, Salta.
n.d.b   The Archaeology of the Inca Ceremonial Center on Mount Llullaillaco. Vol. 1. (in press)

REINHARD, JOHAN, AND JOSÉ ANTONIO CHÁVEZ
1996   Proyecto de Investigación Arqueológica "Santuarios de Altura del Sur Andino": Informe Temporada 1995. ms. Instituto Nacional de Cultura, Lima.
1998   Proyecto de Investigación Arqueológica "Santuarios de Altura del Sur Andino": Informe Temporada 1996. ms. Instituto Nacional de Cultura, Lima.
2001   Proyecto de Investigación Arqueológica "Santuarios de Altura del Sur Andino": Informe Temporada 1997-1998. ms. Instituto Nacional de Cultura, Lima.
n.d.a   Ampato: Investigaciones Arqueológicas en una Montaña Sagrada del Sur Andino. ms. Proyecto Santuarios de Altura del Sur Andino, Arequipa.
n.d.b   El Santuario Incaico del Nevado Pichu Pichu. ms. Proyecto Santuarios de Altura del Sur Andino, Arequipa.
n.d.c   El Santuario Incaico del Volcán Misti. ms. Proyecto Santuarios de Altura del Sur Andino, Arequipa.
n.d.d   Hallazgos Arqueológicos en el Volcán Sara Sara. ms. Proyecto Santuarios de Altura del Sur Andino, Arequipa.

REINHARD, JOHAN, AND JULIO SANHUEZA
1982   Expedición Arqueológica al Altiplano de Tarapacá y sus Cumbres. Revista de Corporación para el Desarrollo de la Ciencia 2(2): 17-42, Santiago.

RENFREW, COLIN, AND PAUL BAHN
2000   Archaeology: Theories, Methods, and Practice. Thames and Hudson, London. (3rd ed.)

RIDGEWAY, RICK
1979   The Boldest Dream. Harcourt, Brace, Jovanovich, New York.
2000   Below Another Sky. Henry Holt, New York.

RIDLEY, MATT
1999   Genome: The Autobiography of a Species in 23 Chapters. HarperCollins Publishers, New York.

ROBERTS, CHARLOTTE, AND KEITH MANCHESTER
1995   The Archaeology of Disease. Cornell University Press, Ithaca. (2nd ed.)

ROBERTS, DAVID
2000   Iron Man of the Andes. National Geographic Adventure January/February: 72-81, 121-123.

ROLANDI DE PERROT, DIANA
1975   Análisis de materiales provenientes del Volcán Llullaillaco y del Nevado de Quehuar (Prov. de Salta). Revista del CIADAM 2: 43-44, San Juan.

RONDÓN, ENRIQUE
1937   Expedición al Volcán Misti. La Colmena, Arequipa.

ROSKAMS, STEVE
2001   Excavation. Cambridge University Press, Cambridge.

ROTH, CHARLES
1986   The Sky Observer's Guidebook. Prentice Hall Press, New York.

ROWE, ANN
1997   Inca Weaving and Costume. The Textile Museum Journal 1995-1996, 34-35: 5-54, Washington D.C.

ROWE, JOHN
1979   Standardization in Inca Tapestry Tunics. The Junius Bird Pre-columbian Textile Conference, Anne Rowe and Elizabeth Benson (eds.). The Textile Museum, Washington D.C., pp. 239-264

ROZAS, WASHINGTON
1992   Sana, Sana Patita de Rana. In El Qosqo: Antropología de la Ciudad, H. Tomoeda and J. Flores (eds.). CEAC, Cuzco, pp. 200-224.

SALAS, DIONISIO
1950   El Nevado Sarasara. In Monografía de la Provincia de Parinacochas (anonymous). Magisterio Primerio de Parinacochas, Lima. pp. 610-626.

SALLNOW, MICHAEL
1987   Pilgrims of the Andes: Regional Cults in Cuzco. Smithsonian Institution Press, Washington, DC.

SALOMON, FRANK, AND JORGE URIOSTE
1991   The Huarochirí Manuscript. University of Texas Press, Austin.

SANTA CRUZ PACHACUTI, JUAN DE
1968 [1571]   Relación de Antiguedades deste reyno del Perú. Biblioteca de Autores Españoles, Madrid.

SARMIENTO DE GAMBOA, PEDRO
1999 [1572]   History of the Incas. Dover Publications, Mineola (NY).

SCHOBINGER, JUAN
2001   Los Santuarios de Altura Incaicos y el Aconcagua: Aspectos Generales e Interpretativos.
       In El Santuario Incaico del Cerro Aconcagua, Juan Schobinger (ed.). Universidad Nacional de
       Cuyo, Mendoza, pp. 415-435.

SCHOBINGER, JUAN (ED.)
1966   La "momia" del Cerro El Toro: Investigaciones arqueológicas en la Cordillera de la Provincia de
       San Juan. Universidad Nacional de Cuyo, Mendoza.
2001   El Santuario Incaico del Cerro Aconcagua. Universidad Nacional de Cuyo, Mendoza.
2004   El Santuario Incaico del Nevado de Chuscha. Fundación CEPPA, Buenos Aires.

SCHOBINGER, JUAN, MÓNICA AMPUERO, AND EDUARDO GUERCIO
2001   Descripción de las Estatuillas Asociadoas al Fardo Funerario Hallado en al Cerro
       Aconcagua. In El Santuario Incaico del Cerro Aconcagua, Juan Schobinger (ed.).
       Universidad Nacional de Cuyo, Mendoza, pp. 266-280.

SEASE, CATHERINE
1994   A Conservation Manual for the Field Archaeologist. Institute of Archaeology, University of
       California, Los Angeles. (3rd ed.)

SEEMAN, NADRIAN
2004   Nanotechnology and the Double Helix. Scientific American, June: 64-75.

SHAH, TAHIR
2001   Trail of Feathers. Arcade Publishing, New York.

SHERMER, MICHAEL
1992   Can Science Cheat Death? Cryonics, Altered States, and the Quest for Transcendence.
       Skeptic 1(2): 46-63.

SILVA, SHANKA DE, AND PETER FRANCIS
1991   Volcanoes of the Central Andes. Springer-Verlag, New York.

SILVERBLATT, IRENE
1987   Moon, Sun, and Witches: Gender Ideologies and Class in Inca and Colonial Peru. Princeton
       University Press, Princeton.

SIMKIN, T., ET AL.
1981   Volcanoes of the World. Hutchinson Ross, Stroudsburg.

SPINDLER, KONRAD
1994   The Man in the Ice: The Discovery of a 5,000-Year-Old Body Reveals the Secrets of the Stone Age.
       Harmony Books, New York.

STARK, PETER
2001   Last Breath: Cautionary Tales from the Limits of Human Endurance. Ballantine Books, New York.

SWIDLER, NINA, KURT DONGOSKE, ROGER ANYON, AND ALAN DOWNER (EDS.)
1997   Native Americans and Archaeologists: Stepping Stones to Common Ground. Altamira Press, Walnut Creek
       (CA).

SYKES, BRYAN
2001   The Seven Daughters of Eve. W. W. Norton & Co., New York.

TAYLOR, TIMOTHY
2002   The Buried Soul: How Humans Invented Death. Beacon Press, Boston.

TERRELL, JOHN
1971   American Indian Almanac. Barnes and Noble, New York.

TIERNEY, PATRICK

1989   The Highest Altar. Viking Penguin, New York.

UCKO, PETER, AND ROBERT LAYTON (EDS.)
1999   The Archaeology and Anthropology of Landscape. Routledge, London.

ULLOA MOGOLLÓN, JUAN DE
1965 [1586]   Relación de la provincia de los Collaguas. In Relaciones Geográficas de Indias-Perú, Marcos Jimenez de la Espada (ed.). Ediciones Atlas, Madrid, v.1, pp. 326-333.

UMAN, MARTIN
1986   All About Lightning. Dover Publications, New York.

URTON, GARY
1981   At the Crossroads of the Earth and the Sky: An Andean Cosmology. University of Texas Press, Austin.

VALDERRAMA, RICARDO, AND CARMEN ESCALANTE
1988   Del Tata Mallku a la Mama Pacha. DESCO, Lima.
1997   La Doncella Sacrificada: Mitos del Valle del Colca. Universidad Nacional de San Agustín, Arequipa.

VARGAS LLOSA, MARIO
2001   El Lenguaje de la Pasión. PEISA, Lima.

VARÓN, RAFAEL
1990   El Taki Onqoy: Las raíces andinas de un fenómeno colonial. In El Retorno de las Huacas, Luis Millones (compiler). Instituto de Estudio Peruanos, Lima, pp. 331-405.

VÁZQUEZ DE ESPINOZA, ANTONIO
1948 [1617]   Compendio y descripción de las Indias occidentales. Smithsonian Miscellaneous Collections, vol. 108. Smithsonian Institution, Washington, D.C.

VERA CRUZ, PABLO DE LA
1987   Cambio en los Patrones de Asentamiento y el Uso y Abandono de los Andes en Cabanaconde, Valle del Colca, Peru. In Pre-Hispanic Agricultural Fields in the Andean Region, William Deneven, Kent Mathewson, and Gregory Knapp (eds.). BAR International Series, Oxford, pp. 89-128.

VERANO, JOHN
1996   Physical Examination of Nevado Ampato Mummies I-III. Department of Anthropology, Tulane University, New Orleans.

VIVAR, GERÓNIMO DE
1987 [1558]   Crónica y Relación Copiosa y Verdadera de los Reinos de Chile. Editorial Universitaria, Santiago.

WAISBARD, SIMONE
1981   Enigmatic Messages of the Nazcas. In The World's Last Mysteries. Readers Digest Association, Pleasantville, pp. 281-287.

WATKINS, JOE
2000   Indigenous Archaeology: American Indian Values and Scientific Practice. Alta Mira Press, Walnut Creek (CA).

WILKINS, ROBERT
1996   Death: A History of Man's Obsessions and Fears. Barnes and Noble, New York.

WILSON, A., C. CERUTI, T. GILBERT, T. TAYLOR, I. BARNES, M. WOROBEY, J. REINHARD, AND M. RICHARDS
n.d.   Diachronic aspects of human sacrifice: The Llullaillaco Maiden. (in press)

YOUNG, MARK (ED.)
1997   The Guinness Book of Records. Bantam Books, New York.

ZUIDEMA, TOM
1978   Shafttombs and the Inca Empire. Journal of the Steward Anthropological Society 9(1-2): 133-179, Urbana (IL).
1991   Guaman Poma and the Art of Empire: Toward an Iconography of Inca Royal Dress. In Transatlantic Encounters, Kenneth Andrien and Rolena Adorno (eds.). Univ. of California Press, Berkeley, pp. 151-202.

ENDNOTES

NOTES

English translations of the Spanish sources are noted whenever possible, as these are more accessible to English readers. References to original Spanish sources can be found in Reinhard 1985, 1993, and 2002a, and Reinhard and Ceruti 2000 and 2005. In Spanish, people normally include their mother's maiden name after their father's name. Since this can cause confusion in English, I have omitted the former, except in those cases where a person is already well known by his full name, such as the writer Mario Vargas Llosa. In the case of Quechua and Aymara words, I have used the spellings that are most commonly found in the literature.

Prologue

1. We do not know if everything happened exactly as described here, but much of it did—and all of it is in accord with the archaeological material, the results of scientific studies undertaken with the Ampato Ice Maiden, and the historical accounts of Inca customs and beliefs (cf. Betanzos 1996, Cobo 1990, and Molina 1959). For a description of one girl's journey to a mountain where she was sacrificed, see Hernández 1923 [1621]. English translations of key parts of Hernández's and Molina's accounts can be found in Silverblatt 1987: 95-99 and Abercrombie 1998: 171-173, respectively. See Zuidema 1978 for a discussion of the description by Hernández.

Chapter 1
Discovery on Ampato
1. The altitudes of several mountains still remain uncertain. Those I have listed are the ones most accepted in the literature (cf. Biggar 1996, Neate 1987, and Reinhard 1990b). Altimeter readings can only be approximate, because they are affected by changes in the atmospheric pressure that varies depending on the weather. The worse the weather, the higher, the reading. See Reinhard 1985 and 1992c and Beorchia 1985 for high-altitude sites as being of Inca origin and Biggar 1996 for climbing routes on some of these peaks.

2. For summaries of these expeditions, see Beorchia 1985.

3. Several chroniclers pointed out that mountains were among the most important traditional deities, cf. Cristóbal de Albornoz (in Duviols 1984), Cieza de León
   1959, and Guaman Poma 1980. However, since there was no writing in the Andes
   prior to the Spanish conquest of 1532, the documents that exist were written
   by Spaniards or men of mixed descent influenced by Spanish culture. Most of
   the chroniclers did not speak the native language, and even when they did, their
   abilities and the interests of the time heavily influenced the material they
   selected. In addition, what they heard was influenced by informants who had
   their own agendas and limitations of knowledge. Fortunately, some of the chroniclers were keen observers and many of their descriptions have withstood the
   test of time. Nonetheless, any interpretations of Inca culture must remain ten-
   tative and be open to revision as new information is obtained. See D'Altroy 2002:
   11-20 for a discussion of some of the best-known chroniclers.

4. Chroniclers noting the reasons for human sacrifice include: Cobo 1990: 111-
   112; Sarmiento 1999: 122-123; Murúa 2001: 416; Polo 1916: 193; and Ulloa 1965:
   330. Chroniclers who described human sacrifices being performed annually
   during major festivals include Avila (in Salomon and Urioste 1991: 112), Cieza
   1959: 151-152, and Cobo 1990: 54-74.

5. Many of the conversations presented in this book have been reconstructed from
   memory. However, most of them are based on journal entries written soon after
   the conversations occurred—usually within a day. No quotations have been know-
   ingly altered to provide meanings different from those the speakers intended.
   See Beorchia 1985 for summaries of sites on Misti and Chachani.

6. Cf. Ulloa 1965.

7. For information about the eruption of Sabancaya see Chávez 1993: 114-139 and
   Silva and Francis 1991: 26-28.

8. Cf. Houston 1987: 227. See Ashcroft 2000: 8 with regard to elevations over 10,000
   feet being considered "high altitude."

9. Descriptions of apachetas can be found in Girault 1988: 391-431. See Ramos
   1976: 68 for an account of apachetas written in the early 1600s.

10. Bowman 1924 provides an interesting overview of life in the Atacama Desert.

11. See Gelles 1990 and 2000.

12. Albornoz in Duviols 1984.

13. For the definition of Ampato, see González Holguín 1952: 145. and Bertonio
    1984: 426. For the significance of frogs in Andean worship, see Berg 1985: 77.

14. The first complete excavation of an artificial platform is described in Reinhard
    1992. See also Beorchia 1985 and 2001 for summaries of excavations. Besom
    (2000: 180-181, 188) described what must be the first well-documented exca-
    vation and plan of an Inca ceremonial platform on a mountain—and it was
    done in 1765!

15. Houston 1987: 122-180 describes high-altitude illnesses.

16. See, e.g., Bradley 2000: 62 and Green 2001.
17. See Burkert 1983 and 1985.
18. Although no Spaniard in Peru personally witnessed a human sacrifice, several chroniclers reported details provided to them by the Incas. See especially Betanzos 1996: 46, 77-78, 132; Cobo 1990: 111-112; Molina 1959; and Murúa 2001. Writing in the early 1600s, Hernández Príncipe (1923) provides the most detailed description of a specific case, including his excavation of the remains of the sacrificial victim. Ramos (1976: 65-66, cf. Cobo 1990: 99) presents the account of a girl who informed Spaniards at Lake Titicaca how she narrowly escaping being sacrificed thanks to Inca priests finding a mole on her body. They decided that she was not perfect enough. However, the most compelling evidence supporting the practice of human sacrifice at high-altitude burial sites comes from the forensic evidence and its close correlation with the chroniclers' accounts, the kinds of high-status ritual items interred with the bodies, and the archaeological contexts in which they are found (such as the types of structures and their locations).

Chapter 2
Return of the Maiden

1. For descriptions of the El Plomo mummy and artifacts see Mostny 1957.
2. Cf. Cobo 1990: 42. Many chroniclers noted the Incas performing human sacrifices; cf. Arriaga (1968: 88), Acosta (2002: 292), Betanzos (1996: 46), Cieza (1959: 151), Cobo (1983: 235), Hernández (1923: 63), Molina (1959: 97), Murúa (2001: 416), Noboa (in Duviols 1986: 248), Polo (1916: 193), Ramos (1976: 25), Santacruz (1968: 292), Sarmiento (1999: 122), and Ulloa (1965: 330).
3. Cobo 1983: 238.
4. See Hernández 1923. For an English translation, see Silverblatt 1987: 95-99.
5. See Ramos 1976: 81; cf. Cobo 1990: 112.
6. This occurred on Cerro Esmeralda on the coast of Chile (cf. Besom 2000). Among those who used the word "capacocha" for Inca human sacrificial offerings were some of the best-known chroniclers, including Betanzos (1996: 46), Cieza (1959: 151), Hernández (1923: 63), Molina (1959: 97), Noboa (in Duviols 1986: 248), Santacruz (1968: 292), and Sarmiento (1999: 122). See also Duviols 1986 and Rostworowski 1988, where the term appears repeatedly in collections of historical documents. Several chroniclers, such as Arriaga (1968: 88), Acosta (1962: 248), Ramos (1976: 25), Polo (1916: 193), Cobo (1983: 235), and Ulloa (1965: 330) noted the practice of human sacrifice among the Inca, but did not use a Quechua word for it.
7. Cf. Cobo 1983: 236-237 and 1990: 172.
8. Cf. Flores 1976.
9. For overviews of Inca culture placed within the context of Andean prehistory in general, see Davies 1997, Morris and von Hagen 1993, and Moseley 1992.

10. Cf. Morris and von Hagen 1993 and Moseley 1992.
11. Volumes devoted exclusively to Inca culture include D'Altroy 2002, Davies 1995, Hemming 1970, and Kendall 1973. McIntyre 1975 presents a popular account. See Bauer 1992 for the development of the Inca state; Bauer and Stanish 2001 for the Inca pilgrimage tradition; Hyslop 1984 and 1990 for Inca roads and settlement patterns; Gasparini and Margolies 1980, Lee 2000, and Niles 1999 for Inca architecture; and Raffino 1981 for an overview of the Inca occupation in the southern part of their empire.
12. Garcilaso de la Vega 1966: 124.
13. For a summary report about my initial research on Huarancante, see Beorchia 1985: 98-99.
14. See Spindler 1994; cf. Fowler 2000.
15. See Niles 1999: 130 for Juana as a name used by one of the Inca coyas (women of royalty) in a document of 1551.

Chapter 3
Extreme Archaeology
1. Cf. Arriaga 1968 written in the early 1600s and Bolin 1998: 34-41 for offerings made today.
2. See Hyslop 1990 for details about Inca way stations (tambos).
3. See Uman 1986: 93.
4. See Houston 1987: 122-180.
5. Ashcroft 2000: 40 notes that the temperature falls by about 3° F for every 1,000 feet because thinner air causes the insulating effect of the atmosphere to diminish.
6. See Baker 2001 and Besom 2000 for information about the headdress found at the Esmeralda burial.
7. Cf. Mostny 1957, Quevedo and Durán 1992, and Schobinger 2001.
8. The ritual breaking of pottery has been noted at other pre-Hispanic sites (cf. Menzel 1977: 54) and in ethnographic contexts (cf. Girault 1988: 55).
9. Cf. Bray 2003 and 2004.
10. For information and plans of the excavations conducted on Ampato, see Reinhard and Chávez 1996 and n.d.a.
11. See Uman 1986: 85-87.
12. Cf. Bastien 1978: 24.
13. Betanzos 1996: 132.
14. Cf. Cobo 1990: 117 and Blower 2000.
15. Cf. Cieza 1959: 250.
16. Cf. Chávez 1993.
17. Ulloa 1965: 330.
18. See Reinhard 1996 for a popular account of the expeditions to Ampato in 1995. For information and plans of the excavations conducted during 1995 on Ampato, see Reinhard and Chávez 1996 and n.d.a.

19. See Backpacker 1999 for the 18,000-foot altitude of the "death zone" and cf. Stark 2001: 48, 65 with regard to the body's inability to permanently adapt above that altitude. Some scientists use the term "death zone" for altitudes above 26,000 feet, when it takes only hours for rapid physical deterioration to set in (cf. Ashcroft 2000: 23).

20. See Vera Cruz 1987.

Chapter 4
Mummies and Media

1. Cf. Iserson 1994: 601.
2. Cf. Iserson 1994: 42-43.
3. Arriaza 1995: 123.
4. Cf. Bahn 1996 and 2003, Chamberlain and Pearson 2001, Fowler 2000, Reid 1999, Spindler 1994, Taylor 2002.
5. For a discussion of the freezing of cells, see Iserson 1994: 42-43.
6. Cf. Beorchia 1985, Schobinger 1966 and 2001, Mostny 1957.
7. Garcilaso 1966: 87.
8. See Endnote #2 of Chapter 2.
9. See Curatola 1977: 69 with regard to a human sacrifice in the late 1500s and Favre (1967: 131), Gose (1994: 241), and Tierney (1989) for information about human sacrifices reported in the 20th century.
10. See Rowe 1997 for Inca women's textiles and cf. Guaman Poma 1980.
11. Cf. Chamberlain and Pearson 2001: 18. Arriaga (1968: 121, 154) noted that the Incas kept a child's hair after it was first cut at age 4-5.
12. Cieza 1959: 55.
13. See Ulloa 1965: 330.
14. Betanzos 1996: 87.
15. Betanzos 1996: 132. For the symbolic marriage of a girl with a deity see Arriaga 1966: 36 for the early 1600s and Favre 1967: 133-134 (cf. Gose 1994: 222) for modern times.
16. Cf. Guaman Poma 1990: 138, 284, 316, 326, 334.
17. O'Neill 2003: cf. Uman 1986.
18. For difficulties in recognizing some skull fractures, see Roberts and Manchester 1995: 73.
19. Unlike rigor mortis, cadaveric spasm is an immediate stiffness of the body at death, which usually occurs under violent physical and emotional circumstances (Lyle 2004: 165). See Iserson 1994: 41-43 and Mims 1999: 120 for the normal process the body goes through immediately following death.

Chapter 5
The Mountains of Power

1. Halliburton 1941.

2. Clark 1953.
3. The film *The Sky Above, the Mud Below* won an Academy Award among documentaries in the early 1960's.
4. Doyle 1963.
5. See Reinhard 1968, 1974a, 1976a, and 1976b. Films I made during my Nepal research are available at the Institute for Scientific Film, Göttingen, Germany, and the Human Studies Film Archives, Smithsonian Institution, Washington, D.C.
6. See Ridgeway 1979.
7. See Reinhard 1978. For a popular account of our 1977 expedition to Khembalung see MacInnes 1981: 189-217. In 1978 BBC Television aired a film about our 1977 expedition titled *North of Kathmandu*. A New Explorers' film titled *In Search of Shangri-La* was made of our 1996 return trip to Khembalung (see www.pbs.org).
8. See Isherwood 1980.
9. See MacInnes 1984: 3-104.
10. See Darwin 1959: 268.
11. See Iensen 1979.
12. Cf. Lamb 2004 and Fisher et al. 1997.
13. Cf. Rachowiecki et al. 2003: 24-25. Given the difficulties of undertaking censuses in Andean countries, percentages can only be approximate.
14. See Arriaga 1966: 72.
15. A compendium of the sites known up to 1984, along with plans and artifact descriptions, has been presented by Beorchia (1985). He compiled a second volume for the period 1987-1999 (Beorchia 2001). The majority of high-altitude (over 17,000 feet) sites have been found in southern Peru and the Chilean and Argentine Andes. Summits of mountains further to the north usually could not be reached because of the lower snowline and the technical climbing difficulties presented by many of these peaks.
16. See Schobinger 1966. Before I began my research, several other publications in Spanish had already dealt with finds made at high-altitude sites (e.g., Beorchia 1975, Linares 1966, Mostny 1957, and Rebitsch 1966). For a description of typical statues found with capacocha burials, see Beorchia 1985, Ceruti 2001a, Dransart 1995, Rowe 1997, and Schobinger et al. 2001. For details about the construction of metal statues found in capacocha burials, see Bárcena 2001. Although statues have been found throughout the Inca Empire, it is not known exactly what the ones recovered from mountain summits represented (cf. Cobo 1990: 45). I believe that most of the male and female statues probably represented deities that inhabited the mountains, along with other principal deities of Inca cosmology, such as the Sun (Inti) and Weather (Illapa). Camelid figurines may have been substitute offerings (cf. MacCormack 1991: 171-173 and Schobinger 2001: 430-431), but I feel that they were usually believed to be power-laden and offered to promote the fertility of livestock.

17. See Reinhard 1983 and 1985. See Echevarría (1977: 3) with regard to 22,000 feet not being "surpassed by modern climbers until the Schlagintweits attempted Abi Gamin in the Himalayas in 1855."

18. Bastien 1978: xx.

19. See Reinhard 1983 for skin diving and Brush 1984 for scuba diving in Licancabur's crater lake. For the lake as being the highest in the world, see Young 1997: 382. (The date of November 14-17 is correct, but the year was 1982, not 1994.) Recently NASA scientists studied Licancabur's summit as providing the closest earthly analog to conditions on Mars (see http://www.extremeenvironment.com/index.htm).

20. Reinhard 1992b.

21. Schobinger 2001.

22. For an archaeological report of this expedition, see Reinhard 1992a.

23. Krahl and González 1966: 117. In undertaking such feats, the Incas had to conquer the fear of ascending mountains thought inhabited by powerful deities. Physical dangers (storms, altitude sickness, rockfall) were attributed to the gods, making a powerful psychological barrier to be overcome. Thus the Incas did more than just conquer the peaks—they conquered themselves.

24. Cobo 1990: 48.

25. Cobo 1990: 74.

26. See Cieza 1959: 152 and the drawing of Guaman Poma 1980: 246.

27. See Reinhard 1999b.

28. Cf. Flores 1997 and Reinhard n.d.a.

29. Guaman Poma 1980: 253.

30. Cf. Flores 1997, Gow and Condori 1982, Randall 1982, and Reinhard n.d.a.

31. Cieza 1959: 262.

32. Only days after I returned from Ausangate, I met my friend Mike Rodman in Bolivia to trace the legendary route of the deity Tunupa. Tunupa figured prominently in beliefs about the origin of several of the main landscape features in a region of Bolivia bordering Chile. While following Tunupa's route, Mike and I located several sites, including those on Mount Tunupa where the deity had been transformed into a volcano. Inca ruins on the summit of Mount Puquintica (19,311 feet) directly overlooked Inca funerary towers (chullpas) built near its base, and their walls were decorated with the best surviving examples of Inca painted designs known. A week after our expedition was over, I was on my way to Arequipa, where the acclimatization gained in Bolivia made possible the recovery of the Ice Maiden—and, by coincidence, textiles with some of the same designs as on the funerary towers.

33. For my publications about these centers, see Reinhard 1985b, 1987a (which has an expanded version of the Chavin section of 1985b), 1988, 1990a, and 2002a. Peter Baumann (1986) published a popular account of my Andean research during 1980-1985.

34. Waisbard 1981: 281.
35. In recent years there have been several studies, mainly in Europe and Mexico, that have demonstrated the need for archaeological sites to be placed within the broader context of sacred features of the landscape. For examples in Europe, cf. Ashmore and Knapp 1999 and Ucko and Layton 1999; for Mexico, cf. Broda et al. 2001 and Freidel et al. 1993; and for pre-Inca sites in the Andes, cf. Bourget 1994 and Reindel 1999. I had analyzed the role sacred landscape played in cultures that had no written histories without intending to become involved in theoretical debates, mainly believing that any theory should be judged on how well it explains the known facts. However, many archaeologists consider this kind of theoretical approach as belonging together with those currently labeled as "interpretative" or "post-processual," where more emphasis is placed upon symbolism and other cognitive factors (cf. Dark 1995: 10, Hodder 1999: 5, Johnson 1999: 98-107, Renfrew and Bahn 2000: 483-494). Readers interested in the methodology of excavations and conservation of artifacts might read Cronyn 1990, Ellis 2000, Joukowsky 1980, Mays 1998, and Roskams 2001.

Chapter 6
Juanita's Journey

1. Cf. Bahn 2003: 119-123.
2. See Beech 2003. Atwood (2004: 240, 242) noted that the number of looters in Peru could easily number more than 15,000 and that at the current pace nearly every site will have been ransacked or destroyed by 2050.
3. See Carrier 1996 and Carrier's website http://www.carrier.com.
4. For a brief overview see Reinhard 1997. Aufderheide and Langsjoen (1998) presented an analysis of the Ampato Ice Maiden's CT scan.
5. See Cobo 1983: 235, Gutierrez 1963: 233, and Ramos 1976: 25. A few chroniclers noted that the Incas cut the throats of some human sacrifices (cf. Acosta 2002: 292) or used human blood in offerings (cf. Cobo 1990: 89, 111 and Murúa 2001: 416). Most Andean scholars, myself included, had thought that these chroniclers either confused blood sacrifices of llamas with that of humans or mistakenly attributed Aztec sacrificial practices to the Incas. Recently, however, scientists examined an Inca human sacrifice found on Mount. Chuscha in northwestern Argentina, and they concluded that the girl's death had been caused by a wound made by a pointed object, probably a lance (Mazziotti and Vargas 2004: 83-87). Assuming that their analysis is correct, the possibility exists that this sacrificial method (and perhaps other similar ones that would have caused bleeding) may have been used on rare occasions. This would run counter to the concept that a flawless child must remain unmarked even at the moment of being sacrificed (cf. MacCormack 2000: 131).
6. See Mims 1999: 52.

7. See Egarter 2003.

8. See Gould 1998.

9. For discussions of some of the issues involved, see Chamberlain and Pearson 2001, Swidler et al. 1997, and Watkins 2000.

10. See Francou et al. 2000.

11. Cf. Beorchia 1985 and 2001.

12. See Watkins 2000: 172.

13. Cf. Watkins 2000: 19 and Nichols et al. 1989: 37 with regard to the concept of "ownership" of ancient remains needing to be reconsidered in terms such as what could be labeled "custodianship."

14. Cf. Terrell 1971: 148, 178, 286. For an overview of the politics surrounding the excavation and display of the dead, see Pearson 1999: 171-192.

15. Cf. Johnson and McGee 1998, Metcalf and Huntington 1991, Taylor 2002, Wilkins 1996.

16. See *Native American News* 1(7) (June 3): 51-53, 1996. One of the guidelines followed by many museums in the West is that mummies can be exhibited, as long as they are treated with respect and are displayed in the country from which they originated. In 1986 the International Council on Museums issued a Code of Ethics, and the section regarding the display of mummies made the following point: "Although it is occasionally necessary to use human remains and other sensitive material in interpretative exhibits, this must be done with tact and with respect for the feeling for human dignity held by different peoples" (cf. Pearson 1999: 185).

17. Often the corpses were simply placed under overhangs and boulders or put in caves and niches. In some areas the bodies of higher-ranking individuals were placed in funerary towers and not actually "buried" at all. One of the problems the Spanish priests had to contend with was the removal of corpses from Christian graveyards (Polo 1916: 194). This was reportedly due to indigenous peoples, fear that the dead would be angered by being buried and thus unable to "breathe" (cf. Doyle 1988: 205; Duviols 1986: 72). The world's oldest artificially preserved mummies (before 4000 B.C.) have been found in coastal regions of southern Peru and northern Chile. Interestingly, the evidence indicates that they were displayed, thus suggesting a long-standing Andean tradition (Arriaza 1995: 152).

18. Sometimes even respectable writers couldn't resist ruining a good story by checking facts. For example, Tahir Shah (2001: 56) wrote, "For three years she [Juanita] criss-crossed the U.S., shuttled about in a giant deep freeze. At an engagement in Connecticut she was even presented to President Clinton." Entertaining tale, but, as we have seen, wrong.

19. The results of the Ice Maiden's DNA were noted on the Institute for Genomic Research's website: http://www.tigr.org/cet/dna/ice/index.html.

20. Bray et al. 2005; cf. Renfrew and Bahn 2000: 361 for a summary of neutron activation analysis.

21. See Reinhard 1992b and Bauer and Stanish 2001 for information about Lake Titicaca's significance in Inca beliefs.
22. Cf. Renfrew and Bahn 2000: 137-145.
23. See Mays 1998: 46 for charts of dental development as a person ages.
24. For more information on Harris lines, see Aufderheide and Rodríguez-Martín 1998: 422-424.

Chapter 7
Peaks, Storms, and Sarita
1. See Sallnow 1987: 70-71.
2. See Valderrama and Escalante 1997: 75.
3. Cf. Linares 1966 and Beorchia 1985.
4. See Nachtigall 1966.
5. For a summary of the 1989 expedition see Beorchia 1985.
6. See Cobo 1990: 201 and Ulloa 1965: 327.
7. Betanzos 1996: 132.
8. See Arriaga 1966: 69 and Parssinen 1992: 75 (ftn. 12) for the reference to the description in an account of Colque Guarache.
9. Cf. Rozas 1992: 203-206.
10. See Reinhard and Sanhueza 1982.
11. Cf. Reinhard 1985: 309.
12. Gow and Condori 1982: 46
13. Bastien 1978: 22.
14. Cf. Allen 1988: 41.
15. Ulloa 1965: 327.
16. Cf. Gelles 2000: 83-85 and Hurley 1978: 291.
17. See Beorchia 1985 for a summary of the find and photo of the puma skin.
18. Cf. Valderrama and Escalante 1988: 115.
19. We know from chroniclers that the bodies of pumas might be worshipped and that puma skins were worn in important ceremonies (cf. Cobo 1990: 67, 133; Avila in Salomon and Urioste 1991: 48).
20. See Vera Cruz 1987.
21. Cf. Hyslop 1990: 69-100.
22. See Gelles 2000: 57
23. Gisbert et al. (1987) have suggested that blue was associated especially with Inca nobility, and Zuidema (1991: 152) noted that only the Incas had the privilege of using tucapu designs on tunics.
24. One possible use was suggested by a colored drawing published in the late 1500s by Murúa (see Ossio 2001: 47 fig. 2; cf. Guaman Poma 1980: 98). A similar looking red and white banded object is held above the head of one of the Inca queens and may have been used to keep away flies, since this was reported in 1534 as being done even for royal mummies (cf. Isbell 1997: 40).

25. Albornoz (in Duviols 1984: 198).
26. Cf. Curatola 1977: 79.
27. Cf. Varón 1990: 331-405.
28. See Salas 1950: 612.
29. The film was to eventually appear with the title Frozen in Time.
30. The site can still (2005) be found on the Web at: www.pbs.org/nova/peru.
31. Cf. Flannery et al. 1989: 154, Paz 1988: 219-221.
32. A moving tribute to Jonathon Wright appears in Ridgeway 2000.
33. Mims 1999: 121.
34. See Reinhard 1998b for a brief discussion of the expeditions to Sara Sara and Pichu Pichu in 1996, and Carey 1999 for a popular account of our Pichu Pichu expedition. For information and plans of the excavations conducted during 1996 on Pichu Pichu, Sara Sara, and Ampato, see Reinhard and Chávez 1998, n.d.b, and n.d.d.

Chapter 8
Earth Mother, Mountain Father

1. Kurtz 1998: 48-49.
2. cf. Kudalis 2003 and Pringle 2001.
3. See Vargas Llosa 2001: 172-175.
4. Reinhard 1998a. (For ages ten and up. In 1999 the National Geographic Society published a Read & Explore Kit, including a teacher's guide, for use with this book.)
5. Other publications for children with information relating to the discovery of the Ice Maiden include: Buell 1997, Chávez 2000, Getz 1998, and Griek 1999 (a fictional book about the Ice Maiden's life). The Sara Sara board game "Mummy Trekking" appeared in Funston 2000: 18-19.
6. Later Daniel Jones won a prestigious Webbie Award—considered the Internet's Oscar—for the website he built. I have only been able to keep updating a small part of it, but it can still be accessed at www.johanreinhard.org.
7. See Iserson 1994: 288-298, Miller 2004, Pringle 2001: 333-335, and Shermer 1992: 50-51 for overviews of cryonics and its difficulties.
8. See Darwin and Wowk 1992 and cf. Iserson 1994: 298. Some scientists and U.S. government officials believe that nanotechnology will form the basis of the next industrial revolution (cf. Atkinson 2003).
9. Davis 1997: 31. See Horgan 1999 for the extreme complexity of the brain and thus the inherent difficulties in ever completely understanding it.
10. See Iserson 1994: 296-298.
11. Ice-free cryopreservation (vitrification) has been posited as a way to avoid the problem of damage to cells after they have been cooled and later rewarmed. Vitrification "involves partly replacing water in cells with a mixture of chemicals that prevent ice formation" (Miller 2004: 24-25). This has been success-

fully carried out with small organs and blocks of tissue, but large organs have not been able to survive the toxicity of the antifreeze chemicals utilized. Optimists point out that there is nothing about liquid nitrogen temperatures or vitrification per se that is fatal to large groups of cells (Harris 2004: 27). Pessimists point to there being no hard evidence to indicate it would work for large organs, let alone entire human bodies (Miller 2004: 25). This has given rise to a joke: How many cryonicists does it take to screw in a light bulb? Answer: None—they just sit in the dark and wait for the technology to improve (Benford 2004: 29).

12. See Chávez 1993 and Silva and Francis 1991 for information about the eruptions of Ubinas in historical times.

13. See Valderrama and Escalante 1988.

14. For a brief report on this expedition, see Beorchia 1985.

15. Writing in the early 1600s, Estrada (1923) wrote that the Huanca (Wanka) people living in the mountains to the east of Lima used flat stones in their rituals.

16. Arriaga 1968: 168.

17. See Valderrama and Escalante 1988: 192.

18. Cf. Pardo 1941: 110.

19. See Reinhard 1998b for a brief discussion of the Ampato expedition in 1997. For information about the archaeological research, see Reinhard and Chávez 2001 and n.d.a. Digital video footage documenting the expedition to Ampato in 1997 is available from the author.

Chapter 9
Misti's Children

1. See Masías 1997 and Chávez 1993.

2. Murúa 2001: 523-524.

3. See Albornoz in Duviols 1984: 198. See Cardona 2002: 127 with regard to Yumina.

4. Cf. Legros n.d., Chávez 1993, Silva and Francis 1991.

5. Quoted in Pearce 2001.

6. See Nachtigall 1966: 278, 287 and Tierney 1990: 355.

7. Bailey 1899: 31.

8. See Beorchia 1985: 139-143.

9. Acosta 2002: 154. See Beorchia 1985: 140 for the 1677 account of a Spanish priest, Alvaro Melendez. See Rondón 1937: 30 for a general plan of the ruins on Misti.

10. See Reinhard 1992c.

11. See Price 1981: 85, 87.

12. See Urton 1981. Cf. Reinhard 2002 for the association of astronomical phenomena with sacred landscape at the Inca site of Machu Picchu.

13. Cf. Sykes 2001: 171.

14. See Murúa 2001: 523-524.

15. For information about the archaeological research, see Reinhard and Chávez 2001 and n.d.c. Digital video footage documenting the expedition to Misti in 1998 is available from the author.

Chapter 10
Quehuar's Headless Mummy

1. Beorchia 1985: 188-200 summarizes these expeditions.
2. See Roth 1986: 37 for a summary of this phenomenon.
3. Because of this tension, the Mamanis became concerned that the team was not in "harmony." Arcadio in particular had a strong spiritual side that focused on maintaining harmony with nature and the universe—indeed, it was one reason he enjoyed working with us. As he once said, "I want to help save the Inca offerings from destruction by looters because that disrupts the harmony that should exist with our past."
4. See Ceruti 2001a for a summary of the archaeological work and Roberts 2000 for a popular account. Digital video footage documenting the expedition to Quehuar in 1999 is available from the author.
5. See Abal 2001 and 2004, Conklin 1997, Mostny 1957, and Rowe 1997 for details about Inca capacocha textiles. See Ceruti 2003 and Abal 2003 for information about the Llullaillaco textiles.
6. Shortly after returning with the Llullaillaco mummies, Constanza and I attended another meeting with representatives of UNSA, this time at the office of the dean of the Faculty of Humanities, Dr. Hipolito Piñeiro. Once again UNSA archaeologists failed to appear, but Dr. Noemí Acreche, a human biologist, was present, and she was the coordinator of UNSA's School of Anthropology (Escuela de Antropología). She accepted our offer to become involved with the Llullaillaco finds, as did later an UNSA historian. Unfortunately, we did not receive any further communication from UNSA representatives in this regard, and my hopes for collaboration between the two universities were not to materialize.

Chapter 11
Mountain of Dreams

1. See Reinhard 1993; cf. Echevarría (1977: 3) with regard to Llullaillaco's altitude not being surpassed by modern climbers until 1855.
2. See Lizárraga 1999: 121 and Vivar 1987: 63.
3. Lizárraga 1999: 121.
4. See Bray et al. 2005.
5. Cf. Houston 1987: 122-180, Stark 2001: 63-64, and Kammler 2004: 216-217.
6. Cf. Guaman Poma 1980 for several depictions of anklets and moccasins.
7. Cf. Kammler 2004: 203.
8. See Lynch 1978.

9. Guaman Poma 1980.

10. See Reinhard 1999a for a popular account of the expedition to Llullaillaco in 1999. For information and plans of the excavations conducted on Llullaillaco, see Reinhard and Ceruti 2000 and n.d.b and Ceruti 2003.

Chapter 12
Past Perfect

1. Later I realized another reason for Mario's insistence on our reaching Salta together: If we had arrived in the city before him, the press would have contacted us first. He knew the Sunday paper would then be full of details about the change of plans that he had made in San Antonio de los Cobres—and my thoughts in this regard. Months later National Geographic TV presented a one-hour program of our expedition titled "Ice Mummies," which unfortunately focused on this disagreement, meaning there was less time available to deal with scientific aspects of our research. Digital video footage documenting the archaeological work undertaken during our 1999 expedition is available from the author.

2. See Previgliano et al. 2003.

3. Lambert 1997: 248.

4. For detailed studies of the pathology of ancient mummies, see Aufderheide 2003 and Aufderheide and Rodríguez-Martín 1998.

5. Cf. Quevedo and Duran 1992, Schobinger 2001.

6. Ramos (1976: 26, 81) noted this in 1621.

7. See John Rowe 1979 and Ann Rowe 1997 for a description of Inca textiles. See Ceruti 2003, Abal 2003, and Rolandi 1975 for descriptions of textiles found on Llullaillaco.

8. Cf. Mims 1999: 120.

9. Cf. Iserson 1994: 42, Mims 1999: 120, Brier 1998: 157.

10. Dr. Gerardo Vides would later point to the blood's lack of coagulation as being evidence that the children had died on the summit. Their blood must have frozen soon after their deaths for this to occur.

11. See Arriaga 1968: 35; cf. Niles 1999: 132.

12. For descriptions of the Llullaillaco chuspas, see Ceruti 2003 and Abal 2003. See Allen 1988 for a description of the importance of coca leaves among indigenous people of Peru today and Niles 1999: 75 with regard to the use of hair and fingernail clippings.

13. Cf. Guaman Poma 1980 for several depictions of anklets and moccasins.

14. A bulge in her left cheek was later shown to have been caused by a cud of chewed coca leaves (cf. Previgliano et al. 2003).

15. She recounted her experience in Cornwell 2001: 37-38.

16. See Jones 2001: 71.

17. Cf. Sykes 2001: 8-9, 233.

18. See Castañeda 2000.

19. See Arias, González, and Ceruti 2002.

20. See Bray et al. 2005.

21. See Wilson et al. 2005.

22. Cf. Iserson 1994: 315.

23. See Chamberlain and Pearson 2001: 48.

24. Cf. Iserson 1994: 288-298 and Mims 1999: 213-214.

25. If there is such a thing as a mummy curse, it must be the volatile cocktail of rumors and "mummy politics" that inevitably follows discovery of a famous mummy. Some people who become involved might be called archaeo-parasites, since they exploit the finds without making constructive contributions and without checking facts. Their motives for doing this vary, but most can be summed up as ways to: 1. Bring a focus to their particular agenda. 2. Gain personal recognition by misusing the fame of the discoveries and the work of others. 3. Obtain greater control over the finds. 4. Let their overactive—often conspiracy inspired—imaginations run wild. For example, our wait for Mario at the gendarmería's check post led to a myth that still persists in Argentina, namely, that we had been stopped to prevent our stealing the mummies! (Of course—and aside from everything else—it ignores the salient fact that mummies were not with us, but rather with Mario.) Even more bizarre were claims such as that the mummies had been frozen so that they could be brought back to life in the future—a modern concept unknown to the Incas. Distortions and wild rumors also arose in the case of the Ampato Ice Maiden, not to mention with other mummies that have gotten into the news, such as the Iceman (cf. Fowler 2000 and Spindler 1994). I came to think of this as the Mummy Maxim: Rumors and mummy politics increase in direct proportion to a mummy's fame. And in the case of Llullaillaco, there are three.

26. Catholic University's Institute of High Mountain Research can be reached at Instituto de Investigaciones de Alta Montaña, Universidad Católica de Salta, Calle Pelligrini 790, 4400 Salta, Argentina. See also Catholic University's website: www.ucasal.net/consceruti/. The Museum of High Altitude Archaeology in Salta has the following address: Museo de Arqueología de Alta Montaña (MAAM), Calle Mitre 77, 4400 Salta, Argentina (website in English and Spanish: www.maam.org).

27. The Museum of Andean Sanctuaries in Arequipa has the following address: Museo Santuarios Andinos, Calle Merced 110, Arequipa, Peru.

28. See Reinhard and Astete n.d. Digital video footage documenting the expedition to Pachatusan in 2002 is available from the author.

29. See Ceruti 2001 and n.d. Digital video footage documenting the expedition to Chañi in 2000 is available from the author.

30. Cf. Bahn 2003: 119-123, Chamberlain and Pearson 2001: 187-188, and Reid 1999: 285.

INDEX